CORPORATE INTERNAL AFFAIRS

CORPORATE
INTERNAL
AFFAIRS

A CORPORATE
AND SECURITIES
LAW PERSPECTIVE

MARC I. STEINBERG
Foreword by Harold M. Williams

Q

Quorum Books
Westport, Connecticut • London, England

Library of Congress Cataloging in Publication Data

Steinberg, Marc I.
  Corporate internal affairs.

  Bibliography: p.
  Includes index.
  1. Securities—United States. 2. Corporation law—
United States. I. Title.
KF1439.S73 1983   346.73'0666   82-16619
ISBN 0-89930-039-1 (lib. bdg.)   347.306666

Library of Congress Catalog Card Number: 82-16619
ISBN: 0-89930-039-1

First published in 1983 by Quorum Books

Greenwood Press
A division of Congressional Information Service, Inc.
88 Post Road West, Westport, Connecticut 06881

Printed in the United States of America

10 9 8 7 6 5 4 3 2 1

Contents

Foreword

I am pleased to write this foreword for Professor Steinberg's analytical treatment of many of the key corporate and securities law issues facing corporations and their legal counsel today. Professor Steinberg is the author of over fifty law review articles; this is his first book. It is a most timely and worthwhile one dealing with the very important subject of internal affairs—which I view as a critical dimension of corporate accountability.

One hears frequent comments from the corporate community and the bar to the effect that corporate accountability is no longer a matter of priority concern. Whether it is depends upon how its importance is defined and the time horizon within which it is viewed. If its importance is viewed primarily defensively and in reaction to the threat of government regulation or legislative intervention, then, in the short term, the urgency has diminished. In the longer term, however, history and experience inform us that the resurgence of the issue and the danger of increased federal intervention into how the American corporation is organized and operated is fully predictable. Only the events that will trigger that intervention cannot be precisely anticipated. The lessons of history are there to be understood and they are quite clear and straightforward.

But the subject of corporate accountability is of more fundamental importance. It is essentially a key element in assuring the effectiveness of American business over time and its contribution to American society and the American way of life. For indeed, the effectiveness of American business *over time* will impact not only the obvious, i.e., the quality of American business, but also will determine the extent to which this country remains a private economy and a democracy. I am satisfied that the two are inexorably intertwined. While a private economy may be able to exist without democracy, democracy as we know it, is dependent upon the existence of a healthy and essentially free private economy, which assures the standard of living and the condition of society. The health of the private economy is, in turn, dependent on the *long term* effectiveness of the corporate community. Whether we continue to be a private economy will depend first and foremost on the extent to which the leaders of that private economy and the people who make it work recognize that interdependency and their responsibility for it and for conduct consistent with the *long term* interests of American business and the American society.

We are well past the point, if we were ever there, when American business can count on the blind support, indulgence or understanding of the American people and American polity. American business will need to exert great efforts to be understood and to be respected, and it must begin with how it governs itself and accounts for its conduct.

Periodic intervention of governmental, administrative and legislative bodies is a predictable reaction to occurrences in the corporate sector that are not acceptable to the public at large and to the body politic. This nonacceptance may stem from failure of public understanding of the business or corporate problems involved or, perhaps even more fundamentally, of the workings of the economy. Or it may result from failure of parts of our business system to deport themselves in socially acceptable and responsible ways. Regardless, governmental intervention, as it occurs, threatens increasingly over time to so fetter American business as to result, largely unintentionally, in the diminution of the potential growth and viability of American business.

The future of American business, and indeed of the American economy and society, is being impacted daily in the corporate board rooms of America. It is imperative that the corporate community and the bar recognize their responsibilities to the future of the system and make their decisions accordingly.

I became acquainted with Professor Steinberg during my tenure as Chairman of the Securities and Exchange Commission, when he served as Special Projects Counsel and confidential legal adviser to the General Counsel. This period was marked by extensive discussion regarding corporate accountability and internal affairs. These issues are as important and controversial today. For example, the proper composition of a corporation's board of directors, the duty of management to disclose "qualitative" rather than solely economically important information, the deference to be given to a special litigation committee's decision to terminate a shareholders' derivative action, the propriety of defensive tactics taken by target management when faced with a hostile take-over bid, and the role of inside counsel are all in need of further clarification.

During my tenure as Chairman, I addressed a number of these issues. With respect to the composition of corporate boards and committees, I am pleased that by the end of my chairmanship the overwhelming number of publicly held corporations had a majority of disinterested directors on their boards and had established audit committees comprised solely of disinterested directors. In this regard, I urged that disinterested directors serve an increasingly meaningful role in the corporate accountability mechanism, even with respect to fundamental corporate changes such as corporate control contests. Along these lines, I also stressed the need for independence on the part of the accountants and attorneys who serve as advisers to publicly held corporations.

There were other difficult and controversial issues that the Commission focused upon during my tenure as Chairman and that continue to be of pressing importance. Examples include the application of the Foreign Corrupt Practices Act, the extent of disclosure required for practices that reflect upon the integrity of corporate management, and the much broader concern relating to the propriety and scope of governmental regulation that impacts on corporate internal affairs.

Professor Steinberg tackles these issues as well as several others. Although I by no means agree with all of the positions taken, Professor Steinberg's insightful analysis merits the attention of the corporate community and the bar. In short, this is a worthwhile book and I strongly recommend it.

Harold M. Williams

Acknowledgments

I owe many thanks to certain individuals for helping to bring this book to fruition. A plentiful source of the material contained in a number of chapters was several of my law review articles. Some of these works were coauthored. In particular:

(1) The chapter on the SEC's programs and policies that affect corporate internal affairs has been substantially expanded and revised, both in content and focus, from a paper coauthored by Paul Gonson, Solicitor, Securities and Exchange Commission, and me for the 1981 Ray Garrett, Jr., Corporate and Securities Law Institute sponsored by Northwestern University School of Law. The basis of the chapter appearing herein has been published, as a solely authored work, in 58 Notre Dame Law Review 173 (1982).

(2) The basis of the chapter on the disclosure of information bearing on management integrity and competency was originally published in 76 Northwestern University Law Review 555 (1981). I thank my coauthors on this piece, Ralph C. Ferrara, former General Counsel, Securities and Exchange Commission, and currently a partner at Debevoise & Plimpton in Washington, D.C., and Richard M. Starr, former Legal Assistant to SEC Commissioner Barbara S. Thomas and currently associated with Paul, Weiss, Rifkind, Wharton & Garrison in New York City. Also, portions of this chapter which discuss the "true purpose" cases and disclosure of antisocial conduct were separately published by me in 5 Corporation Law Review 249 (1982)[1] and 30 Emory Law Journal 169 (1981).

(3) The chapter on the use of special litigation committees to terminate shareholder derivative suits is largely derived from three separate articles

---

1. Reprinted by permission from the Corporation Law Review, Summer 1982, Volume 5, Number 3, Copyright © 1982, Warren, Gorham and Lamont, Inc., 210 South Street, Boston, Massachusetts. All Rights Reserved.

by the author which were published in 35 University of Miami Law Review 1 (1980),[2] 9 Securities Regulation Law Journal 381 (1982),[3] and 7 Delaware Journal of Corporate Law 1 (1982) (coauthored with Ralph C. Ferrara).

(4) The chapter on the corporate mismanagement-nondisclosure cases is principally derived from two articles, coauthored with Ralph C. Ferrara, which appeared in 129 University of Pennsylvania Law Review 263 (1980)[4] and in 7 Delaware Journal of Corporate Law 1 (1982). In addition, portions of the chapter which discuss state court decisions were addressed by the author in 9 Securities Regulation Law Journal 85 (1981).[5]

(5) The chapter on the duties of boards of directors and management in tender offer contests is derived, in substantial part, from an article published by the author in 30 Emory Law Journal 169 (1981). Also, portions of the chapter which recommend a framework for assessing the legitimacy of defensive tactics were originally addressed in 64 Cornell Law Review 901 (1979) (coauthored with Gary G. Lynch, Associate Director of Enforcement, Securities and Exchange Commission).[6]

(6) The basis of the chapter on application of the business judgment rule and related judicial principles was originally published in 56 Notre Dame Lawyer 903 (1981).

(7) The chapter on the role of inside counsel was derived in part from an article, coauthored with Ralph C. Ferrara, which appeared in 4 Corporation Law Review 3 (1981).[7]

The chapters contained herein have been expanded, revised, and edited from any article(s) from which they may have been derived. Moreover, as a former attorney at the Securities and Exchange Commission, I wish to make clear that, as a matter of policy, the SEC disclaims responsibility for any private publication by any of its employees. The views expressed herein are solely my own and do not necessarily reflect the views of the Commission or of my former colleagues on the staff of the Commission.

---

2. Reprinted from the University of Miami Law Review [35 U. MIAMI L. REV. 1 (1980)], which holds copyright on this article. All Rights Reserved.

3. Reprinted by permission from the Securities Regulation Law Journal, Winter 1982, Volume 9, Number 4, Copyright © 1982, Warren, Gorham and Lamont, Inc., 210 South Street, Boston, Massachusetts. All Rights Reserved.

4. Reprinted from the University of Pennsylvania Law Review [129 U. PA. L. REV. 263 (1980)], which holds copyright on this article. All Rights Reserved.

5. Reprinted by permission from the Securities Regulation Law Journal, Fall 1981, Volume 9, Number 1, Copyright © 1981, Warren, Gorham and Lamont, Inc., 210 South Street, Boston, Massachusetts. All Rights Reserved.

6. Reprinted from the Cornell Law Review [64 CORNELL L. REV. 901 (1979)], which holds copyright on this article. © Copyright 1979 by Cornell University. All Rights Reserved.

7. Reprinted by permission from the Corporation Law Review, Winter 1981, Volume 4, Number 1, Copyright © 1981, Warren, Gorham and Lamont, Inc., 210 South Street, Boston, Massachusetts. All Rights Reserved.

Acknowledgments

I wish also to thank certain individuals in addition to those mentioned above. In particular, I thank Valerie G. Richardson, whose editorial and research assistance was invaluable, and I express my gratitude to Samuel H. Gruenbaum who practices at Cohen & Ziskin in Los Angeles for his keen insight and helpful advice. Last, but certainly not least, I thank my mother and father, to whom I dedicate this book.

CORPORATE
INTERNAL
AFFAIRS

Introduction

This book represents an effort to compile in one source many of the significant issues that confront corporate management and its legal counsel. A number of these issues are in a state of flux; others, although more firmly defined, remain vitally important.

Although some subjects addressed herein concern corporate accountability and governance, the primary focus is on the broader theme of corporate internal affairs. Many of the divergent issues contained in the book are addressed from this broad perspective, the pertinent trends in the case law are analyzed and, where relevant, suggestions are proffered on how certain issues should be resolved by the courts.

The book is designed to be useful to a wide audience, including corporations, the corporate bar, accountants, and academicians. It presents a broad overview and analysis of seven topical and controversial subjects: the Securities and Exchange Commission's programs and policies that influence corporate internal affairs, disclosure of information bearing on management integrity and competency, the use of special litigation committees to terminate shareholder derivative suits, the corporate mismanagement-nondisclosure lines of cases, the duties of directors and management in tender offer contests, a corporate accountability analysis of the business judgment rule and related judicial principles, and the role of inside counsel.

The first subject addressed, the influence that the SEC's administrative, enforcement and legislative programs have on corporate internal affairs, takes the position that, while the Commission in the past has been interested in raising the level of corporate consciousness, its primary focus has been on addressing particular conditions, wrongdoings, and deficiencies. This point is reinforced by the Commission's direction under the present Chairman, John S. R. Shad. Hence, although there currently is little attention paid to the subject of corporate accountability, the actions taken recently by the Commission, while having a very different focus, nevertheless indicate that corporate internal processes necessarily will be affected.

From this perspective, the discussion centers on a number of Commission programs and policies, including such diverse topics as the Staff's 1980 Corporate Accountability Report, accounting and financial reporting developments, proxy disclosure regulations, the adoption of the director-signature requirement with respect to Form 10-K, enforcement practices, developments in regard to the Foreign Corrupt Practices Act, the *amicus curiae* program, and the Commission's impact on advisers to corporate management, namely, lawyers and accountants.

Chapter 2 addresses an issue that is of considerable importance to corporations, the SEC, and the courts: the disclosure of information, not because such information is quantitatively material (because it does not impact significantly on an issuer's assets), but because such information reflects on the integrity and competency of corporate management. The proposition advanced is that, notwithstanding the broad statutory language contained in the securities acts, the Commission generally has suggested that the thrust of the disclosure requirements is to mandate the dissemination of information that is economically significant.[1] Three notable exceptions, however, have developed to this principle. First, the Commission has required affirmative disclosure by registrants of certain information routinely called for in registration statements, periodic reports, and proxy solicitations.[2] Second, under Section 14(a) of the Securities Exchange Act, subject parties may be required to include in their proxy materials information that is not quantitatively

---

1. *See* Securities Act Release No. 5627, 8 SEC DOCKET 41, 43, [1975-1976 Transfer Binder] FED. SEC. L. REP. (CCH) ¶ 80,310, at 85,710 (Oct. 14, 1975) (hereinafter cited as SEC Release No. 5627), where the Commission stated that "[t]he Acts and the relevant legislative history also suggest that a prime expectation of the Congress was that the Commission's disclosure authority would be used to require the dissemination of information which is or may be economically significant."

This apparently narrow interpretation of the Commission's mandate has also been endorsed by a number of courts. *See, e.g.,* NAACP v. Federal Power Comm'n, 520 F.2d 432, 443 (D.C. Cir. 1975), *aff'd,* 425 U.S. 662 (1976), where the court, in commenting upon a Commission release addressing disclosure requirements pertaining to the pendency of civil rights proceedings, stated: "[i]n thus acting, however, the SEC appears to us merely to have been fulfilling its proper role of seeing that investors are fully informed of circumstances which bear on the financial prospects of securities-issuing corporations." *See also* Gaines v. Haughton, 645 F.2d 761 (9th Cir. 1981), *cert. denied,* 102 S. Ct. 1006 (1982).

2. *See, e.g.,* Item 402, Regulation S-K, 17 C.F.R. § 229.402 (1982). This item requires registrants to disclose affirmatively information about management remuneration in registration statements filed under the Securities Act, and in periodic reports and proxy solicitations regulated under the Exchange Act, irrespective of the economic materiality of the information. *See also* Securities and Exchange Commission, Brief for Appellee, at 27, SEC v. Falstaff Brewing Corp., 629 F.2d 62 (D.C. Cir. 1980), where the Commission argued that it is authorized to require disclosure of information called for in its rules, irrespective of economic materiality: "In addition, Rule 14a-3 and Schedule 14A establish certain minimum disclosure requirements that must be met regardless of a finding of materiality."

4

material to ensure that shareholders are adequately informed about issues to be voted upon at shareholder meetings.³ This exception recognizes the vital distinction between information important to a voting decision and an investment decision. Third, the Commission has departed from economic materiality as the basis for disclosure when other criteria are mandated by an independent federal statute, for example, the National Environmental Policy Act (NEPA).⁴

With this background in focus, the chapter addresses the concept of qualitative materiality and the duty to disclose in the context of the securities acts. The chapter first presents an overview of relevant case law and Commission proceedings. Thereafter, the chapter addresses management self-dealing (including the "true purpose" cases), questionable and illegal payments, unethical or unlawful company policies, adjudicated illegalities and pending lawsuits against officers and directors, and business expertise and reputation of corporate officials. Finally, a standard for the disclosure of qualitatively material information—in both an investing and a voting context—is proposed.

Chapter 3 addresses the very topical subject of the use of special litigation committees to terminate shareholder derivative suits. At the outset of the discussion, it is pointed out that a corporation's board of directors will frequently appoint a special litigation committee when faced with a shareholder's derivative action against fellow directors. Not surprisingly, dismissal motions sought by such committees is the subject of increasing scrutiny by the courts.⁵ The discussion thereupon analyzes the relevant federal and state

---

3. *See* SEC Release No. 5627, *supra* note 1, at 44, [1975-1976 Transfer Binder] FED. SEC. L. REP. (CCH) ¶ 80,310, at 85,711: "It is also evident, however, that, insofar as the Commission's rulemaking authority under Section 14(a) of the Securities Exchange Act is concerned, the primacy of economic matters, particularly with respect to shareholder proposals, is somewhat less." *See also* Mills v. Electric Auto-Lite Co., 396 U.S. 375 (1970), where the Court stated that the underlying purpose of Section 14(a) of the Exchange Act is to promote " 'the free exercise of the voting rights of stockholders' by ensuring that proxies [are] solicited in 'explanation to the stockholder of the real nature of the questions for which authority to cast his vote is sought.' " *Id.* at 381 (quoting H.R. REP. No. 1383, 73d Cong., 2d Sess. 14 (1934) and S. REP. NO. 792, 73d Cong., 2d Sess. 12 (1934)).

4. Section 102(1) of NEPA provides that "to the fullest extent possible . . . the policies, regulations and public laws of the United States shall be interpreted and administered in accordance with the policies set forth in [NEPA]." *Id.* § 4332(1). Section 101(a) of NEPA provides that the "continuing policy" of the federal government is "to use all practicable means and measures" to protect environmental values. 42 U.S.C. § 4331(a) (1976 & Supp. III 1979).

5. *See, e.g.,* Burks v. Lasker, 441 U.S. 471 (1979); Abramowitz v. Posner, [1981-1982 Transfer Binder] FED. SEC. L. REP. (CCH) ¶ 98,458 (2d Cir. 1982); Maldonado v. Flynn, [1981-1982 Transfer Binder] FED. SEC. L. REP. (CCH) ¶ 98,457 (2d Cir. 1982); Gaines v. Haughton, 645 F.2d 761 (9th Cir. 1981), *cert. denied,* 102 S. Ct. 1006 (1982); Galef v. Alexander, 615 F.2d 51 (2d Cir. 1980); Lewis v. Anderson, 615 F.2d 778 (9th Cir. 1979), *cert. denied,* 101 S. Ct. 206 (1980); Abbey v. Control Data Corp., 603 F.2d 724 (8th Cir. 1979), *cert. denied,* 444 U.S. 1017 (1980); Genzer v. Cunningham, 498 F. Supp. 682 (E.D. Mich. 1980); Abella v. Universal Leaf Tobacco, Inc., 495 F. Supp. 713 (E.D. Va. 1980); Maher v. Zapata Corp.,

court decisions and focuses on special procedures that should be employed to help insulate the decision reached by the special litigation committee from successful challenge. These procedures include that:

1. The board appoint only nondefendant, disinterested, and independent persons to the special litigation committee;

2. The board delegate binding, nonreviewable authority to the committee to investigate and determine whether the suit is in the corporation's best interests;

3. The committee employ thorough investigative procedures and resources, including the appointment of a reputable special counsel and law firm to assist in the investigation;

4. Reasonable measures be taken to help ensure that the directors and other relevant parties inform committee members of all facts material to the committee's decision; and

5. The committee conduct itself so as to withstand strict judicial scrutiny.

Chapter 4 addresses the corporate mismanagement-nondisclosure lines of cases. In *Santa Fe Industries, Inc. v. Green,*[6] the Supreme Court held that in order to state a cause of action under Section 10(b) and Rule 10b-5 of the Securities Exchange Act, deception or manipulation must be alleged.[7] In other words, under Section 10(b) and Rule 10b-5, breaches of fiduciary duty that do not involve any misrepresentation or nondisclosure are not actionable. In what has become a most significant footnote, however, the *Santa Fe* Court rejected the plaintiff's contention that the majority stockholder's failure to give them advance notice of the merger was a material nondisclosure. The Court pointed out that the plaintiffs had not indicated how they might have acted differently had they received prior notice of the merger. Indeed, the Court noted that the plaintiffs accepted the conclusion that they could not have enjoined the merger for alleged unfairness because an appraisal proceeding was their sole remedy under Delaware law. It therefore concluded that the failure to give advance notice to the minority shareholders was not a material nondisclosure within the meaning of Section 10(b) or Rule 10b-5.[8]

Shortly thereafter, however, the Delaware Supreme Court in *Singer v. Magnavox Co.,*[9] viewing *Sante Fe* as a "current confirmation of the Supreme Court of the responsibility of a State to govern the internal affairs of cor-

---

490 F. Supp. 348 (S.D. Tex. 1980); Zapata Corp. v. Maldonado, 430 A.2d 779 (Del. 1981); Auerbach v. Bennett, 47 N.Y.2d 619, 393 N.E.2d 994, 419 N.Y.S.2d 920 (1979).

   6. 430 U.S. 462 (1977).

   7. *Id.* at 474.

   8. *Id.* at 474 n.14.

   9. 380 A.2d 969 (Del. 1977).

porate life,"[10] concluded that under Delaware law, appraisal was not a minority shareholder's sole remedy. Moreover, it held that if it is alleged that the purpose of the merger is improper, the majority shareholders must prove a proper business purpose. Additionally, the court concluded that even if a proper business purpose were shown, a court must scrutinize the transaction for its entire fairness and award appropriate relief if a violation is found.[11]

Subsequent Delaware cases have expanded upon *Singer*. The overwhelming rationale of these cases is that, regardless of whether a short- or long-form merger is effected, the merger must be for a proper purpose and must be entirely fair to minority shareholders.[12] Although other state court decisions have not strictly followed *Singer,* they generally stand for the proposition that a shareholder may enjoin a merger that has not been consummated if it is not being effected for a proper business purpose.[13]

Construing these recent Delaware and other state court decisions together with footnote fourteen of *Santa Fe,* a number of federal courts have found actionable claims under Section 10(b) when there has been a lack of adequate and fair disclosure that would have enabled the aggrieved shareholder to seek injunctive relief in a state court. Indeed, subject to a number of caveats which will be discussed in the chapter, this rationale has been adopted by

---

10. *Id.* at 976 n.6.

11. *Id.* at 975, 980.

12. *See, e.g.,* Roland Int'l Corp. v. Najjar, 407 A.2d 1032, 1034 (Del. 1979); Tanzer v. Int'l Gen. Indus., Inc., 379 A.2d 1121, 1123 (Del. 1977); Young v. Valhi, Inc., 382 A.2d 1372, 1374 (Del. Ch. 1978); Kemp v. Angel, 381 A.2d 241, 244 (Del. Ch. 1977). *See also* Harman v. Masoneilan International Inc., 442 A.2d 487 (Del. 1982); Lynch v. Vickers Energy Corp., 429 A.2d 497 (Del. 1981). *But see* discussion at 182 n. 97 *infra.*

13. *See* Perl v. IU Int'l Corp., 607 P.2d 1036, 1046 (Hawaii 1980) (followed *Singer*); Gabhart v. Gabhart, 267 Ind. 370, 388, 370 N.E.2d 345, 356 (1977) (followed *Singer's* first prong in holding that the effectuation of a merger that eliminated a minority shareholder, even though in compliance with the technical requirements of the state's merger statute, must advance a corporate purpose in order to withstand scrutiny under Indiana law). *See also* Masinter v. Webco Co., 262 S.E.2d 433 (W. Va. 1980). Interpreting the California Supreme Court's decision in Jones v. H. F. Ahmanson & Co., 1 Cal. 3d 93, 460 P.2d 464, 81 CAL. RPTR. 592 (1969), the Hawaii Supreme Court in *Perl* opined that the court would adopt the *Singer* principles: "Although *Ahmanson* did not involve a merger, it appears clear from the language of the opinion that the California Supreme Court would apply the fiduciary duty of good faith and inherent fairness to such a situation." 607 P.2d at 1047 n.12. However, in *In re* Jones & Laughlin Steel Corp., 488 Pa. 524, 412 A.2d 1099 (1980), the Pennsylvania Supreme Court rejected the approach adopted by the Delaware courts. The Pennsylvania court held that the appraisal statute served as the sole postmerger remedy for aggrieved minority shareholders. 488 Pa. at 531, 412 A.2d at 1103. In the premerger stage, the court recognized the minority's right to seek injunctive relief in order to prevent the merger's consummation. *Id.,* 412 A.2d at 1103. The majority's holding occasioned a fairly vigorous dissent. *Id.,* 412 A.2d at 1104 (Larsen, J., dissenting). *But see* Yanow v. Teal Industries, Inc., 178 Conn. 263, 422 A.2d 311 (1979) (appraisal exclusive remedy); discussion at 182 n. 97 *infra.*

the Second, Third, Fifth, Seventh, and Ninth Circuits.[14] Moreover, as recently held by the Ninth Circuit, as well as other courts, the availability of state court relief is not determinative. Rather, according to these courts, a fact is material under Section 10(b) in this context if a reasonable investor "could respond to the fact's disclosure by protecting himself from possible financial loss."[15] Thus, the lesson of these cases is that, although a breach of fiduciary duty by itself is not a sufficient basis for a federal law claim, there are circumstances, subject to certain limitations, under which such a breach coupled with either nondisclosure or affirmative misrepresentation remains a firm foundation for a federal claim.

Chapter 5 examines the duties of boards of directors and management in tender offer contests. The subjects addressed include the general duty to disclose in the tender offer context, pertinent SEC tender offer rules, and the legitimacy of defensive tactics. In addition, recent judicial decisions and their ramifications are discussed at length.[16]

Perhaps the most controversial and stimulating issue in the tender offer setting is the extent to which target management can take defensive measures to defeat a hostile takeover bid. As discussed in the chapter, the majority of courts appear to apply the business judgment rule in assessing the legality of such tactics.[17] The Seventh Circuit's decision in *Panter v. Marshall Field & Co.*[18] serves as such an example. A number of recent cases, however, have not been as favorable to target management. As stated by one court, "[w]hat is sometimes lost sight of in these tender offer controversies is that

---

14. *See* Healey v. Catalyst Recovery, Inc., 616 F.2d 641 (3d Cir. 1980); Alabama Farm Bureau Mut. Cas. Co. v. American Fidelity Life Ins. Co., 606 F.2d 602 (5th Cir. 1979), *cert. denied,* 446 U.S. 933 (1980); Kidwell v. Meikle, 597 F.2d 1273 (9th Cir. 1979); Goldberg v. Meridor, 567 F.2d 209 (2d Cir. 1977), *cert. denied,* 434 U.S. 1069 (1978); Wright v. Heizer Corp., 560 F.2d 236 (7th Cir. 1977), *cert. denied,* 434 U.S. 1066 (1978).

15. United States v. Margala, [1981-1982 Transfer Binder] FED. SEC. L. REP. (CCH) ¶ 98,363 at 92,221 (9th Cir. 1981). *See* SEC v. Blatt, 583 F.2d 1325, 1331-32 (5th Cir. 1978) ("*Santa Fe* does not control a case in which information that would prove useful to investors is withheld"); Wright v. Heizer Corp., 560 F.2d 236, 250 (7th Cir. 1977), *cert. denied,* 434 U.S. 1066 (1978) ("If these shareholders would have been powerless to prevent the proposed self-dealing by the controlling shareholders even if they had possessed knowledge of all the facts, the failure to disclose to them would presumably be immaterial and reliance could not be shown").

16. *See, e.g.,* Mobil Corp. v. Marathon Oil Co., 669 F.2d 366 (6th Cir. 1981); Panter v. Marshall Field & Co., 646 F.2d 271 (7th Cir.), *cert. denied,* 102 S. Ct. 658 (1981); Treadway Cos. v. Care Corp., 638 F.2d 357 (2d Cir. 1980); Crouse-Hinds Co. v. InterNorth, Inc., 634 F.2d 690 (2d Cir. 1980); Lewis v. McGraw, 619 F.2d 192 (2d Cir. 1980); Berman v. Gerber Products Co., 454 F. Supp. 1310 (W.D. Mich. 1978).

17. *See, e.g.,* Panter v. Marshall Field & Co., 646 F.2d 271 (7th Cir.), *cert. denied,* 102 S. Ct. 658 (1981); Treadway Cos. v. Care Corp., 638 F.2d 357 (2d Cir. 1980); Crouse-Hinds Co. v. InterNorth, Inc., 634 F.2d 690 (2d Cir. 1980); Berman v. Gerber Products Co., 454 F. Supp. 1310 (W.D. Mich. 1978).

18. 646 F.2d 271 (7th Cir.), *cert. denied,* 102 S. Ct. 658 (1981).

the shareholders, not the directors, have the right of franchise with respect to the shares owned by them."[19] Moreover, the Sixth Circuit in *Mobil Corporation v. Marathon Oil Company*[20] held that the option agreement between the white knight, U.S. Steel, and the target, Marathon, constituted a manipulative practice proscribed by Section 14(e) of the Securities Exchange Act.[21]

Interestingly, a number of commentators have expressed divergent views regarding target management's duties in the tender offer context. While some of these views have found judicial acceptance, others have not. The first view basically advocates that management may oppose a hostile tender offer if it determines in its good faith judgment that the offer is not in the best interests of the corporation. Consistent with this policy, directors may undertake any policy which they believe, in their good faith business judgment, is necessary to defeat the offer.[22] In addition, some commentators who favor this view advocate that management should control the corporation's response to a takeover bid after considering both investor and noninvestor interests. This signifies that directors may consider not only shareholder interests but also those of the corporation's employees, the community in which it resides, and the general public.[23] This view appears to have been accepted by a number of courts.[24]

A second view, which is diametrically opposed to the preceding, is that because cash tender offers are beneficial and lead to more efficient management, any attempt by a target's management to impede a tender offer should be prohibited. In short, when confronted with a tender offer, target management "should relax, not consult any experts, and let the shareholders decide."[25]

A third approach proposes that a subject tender offer should be submitted to a vote of the target corporation's shareholders, with the bidder having a right to proceed only if at least a majority of the shareholders who are

---

19. Conoco Inc. v. Seagram Company Ltd., 517 F. Supp. 1299, 1303 (S.D.N.Y. 1981). *See* Joseph F. Seagram & Sons, Inc. v. Abrams, 510 F. Supp. 860, 861-62 (S.D.N.Y. 1981).

20. 669 F.2d 366 (6th Cir. 1981).

21. *Id.* at 373-77.

22. *See* Fleischer, *Business Judgment Rule Protects Takeover Targets,* Legal Times (Wash.), April 14, 1980, at 15, col. 1; Lipton, *Takeover Bids in the Target's Boardroom,* 35 Bus. Law. 101 (1979); Steinbrink, *Management's Response to the Takeover Attempt,* 28 Case W. Res. L. Rev. 882 (1978).

23. *See, e.g.,* Lipton, *supra,* note 22, at 130-31; Steinbrink, *supra,* note 22, at 901. *See generally* Herald Co. v. Seawell, 472 F.2d 1081, 1094-95 (10th Cir. 1972) (Colorado law).

24. *See* cases cited *supra* note 17.

25. Easterbrook & Fischel, *Takeover Bids, Defensive Tactics, and Shareholders' Welfare,* 36 Bus. Law. 1733, 1750 (1981). *See* Easterbrook & Fischel, *The Proper Role of a Target's Management in Responding to a Tender Offer,* 94 Harv. L. Rev. 1161 (1981); Gilson, *A Structural Approach to Corporations: The Case Against Defensive Tactics in Tender Offers,* 33 Stan. L. Rev. 819 (1981).

unaffiliated with the offeror approves.[26] Although a comparable approach has received judicial attention in going-private mergers,[27] no court has yet adhered to this approach in the tender offer setting.

A fourth view has been presented by former SEC Chairman Harold M. Williams. According to Mr. Williams, the judicial deference incorporated into the business judgment rule should not apply in a takeover situation, absent a board's establishing that it has, in fact, satisfied certain criteria.[28] First, he asserts that the board must be competent and objective. Obviously, therefore, a management director whose very livelihood may be affected by the board's decision—as well as other directors who have a substantial economic interest in the continued separate existence of the corporation— should not be considered to act solely in the corporation's and shareholders' best interests. Therefore, to satisfy the above requirement, a corporation's board should delegate to a special committee of independent directors the responsibility to investigate the offer and to recommend to the full board an appropriate response. It is not necessary to require that management directors and others having a substantial economic interest in the outcome abstain from participating in the board's ultimate decision; however, if these directors provide the margin in rejecting the tender offer, they should have a difficult burden in establishing that they acted objectively in the corporation's and shareholders' best interests. In addition, according to Mr. Williams, the board has an institutional responsibility to consider concerns other than those of the shareholders, including the potential adverse impact on employees, suppliers, and communities. If these steps are complied with, management should be able to engage in legal ethical acts to resist the takeover bid. Such acts themselves, however, cannot be inconsistent with the corporation's viability. Therefore, as part of its defensive tactics, a corporation should not have the right to waste corporate assets by, for example, an otherwise senseless acquisition, or to make vacuous charges against the bidder or to engage in other unethical behavior.[29]

---

26. Herzel, Schmidt & Davis, *Why Corporate Directors Have a Right To Resist Tender Offers,* 3 Corp. L. Rev. 107, 116 (1980).

27. *Cf.* Harman v. Masoneilan International Inc., 442 A.2d 487 (Del. 1982).

28. Williams, *Role of Directors in Takeover Offers,* 13 Rev. Sec. Reg. 963 (1980).

29. *Id.* at 965-66. *See* Gelfond & Sebastian, *Reevaluating the Duties of Target Management in a Hostile Tender Offer,* 60 B.U.L. Rev. 403, 472 (1980):

> If the target corporation's actions are made pursuant to the recommendations of a truly independent committee of the board of directors, courts should apply the traditional business judgment rule. However, if the decisions are made by interested management, courts should not defer to management but should scrutinize the decision under a stringent liability, or fairness, standard of review.

Also, it is arguable that some courts are beginning to place increasing emphasis on objective criteria. Such criteria might include the subject corporation's financial structure, the rendition of independent professional advice, and the extent to which the surrounding circumstances indicate biased or unbiased action. Under this framework, courts may substitute their own

A fifth approach, and the one proposed herein, posits that under the Williams Act, as evidenced by its legislative history, and also possibly under state law, the shareholders and not the directors are entitled to decide the fate of the company when it becomes the subject of a tender offer. In other words, a target's management should not be allowed to effectively deprive shareholders of the right to tender by taking actions that preclude or materially impede a shareholder's right to decide. Thus, if management takes actions that are designed to preclude a shareholder from having the right to tender, such a tactic is illegitimate no matter how complete the disclosure may be surrounding the use of the tactic. On the other hand, if management undertakes tactics that are designed to defeat the tender offer but that do not materially impede the shareholder's right to tender, such tactics are proper if there is full disclosure. This approach, while it has not yet been explicitly adopted, has received implicit judicial approbation in a number of recent decisions, particularly the Sixth Circuit's holding in *Mobil Corporation v. Marathon Oil Company*.[30]

Chapter 6 focuses on the concept that, in the context of shareholder challenges to management actions, courts have enunciated several principles which, if construed too broadly, serve as a subterfuge allowing recalcitrant management to rationalize and defend its otherwise illegal conduct. The principles permitting management to avoid shareholder scrutiny include the inveterate business judgment rule, the *Burks v. Lasker*[31] special litigation committee scenario, certain limitations on the *Goldberg v. Meridor*[32] rationale, the true purpose cases, and the somewhat related disclosure of antisocial, unethical or unlawful policies rationale. The author, however, is by no means urging that the foregoing principles be abrogated. If interpreted properly, these principles advance both the corporation's and shareholders' best interests. Accordingly, it is asserted that, before holding that a particular action taken by management is insulated from challenge by one of these principles, courts should scrutinize the purposes underlying the relevant principle and determine whether applying the principle in that setting would effectuate its purposes. Moreover, the importance of affording shareholders, suing either derivatively or individually, the opportunity for redress should be a relevant consideration in determining whether a particular principle should be applied in a given case. Thus, although courts should apply the

---

view of "unreasonableness" in assessing how a "reasonable" director should have acted in a tender offer setting. *See generally* Consolidated Amusement Co. v. Rugoff, [1978 Transfer Binder] FED. SEC. L. REP. (CCH) ¶ 96,584 (S.D.N.Y.) (applying New York law); Podesta v. Calumet Indus., Inc., [1978 Transfer Binder] FED. SEC. L. REP. (CCH) ¶ 96,433 (N.D. Ill.) (applying Delaware law); Zapata Corp. v. Maldonado, 430 A.2d 779 (Del. 1981); Gelfond & Sebastian, *supra*, at 443-46.

30. 669 F.2d 366 (6th Cir. 1981).

31. 441 U.S. 471 (1979).

32. 567 F.2d 209 (2d Cir. 1977), *cert. denied,* 434 U.S. 1069 (1978).

business judgment rule and related judicial principles in appropriate situations to shield management's conduct, they should be careful to ensure that their processes are not used as a sword by recalcitrant management to pierce legitimate shareholder interests.

Chapter 7 addresses the role of inside counsel. There can be little question that inside counsel walks a tightrope: inside counsel is an employee of a corporation but also an attorney who must comply with the profession's obligations. In this context, the chapter analyzes the questions that inside counsel must face as well as the opportunities that exist to help mold corporate standards. With this framework established, the chapter focuses on five subject areas: who is inside counsel's client, counsel's role as an adviser rather than an advocate, counsel's general duty to inquire and to offer advice, counsel's obligation to take appropriate actions where a corporate fraud or crime is discovered, and the propriety of inside counsel serving as a director to the corporation.

As a final point, the diverse issues addressed herein are of paramount significance to corporations and their counsel. Many of the issues discussed go far beyond the theme of corporate accountability and governance. Rather, they concern the much broader concept of corporate internal affairs. In short, while corporate accountability and governance are important issues that should continue to receive considerable attention, the subjects addressed focus primarily on many of the recurring and perplexing problems that corporations and their counsel must all too frequently face. Hopefully, the analysis provided herein will serve as a useful corporate and securities law framework for assessing these significant issues.

1

The SEC's Administrative, Enforcement, and Legislative Programs and Policies—Their Influence on Corporate Internal Affairs

I. INTRODUCTION

Less than two years ago, the Securities and Exchange Commission's ("SEC" or "Commission") programs and policies were criticized by some authorities on the rationale that the Commission was overstepping its statutory authority. These authorities argued that the SEC's myriad activities were all pieces in a carefully wrought and exquisitely detailed master plan to raise the level of corporate accountability. In short, the Commission's administrative, enforcement, and legislative programs and policies, according to these critics, were aimed at regulating corporate internal affairs.[1]

This assertion was an overstatement. Life is much more prosaic at the Commission. SEC regulation during the chairmanship of Harold M. Williams,[2] although undoubtedly affecting corporate processes, was principally directed to addressing particular conditions, wrongdoings, and deficiencies. Nonetheless, there is much truth to the statement that the Commission desired to raise the level of corporate consciousness. Indeed, while former Chairman Williams' speeches reflected generalized views on corporate governance and accountability,[3] the Commission's disclosure, enforcement, and legislative policies represented significant regulatory actions that had the effect of inducing corporations to be more accountable to their shareholders and the public.

---

1. *See generally* Kripke, *The SEC, Corporate Governance, and the Real Issues,* 36 Bus. Law. 173 (1981); Wolfson, *A Critique of the Securities and Exchange Commission,* 30 Emory L.J. 119 (1981).

2. Harold M. Williams served as Chairman of the SEC from 1977 to 1981.

3. *See* notes 33-44 and accompanying text *infra.*

In the last two years, times have unquestionably changed at the SEC. For example, Commission policies appear to be more concerned with aiding the capital formation process.[4] The theme of corporate accountability has all but vanished. Nonetheless, the present chairmanship of John S. R. Shad perhaps exemplifies that, even though there is little focus on the subject of corporate accountability, the nature of the Commission's activities necessarily signifies that, regardless of the particular position taken on a given issue, internal corporate processes will be thereby affected.

Viewed from this perspective, a plausible argument can be made that, although there may be a difference in focus, SEC disclosure and enforcement activities are not that much different. There is a degree of truth in this proposition upon which this chapter will elaborate. On the other hand, from both a rhetoric and action standpoint, there undoubtedly has been a shift in Commission philosophy.

A crucial point, however, is that the Commission, by pursuing its various and sometimes changing policies, exerts a very significant influence on corporate internal affairs. This chapter will examine the methods by which the Commission affects internal corporate processes. First, the Commission's and staff's use of the exhortatory approach, which apparently has been abandoned to a large extent during the Shad chairmanship, will be discussed. Thereafter, the chapter will examine the SEC's disclosure processes, focusing on their impact on corporate internal affairs. Next, the subject of SEC substantive "non-enforcement" regulation from this perspective will be discussed. The following section will address in this context law enforcement and related proceedings. Then, the SEC's legislative program will be discussed, with an emphasis on the Foreign Corrupt Practices Act. The Commission's *amicus curiae* program is highlighted thereafter with an illustrative discussion of the agency's views in *Burks v. Lasker*.[5] Finally, the chapter describes how the various Commission initiatives respecting the principal advisers to corporations—lawyers and accountants—may affect their clients' internal affairs.

Before delving into the subject matter, a preliminary point will be addressed. In undertaking its administrative and enforcement responsibilities, regardless of the particular area involved, the Commission has generally done so through adjudication, rulemaking, and, occasionally, legislation. For example, in *in re Cady, Roberts & Co.*,[6] the Commission in an administrative proceeding extended liability under Section 10(b) of the Securities

---

4. *See* notes 158-80 and accompanying text *infra*.
5. 441 U.S. 471 (1979).
6. 40 S.E.C. 907 (1961).

Exchange Act[7] and rule 10b-5 prescribed thereunder[8] to hold that a broker-dealer who received material nonpublic information from a corporate director had an affirmative duty to disclose that information to purchasers to whom he sold the corporation's stock.[9] *Cady, Roberts* represented, as the Supreme Court recently perceived, "an important step in the development of § 10(b)."[10] Subsequent Commission actions and judicial decisions have refined and textured the obligation to disclose or refrain from trading under Section 10(b) and Rule 10b-5.[11] Indeed, it was partially due to one such

---

7. Section 10(b) of the Securities Exchange Act of 1934 provides:

It shall be unlawful for any person, directly or indirectly, by the use of any means or instrumentality of interstate commerce or of the mails, or of any facility of any national securities exchange—

(b) To use or employ, in connection with the purchase or sale of any security registered on a national securities exchange or any security not so registered, any manipulative or deceptive device or contrivance in contravention of such rules and regulations as the Commission may prescribe as necessary or appropriate in the public interest or for the protection of investors.

15 U.S.C. § 78j(b) (1976).

8. 17 C.F.R. § 240.10b-5 (1982). Rule 10b-5 provides:

It shall be unlawful for any person, directly or indirectly, by the use of any means or instrumentality of interstate commerce, or of the mails or of any facility of any national securities exchange,

(a) To employ any device, scheme, or artifice to defraud,

(b) To make any untrue statement of a material fact or to omit to state a material fact necessary in order to make the statements made, in light of the circumstances under which they were made, not misleading, or

(c) To engage in any act, practice, or course of business which operates or would operate as a fraud or deceit upon any person, in connection with the purchase or sale of any security.

9. 40 S.E.C. 907, 911 (1961). The Commission premised its extension of liability by pointing to the broad remedial purpose of the Securities Exchange Act which was aimed at reaching deceptive and manipulative practices, regardless of whether such practices would have been actionable at common law. *See* notes 10-14 *infra*.

10. Chiarella v. United States, 445 U.S. 222, 226 (1980). The *Chiarella* Court held that silence, absent a duty to disclose, will not give rise to Section 10(b) liability. Insofar as insiders and their tippees are concerned, however, the Court appears to have reinforced the principle that a duty to disclose or abstain from trading does arise when such persons are in possession of material nonpublic information. *Id.* at 226-27.

11. *See, e.g.,* Chiarella v. United States, 445 U.S. 222 (1980) (financial printer not liable); Affiliated Ute Citizens v. United States, 406 U.S. 128 (1972) (bank held liable); Dirks v. SEC, 681 F.2d 824 (D.C. Cir.), *cert. granted,* 51 U.S.L.W. 3378 (1982) (securities analyst liable); United States v. Newman, 664 F.2d 12 (2d Cir. 1981) (employees of an investment banking firm and their tippees held liable on misappropriation rationale); Elkind v. Liggett & Myers, Inc., 635 F.2d 156 (2d Cir. 1980) (corporate officer, tipper liability); SEC v. Monarch Fund, 608 F.2d 938 (2d Cir. 1979) (investment manager not liable); Zweig v. Hearst Corp., 594 F.2d 1261 (9th Cir. 1979) (financial columnist liable); SEC v. Geon Indus., 531 F.2d 39 (2d Cir. 1976) (corporate officer held liable for tip at bar of country club); Shapiro v. Merrill

subsequent decision that the Commission responded through the *rulemaking* process. In *Chiarella v. United States*,[12] the Supreme Court held that under Section 10(b) and Rule 10b-5 a financial printer, who purchased stock after deciphering information gleaned from confidential documents entrusted to his employer that certain companies were to be the subjects of mergers or tender offers, did not breach a duty to the investing public.[13] In the aftermath of *Chiarella*, as an effort to regulate, *inter alia*, insider and tippee trading in the tender offer context, the SEC promulgated Rule 14e-3 which establishes a "disclose or abstain from trading" rule under Section 14(e) of the Williams Act.[14]

Lynch, Pierce, Fenner & Smith, Inc., 495 F.2d 228 (2d Cir. 1974) (institutional investor liable); Chasins v. Smith, Barney & Co., 438 F.2d 1167 (2d Cir. 1970) (market maker liable); Crane Co. v. Westinghouse Air Brake Co., 419 F.2d 787 (2d Cir. 1969) (person acquiring information in course of negotiations with company liable); SEC v. Texas Gulf Sulphur Co., 401 F.2d 833 (2d Cir. 1968), *cert. denied*, 404 U.S. 1005 (1971) (insider and tippee liability); SEC v. Roussel, 485 F. Supp. 295 (D. Kan. 1980) (securities broker-dealer liable); United States v. Hall, [1980 Transfer Binder] FED. SEC. L. REP. (CCH) ¶ 97,675 (S.D.N.Y. 1980) (attorney liable); SEC v. Wyman, 22 SEC DOCKET 391 (March 17, 1981) (registered representative; court entered consent order); In re Fleiss, [1979-1980 Transfer Binder] FED. SEC. L. REP. (CCH) ¶ 82,471 (S.E.C. 1980) (salesman employed by broker-dealer; court entered consent order); SEC v. Lerner, David, Littenberg & Samuel, 19 SEC DOCKET 1153 (April 2, 1980) (law firm; court entered consent order); In re Van Alstyne, Noel & Co., 43 S.E.C. 1080 (1969) (underwriters liable). *See Insider Trading by Law Firm Employees*, SEC Securities Exchange Act Release No. 13,437, [1977-1978 Transfer Binder] FED. SEC. L. REP. (CCH) ¶ 81,116 (S.E.C. 1977) (the obligation not to trade on confidential nonpublic information "extends not only to partners in the law firm but also to associated lawyers and service personnel employed by the firm"). *See generally* Branson, *Discourse on the Supreme Court Approach to SEC Rule 10b-5 and Insider Trading*, 30 EMORY L.J. 263 (1981); Dooley, *Enforcement of Insider Trading Restrictions*, 66 VA. L. REV. 1 (1980); Hazen, *Symposium Introduction—The Supreme Court and the Securities Laws: Has the Pendulum Slowed?* 30 EMORY L.J. 5, 22-24 (1981); Herlihy & Weir, *Insiders, Outsiders: The Commission's Efforts to Outlaw Insider Trading*, in PROXY CONTESTS AND BATTLES FOR CORPORATE CONTROL 421 (Practising Law Institute, 1981); Langevoort, *Insider Trading and the Fiduciary Principle: A Post-Chiarella Restatement*, 70 CALIF. L. REV. 1 (1982); Morrison, *Silence Is Golden: Trading on Nonpublic Market Information*, 8 SEC. REG. L.J. 211 (1980); Steinberg, *Fiduciary Duties and Disclosure Obligations in Proxy and Tender Contests for Corporate Control*, 30 EMORY L.J. 169, 171-73 (1981); Wang, *Trading on Material Nonpublic Information on Impersonal Stock Markets: Who Is Harmed and Who Can Sue Whom Under SEC Rule 10b-5?* 54 S. CAL. L. REV. 1217 (1981).

12. 445 U.S. 222 (1980).

13. *Id.* Thus, the Court held that silence, absent a duty to disclose, will not give rise to Section 10(b) liability. *Id.* at 230.

14. *See* 17 C.F.R. § 240.14e-3 (1982), Securities Exchange Act Release No. 17120, Inv. Co. Act No. 11336, [1980 Transfer Binder] FED. SEC. L. REP. (CCH) ¶ 82,646. As adopted, with certain exceptions, Rule 14e-3 applies this disclose-or-abstain provision to the possession of material information relating to a tender offer where the person knows or has reason to know that the information is nonpublic and was received directly or indirectly from the offeror, the subject corporation, any of their affiliated persons, or any person acting on behalf of either company. Moreover, the rule contains a broad anti-tipping provision and provides for certain exceptions pertaining to sales to the offeror and to certain activities by multiservice financial

The Commission occasionally has employed both adjudication and rule-making in a single proceeding. One such example is *In the Matter of Carter and Johnson*[15] where the Commission in a Rule 2(e) proceeding,[16] while declining to discipline the subject attorneys, set forth a standard for ethical conduct that had prospective application.[17] In that decision, the Commission also stated that it intended to solicit public comment in regard to the standard adopted[18] which it subsequently did.[19]

Thus, by exercising its discretion to choose between adjudication and rulemaking, the Commission has been able to pursue efficiently its statutory mandates.[20] As a general proposition, this practice has received judicial approbation.[21] As the Supreme Court stated in *SEC v. Chenery Corp.*,[22] "the choice made between proceeding by general rule or by individual, *ad hoc* litigation is one that lies primarily in the informed discretion of the administrative agency."[23] The fact that the adjudication will have far-reaching impact is not normally dispositive of whether the agency abused its discretion in selecting adjudication over rulemaking.[24] This principle, how-

---

institutions. *See* O'Connor & Assoc. v. Dean Witter Reynolds, Inc., [1981-1982 Transfer Binder] Fed. Sec. L. Rep. (CCH) ¶ 98,443, at 92,629-32 (S.D.N.Y. 1982) (upholding validity of Rule 14e-3). For discussion on Rule 14e-3, *see* Gruenbaum, *The New Disclosure or Abstain from Trading Rule: Has the SEC Gone Too Far?* 4 Corp. L. Rev. 350 (1981); Heller, Chiarella, *SEC Rule 14e-3 and Dirks: "Fairness" versus Economic Theory*, 37 Bus. Law. 517, 557 (1982); Steinberg, note 11 *supra*, at 174-76; Note, *Trading on Material, Nonpublic Information Under Rule 14e-3*, 49 Geo. Wash. L. Rev. 539 (1981).

15. [1981 Transfer Binder] Fed. Sec. L. Rep. (CCH) ¶ 82,847 (S.E.C. Feb. 28, 1981), 22 SEC Docket 292 (March 17, 1981).

16. 17 C.F.R. § 201.2(e) (1982). For a description of Rule 2(e), *see* note 255 *infra*.

17. [1981 Transfer Binder] Fed. Sec. L. Rep. (CCH) ¶ 82,847, at 84,172-73 (S.E.C. Feb. 28, 1981). For more discussion on this standard, *see* notes 252-68 and accompanying text *infra*. *See also* pages 251-68 herein *infra*.

18. *Id.* at 84,170.

19. Securities Act Release No. 6344 [Current] Fed. Sec. L. Rep. (CCH) ¶ 83,026 (Sept. 21, 1981). For more discussion, *see* notes 252-68 and accompanying text *infra*.

20. *See* Brief *Amicus Curiae* of Federal Administrative Agencies in Support of Petition for Rehearing and Suggestion for Rehearing *En Banc*, Ford v. FTC, 673 F.2d 1008 (9th Cir. 1981).

21. *See* cases cited in notes 22-24 *infra*.

22. 332 U.S. 194 (1947).

23. *Id.* at 203. *See* NLRB v. Bell Aerospace Co., 416 U.S. 267, 294 (1974) (the NLRB "is not precluded from announcing new principles in adjudicative proceedings and that the choice between rulemaking and adjudication lies in the first instance within the Board's discretion"); NLRB v. Wyman-Gordon Co., 394 U.S. 759, 765 (1969) ("Adjudicated cases may, and do, of course, serve as vehicles for the formulation of agency policies which are applied and announced therein").

24. *See* 3 Mezines, Stein & Gruff, Administrative Law § 14.01 (1981). *See also* British Caledonian Airways, Ltd. v. CAB, 584 F.2d 982, 994 (D.C. Cir. 1978); Drug Package, Inc. v. NLRB, 570 F.2d 1340, 1346 n.5 (8th Cir. 1978); Giles Lowery Stockyards, Inc. v. Department of Agriculture, 565 F.2d 321, 325 (5th Cir. 1977); NLRB v. A.P.W. Products Co., 316 F.2d 899, 905 (2d Cir. 1963); cases cited in note 23 *supra*; 2 Davis, Administrative Law Treatise § 7.25, at 118 (1979).

ever, may have been eroded, at least somewhat, by the Ninth Circuit's recent decision in *Ford v. FTC*.[25] There, the court, in holding that the Federal Trade Commission exceeded its authority by proceeding to create new law through adjudication rather than rulemaking, premised its decision on the consequence that the FTC's order would have widespread application.[26]

The above discussion serves to focus that the SEC generally has relatively broad discretion to select the forum which it believes will most effectively enable it to carry out its legitimate functions and policies in a particular proceeding. The result of such is that the Commission's diverse programs and their concomitant impact on corporate internal affairs are usually effectuated by either adjudication or rulemaking. Moreover, the Commission may seek or urge the adoption of legislation to resolve widespread and egregious misconduct. The enactment of the Foreign Corrupt Practices Act[27] serves as such an example. It should be further noted that before the passage of that legislation, the SEC through its Questionable Payments Program and the bringing of enforcement actions effectively dealt with this problem.[28]

II. EXHORTATION

The exhortatory approach, perhaps more appropriately viewed as jawboning, was frequently employed during the Williams chairmanship in an effort to help remedy certain perceived problems in the corporate machinery. Undoubtedly, the thrust of this approach was directed at corporate management and the self-regulatory organizations. In the past, the SEC has also affected corporate conduct through the issuance of reports and the holding of conferences, a number of which have been conducted with the assistance

---

25. 673 F.2d 1008 (9th Cir. 1981).

26. *Id.* at 1009-10. *See* Patel v. Immigration and Naturalization Service, 638 F.2d 1199 (9th Cir. 1980). *But see* Brief, note 20 *supra,* where nine federal administrative agencies jointly filed an *amicus curiae* brief in support of the FTC's petition for rehearing and suggestion for rehearing *en banc.* Referring to the Ninth Circuit's opinion, the agencies argued that "[t]o state, as the present opinion does, that articulation of 'new law' in an adjudication with potentially widespread applicability constitutes an abuse of discretion is to effect a major alteration in the way in which administrative agencies operate, and to cast substantial doubt upon the validity of ongoing and future adjudication." *Id.* at 4. The petition was denied. *See* 673 F.2d at 1010-12.

27. Pub. L. No. 95-213, title I, 91 Stat. 1494 (1977). For discussion on the Act, *see* notes 224-33 and accompanying text *infra.* For further discussion herein on the FCPA, *see* pages 106-08 *infra.*

28. *See, e.g.,* SEC v. Jos. Schlitz Brewing Co., 452 F. Supp. 824 (E.D. Wis. 1978); SENATE COMM. ON BANKING, HOUSING AND URBAN AFFAIRS, 94TH CONG., 2D SESS., REPORT OF THE SECURITIES AND EXCHANGE COMMISSION ON QUESTIONABLE AND ILLEGAL CORPORATE PAYMENTS PRACTICES 20 (Comm. Print, 1976) (hereinafter cited as SEC QUESTIONABLE PAYMENTS REPORT). For further discussion herein on this subject, *see* pages 56-57 *infra.*

of leading members of the securities bar and others of which the staff alone has been responsible.[29] Regardless of the particular problem addressed, however, the hallmark of the SEC's exhortatory approach in this area generally has been that it seeks to ameliorate or address particular weaknesses in the corporate accountability mechanism without the imposition of government regulation.

A. Jawboning

In a variety of contexts, SEC Commissioners have addressed corporate mechanisms and procedures that, in their views, were in need of increased accountability. For example, former Commissioner Phillip A. Loomis, Jr., urged that corporations should adopt their own codes of conduct to provide officers and employees with sufficient guidance as to the types of behavior that are deemed acceptable in connection with business dealings.[30] According to Commissioner John Evans, disclosure should extend beyond financial matters to social issues, thereby enhancing accountability to shareholders and the public.[31] On the other hand, former Commissioner Roberta Karmel, an outspoken critic during the Williams era, cautioned that SEC policies to promote corporate accountability should "go forward in an atmosphere of respectful, creative tension."[32]

Undoubtedly, the most active Commissioner in addressing perceived problems of corporate accountability was former Chairman Williams. During his tenure, Chairman Williams described his preferred corporate structure as requiring that those who wield corporate powers be held accountable for the consequences of their stewardship. To help effectuate this objective, his ideal board of directors would consist of independent directors except for the chief executive officer who would not serve as chairman of the board. In defining directors who would be independent of management, Chairman Williams excluded such persons as the corporation's outside counsel, in-

---

29. *See* notes 30-72 and accompanying text *infra.*

30. Loomis, speech before the National Association of Corporate Directors and the Institute of Auditors, reported in SEC REG. & L. REP. (BNA) No. 581, D-1 (Dec. 3, 1980).

31. *See* FED. SEC. L. REP. (CCH) No. 886, Part I, at 4 (Nov. 19, 1980). *But see* SENATE COMM. ON BANKING, HOUSING AND URBAN AFFAIRS, 96TH CONG., 2D SESS., SECURITIES AND EXCHANGE COMMISSION STAFF REPORT ON CORPORATE ACCOUNTABILITY 277 (Comm. Print, 1980) (hereinafter cited as SEC STAFF CORPORATE ACCOUNTABILITY REPORT) ("Proposals that the Commission move away from primarily an economic test of materiality [to require disclosure of socially significant information] are troubling to the staff because there is no readily available alternative basis for determining the materiality of information").

32. Karmel, "The Quest for Accountability," before the Middle Atlantic Regional Group of the American Society of Corporate Secretaries, at 12 (Jan. 9, 1980).

vestment bankers and major suppliers.[33] Moreover, he stressed that audit, nominating, and compensation committees should play an integral part in the accountability process.[34]

Chairman Williams also addressed the roles of the lawyer and the accountant in this process. Referring to the lawyer's role, he stated that counsel has the opportunity to bring considerations of both ethics and law to bear on a corporation's behavior.[35] Noting that the responsibility and prestige of inside counsel have increased dramatically in recent years, Chairman Williams asserted that such persons should play an active role in shaping corporate events as they occur, in assessing and determining corporate policies, and in establishing the tone and standard for what may be called "the

---

33. See Williams address, "Corporate Accountability," at 26, before the Fifth Annual Securities Regulation Institute, San Diego, Calif. (Jan. 18, 1978); Williams address, "Corporate Accountability and Corporate Power," presented at the Fairless Lecture Series, Carnegie-Mellon University, Pittsburgh, Pa. (Oct. 24, 1979). In this regard, the Corporate Directors Guidebook, published by the American Bar Association's Section of Corporation, Banking and Business Law, recommended that corporate boards be composed of a majority of non-management directors and that each important committee, except for the executive committee, have only non-management members. See 33 Bus. Law. 1591 (1978). But see Kripke, note 1 supra, at 175-79.

34. See Williams, speech before the Institute of Advanced Legal Studies, reported in Fed. Sec. L. Rep. (CCH) No. 885, Part I, at 6 (Nov. 12, 1980). See also Brudney, The Independent Director—Heavenly City or Potemkin Village? 95 Harv. L. Rev. 597 (1982). At Chairman Williams' request, the New York Stock Exchange (NYSE) required that, as a listing requirement, domestic firms maintain audit committees composed solely of outside directors. Some commentators contend that the Commission compelled the NYSE to adopt this measure. See Coffee, Beyond the Shut-Eyed Sentry: Toward a Theoretical View of Corporate Misconduct and an Effective Legal Response, 63 Va. L. Rev. 1099, 1274 (1977) ("the SEC virtually thrust the audit committee rule upon the New York Stock Exchange"); Kirpke, note 1 supra, at 190 ("to characterize the New York Stock Exchange's action as that of a self-regulatory agency providing voluntary leadership . . . is unreal"). More recently, the American Stock Exchange and the Board of Governors of the National Association of Securities Dealers have taken action in regard to the establishment of audit committees. See SEC Staff Corporate Accountability Report, note 31 supra, at 637-39.

It is possible that this "exhortatory" approach, along with other factors, has achieved, at least in part, its objective. For example, in the fall of 1978, the NYSE conducted a corporate governance survey. Questionnaires were mailed by the American Association of Corporate Secretaries to their 1700 members, of which 993 responded (58 percent). Six hundred fifty-five of these respondents were NYSE companies. The survey indicated that approximately 80 percent of the companies responding had a board of directors composed of a majority of non-managerial directors; there was a marked increase in the number of companies that had established audit, compensation, and nominating committees as compared to 1975; there was a marked increase in the number of such committees being composed of non-managerial directors as compared to 1975; and out of the companies responding (both NYSE and non-NYSE companies) 92 percent maintained an audit committee composed of non-managerial directors. Both 1980 and 1981 studies indicate that, from a corporate accountability perspective, these figures have improved. See notes 61, 73, 277-78 and accompanying text infra.

35. Williams, Corporate Accountability and the Lawyer's Role, 34 Bus. Law. 7, 13 (1978).

conduct of corporations."[36] Finally, respecting the accountant's role, Chairman Williams, among other things, encouraged the American Institute of Certified Public Accountants to adopt a professional standard mandating independent audit committees.[37]

It bears emphasis that, while Chairman Williams and other Commissioners exhorted those involved in the corporate machinery to effect changes in order to remedy certain perceived deficiencies, they, for the most part, called for voluntary initiatives rather than governmental intervention. While some commentators have suggested that such statements of voluntary action in actuality represent an *in terrorem* approach,[38] the fact of the matter is that the Commission has frequently opposed undue federal incursion into the corporate accountability area. In this regard, Chairman Williams stated that he "ha[d] little confidence in Government's ability to dictate corporate governance structure without becoming oppressively destructive."[39] Thus, for example, in testimony before the Senate Subcommittee on Securities regarding the proposed Protection of Shareholders' Rights Act of 1980, which was an effort to establish federal minimum standards relating to composition of corporate boards, duties of corporate directors, audit and nominating committees, and shareholders' rights,[40] Chairman Williams expressed his

---

36. Williams, *The Role of Inside Counsel in Corporate Accountability,* FED. SEC. L. REP. (CCH) ¶ 82,318, at 82,369 (Oct. 4, 1979). For further discussion herein on this issue, *see* pages 251-68 *infra.*

37. Williams, "The Role of the Director in Corporate Accountability," at 24, before the Economic Club of Detroit (May 1, 1978).

38. *See* Kripke, note 1 *supra,* at 191 ("The constant repetition of the refrain—that experts and institutions of the financial world, *i.e.,* the accounting standard setters, the auditors, the lawyers, must voluntarily improve the arrangements for internal control and corporate governance or government will step in—is too insistent to be passed off as mere exhortation to voluntary action"). *See also* Wolfson, *A Critique of Corporate Law,* 34 U. MIAMI L. REV. 959, 987-94 (1980).

39. FINANCIER (Correspondence) at 15-16 (Aug. 1980).

40. S. 2567, 96th Cong., 2d Sess. (1980). *See* Corporation Democracy Act of 1980, H.R. 7010, 96th Cong., 2d Sess. (1980). Pertinent provisions of the bills, if they had been enacted, would have required that a majority of a corporation's board be composed of independent directors, that the audit and nominating committees be composed solely of independent directors, that each director has a "duty of loyalty" and a "duty of care" to the corporation and its shareholders, that cumulative voting be required, that shareholders be entitled to vote on major corporate transactions, and that extensive disclosure be required in regard to such matters as employment discrimination, compliance with environmental controls, tax rates, cost of legal and accounting fees, and planned plant closings. *See generally* Metzenbaum, *Legislative Approaches to Corporate Governance,* 56 NOTRE DAME LAW. 926 (1981) ("There is widespread agreement within and without the business community that reforms are necessary in the governance of the nation's major corporations"); Millspaugh, *The Corporate Democracy Act— A Renaissance or Death Knell for the Corporate World?* 4 CORP. L. REV. 291 (1981). For further discussion herein on this subject, *see* pages 252-53 *infra.*

opposition to such government intervention.[41] While sensing the need for enhancing corporate accountability by means of increasing the role and responsibility of independent directors, he concluded that he "ha[d] severe reservations about the wisdom of legislation designed to regulate the corporate boardroom" and that enactment of the bill might well "retard" the goals that it intended to achieve.[42] Other examples of deference to voluntary action have been the Commission's long-held view of deferring to the private sector for the promulgation of accounting standards, notwithstanding its statutory authority in this area, and its urging of Congress that the accounting profession be given the opportunity to reform itself.[43] On the other hand, the Commission strongly advocated legislation to deal with the question of improper payments and off-books slush funds, when it perceived that only legislation would serve to correct the widespread abuses that then existed.[44]

This rhetoric urging improved standards of corporate accountability and governance has largely disappeared during the Shad chairmanship. Indeed, jawboning currently focuses on the capital formation process and stresses that the abuse of inside information is a matter of major enforcement priority.[45] In this regard, Chairman Shad has called upon investment banking, brokerage, and law firms, as well as publicly held corporations, to help ferret out such abuses.[46] An argument can be made that the Commission's apparent abandonment of the corporate accountability rhetoric is correct. During a recessionary period, capital formation will help stimulate the econ-

---

41. Statement of Chairman Williams Before the Subcommittee on Securities of the Senate Committee on Banking, Housing, and Urban Affairs in Connection with Hearings on S. 2567 (Nov. 19, 1980). In his testimony, Chairman Williams stated that "the views which I express today are my own and not necessarily those of my fellow Commissioners—although I believe that at least a majority would agree with my conclusion at this time."

42. *Id.* at 23.

43. *See* Securities and Exchange Commission, *Report to Congress on the Accounting Profession and the Commission's Oversight Role,* FED. SEC. L. REP. (CCH) ¶ 82,120 (June 28, 1979). In its concluding remarks in its second report to Congress, the Commission stated that it was not recommending legislation to supersede or control the regulation of accountants. *Id.* at 81,973. For more discussion on this point, *see* Gruenbaum & Steinberg, *Accountants' Liability and Responsibility: Securities, Criminal and Common Law,* 13 LOY. L.A.L. REV. 247, 292-94 (1980).

44. *See* Statement of Roderick Hills, Chairman of the Securities and Exchange Commission, Hearings Before the Senate Committee on Banking, Housing and Urban Affairs at 111 on S. 305 (95th Cong., 1st Sess.) (1977); Statement of Harold M. Williams, Chairman of the Securities and Exchange Commission, Hearings Before the House Subcommittee on Consumer Protection and Finance of the Committee on Interstate and Foreign Commerce at 196 on H.R. 3815 and H.R. 1602 (95th Cong., 1st Sess.) (1977).

45. *See, e.g.,* Hudson, *SEC May Be Losing Its Former Toughness, Some Observers Think,* Wall St. J., March 22, 1982, at 1, col. 1; *The SEC Swats at Insider Trading,* BUSINESS WEEK (April 19, 1982), at 96. *See* notes 121-27 and accompanying text *infra.*

46. *See* Hudson, note 45 *supra,* at 18; SEC. REG. & L. REP. (BNA) No. 612, A-4 (July 15, 1981).

omy, not the number of independent directors on corporate boards. Moreover, insider trading constitutes one of the greatest threats to maintaining the integrity of the marketplace and investor protection.[47] Nonetheless, it may be argued that the Commission's focus is too narrow. Such rhetoric may imply that the SEC is concerned only with so-called traditional frauds, thereby greatly diminishing the advances made in the Stanley Sporkin era[48] to seek enforcement solutions for a wide range of corporate activities that implicate the federal securities laws.[49] Moreover, it may be argued that, while capital formation is laudable, the SEC is not a chamber of commerce. In short, the Commission was created primarily to protect the investing public, not to serve the interests of business.[50]

B. Reports and Conferences

During the past decade, the Commission and its staff, with substantial input from the private sector, have sponsored or participated in at least three major reports or conferences: the SEC Major Issues Conference,[51] the Advisory Committee Report on Corporate Disclosure,[52] and the SEC Staff Corporate Accountability Report.[53] These undertakings shared the common thread that each, at least in part, concerned the impact that SEC regulation and exhortation had upon certain developments in corporate internal affairs. For example, the Final Report of the SEC Major Issues Conference discussed the desirability of reporting companies maintaining audit committees com-

---

47. *See generally* authorities cited in notes 10-14 *supra*.

48. Stanley Sporkin was Director of the SEC's Division of Enforcement from 1974 to 1981.

49. As stated in a recent Wall Street Journal article: "Under Mr. Sporkin, the SEC brought about 60 cases alleging corporate bribery overseas, uncovered several instances of secret self-dealing by top corporate officers and tackled some of the most prestigious accounting firms, underwriters and law firms." Hudson, note 45 *supra*, at 18.

50. *See id.;* Vilkin, *SEC: An Agency in Turmoil?* National Law Journal, March 29, 1982, at 1, col. 1.

51. FINAL REPORT OF THE SEC MAJOR ISSUES CONFERENCE (1977). This conference, sponsored by the SEC, was attended by sixty-four participants, including former SEC Commissioners, industrialists, academicians, members of public interest organizations, and members of the law and accounting professions to consider major policy issues which would be affected by many of the important individual decisions which were to be made by the Commission. *See also* SEC, DISCLOSURE TO INVESTORS—A REAPPRAISAL OF ADMINISTRATIVE POLICIES UNDER THE '33 AND '34 ACTS (1969) ("Wheat Report").

52. HOUSE COMM. ON INTERSTATE AND FOREIGN COMMERCE, REPORT OF THE ADVISORY COMM. ON CORPORATE DISCLOSURE TO THE SEC, 95TH CONG., 1ST SESS. (Comm. Print 95-29, 1977). The Advisory Committee was established to study the mandatory disclosure system. *But see* Kripke, *Where Are We on Securities Disclosure After the Advisory Committee Report?* 6 SEC. REG. L.J. 99 (1978).

53. SEC STAFF CORPORATE ACCOUNTABILITY REPORT, note 31 *supra*.

posed of independent directors.[54] Along similar lines, the Advisory Committee Report on Corporate Disclosure recommended that the Commission should promulgate requirements that enhance "the ability of directors—as the representative shareholders—to serve as the independent, effective monitors of management."[55]

Undoubtedly, the most intensive study of corporate internal affairs was the 1980 Staff Report on Corporate Accountability. This study, the result of a three-year effort, drew upon public hearings and comments received from several different groups, including corporations, self-regulatory organizations, law firms, financial institutions, public interest groups, academicians and government officials.[56] Its genesis lay not in a generalized academic concept of ideal corporate structure, but in the wake of "the collapse of several major companies, the hundreds of corporations involved in questionable payments, and corporate non-compliance with environmental and other laws [which] astonished the public, shareholders, and, in many cases, even the affected companies' directors."[57] The Report noted that successive investigations and reports added support to the proposition that, as a whole, the corporate accountability framework needed strengthening.[58] The Report carefully and narrowly focused on accountability of the corporation to shareholders and investors, leaving it to "others" to consider the "larger corporate accountability issues [which] transcend the jurisdiction and expertise of this Commission . . ."—the obligations of corporations to noninvestor constituencies such as "employees, consumers, communities, federal, state and local governments and the public generally."[59]

Far from containing major innovations of either a substantive or procedural nature, however, the Report, although making several specific recommendations, generally consists of staff discussion on a broad range of

---

54. SEC Major Issues Conference, note 51 supra, at 8. The conferees also "urged that the establishment of such committees should be expanded beyond companies listed on the New York Stock Exchange. . . ." Id.

55. Report of the Advisory Comm., note 52 supra, at D-22. Other recommendations that the Advisory Committee made included that: shareholders be given information regarding "the identification of the nominating committee members and a requirement that if a director resigns and submits a letter stating a reason, that letter should be filed with a Form 8-K if the director so requests." Id. at 413. Also, the Committee recommended that "particularly in those areas of possible conflicts of interest, such as antitakeover and compensation plans, the Commission should attempt to get better, more uniform disclosure in proxy statements of the disadvantages as well as the advantages of management's proposals. Id. at 416.

56. SEC Staff Corporate Accountability Report, note 31 supra, at 1, 29-30.

57. Id. at 29.

58. Id.

59. Id. at 33 ("Inevitably, the effectiveness of a corporation's board of directors and the degree of concern and participation by its shareholders will affect the corporation's relationships with other constituencies, but the Report is, first and foremost, about accountability of the corporation to shareholders and investors"). Id.

significant and controversial issues. Among the subjects the staff addresses are shareholder participation in the corporate electoral process, the shareholder proposal rule, disclosure of socially significant information, the role of the board of directors in the corporate accountability process, and the role of institutional investors in this process. Although the Report is far too comprehensive to thoroughly examine for the purposes of this chapter, the following discussion will highlight some of the major issues.[60]

One such issue considered by the staff was whether the Commission should adopt a rule requiring all of the country's more than 10,000 publicly held corporations to have audit committees composed of independent directors. A staff survey of 1,200 companies found that 85 percent of them already have such committees and that the majority of these are composed of independent directors. In light of this development, the staff recommended that the Commission should not proceed with consideration of such a rule at that time.[61]

Another issue considered was the extent to which corporations used nominating committees as a means of fostering accountability in selecting, evaluating, and reviewing nominee incumbent directors. The staff found that only 29 percent of publicly held companies, principally the larger ones, had created such committees. Despite this percentage, the staff recommended that the Commission delay the development of a nominating committee rule until it could assess whether more corporations would initiate such committees on their own. The staff indicated, however, a position on which subsequently it has arguably retreated, that if there was not a substantial increase in the number of companies that have independent nominating committees that consider shareholder nominations, it would urge the Commission to authorize the development of a rule to require companies to adopt procedures for considering such nominations.[62]

---

60. For an excellent discussion of the Report, *see* Vandegrift, *SEC Discusses Wide Range of Accountability Issues,* Legal Times (Wash.), Oct. 20, 1980, at 20, col. 1.

61. SEC STAFF CORPORATE ACCOUNTABILITY REPORT, note 31 *supra,* at 28-29, 587 ("The audit committee today has become so well established that any company which has chosen not to establish such a committee, composed solely of directors independent of management, should weigh carefully the costs of such a decision in terms of liability and loss of control against the reasons, if any, for not establishing an audit committee"). *Id.* at 583. *See also* American Law Institute, PRINCIPLES OF CORPORATE GOVERNANCE AND STRUCTURE: RESTATEMENT AND RECOMMENDATIONS § 3.05 (Tentative Draft No. 1 1982) (stating that "[c]orporate law should provide that every large publicly held corporation shall have an audit committee. . .").

62. *Id.* at 57-58, 583-84 ("It is essential to recognize . . . that under corporate statutes the power to elect the board is vested in the shareholders, and to the extent that boards of directors are not more forthcoming in their efforts to facilitate shareholder participation in the electoral process, a shareholder nomination rule may be necessary"). *Id.* at 584. Recently, in Securities Exchange Act Release No. 18532, 24 SEC DOCKET 1224 (March 16, 1982), the staff stated that in view of the "dramatic" increase in the number of nominating committees from 19.4 percent of companies in 1979 to 30.4 percent in 1981, it "has determined not to recommend

The staff also considered the adequacy of the Commission's approach to the disclosure of socially significant corporate information. During the decade of the 1970s, the Commission increasingly was called upon to address questions relating to the disclosure of such information.[63] Although not necessarily material from an economic perspective and although many shareholders desire solely to maximize their investments, a number of reasonable shareholders are concerned that the companies in which they have an equity interest adhere to certain minimal ethical and legal standards.[64] With these policies in mind, the Report examined the extent to which socially significant information should be disclosed in proxy statements. The conclusion reached was that "unless issuers know that there is a reasonable probability that shareholders would consider information about a particular social topic important when voting, the economic materiality standard, in conjunction with the Commission's proxy rules, are sufficient guides to issuers in determining what socially significant information should be disclosed in the proxy statement."[65] While the staff's recommendation probably did not go far enough for some advocates,[66] it is highly significant that the Report recognizes the crucial distinction between an investment decision and a voting decision. For example, although a corporation's antisocial conduct may not be considered material in an investment context due to the remote possibility that economic consequences would ensue, such conduct may be viewed as important to shareholders voting in an election of directors because it reflects upon the directors' competency and integrity to assume a corporate position of trust.[67]

---

such a rule." *Id.* at 1226. It is questionable whether such an increase is "dramatic" under these circumstances. *See also* ALI Draft Restatement, note 61 *supra*, at § 3.06 (stating that "[c]orporate law should provide that [with certain exceptions] every large publicly held corporation shall have a nominating committee. . .". For further discussion on this point, *see* note 73 and accompanying text *infra*.

63. *See, e.g.,* Natural Resources Defense Council, Inc., 606 F.2d 1031 (D.C. Cir. 1979); Committee for Human Rights v. SEC, 432 F.2d 659 (D.C. Cir. 1970), *vacated on mootness grounds,* 404 U.S. 403 (1972).

64. *See, e.g.,* Natural Resources Defense Council, Inc. v. SEC, 389 F. Supp. 689 (D.D.C. 1974), in which the court alluded to the qualitative nature of information relating to a corporation's environmental policy. For discussion herein on this case, *see* pages 110-13 *infra*. *See generally* Stevenson, *The SEC and the New Disclosure,* 62 CORNELL L. REV. 50 (1976); Comment, *Disclosure of Regulatory Violations Under the Federal Securities Laws: Establishing the Limits of Materiality,* 30 AM. U.L. REV. 225 (1980); pages 108-13 herein *infra*.

65. SEC STAFF CORPORATE ACCOUNTABILITY REPORT, note 31 *supra*, at 234. *See id.* at 44-45; note 31 *supra*.

66. *See* note 63 *supra*.

67. *See* pages 102-04 herein *infra*. *See also* Weiss, *Social Regulation of Business Activity: Reforming the Corporate Governance System to Resolve an Institutional Impasse,* 28 UCLA L. REV. 343 (1981).

Another interesting area addressed in the Report was the impact of the Supreme Court's 1978 decision in *First National Bank of Boston v. Bellotti*.[68] That decision found unconstitutional a state statute which prohibited a corporation from expending corporate funds to make its views known on a political referendum unless the subject matter was materially related to the corporation's business. In so holding, the Supreme Court reasoned that, through the process of corporate democracy, shareholders could be informed of such corporate expenditures.[69] In light of that holding, the staff Report urged the Commission to request comments on possible ways of enabling shareholders to be aware of such expenditures, including the need for a general disclosure requirement regarding corporate political activities and expenditures.[70]

As stated before, the Staff Corporate Accountability Report contained no major or startling recommendations. Yet, this moderate nature of the Report says something significant about the Commission's role in the corporate governance process. Less than a decade ago, few would have predicted that, by the end of the 1970s, most publicly held corporations in this country

---

68. 435 U.S. 765 (1978). For commentary on *Bellotti, see, e.g.,* Brudney, *Business Corporations and Stockholders' Rights Under the First Amendment,* 91 YALE L.J. 235 (1981); O'Kelley, *The Constitutional Rights of Corporations Revisited: Social and Political Expression and the Corporation After* First National Bank v. Bellotti, 67 GEO. L.J. 1347 (1979); Rome & Roberts, *Bellotti and the First Amendment: A New Era in Corporate Speech?* 3 CORP. L. REV. 28 (1979); Shaw, *Corporate Speech in the Marketplace of Ideas,* 7 JOUR. CORP. L. 265 (1982).

69. 435 U.S. at 794 ("Ultimately shareholders may decide, through the procedures of corporate democracy, whether their corporations should engage in debate on public issues").

70. SEC STAFF CORPORATE ACCOUNTABILITY REPORT, note 31 *supra,* at 39-40, 194-202. Another concern expressed by the staff was the role of institutional shareholders. The staff concluded that institutions, in discharging their fiduciary duties, should exercise their voting authority that accompanies their management of securities in such a manner so as to promote corporate accountability. Specifically, the staff recommended that such institutions: (1) establish formalized procedures for reaching proxy voting decisions; (2) establish voting criteria designed to produce objective voting decisions, including criteria for reaching decisions on matters having no investment impact; and (3) discontinue treating an uncontested election of directors as a matter of warranting an automatic vote for the slate of nominees. The staff also urged institutions to make their voting procedures and practices readily available to customers and the public. The staff sought Commission authorization to study the public availability of such information and, if necessary, to develop a legislative proposal designed to increase disclosure in this area. *Id.* at 50-54, 409-25. *See also* Securities Exchange Act Release No. 15385 (Dec. 6, 1978); Securities Exchange Act Release No. 14970 (July 18, 1978). These releases involve the Commission's proposal, and ultimate withdrawal thereof, of a rule requiring certain institutions which are subject to the SEC's proxy provisions to disclose their voting policies and procedures in their annual reports to stockholders. The major drawback to the proposed rule was that many large institutions, such as pension funds and banks, other than bank holding companies, are not subject to the proxy provisions. In withdrawing the proposed rule, however, the Commission reaffirmed its belief that "there is shareholder interest in institutional voting policies and procedures."

would have boards composed of a majority of outside directors and audit committees comprised solely of such outside directors. [71] This development may be viewed as part of an evolutionary process in the corporate accountability framework in which the Commission's exhortatory approach played a crucial part.[72]

On the other hand, it may be argued that there already has been a retreat from the Staff Corporate Accountability Report. For example, less than two years after the Report, the staff declined to recommend that the Commission promulgate a rule requiring independent nominating committees even though there was only a slight increase in the number of corporations that had such committees.[73] Moreover, despite the recommendation contained in the staff Report, the Commission has yet to request comments on providing a means by which shareholders can be informed of corporate political activities and expenditures. Most recently, the Commission's decision not to take action against Citicorp for not disclosing alleged foreign exchange trading impropriety in order to avoid foreign taxes and currency exchange controls[74] has been viewed by some commentators as a significant step backward from the prior positions taken by the Commission in the management integrity area.[75] In sum, although much of the Corporate Accountability Report remains viable, recent Commission actions (or inaction) signal an apparent retreat from some of the corporate accountability themes stressed in that Report.

III. SEC DISCLOSURE

Undoubtedly, the central focus of the federal securities laws as they apply to publicly held corporations is that of disclosure. Although crucial, disclosure requirements are flanked by two other Commission sources that impact

---

71. *See* notes 34, 61 and accompanying text *supra*.

72. *See* Vandegrift, note 60 *supra*, at 24.

73. Securities Exchange Act Release No. 18532 (March 8, 1982), 24 SEC DOCKET 1224, 1226 (March 16, 1982) (stating that, according to the 1981 results, 30.4 percent of companies, compared to 19.4 percent in 1979, had nominating committees). *But see* SEC STAFF CORPORATE ACCOUNTABILITY REPORT, note 31 *supra*, at 525 ("The staff's own statistics indicate that 28.9 percent of the category of all companies have nominating committees. . .").

74. *See* SEC Statement on Citicorp (March 5, 1982).

75. *See* Hudson, note 45 *supra*; Vilkin, note 50 *supra*. For further discussion, *see* notes 115-27 and accompanying text *infra*. *See also* Securities Exchange Act Release No. 19135 (Oct. 14, 1982), where the Commission proposed "sweeping changes in its shareholder-voting rules, including some that would make it harder for social activists to press their causes at corporate meetings." Hudson, *SEC Proposes Rule Changes on Holder Votes*, WALL ST. J., Oct. 15, 1982, at p.3, col. 1. Some of these proposed changes would enable corporations to exclude shareholder proposals on a much easier basis than current practice. In this regard, "Commissioner John Evans defended the current system, saying the shareholder-proposal process 'is one of the trappings of corporate democracy, and we have to be careful not to snuff out that little light' of democracy." *Id.*

on such corporations. The first, discussed in the preceding section, is what may be viewed as the Commission's exhortatory approach. The second, to be examined in the following sections, is substantive regulation by means of rules and enforcement measures.[76] The present discussion addresses the Commission's influence on corporate internal affairs from the perspective of disclosure. As will be seen, the Commission's current approach toward disclosure, although to a large extent consistent with prior practice, appears in certain respects to take a narrower perspective.

Although the rationale underlying disclosure is not based primarily on influencing corporate internal affairs but rather on providing shareholders and the marketplace with sufficient information to make intelligent decisions and to be apprised of significant developments, there is little question that disclosure has a substantial impact on the normative conduct of corporations.[77] In this regard, the Commission's disclosure policies, in Brandeisian manner,[78] have not only had an effect of deterring unlawful or questionable conduct but have played a positive role in influencing the establishment of improved standards of conduct.[79]

Certain of these disclosure mandates directly impact on the integrity and competency of corporate management. For example, self-dealing by management must be disclosed pursuant to the Commission's disclosure requirements relating to remuneration and conflicts of interest.[80] Generally,

---

76. See Cohen, *S.E.C. Power to Regulate Corporate Internal Affairs Through Disclosure*, in STANDARDS FOR REGULATING CORPORATE INTERNAL AFFAIRS 292 (The Ray Garrett, Jr., Corporate and Securities Law Institute, sponsored by Northwestern University School of Law) (D. Fischel ed., 1981).

77. *See, e.g.* L. BRANDEIS, OTHER PEOPLE'S MONEY 62 (1914) ("Sunlight is said to be the best of disinfectants"). R. STEVENSON, CORPORATIONS AND INFORMATION—SECRECY, ACCESS AND DISCLOSURE 81-82 (1980) ("Today the disclosure requirements of the securities laws are used, in a variety of ways, for the explicit purpose of influencing a wide range of corporate primary behavior. . ."); Frankfurter, *The Federal Securities Act II*, FORTUNE (Aug. 1933), at 53, 55 (disclosure has a "shrinking quality"); Sommer, Book Review (H. KRIPKE, THE SEC AND CORPORATE DISCLOSURE: REGULATION IN SEARCH OF A PURPOSE), 93 HARV. L. REV. 1595, 1601 (1980) ("the frequency with which corporations have withheld [disclosure of] adverse information, even when it posed the danger of Commission and private action, suggests that if the potential sanctions were reduced at all the incidence of such withholding would increase"); Weiss, *Disclosure and Corporate Accountability*, 34 BUS. LAW. 575 (1979) ("one of the central themes of the system by which large corporations are governed [is] that corporate decision-making be regulated through mandatory disclosure requirements rather than direct government intervention").

78. *See* Brandeis, note 77 *supra.*

79. *See* Cohen, note 76 *supra*, at 296 ("on the positive side, if specific facts as to the independence and diligence of directors, or as to the use of special board committees or particular types of internal controls, are required to be openly discussed, many a corporation will prefer to report progress in these areas rather than backwardness, and progress will indeed occur"). *See also* 14 SEC. REG. & L. REP. (BNA) 1575-76 (Sept. 17, 1982) (*Wharton Economics Professor Says SEC Disclosure Rules Benefit Economy*).

80. *See* Item 402, Regulation S-K, 17 C.F.R. § 229.402 (1982); Item 404, Regulation

Commission forms require disclosure of adjudicated illegal activities by officers and directors, provided that such violations are material to an evaluation of the ability or integrity of such persons.[81] Also, disclosure is mandated of certain "events" transpiring during the previous five years which are material to an evaluation of the competency or integrity of any director, director-nominee or executive officer.[82] Although the extent to which these disclosure requirements affect corporate internal affairs is uncertain, it may be safely stated that they have such an impact.[83]

Turning to rulemaking proceedings that have centered on disclosure obligations, the Commission has addressed such subjects as the structure and role of corporate boards of directors, financial reporting and accounting developments, extraordinary events (such as going-private transactions and tender offers), and developments in the corporation finance area (such as changes in management remuneration). With respect to corporate boards, the Commission has adopted rules that require disclosure of whether the board has auditing, nominating, or compensation committees, require a brief description of functions performed by each of these committees, require disclosure of the total number of board and committee meetings held, and require the disclosure of the identity of directors who do not attend 75 percent of the total number of board or committee meetings held.[84] In this regard, the Commission declined to adopt the staff suggestion of labeling directors as management, affiliated non-management, and unaffiliated non-management.[85] Disclosure, however, is required with respect to substantial business and personal relations of directors with issuers.[86] Further, the

---

S-K, *as adopted,* Securities Exchange Act Release No. 19290 (Dec. 2, 1982), 14 SEC. REG. & L. REP. (BNA) 2166 (Dec. 10, 1982). For further discussion on Items 402 and 404 herein, *see* pages 83, 86 *infra.*

81. *See* Item 401, Regulation S-K, 17 C.F.R. § 229.401 (1982).

82. *Id.* For further discussion on this subject herein, *see* pages 116-19 *infra.* For a description of such "events" requiring disclosure, *see* page 116, n.183 *infra.*

83. As another disclosure item example, Item 401(e) of Regulation S-K, 17 C.F.R. § 229.401 (1982), requires a brief account of the business experience of management and nominees during the prior five years. For further discussion on this subject herein, *see* pages 122-24 *infra.*

84. Securities Exchange Act Release No. 15384 (Dec. 6, 1978). The rule amendments also required, *inter alia,* (1) that a resigning director can submit a description, required to be disclosed by the issuer, of the reasons for resignation but that the issuer can give its own views of the disagreement and (2) that the settlement terms of an election contest must be disclosed.

85. *Id.*

86. *Id.* In this regard, disclosure of such substantial personal and business relations include that the nominee or director is a relative of an executive officer, that the nominee or director is a former officer or director of the issuer, that the nominee or director is an officer or director of a customer or supplier of the issuer, and that the law firm of the nominee or director has been retained by the issuer for the prior two years. On this last point, the Commission stated that "[i]n view of inherent conflicts faced by lawyers who serve both as directors and as counsel to corporations, the Commission is reluctant to limit disclosure of such relationships solely on the basis of the economic test." *See also* Securities Exchange Act Release No. 19290 (Dec. 2, 1982) (placing certain limitations on the foregoing disclosure requirements).

Commission has revised Item 402 of Regulation S-K on management remuneration.[87]

These disclosure developments, while important, should not be viewed in isolation but rather in conjunction with Commission exhortation and the bringing of enforcement actions that obtained, as ancillary or other equitable relief, the restructuring of corporate boards composed of a majority of non-management directors as well as the establishment of independent audit committees.[88] When viewed in their entirety, these Commission activities had the beneficial effect of inducing corporate boards to have a larger number of outside directors and to establish audit committees.

Regarding accounting and financial reporting developments, the most important recent development has been the Foreign Corrupt Practices Act.[89] One consequence of the Act is that disclosure of such questionable payments may be required, not necessarily because they impact on the earnings of the corporation, but because they bear on management integrity.[90] Thus, the required disclosure of such payments may well have the effect of deterring the making of such payments.

An important development in the Commission's administration of that Act was its proposal of new rules which, had they been adopted, would have mandated that corporate annual reports contain a statement by management as to the adequacy of internal accounting controls, which statement itself would have been required to be examined and reported on by an independent accountant.[91] Not surprisingly, the proposed rule was the subject of heavy criticism and was characterized as a compliance certificate having exorbitant costs.[92] Subsequently, the Commission declined to adopt the proposal "to allow existing voluntary and private-sector initiatives to continue to develop."[93] In its release, however, in a further effort to encourage voluntary initiatives in this field, the Commission took the oppor-

---

87. Securities Act Release No. 6003 (Dec. 4, 1978). *See* note 80 *supra*.

88. For discussion of such enforcement actions and the ancillary or other equitable relief obtained, *see* notes 183-91 and accompanying text *infra*.

89. Pub. L. No. 95-213, title I, 91 Stat. 1494 (1977). For further discussion of the Act, *see* notes 224-33 and accompanying text *infra*. For further discussion of the FCPA herein, *see* pages 56-59 *infra*.

90. *See, e.g.,* Berman v. Gerber Products Co., 454 F. Supp. 1310, 1322-23 (W.D. Mich. 1978). SEC v. Joseph Schlitz Brewing Co., 454 F. Supp. 824, 830 (E.D. Wis. 1978) *But see* Gaines v. Haughton, 645 F.2d 761, 776-79 (9th Cir. 1981), *cert. denied*, 102 S. Ct. 1006 (1982). For further discussion on this subject herein, *see* pages 106-08 *infra*.

91. Securities Exchange Act Release No. 15772, [1979 Transfer Binder] FED. SEC. L. REP. (CCH) ¶ 82,063 (April 30, 1979).

92. *See* Cohen, note 76 *supra*, at 311. *See also* Gruenbaum & Steinberg, note 43 *supra*, at 292 (the proposed rules concerning management's statement on internal accounting controls, had they been adopted, would have generated claims of liability against accountants if management's statement was found deficient).

93. Accounting Series Release No. 278, 6 FED. SEC. L. REP. (CCH) ¶ 72,300, at 62,791 (June 6, 1980).

tunity to provide some guidance regarding these developing matters. This guidance, although not necessarily required to be followed by companies, may have an influential role in improving internal accounting control practices and systems.[94]

Fundamental corporate changes that have been impacted by SEC disclosure policy are tender offers and going-private transactions. In regard to tender offers, corporate antitakeover amendments have been an issue of some significance. In October 1978, the Division of Corporation Finance issued a statement regarding disclosure in proxy and information statements of antitakeover or similar proposals.[95] Noting that the increased use to obtain corporate control has prompted many companies to consider defensive techniques to fend off hostile offers, the staff expressed concern over the adequacy of disclosure made to investors when the corporation seeks shareholder approval to amend its charter or by-laws to incorporate antitakeover or similar proposals.[96] Disclosure recommended by the staff included: (1) the reasons for the antitakeover proposals and basis for such reasons; (2) the overall effects of the proposal, including the impact upon management tenure; (3) the advantages and disadvantages of the proposal; (4) disclosure of how the proposal will operate; (5) whether the proposal was the subject of a vote of the issuer's board of directors and, if so, the result of such vote; and (6) a statement of the limitations or restrictions, if any, on the adoption of such proposals.[97]

---

94. *See* Cohen, note 76 *supra*, where the author stated:

"Some guidance" amounted to many pages of elaborate exposition, including endorsement of the original objectives and coverage of some matters going beyond what would have been included in the compulsory statements originally proposed. The end result is that there is no SEC rule requiring any specific conduct or any specific disclosure concerning conduct in respect of internal accounting controls, but—an unusual case where jawboning may be said to be a triumphant end rather than a modest beginning of the process—there is an elaborate guidebook promulgated by the SEC, not having the force of law, but perhaps affecting corporate conduct more broadly and pervasively than a formal rule would have done.

Id. at 312. Most recently, the Commission announced that it will take no further action in this regard. Significantly, the Commission stated: "In reaching this conclusion the Commission has considered the significant private-sector initiatives in this area, including the increased number of management reports included in annual reports to security holders of large companies." Accounting Series Release No. 305, 24 SEC DOCKET 888 (Feb. 9, 1982).

95. Securities Exchange Act Release No. 15230, [1978 Transfer Binder] FED. SEC. L. REP. (CCH) ¶ 81,748.

96. *Id.* at 80,985. *See* Steinberg, note 11 *supra*, at 223-24. For further discussion on this subject, *see* pages 201-02 *infra*.

97. In particular, the staff expressed its opinion that "the issuer's proxy material or information statements should disclose in a prominent place that the overall effect of the proposal

Another disclosure development in this area has been the Commission's promulgation of tender offer rules.[98] These rules establish a number of disclosure obligations, including an express duty for the tender offeror to promptly reveal material changes in the information published, sent, or delivered to shareholders.[99] In addition, Rule 14d-9 calls for the subject company to file with the SEC a Schedule 14D-9 which requires the disclosure of certain information, including a description of any material contract, agreement, arrangement, or understanding and any actual or potential conflict of interest between, among others, the offeror, the subject company, and their affiliates,[100] and disclosure in regard to certain negotiations and transactions by the subject company.[101] Perhaps the most pertinent provision for the purposes here is Rule 14e-2 which requires the subject company to publish or send to security holders a statement disclosing its position with respect to the tender offer within ten business days of the commencement of the tender offer by a person other than the issuer.[102] The statement of position can take one of three forms: (1) recommendation or rejection of the tender offer; (2) no opinion, and will remain neutral toward the tender offer; or (3) the subject company is unable to take a position with respect to the tender offer.[103] In addition, the company is required to include the reasons for its position with respect to the tender offer, including the inability

---

is to render more difficult the accomplishment of mergers or the assumption of control by a principal shareholder, and thus to make difficult the removal of management." [1978 Transfer Binder] FED. SEC. L. REP. (CCH) ¶ 81,748, at 80,985.

98. Securities Exchange Act Release No. 16384, 44 FED. REG. 70,326 (1979). In general, the rules are grouped into two regulations, Regulations 14D and 14E. If the tender offer is subject to Section 14(d)(1) of the Exchange Act, which concerns securities registered under Section 12 of that Act or securities of certain insurance and investment companies, both regulations are applicable. If the tender offer is not subject to Section 14(d)(1), only Regulation 14E is applicable. *See generally* Bloomenthal, *The New Tender Offer Regimen, State Regulation and Preemption*, 30 EMORY L.J. 35 (1981).

99. SEC Rule 14d-6(d), 17 C.F.R. § 240.14d-6(d) (1982). According to the SEC, this rule "comports with current practice and avoids any possible ambiguity, thus ensuring for disclosure of material information during the course of a tender offer." 44 FED. REG. at 70,333. *See generally* Bauman, *Rule 10b-5 and the Corporation's Affirmative Duty to Disclose*, 65 GEO. L.J. 935 (1979); Note, *Disclosure of Material Inside Information: An Affirmative Corporate Duty?* 1980 ARIZ. ST. L.J. 795.

100. SEC Schedule 14D-9, Item 3(b), 17 C.F.R. § 240.14d-101 (1982). In adopting Schedule 14D-9, the SEC "believe[d] that the disclosure elicited by the Schedule will assist security holders in making their investment decision and in evaluating the merits of a solicitation/recommendation." 44 FED. REG. at 70,336.

101. SEC Schedule 14D-9, Item 7, 17 C.F.R. § 240.14d-101 (1982). *See* Rowe, *Tender Offer Regs: Changing the Game Rules*, Legal Times (Wash.), Dec. 31, 1979, at 9, col. 1.

102. SEC Rule 14e-2, 17 C.F.R. § 240.14e-2 (1982).

103. *Id.*

to take a position.[104] In this regard, conclusory or "boilerplate" statements are not considered sufficient disclosure.[105]

Rule 14e-2 may have a significant effect on how target management responds to a hostile tender offer. Prior to the rule, a number of court decisions permitted management to remain silent during the course of a tender offer.[106] Of course, target management rarely, if ever, would remain silent during a hostile battle for control.[107] What the rule does seemingly accomplish, however, is that it compels target management to articulate its position in a conscientious manner with the ultimate objective of permitting shareholders to make their investment decisions after hearing all sides.[108] Failure on management's part to abide by this disclosure obligation under Rule 14e-2 may result in antifraud liability under the federal securities laws, even if a valid business purpose defense exists under state law.[109]

---

104. *Id.* Significantly, in order to comport with the disclosure duties of Rule 14e-2, a target company will be required in the Schedule 14D-9 to state its position and the reasons therefor. SEC Schedule 14D-9, Item 4, 17 C.F.R. § 240.14d-101 (1982). Also, if the subject company changes its position or other material changes occur, the subject company is required to promptly publish, send, or give to security holders a statement disclosing such material change. *See* Sommer & Feller, *Takeover Rules: A Cohesive Comprehensive Code,* Legal Times (Wash.), Dec. 17, 1979, at 18, col. 1.

105. SEC Schedule 14D-9, Item 4(b), 17 C.F.R. § 240.14d-101 (1982). *See* Bloomenthal, note 98 *supra,* at 50-51; Steinberg, note 11 *supra,* at 219-22.

106. *See, e.g.,* Berman v. Gerber Products Co., 454 F. Supp. 1310, 1325 (W.D. Mich. 1978) ("It is true that in general the Williams Act does not appear to impose upon the management of a target company an affirmative duty to respond to a tender offer at all"). *See also* Gelfond & Sebastian, *Reevaluating the Duties of Target Management in a Hostile Tender Offer,* 60 B.U.L. REV. 403, 410 (1980), *referring to* Piper v. Chris-Craft Industries, Inc., 430 U.S. 1 (1977) (defeated tender offeror has no implied right of action for damages for violations of Section 14(e)).

107. *See* Electronic Specialty Co. v. International Controls Corp., 409 F.2d 937 (2d Cir. 1969).

108. The legislative history of the Williams Act indicates that it was designed to protect the legitimate interests of the target corporation, its management and its shareholders, and simultaneously to allow both the target and the bidder to present fairly their views to the shareholders. As the Act's sponsor Senator Harrison Williams stated: "We have taken extreme care to avoid tipping the scales either in favor of management or in favor of the person making the takeover bid." 173 CONG. REC. 24,664 (1967) (remarks of Sen. Williams). Apparently, however, the Supreme Court took a more restrictive view of the Act's objective in Piper v. Chris-Craft Industries, Inc., where the Court stated that "[t]he sole purpose of the Williams Act was the protection of investors who are confronted with a tender offer." 430 U.S. 1, 35 (1977). For further discussion on this general subject, *see* pages 199-231 *infra.*

109. *See* Mobil Corp. v. Marathon Oil Co., 669 F.2d 366 (6th Cir. 1981) ("manipulation under the Williams Act cannot be justified by the good faith performance of fiduciary duties"). For recent cases dealing with the business judgment rule under state law, *see* Panter v. Marshall Field & Co., 646 F.2d 271 (7th Cir.), *cert. denied,* 102 S. Ct. 658 (1981); Treadway Cos. v. Care Corp., 638 F.2d 357 (2d Cir. 1980); Crouse-Hinds Co. v. Inter-North, Inc., 634 F.2d 690 (2d Cir. 1980); Johnson v. Trueblood, 629 F.2d 287 (3d Cir. 1980); Berman v. Gerber Products Co., 454 F. Supp. 1310 (W.D. Mich. 1978). For a discussion of these cases, *see* Steinberg, note 11 *supra,* at 245-60.

In regard to going-private transactions, the most relevant Commission action in this area is the promulgation of Rule 13e-3.[110] In the proposal stage, the rule included that a going-private transaction must be both substantively and procedurally fair to minority shareholders.[111] Relying on *Santa Fe Industries, Inc. v. Green*,[112] a number of commentators asserted that the proposal was an attempt to usurp state law.[113] Although adhering to the soundness of the proposal, the Commission declined to adopt a "fairness" requirement.[114] Rather, as adopted, the rule requires the issuer to disclose material facts about the transaction, including giving its opinion whether it *reasonably believes* that the going-private transaction is fair or unfair to unaffiliated security holders and the factors upon which the belief is based.[115]

---

110. Securities Exchange Act Release No. 16075 (1979). In short, a going-private transaction is one in which the controlling persons of a corporation eliminate public shareholders while retaining their ownership of the business. In general, the SEC's rules prohibit fraudulent, deceptive, or manipulative acts or practices in connection with going-private transactions and prescribe new filing, disclosure, and dissemination requirements as a means reasonably designed to prevent such acts or practices. *See also* Securities Exchange Act Release No. 16112 (1979), in which the Commission adopted Rule 13e-4 which governs issuer tender offers for their own securities. In general, Rule 13e-4 requires that a Schedule 13E-4 be filed with the SEC, and establishes, *inter alia*, disclosure, dissemination, and compliance requirements. In addition, Rule 13e-4 proscribes manipulative, deceptive and fraudulent conduct in connection with issuer tender offers. Note also that an issuer tender offer regulated by Rule 13e-4, that is also a going-private transaction subject to Rule 13e-3, is required to be effected in compliance with both rules. Importantly, an issuer tender offer under state law "must be premised upon a valid business purpose consistent with the interests of the issuer's security holders and not with the primary objective of preserving management in office." Manges, *SEC Regulation of Issuer and Third-Party Tender Offers*, 8 SEC. REG. L.J. 275, 278 (1981).

111. *See* Securities Exchange Act Release No. 14185 (Nov. 17, 1977).

112. 430 U.S. 462 (1977). In *Santa Fe*, the Supreme Court held that in order to state a cause of action under Section 10(b) and Rule 10b-5 of the Securities Exchange Act, deception or manipulation must be alleged. In other words, under Section 10(b) and Rule 10b-5, mere breaches of fiduciary duty that do not involve any misrepresentation or nondisclosure are not actionable. For an analysis of *Santa Fe* and its progeny herein, *see* pages 163-98 *infra*.

113. *See* Cohen, note 76 *supra*, at 309; Connolly, *New Going-Private Rule*, 13 REV. SEC. REG. 975, 977 (1980); notes 110-11 *supra*.

114. The Commission stated that "the views expressed in the 1977 release are sound and therefore [it] specifically affirms those views." Securities Exchange Act Release No. 16075 (1979).

115. *Id.* For commentary on Rule 13e-3, *see, e.g.*, Connolly, note 113 *supra*; Rothschild, *Going Private, Singer, and Rule 13e-3: What Are the Standards for Fiduciaries*, 7 SEC. REG. L.J. 195 (1979); Note, *Regulating Going Private Transactions: SEC Rule 13e-3*, 80 COLUM. L. REV. 782 (1980); Comment, *Rule 13e-3 and the Going-Private Dilemma: The SEC's Quest for a Substantive Fairness Doctrine*, 58 WASH. U.L.Q. 883 (1980). *See also* Note, *Fairness in Freezeout Transactions: Observations on Coping with Going Private Problems*, 69 KENT. L.J. 77 (1980-1981). In a fairly recent administrative proceeding, with the defendant neither admitting nor denying, the Commission concluded that, in a going-private transaction, "FSC's disclosure concerning 'fairness' of the offering price was inadequate," and hence constituted a violation of Section 13e-3 and Rule 13e-3 thereunder. In the Matter of FSC Corporation, 22 SEC DOCKET 1374, 1378 (June 24, 1981).

The Commission, in prescribing this requirement, has arguably stayed on the disclosure, rather than the substantive regulatory, side of the line.[116] Nonetheless, by requiring such disclosure, and, in that an issuer may well be reluctant to disclose that the going-private transaction is unfair, it is quite possible that these transactions today are fairer to minority shareholders than before the adoption of the rule.[117]

Although the above rules were adopted during the Williams era, it appears that the present Commission generally supports them.[118] Although it is premature, an area may develop where the present Commission diverges from its predecessor, namely, disclosure of qualitatively material information in the context of unadjudicated illegalities and perhaps similar improprieties. Participating as *amicus curiae* in a case before the Second Circuit which involved alleged nondisclosures of the directors' intent to thwart or violate the federal labor laws,[119] the Williams Commission stated that "it is clear that future plans of a corporation must be disclosed where they are material and *legal,* and there is no basis for concluding that disclosure obligations may be avoided by making future *illegal* plans."[120] Most recently, however,

---

116. *See generally* authorities notes 113, 115 *supra.*

117. *See* Cohen, note 76 *supra,* at 309-10. A number of commentators, however, contend that the Commission has engaged in substantive regulation. *See* Comment, note 115 *supra,* at 883-84 ("Although Rule 13e-3 does not impose an explicit substantive fairness standard on going private transactions, the rule prescribes such rigid disclosure requirements regarding the effects, purposes, and fairness of the transaction that a fairness objective is clearly implicit in its objectives"). *See also* authorities cited in note 113 *supra.*

In response to a number of proxy statements involving novel, multi sale-of-assets transactions, the Division of Corporation Finance in February 1979 issued a statement of its views and practices in administering the existing disclosure requirements of the proxy rules as they may pertain to such transactions. Securities Exchange Act Release No. 15572. *See also* Securities Exchange Act Release No. 16883 (May 23, 1980), 20 SEC DOCKET 124 (June 10, 1980) (reflecting the views of the Division of Corporation Finance in regard to disclosure in proxy contests where a principal issue in contention is the liquidation of all or a part of the equity of an issuer).

118. *See, e.g.,* In the Matter of FSC Corporation, 22 SEC DOCKET 1374 (June 24, 1981). *But see* Securities Act Release No. 6383 (March 3, 1982) (adopting rules setting forth certain thresholds for disclosure under Regulation S-K of environmental legal proceedings).

119. Amalgamated Clothing & Textile Workers Union v. J. P. Stevens, 475 F. Supp. 328 (S.D.N.Y. 1979), *vacated as moot,* 638 F.2d 7 (2d Cir. 1980).

120. Brief of the Securities and Exchange Commission as *Amicus Curiae* at 17 (emphasis in original), Amalgamated Clothing & Textile Workers Union v. J. P. Stevens, 638 F.2d 7 (2d Cir. 1980). Continuing, the Commission asserted:

> The very concept of disclosure may be contrary to human nature, in that management might prefer to conceal all unfavorable information about a company, including such matters as financial losses. Nevertheless, the essence of the federal securities laws, as stated in the preamble to the Securities Act of 1933, is "to provide full and fair disclosure."

Id. at 17-18.

the present Commission refused to bring an action against Citicorp,[121] reasoning in part that "[t]he law concerning disclosure of unadjudicated allegations is unclear."[122] If this analysis is reflective of the Commission's current thinking on the subject, possible SEC action in future such cases is virtually nil.[123] Moreover, the SEC refused to take action against Citicorp on a much broader rationale, stating that "[e]ven if [the improprieties were] established, the alleged amounts for the years in question were not material to Citicorp."[124] Although this language should not at this point be considered determinative in future cases, such language arguably implies a rejection of a corporation's duty to disclose qualitatively material information, particularly where explicit Commission rules, self-dealing or kickbacks are not involved.[125] Application of such a standard could well signal the death knell to the bringing of enforcement actions where the subject directors and management did not directly benefit from the illegalities.[126] It would also

---

121. *See* SEC Statement in Citicorp (March 5, 1982).

122. *Id.* The Commission added that "[t]here would have been a serious possibility of court reversal of the Commission's action, which would have been bad precedent." Other reasons given by the Commission included that the allegations were not adequately established, that the Comptroller of the Currency had concluded that no action was justified under the federal banking laws, that the case was basically a banking or tax matter, not a securities case, and that the case was old, as the alleged practices occurred between 1973 and 1978. *Id. See* 14 SEC. REG. & L. REP. (BNA) 419 (March 10, 1982).

123. *See* SEC. REG. & L. REP. (BNA) 1564 (Sept. 17, 1982). *See also* Vilkin, "Doe Corp. Inquiry to Expand," NAT. L. J. at p. 3, col. 1 (Sept. 27, 1982).

124. SEC Statement, note 118 *supra*.

125. *See* Fedders, "Law Enforcement Against Those Who Fail to Disclose Illegal Behavior," [Current] FED. SEC. L. REP. (CCH) ¶ 83,279 (Nov. 19, 1982) ("Absent quantitatively material information, self-dealing or failure to comply with other mandated disclosure requirements, the antifraud provisions of the securities laws generally should not be utilized where there is a failure to disclose qualitative information"). *Compare* Gaines v. Haughton, 645 F.2d 761 (9th Cir. 1981), *cert. denied,* 102 S. Ct. 1006 (1982), *with* Weisberg v. Coastal States Gas Corp., 609 F. 2d 650 (2d Cir. 1979), *cert. denied,* 445 U.S. 951 (1980). The Commission did, however, file a memorandum as *amicus curiae* in support of the Petition for Rehearing and Rehearing *En Banc* in *Gaines.* The position taken in the brief, filed in 1981, indicated that the Commission supported the application of the qualitative materiality rationale in the proxy context, even when no kickbacks or self-dealing were involved. *See also* SEC v. Vornado, Inc., [1981-1982 Transfer Binder] FED. SEC. L. REP (CCH) ¶ 98,377 (D.D.C. 1981) (pursuant to consent decree, Commission alleged, *inter alia,* that corporate officers violated the proxy provisions by not disclosing that management countenanced off-the-books slush funds, falsification of records and bribery).

126. According to Congressman Dingell, Chairman of the House Subcommittee on Oversight and Investigations (of the House Energy and Commerce Committee): "In rejecting a recommendation to bring an enforcement action against Citicorp, the Commission overturned long-established precedents and introduced new criteria for disclosure." 14 SEC. REG. & L. REP. (BNA) 1564, 1565 (Sept. 17, 1982). Congressman Dingell also opined that there has been "a fundamental shift in the attitude of the Commission towards its responsibilities." *Id.* Former SEC Enforcement Director Stanley Sporkin testified before the House Subcommittee that "an action against Citicorp was warranted. . . ." *Id.* at 1564.

constitute a marked deviation from previously established Commission policy.[127]

IV. SUBSTANTIVE "NON-ENFORCEMENT" REGULATION

SEC substantive regulation is most often based on a fraud or enforcement rationale. What is sometimes lost sight of, however, is that, in pursuing its statutory mandates, the Commission frequently engages in substantive regulation premised on other grounds. In this context, the following discussion will address, through various examples, SEC substantive "non-enforcement" regulation that affects or influences corporate internal affairs. As will be discussed, although the present Commission apparently supports many of the actions previously taken, the recent promulgation of Regulation D[128] serves as an example of the extent to which the Commission's focus has changed.

While the previous section of this chapter addressed recent developments in proxy disclosure policy,[129] the Commission has also engaged in substantive regulation in this area. Perhaps most notably, the Commission in November 1979 promulgated rules that require shareholders to be provided with a form of proxy that (1) contains the names of persons nominated to the board of directors; (2) permits shareholders to withhold authority to vote for each nominee for election as a director (or to vote against each nominee in those jurisdictions so permitting); (3) may provide for a shareholder to grant authority to vote for nominees set forth as a group, provided that there is a similar means to withhold such authority (or to vote against such nominees in those jurisdictions so permitting); (4) permits shareholders to specify, by boxes, a choice to abstain with respect to each matter to be acted upon, as well as to approve or disapprove each matter, other than elections to office; and (5) indicates whether the proxy is solicited on behalf of the issuer's board of directors or on behalf of persons opposing the issuer's

---

127. *See* note 126 *supra. See also* Memorandum of *Amicus Curiae,* SEC, in Support of Petition for Rehearing and Rehearing *En Banc,* Gaines v. Haughton, 645 F.2d 761 (9th Cir. 1981); SEC v. Joseph Schlitz Brewing Co., 452 F. Supp. 824 (E.D. Wis. 1978). In *Schlitz,* the SEC alleged that the defendant had failed to disclose a nationwide scheme of bribing retailers of beer and malt beverages to purchase Schlitz' products and also had failed to disclose its alleged violation of Spanish law in falsifying its books and records regarding payments and transactions with certain Spanish corporations described as affiliates. Denying Schlitz' motion to dismiss, the court concluded that "the question of the integrity of management gives materiality to the matters the Commission claims should be disclosed." *Id.* at 830. For further discussion herein on this case, *see* pages 99-106 *infra.*

128. Securities Act Release No. 6389 (March 3, 1982), 14 SEC. REG. & L. REP. (BNA) 495 (March 17, 1982).

129. *See* notes 84-87 and accompanying text *supra.*

solicitation.[130] These rules, based on the Commission's broad rulemaking authority under Section 14(a), have the direct impact of enabling shareholders to participate more actively in the corporate decision-making process. At the same time, by providing shareholders with the right to abstain or vote against matters in both election and other contests, these rules may have the indirect effect of promoting revitalized shareholder interest. The ultimate result may be that otherwise recalcitrant management will be more circumspect in selecting questionable director-nominees or putting forth contemplated proposals of dubious benefit to the corporation, due to apprehension that a significant percentage of shareholders will disapprove or abstain or that a lawsuit based on the contemplated nomination or transaction will ensue.[131]

The SEC has also engaged in substantive "non-enforcement" regulation in the tender offer setting. In particular, the Commission, in November 1979, adopted new tender offer rules,[132] including Rule 14d-2(b).[133] That rule generally provides that an announcement of an intent to make a tender offer disclosing the amount of shares sought to be purchased and the price to be offered triggers the commencement of a tender offer.[134] The effect of the rule is that it preempts many of the state takeover statutes which provide

---

130. Securities Exchange Act Release No. 16356 (Nov. 23, 1979). Also, of interest in this regard is Rule 14a-8, 17 C.F.R. § 240.14 (1982), the stockholder proposal rule. Although the Commission's justification for the rule is principally based on fraud (see Hearings on SEC Proxy Rules Before the House Committee on Interstate and Foreign Commerce, 169-71 (78th Cong., 1st Sess.) (1943)), "it is clear that, over the years, the rule has come to carry a substantial amount of corporate governance baggage as well." Cohen, note 76 *supra*, at 313. For commentary on Rule 14a-8, *see* Black & Sparks, *SEC Rule 14a-8: Some Changes in the Way the SEC Staff Interprets the Rule*, 11 TOL. L. REV. 957 (1980); Curzan & Pelesh, *Revitalizing Corporate Democracy: Control of Investment Manager's Voting on Social Responsibility Proxy Issues*, 94 HARV. L. REV. 670, 672-75 (1980); Williams, *Improper Shareholder Proposals*, 13 REV. SEC. REG. 841 (1980); SEC. REG. & L. REP. (BNA) No. 578, A-7 (Nov. 12, 1980). The Commission recently has proposed "sweeping" changes in its shareholder-voting rules. *See* note 75 *supra*; Hudson, note 75 *supra*.

131. Such lawsuits may be based on breach of fiduciary duty under state law or a failure adequately to disclose under federal law. For a discussion of relevant case law herein, *see* pages 163-98 *infra*.

132. Securities Exchange Act Release No. 16384 (Nov. 29, 1979).

133. 17 C.F.R. § 240.14d-2(b) (1982).

134. More specifically, a public announcement by means of a newspaper advertisement, press release, or public statement triggers Rule 14d-2(b) if the material terms of such announcement include the identity of the bidder and target corporation, disclosure of the class and amount of securities that are sought, and a statement of the price or range of prices being offered. *Id.* The rule, however, provides a grace period of five business days for the bidder to file the requisite information with the SEC and disseminate such information to shareholders, or alternatively to publicly announce that it has discontinued the tender offer. *See* Sommer & Feller, *Takeover Rules: A Cohesive Comprehensive Code*, Legal Times (Wash.), Dec. 17, 1979, at 18-19.

for a significant precommencement waiting period and a hearing to be held before a tender offer can commence.[135]

In promulgating the rule, the SEC relied on its broad rulemaking authority under Section 14(d) as well as other provisions.[136] The Commission reasoned that the rule was necessary to protect investors and to effectuate the purposes underlying the Williams Act.[137] According to the Commission, once a contemplated tender offer is announced at a price significantly higher than the then-prevailing market price, shareholders are confronted with the immediate investment decision of selling in the rising market or holding their stock in the hope that the offer will be successful. Under such circumstances,

---

135. The adoption of Rule 14d-2(b) has added to "[t]he confrontation between state requirements and federal law. . . ." Bloomenthal, note 98 *supra,* at 58. At the time it adopted the rule, the SEC recognized the conflict with state laws:

> Thus, the conflict between Rule 14d-2(b) and such state statutes is so direct and substantial as to make it impossible to comply with both sets of requirements as they presently exist. While recognizing its long and beneficial partnership with the states in the regulation of securities transactions, the Commission nevertheless believes that the state takeover statutes presently in effect frustrate the operation and purposes of the Williams Act and that . . . Rule 14d-2(b) is necessary for the protection of investors and to achieve the purposes of the Williams Act.

Securities Exchange Act Release No. 16384, [1979-1980 Transfer Binder] FED. SEC. L. REP. (CCH) ¶ 82,373 at 82,584 (footnote omitted). In response to Rule 14d-2, some states have taken legislative action in an attempt to harmonize their regulatory requirements with those of the Williams Act. Such states include Indiana, Maryland, Nevada, Pennsylvania and Wisconsin. *See* Bloomenthal, note 98 *supra,* at 59-60; SEC. REG. & L. REP. (BNA) No. 605, F-1 (May 27, 1981).

The constitutionality of Rule 14d-2 has not been definitively settled. A number of courts, however, have upheld the validity of the rule and, accordingly, have held that the applicable state takeover statute was preempted. *See, e.g.,* Kennecott Corp. v. Smith, 637 F.2d 181 (3d Cir. 1980); Canadian Pacific Enterprises v. Campbell, [1981 Transfer Binder] FED. SEC. L. REP. (CCH) ¶ 97,804 (D.S.C. 1980). The Supreme Court in Edgar v. MITE Corporation, 102 S. Ct. 2629 (1982), held that the Illinois Business Takeover Act was unconstitutional under the Commerce Clause. *See generally* Langevoort, *State Tender Offer Legislation: Interests, Effects, and Political Competency,* 62 CORNELL L. REV. 213 (1977).

136. The Commission also relied on Sections 3(b), 14(e), and 23(a) of the Exchange Act. *See* SEC Release, note 135 *supra;* Brief of the SEC, *amicus curiae,* GM Sub Corporation v. Liggett Group, Inc., No. 98, 1980, at 15 (Del. filed April 24, 1980).

137. SEC Release, note 135 *supra,* where the Commission stated:

> Such pre-commencement public announcements cause security holders to make investment decisions with respect to a tender offer on the basis of incomplete information and trigger market activity normally attendant to a tender offer, such as arbitrageur activity. Since they constitute the practical commencement of a tender offer, such pre-commencement public announcements cause the contest for control of the subject company to occur prior to the application of the Williams Act and therefore deny security holders the protections which that Act was intended by Congress to provide.

Id.

"[p]rotection of investors requires that when confronted with these decisions, the shareholders have the protection of the Williams Act, including full disclosure concerning the offer, and the opportunity to accept it rather than being held in limbo for some considerable period of confusion before the offer is actually made."[138]

The effect of Rule 14d-2(b) on corporate internal affairs may well be to help neutralize the advantage that target management enjoyed under these state statutes. There is little question that these statutes, particularly those providing for extensive precommencement delays or for substantive fairness determinations, gave the subject company time to implement defensive measures and to find a "white knight."[139] Thus, Rule 14d-2(b) may have a significant impact on a target corporation's internal processes when it is the subject of a hostile tender offer.

One of the more significant measures that the SEC has recently taken in "non-enforcement" substantive regulation has been to require that a majority of a registrant's directors must sign the Form 10-K.[140] In adopting this measure as part of its integration package,[141] the Commission reasoned that the shift in emphasis toward relying on periodic disclosure under the 1934 Act demands that the attention of the private sector, including directors and professionals, must also be refocused toward such Exchange Act filings. Such increased attention is needed if adequate discipline is to be instilled to ensure that the integrated system properly functions. By implementing the signature requirement, the Commission "anticipate[d] that directors will be encouraged to devote the needed attention to reviewing the Form 10-K and to seek the involvement of other professionals to the degree necessary to give themselves sufficient comfort."[142]

---

138. SEC Brief, note 136 *supra*, at 20. *See* note 112 *supra*.

139. *See generally* Langevoort, note 135 *supra*. Such a consequence appears to be contrary to the purposes underlying the Williams Act. Both the House and Senate Reports stated that "[the bill] is designed to require full and fair disclosure for the benefit of investors while at the same time providing the offeror and management equal opportunity to fairly present their case." HOUSE COMM. ON INTERSTATE AND FOREIGN COMMERCE, DISCLOSURE OF CORPORATE EQUITY OWNERSHIP, H.R. REP. NO. 1711, 90th Cong., 2d Sess. 4, reprinted in [1968] U.S. CODE CONG. AD. NEWS 2811, 2813; SENATE COMM. ON BANKING AND CURRENCY, FULL DISCLOSURE OF CORPORATE EQUITY OWNERSHIP AND IN CORPORATE TAKEOVER BIDS, S. REP. NO. 550, 90th Cong., 1st Sess. 3 (1967). For further discussion herein on tender offers, *see* pages 199-231 *infra*.

140. *See* Securities Act Release No. 6383, 24 SEC DOCKET 1318 (March 16, 1982); Securities Act Release No. 6231 (Sept. 2, 1980), 20 SEC DOCKET 1060 (Sept. 16, 1980).

141. *Id.* These amendments are designed to facilitate integration of the Securities Act and Exchange Act disclosure systems. The annual report to shareholders, under the amendments, may become the cornerstone disclosure document upon which the integrated system is to be built.

142. 20 SEC DOCKET at 1067. The Commission concluded that "this added measure of discipline is vital to the disclosure objectives of the federal securities laws, and outweighs the

The effect of this signature requirement on directors' standard of care in reviewing the Form 10-K and on their reliance on counsel and accountants should be substantial. Arguably, by signing the Form 10-K, it may be presumed that the subject directors reviewed the document with care.[143] Accordingly, increased liability upon such directors may be premised on the following rationales: (1) that under Section 18(a) of the Exchange Act,[144] the directors "caused" the filing;[145] (2) that such signing indicates that the directors may have acted with scienter,[146] or at least recklessly,[147] for recovery purposes in private damage and SEC injunctive actions under Section 10(b)[148] and at least negligently in SEC injunctive actions under Section 17(a)(2) and 17(a)(3) of the Securities Act;[149] and (3) that , with respect to control person

---

potential impact, if any, of the signature on legal liability." *Id.* The Commission did state, however, that "[i]t has . . . instructed the staff to report to it on the results of imposing the requirement after an appropriate time has passed, and the Commission will revisit the question if such action appears necessary or appropriate at that time." *Id.*

143. *See* Ferrara, *Current Issues Between Corporations and Shareholders: Federal Intervention into Corporate Governance,* 36 Bus. Law. 759, 766 (1981).

144. 15 U.S.C. § 78r(a) (1976).

145. Section 18(a) imposes liability upon any person "who shall make or cause to be made" any materially false or misleading statement contained in a document filed with the SEC. Relief may be granted to only purchasers and sellers. Strict standards of reliance and causation apply, with the result that, in no reported case, has the plaintiff obtained relief. *See* Greene, *Determining the Responsibilities of Underwriters Distributing Securities within an Integrated Disclosure System,* 56 Notre Dame Law. 755, 758 (1981). For discussion on Section 18(a), *see* Steinberg, *The Propriety and Scope of Cumulative Remedies Under the Federal Securities Laws,* 67 Cornell L. Rev. 557 (1982).

146. In Ernst & Ernst v. Hochfelder, 425 U.S. 185, 193 n.12 (1976), and SEC v. Aaron, 100 S. Ct. 1945, 1950 n.5 (1980), the court defined scienter as "a mental state embracing intent to deceive, manipulate, or defraud." *See generally* Bucklo, *The Supreme Court Attempts to Define Scienter Under Rule 10b-5: Ernst & Ernst v. Hochfelder,* 29 Stan. L. Rev. 213 (1977).

147. The Court in both *Hochfelder* and *Aaron* expressly left this issue open. *See* 100 S. Ct. at 1950 n.5; 425 U.S. at 193. Subsequent to *Hochfelder,* the overwhelming majority of courts have held that recklessness constitutes sufficient scienter. *See, e.g.,* Healey v. Catalyst Recovery of Pa., Inc., 616 F.2d 641 (3d Cir. 1981); Mansbach v. Prescott, Ball & Turben, 598 F.2d 1017 (6th Cir. 1979); Nelson v. Serwold, 576 F.2d 1332 (9th Cir.), *cert. denied,* 439 U.S. 970 (1978); Rolf v. Blyth, Eastman, Dillon & Co., 570 F.2d 38 (2d Cir.), *cert. denied,* 439 U.S. 1039 (1978). *See generally* Steinberg & Gruenbaum, *Variations of "Recklessness" After Hochfelder and Aaron,* 8 Sec. Reg. L.J. 179 (1980).

148. In *Aaron,* 100 S. Ct. 1945 (1980), the Supreme Court held, *inter alia,* that the SEC must prove scienter in SEC injunctive actions brought for violations of Section 10(b) and Section 17(a)(1) of the Securities Act. In *Hochfelder,* 425 U.S. 185 (1976), the Court held that scienter must be shown in private damage actions under Section 10(b.)

149. In *Aaron,* 100 S. Ct. 1945 (1980), the Court held, *inter alia,* that the SEC need not prove scienter in injunctive actions based on violations of Section 17(a)(2) or 17(a)(3). *See* Steinberg, *SEC and Other Permanent Injunctions: Standards for Their Imposition, Modification, and Dissolution,* 66 Cornell L. Rev. 27 (1980).

liability under Section 20(a) of the Exchange Act,[150] such signing may indicate that the subject directors did not act in good faith and may have induced the acts causing the violation.[151] Although the above rationales may ultimately be rejected by the courts, signifying that the signature requirement may not alter existing legal liabilities,[152] it is likely that the potential impact of this requirement will impel directors to examine and review the Form 10-K and to rely on corporate counsel and accountants in this exercise to a much greater extent than has previously been the practice.

A further issue relating to SEC "non-enforcement" substantive regulation is whether the Commission has the authority under Section 19(c) of the Exchange Act[153] to compel self-regulatory organizations to alter their listing standards that relate to the internal corporate affairs of listed companies. In the Corporate Governance Report, the staff contended that Commission authority under Section 19(c) seems clear on its face. The Report stated that the exchanges' listing standards currently impact on the internal governance of listed companies to some extent, requiring such companies to take corporate action that they may not otherwise be inclined to pursue, such as the adoption of the New York Stock Exchange's audit committee rule.[154] While the listing standards of individual exchanges may become less important in the context of a national market system than they currently are, the staff observed that the Commission's authority pursuant to Section 19(c) extends to all national securities exchanges as well as the National Association of Securities Dealers. In addition, the staff noted that the Commission has broad and direct rulemaking power under Section 11A(a)(2) of the Exchange Act[155] to designate the securities or classes of securities that are deemed qualified for trading in the national market system.[156] In this regard,

---

150. 15 U.S.C. § 78t(a) (1976).

151. *See* Ferrara, note 143 *supra,* at 766.

152. *See* note 142 *supra.*

153. 15 U.S. 78s(c) (1976). Pursuant to Section 19(c), the Commission "by rule, may abrogate, add to, and delete from . . . the rules of a self-regulatory organization . . . as the Commission deems necessary or appropriate to insure the fair administration of the self-regulation organization, to conform its rules to requirements of this title and the rules and regulations thereunder applicable to such organization, or otherwise in furtherance of the purposes of this title. . . ."

154. SEC STAFF CORPORATE ACCOUNTABILITY REPORT, note 31 *supra,* at 643-44. *But see* Cary, *Federal Minimum Standards* 319, 370 in COMMENTARIES ON CORPORATE STRUCTURE AND GOVERNANCE, ALI-ABA (D. Schwartz ed., 1976).

155. 15 U.S.C. § 78KA(a)(2) (1976).

156. SEC STAFF CORPORATE ACCOUNTABILITY REPORT, note 31 *supra,* at 646. In this regard, the staff concluded that self-regulatory organizations

> are confronted with somewhat of a dilemma between their marketing efforts to attract companies to list or otherwise qualify their securities for trading and their regulatory efforts to enhance investor confidence through corporate accountability requirements. Thus, while they cannot be expected to be at the forefront of changes in corporate

if "qualification" were to extend to conduct of corporate internal affairs, and not merely suitability for trading, the Commission's leverage "to move the world of corporate governance" would be even stronger.[157] At this point, however, it seems highly unlikely that the present Commission would move in this direction.

Indeed, an argument can be made that the Commission currently is very concerned with facilitating the capital formation process. The recent adoption of Regulation D, particularly certain aspects of Rule 506 contained therein,[158] may be indicative of this position. Essentially, Regulation D contains new rules that govern certain offers and sales of securities without registration under the Securities Act.[159] One such rule, Rule 506, replaces

---

> accountability, they should continue to be concerned about the governance of their listed companies and can play an important role in assuring communication among their listed companies, their member firms and shareholders. The Commission, for its part, should consider carefully further suggestions for SRO rule changes related to the internal corporate structure of listed companies, but, as a matter of policy, should not require such changes at this time.

Id. at 647.

157. *See* Cohen, note 76 *supra*, at 314-16. *See also* Comment, *Stock Exchange Listing Agreements as a Vehicle for Corporate Governance*, 129 U. PA. L. REV. 1427 (1981).

158. Rule 506 is one of six rules adopted by the Commission pursuant to Regulation D. As outlined by the Commission:

> Rules 501-503 set forth definitions, terms, and conditions that apply generally throughout the regulation. The exemptions of Regulation D are contained in Rules 504-506. Rules 504 and 505 replace [*sic*] Rules 240 and 242, respectively, and provide exemptions from registration under Section 3(b) of the Securities Act. Rule 506 succeeds Rule 146 and relates to transactions that are deemed to be exempt from registration under Section 4(2) of the Securities Act.

Securities Act Release No. 6389 (March 3, 1982), 14 SEC. REG. & L. REP. (BNA) 495, 497 (March 17, 1982). For discussion on Regulation D, *see, e.g.,* Donahue, *New Exemptions from the Registration Requirements of the Securities Act of 1933: Regulation D*, 10 SEC. REG. L.J. 235 (1982); Ketels, *Regulation D—The New Regulation World for Limited Offerings*, 5 CORP. L. REV. 268 (1982); Schneider, *Introduction to Regulation D*, 15 REV. SEC. REG. 990 (1982).

159. As stated previously, Rules 504 and 505 were promulgated pursuant to Section 3(b) of the Securities Act which empowers the Commission to exempt from the registration requirements any issue of securities providing that the aggregate amount that such issue is offered to the public does not exceed $5 million. Under Rule 504, a total amount of $500,000 of securities may be sold during any twelve-month period to an unlimited number of investors. The rule contains no specific disclosure requirements and is available only to companies that are neither subject to reporting obligations under the Exchange Act nor defined as investment companies under the Investment Company Act of 1940. Under Rule 505, up to $5 million of an issuer's securities may be sold during any twelve-month period to thirty-five purchasers and to an unlimited number of accredited investors. The rule contains certain informational delivery requirements and prohibits the use of general advertising or solicitation. *See* note 158 *supra*. For discussion of Rule 506, *see* notes 162-63 and accompanying text *infra*.

Rule 146[160] and relates to transactions that are exempt under Section 4(2) of that Act.[161] Under Rule 506, offers and sales are exempt from registration when the securities are purchased by no more than thirty-five purchasers. Accredited investors, including individuals meeting certain financial standards,[162] are excluded in computing the number of purchasers. Moreover, the rule eliminates the economic risk test and requires that only purchasers meet the sophistication standards.[163]

---

160. The Commission adopted Rule 146 in 1974. Securities Act Release No. 5487 (April 23, 1974). Until recently, the Commission had continued to support the rule. *See, e.g.,* Securities Act Release No. 5913, [1978 Transfer Binder] FED. SEC. L. REP. (CCH) ¶ 81,532 (March 6, 1978). As stated by the Commission in that release:

> Section 4(2) of the Securities Act of 1933 provides that offers and sales of securities by an issuer not involving any public offering are exempt from the registration provisions of the Act. Rule 146 provides objective standards for determining when the exemption is available. The main conditions of the rule require that (1) there be no general advertising or soliciting in connection with the offering; (2) offers be made only to persons the issuer reasonably believes have the requisite knowledge and experience in financial and business matters or who can bear the economic risk; (3) sales be made only to persons as described above except that persons meeting the economic risk test must also have an offeree representative capable of providing the requisite knowledge and experience; (4) offerees have access to or be provided information comparable to that elicited through registration; (5) there be no more than 35 purchasers in the offering; and (6) reasonable care be taken to ensure that the securities are not resold in violation of the Act's registration provisions.

Id. at 80,171. For further discussion on Rule 146 as well as former Rules 240 and 242, *see, e.g.,* Deaktor, *Integration of Securities Offerings,* 31 U. FLA. L. REV. 465 (1979); Schneider, *The Statutory Law of Private Placements,* 14 REV. SEC. REG. 869 (1981); Soraghan, *Private Offerings: Determining "Access," "Investment Sophistication," and "Ability to Bear Economic Risk,"* 8 SEC. REG. L.J. 3 (1980); Thomforde, *Exemptions from SEC Registration for Small Businesses,* 47 TENN. L. REV. 1 (1979). For discussion of Section 4(6) of the Securities Act, *see* note 222 *infra.*

161. Section 4(2) states that "[t]he provisions of section 5 shall not apply to transactions by an issuer not involving any public offering." *See* note 158 *supra.* Note that under Section 19(c)(3)(C) of the Securities Act the Commission is empowered to adopt for federal securities law purposes "a uniform exemption from registration for small issuers which can be agreed upon among several States or between the States and the Federal Government." Significantly, the Commission did not rely on this provision as the basis for promulgating Rule 506. This position is correct. Even if the rule were ultimately adopted by some states, Rule 506, unlike the exemptive authority provided by Section 19(c)(3)(C), applies to all issuers regardless of size.

162. Rule 501 defines an "accredited investor" to include any person who purchases at least $150,000 of the securities if the total purchase price does not exceed 20 percent of the person's net worth at the time of sale, any natural person who has an income greater than $200,000 during each of the prior two years and who reasonably anticipates an income greater than $200,000 for the current year, and any natural person whose net worth at the time of purchase is $1 million. *See* SEC Release, note 158 *supra.* 14 SEC. REG. & L. REP. (BNA) 495, 498-99 (March 17, 1982).

163. *Id.* at 503. *Compare* Rule 146, note 160 *supra.*

The Commission's release in adopting Regulation D makes clear that Rule 506 transactions are deemed to be exempt under Section 4(2).[164] As such, it appears, as the Supreme Court in an analogous situation held in *Ernst & Ernst v. Hochfelder*,[165] that the rule's scope cannot exceed that given to its statutory source.[166] Viewed from this perspective, a plausible, if not persuasive, argument can be made that Rule 506 is invalid because it contravenes established judicial construction of Section 4(2), dating back nearly thirty years to the Supreme Court's seminal decision in *Securities and Exchange Commission v. Ralston Purina Co.*[167] Under such judicial interpretation, courts have uniformly held that the section applies not only to purchasers but to offerees as well,[168] and that the financial sophistication or wealth of an offeree is not a sufficient basis for a subject issuer to qualify for the exemption provided by the section.[169] By deleting these requirements, Rule 506 arguably exceeds the Commission's authority.[170]

---

164. *See* note 153 *supra.*

165. 425 U.S. 185 (1976) (concluding that despite the language of Rule 10b-5, which could be read as not requiring scienter, the language of Section 10(b) was controlling and required scienter).

166. By its terms, however, Section 4(2) does not confer rulemaking authority upon the Commission. It would appear that such authority is derived from Section 19(a) of the Securities Act ("The Commission shall have authority from time to time to make, amend, and rescind such rules and regulations as may be necessary to carry out the provisions of this title, including rules and regulations governing registration statements and prospectuses for various classes of securities and issuers, and defining accounting, technical, and trade terms used in this title").

167. 346 U.S. 119 (1953) (the Section 4(2) exemption turns on, *inter alia,* whether the offerees were shown to be able to fend for themselves and whether they were shown to have access to the kind of information which registration would have disclosed).

168. *See, e.g.* SEC v. Murphy, 626 F.2d 633 (9th Cir. 1980); Swenson v. Engelstad, 626 F.2d 421 (5th Cir. 1980); Lawler v. Gilliam, 569 F.2d 1283 (4th Cir. 1978); SEC v. Asset Management Corp., [1979-1980 Transfer Binder] Fed. Sec. L. Rep. (CCH) ¶ 97,278 (S.D. Ind. 1979); Barrett v. Triangle Mining Corp., [1975-1976 Transfer Binder] Fed. Sec. L. Rep. (CCH) ¶ 95,438 (S.D.N.Y 1976). *Compare* Section 202 (41)(B) of the American Law Institute Federal Securities Code which focuses on the number of *purchasers* rather than offerees.

169. *See, e.g.,* Lawler v. Gilliam, 569 F.2d 1283 (4th Cir. 1978); Doran v. Petroleum Management Corp., 545 F.2d 893 (5th Cir. 1977); Hill York Corp. v. American Int. Franchises, Inc., 448 F.2d 680 (5th Cir. 1971); Lively v. Hirschfeld, 440 F.2d 631 (10th Cir. 1971); United States v. Custer Channel Wing Corp., 376 F.2d 675 (4th Cir. 1967).

170. Indeed, in 1975, the American Bar Association's Section of Corporation, Banking and Business Law stated that the Commission's administrative authority with respect to the Section 4(2) exemption "is somewhat circumscribed by relevant judicial decisions." *Position Paper of the Federal Regulation of Securities Committee, Section of Corporation, Banking and Business Law of the American Bar Association,* 31 Bus. Law. 485, 486 (1975). Interestingly, the Commission's former Rule 146 was apparently more restrictive than the statutory case law construing Section 4(2). As the Fifth Circuit stated:

> [Rule 146] is more restrictive than the cases in this Circuit in that it requires that the offeree either be sophisticated or advised by an offeree representative who is, in addition to the requirement that offerees receive or have access to information that registration

More importantly, the rule's promulgation will provide certain investors with far less protection than they previously had enjoyed. This fact is graphically illustrated by the Fourth Circuit's decision in *Lawler v. Gilliam*,[171] decided in 1978. There, 100 investors lost approximately $21 million.[172] The defendants claimed that the private offering exemption of Section 4(2) was available. The Fourth Circuit disagreed, relying on the Supreme Court's decision in *Ralston Purina* as well as a long line of federal appellate cases.[173] Accordingly, the status of the investors as wealthy or financially sophisticated was not sufficient for the exemption to apply. In short, such status "is not a substitute for 'access to the kind of information which registration would disclose.' "[174] The court therefore held the defendants liable under Section 12(1) of the Securities Act.[175] In contrast, under the SEC's Rule 506, the

---

would disclose. Moreover, the requirement that the offerees be able to bear the economic risk of the investment is one that our cases never dealt with. . . .

Woolf v. S. D. Cohn & Co., 515 F.2d 591, 612 n.14 (5th Cir. 1975), *vacated and remanded on other grounds*, 426 U.S. 944 (1976). *See* Doran v. Petroleum Management Corp., 545 F. 2d 893, 902 (5th Cir. 1977); Schneider, note 160 *supra*, at 874-75. *But see ABA Position Paper, supra*, 31 Bus. Law. at 491 ("[U]nder Statutory Law as well as Rule 146, we believe that both the total amount of money invested, and also the likelihood that all or part of it will be lost, must be considered"). *See also North American State Securities Administrators (NASSA) Uniform Limited Offering Exemption*, 14 Sec. Reg. & Rep. (BNA) 834 (May 7, 1982) (requiring, unlike Rule 506, that for such accredited investor as discussed above, "the issuer and any person acting on its behalf shall have reasonable grounds to believe and after making reasonable inquiry shall believe that the purchaser either alone or with his/her purchaser representative(s) has such knowledge and experience in financial and business matters that he/she is or they are capable of evaluating the merits and risk of the prospective investment and that the investment does not exceed 20% of the investor's net worth (excluding principal residence, furnishings therein and personal automobiles)." The exemption does provide, however, that "[i]n those states where facts and circumstances permit, it would not be inconsistent with the regulatory objectives of this exemption to omit this section").

171. 569 F.2d 1283 (5th Cir. 1978).

172. *Id.* at 1290.

173. *Id.* at 1289-91, *citing* SEC v. Ralston Purina Co., 346 U.S. 119 (1953); Doran v. Petroleum Management Corp., 545 F. 2d 893 (5th Cir. 1977); United States v. Custer Channel Wing Corp., 376 F. 2d 675 (4th Cir. 1967); Gilligan, Will & Co. v. SEC, 267 F 2d. 461 (2d Cir. 1959).

174. 569 F.2d at 1289, *quoting* United States v. Custer Channel Wing Corp., 376 F.2d 675, 678 (4th Cir. 1967), *quoting* SEC v. Ralston Purina Co., 346 U.S. 119, 127 (1953). *Accord,* Doran v. Petroleum Management Corp., 545 F. 2d 893, 902 (5th Cir. 1977) ("[E]vidence of a high degree of business or legal sophistication on the part of all offerees does not suffice to bring the offering within the private placement exemption").

175. 569 F.2d at 1289-91. Section 12(1) provides that "[a]ny person who offers or sells a security in violation of Section 5 . . . shall be liable to the person purchasing such security from him. . . ." Some courts have limited liability under Section 12 to only those persons who are in a privity relationship with the aggrieved purchaser. *See, e.g.,* McFarland v. Memorex Corp., 493 F. Supp. 631, 647-48 (N.D. Cal. 1980). The Fifth Circuit in *Lawler* rejected this rationale, holding that liability may be imposed under Section 12 upon those who are integrally connected with or substantially involved in the offer or sale. 569 F.2d at 1287, *following,*

defendants in *Lawler* apparently would have been successful in claiming the exemption, thereby precluding the plaintiffs from their Section 12(1) remedy. This result is due to the fact that the plaintiffs apparently would be considered "accredited investors" as defined in Commission rules.[176] As such, they would not be entitled to delivery of any information as the rule presumes that such investors can fend for themselves.[177]

Rule 506's departure from established case law construing Section 4(2) calls into question whether the rule will ultimately be upheld by the courts. For our purposes here, the rule, perhaps more so than any other recent SEC action, brings into focus the apparently changed philosophy at the Commission, at least with respect to its excessive concern for the capital-raising process. In this context, a former SEC Commissioner has recommended that the preambles of the 1933 and 1934 Acts should be amended to elevate the promotion of the capital formation process as one of the Commission's specified objectives.[178] Although this is certainly a laudable objective, it is clear that Congress was far more concerned with the SEC's role in protecting the investing public and the integrity of the marketplace.[179] Accordingly,

---

Lewis v. Walston & Co., 487 F.2d 617, 621-22 (5th Cir. 1973). In addition, some courts have premised liability under the section on an aiding and abetting basis. *See generally* Collins v. Signetic Corp., 605 F.2d 110, 112-13 (3d Cir. 1979).

176. Since investors lost an average of $210,000 each, this conclusion seems supportable. The decision, however, does not discuss each investor's loss. For Regulation D's definition of "accredited investor," *see* Rule 501, note 162 *supra*.

177. *See* Rule 502(b), SEC Release, note 158 *supra*, 14 SEC. REG. & L. REP. (BNA) 495, 500-01 (March 17, 1982).

178. R. KARMEL, REGULATION BY PROSECUTION: THE SECURITIES AND EXCHANGE COMMISSION VERSUS CORPORATE AMERICA 297-305 (1982). *See* Klein, *Karmel's 'Good Book' Flawed by Rhetorical Excess,* Legal Times (Wash.), April 5, 1982, at 13, col. 1. *See also* KARMEL at 297 ("The Commission's traditional concern with acting in the public interest to protect investors must be broadened so that investor protection is equated with capital formation").

179. *See* Preamble to the Securities Act of 1933 ("To provide full and fair disclosure of the character of securities sold in interstate and foreign commerce and through the mails, and to prevent frauds in the sale thereof, and for other purposes"); Preamble to the Securities Exchange Act of 1934 ("To provide for the regulation of securities exchanges and over-the-counter markets operating in interstate and foreign commerce and through the mails, to prevent inequitable and unfair practices on such exchanges and markets, and for other purposes"). Interestingly, when Congress amended the Securities Act in 1980, it urged "greater Federal and State cooperation in securities matters, including . . . minimum *interference* with the business of capital formation. . . . " Section 19(c)(2)(C) (emphasis supplied). The term "interference" is far different from the terms "facilitating" or "encouraging," which Congress could have elected to employ.

The Commission's adoption of Rule 415, the temporary "shelf" registration rule, Securities Act Release No. 6383, 24 SEC DOCKET 1318 (March 16, 1982), and the Commission's subsequent extension of that rule, Securities Act Release No. 6423, 14 SEC. REG. & L. REP. (BNA) 1593 (Sept. 17, 1982), have come under attack. Generally, Rule 415 governs the registration of securities to be offered and sold on a delayed or continuous basis in the future. Significantly, for the first time, the rule permits primary at-the-market offerings of equity securities which

the Commission's promulgation of Rule 506, although perhaps beneficial by replacing the cumbersome and much criticized Rule 146,[180] goes too far in facilitating capital formation at the expense of the investing public.

V. ENFORCEMENT

During the 1970s, the trilogy of (1) the Commission's enforcement program, (2) the voluntary disclosure program, and (3) the Foreign Corrupt Practices Act had a profound collective impact on corporate accountability. The enforcement program in the area of questionable payments is well known and need not be detailed here.[181] Equally well known are the many cases brought for violations involving other misconduct.[182] Again, the point should be made, however, that these and other cases were brought in re-

---

the issuer expects to offer within two years of the registration statement's effective date. *See* Ferrara & Sweeney, *Shelf Registration Under SEC Temporary Rule 415,* 5 Corp. L. Rev. 308 (1982). Following public hearings and comment regarding Rule 415, the Commission extended the effective period for the rule until December 31, 1983, to obtain additional experience before taking final action on the rule. Securities Act Release No. 6423 (Sept. 2, 1982). Arguing that the rule should be limited to debt offerings, Commissioner Thomas dissented. She asserted that Rule 415, when applied to equity offerings,

> jeopardizes the liquidity and stability of our primary and secondary securities markets by encouraging greater concentration of underwriters, market-makers, and other financial intermediaries and by discouraging individual investor participation in the capital markets thereby furthering the trend toward institutionalization of securities holders, and (2) reduces the quality and timeliness of disclosure available to investors when making their investment decisions. Incurring these risks is antithetical to the statutory duty of the Commission to protect investors and to maintain the integrity of our capital markets.

14 Sec. Reg. & L. Rep. (BNA) at 1597. Also, commenting on the rule, John C. Whitehead, Senior Partner of Goldman, Sachs & Co., stated: "There have been times when its zealous protection of the interests of investors have seemed to make it unduly difficult for corporations to raise needed capital. But now the Commission has seemingly taken a 180-degree turn, abandoning its traditional role of protecting investors. . . ." Whitehead, *SEC Abandons Investor Protection,* Financier (Correspondence) 59, 60 (April 1982).

180. Thus, Rule 146 was subject to two major criticisms: "(1) It [did] not relieve all ambiguity and uncertainty regarding the necessary requirements for the private placement exemption, and (2) full compliance with the Rule [was] a time consuming and financially expensive procedure." Thomforde, note 160 *supra,* at 21. *See* authorities cited in note 160 *supra.* As noted before, former Rule 146 apparently was more restrictive than the statutory case law construing Section 4(2). *See* note 170 *supra.* Irrespective of whether Rule 506 is ultimately upheld by the courts, the rule's adoption by the Commission may in itself represent a change in focus.

181. *See* SEC Questionable Payments Report, note 27 *supra.*

182. *See generally* Hazen, *Administrative Enforcement: An Evaluation of the Securities and Exchange Commission's Use of Injunctions and Other Enforcement Methods,* 31 Hastings L. J. 427 (1979).

sponse to specifically perceived wrongdoings and deficiencies and not with an aim to influence internal corporate affairs. While the express statutory remedy sought in such cases was an injunction against future violations, the Commission also obtained a variety of ancillary or other equitable relief. Such relief was designed to establish mechanisms by which repetition of the questionable conduct was to be avoided. In this process, the Commission influenced internal corporate mechanisms, sometimes dramatically. For example, corporate boards were restructured,[183] independent directors were appointed,[184] audit and other committees were established,[185] special counsel was appointed to investigate and report,[186] and corporate officials were removed or ordered not to serve in public companies.[187]

While the SEC has often procured such relief through the consent negotiation process, usually with the defendant neither admitting nor denying the allegations of the complaint,[188] in a number of cases, the Commission has obtained these orders through litigation.[189] In addition, pursuant to Section 15(c)(4) of the Exchange Act,[190] the Commission through the ad-

---

183. *See, e.g.,* SEC v. Mattel, Inc., [1974-1975 Transfer Binder] FED. SEC. L. REP. (CCH) ¶ 94,807 (D.D.C. 1974); SEC v. Westgate Cal. Corp., SEC Litigation Release No. 6142 (S.D. Cal. 1973).

184. *See, e.g.,* SEC v. The Fundpack, Inc., [1979-1980 Transfer Binder] FED. SEC. L. REP. (CCH) ¶ 97,125 (D.D.C. 1979); SEC v. Marlene Industries, Inc., SEC Litigation Release No. 8733 (S.D.N.Y. 1979); SEC v. Inflight Services, Inc., SEC Litigation Release No. 8182 (S.D.N.Y. 1977).

185. *See, e.g.,* SEC v. International Systems & Controls Corp., [1979-1980 Transfer Binder] FED. SEC. L. REP. (CCH) ¶ 97,207 (D.D.C. 1979); SEC v. Aydin Corp., [1979-1980 Transfer Binder] FED. SEC. L. REP. (CCH) ¶ 97,111 (D.D.C. 1979); SEC v. Sharon Steel Corp., SEC Litigation Release No. 8119 (D.D.C. 1977).

186. SEC v. The Fundpack, Inc., [1979 Transfer Binder] FED. SEC. L. REP. (CCH) ¶ 96,951 (D.D.C. 1979); SEC v. Occidental Petroleum Corp., SEC Litigation Release No. 8121 (D.D.C. Sept. 21, 1977); SEC v. Lockheed Aircraft Corp., [1975-1976 Transfer Binder] FED. SEC. L. REP. (CCH) ¶ 95,509 (D.D.C. 1976). For an excellent article on this subject, see Gruenbaum & Oppenheimer, *Special Investigative Counsel: Conflicts and Roles,* 33 RUTGERS L. REV. 965 (1981).

187. *See, e.g.,* SEC v. Ormand Indus., [1977-1978 Transfer Binder] FED. SEC. L. REP. (CCH) ¶ 96,046 (D.D.C. 1977); SEC v. Clinton Oil, SEC Litigation Release No. 5798 (N.D. Ohio 1973). *See generally* Farrand, *Ancillary Remedies in SEC Civil Enforcement Suits,* 89 HARV. L. REV. 1779 (1976).

188. *See, e.g.,* SEC v. International Systems & Controls Corp., [1979-1980 Transfer Binder] FED. SEC. L. REP. (CCH) ¶ 97,207 (D.D.C. 1979); SEC v. Lockheed Aircraft Corp., [1975-1976 Transfer Binder] FED. SEC. L. REP. (CCH) ¶ 95,509 (D.D.C. 1976). *See generally* Levine & Herlihy, *How SEC Will Continue to Use Consent Decrees,* Legal Times (Wash.), June 5, 1978, at 16, col. 2; Mathews, *Recent Trends in SEC Requests for Ancillary Relief in SEC Civil Injunctive Actions,* 31 BUS. LAW. 1323 (1976).

189. *See, e.g.,* SEC v. Aydin Corp., [1979-1980 Transfer Binder] FED. SEC. L. REP. (CCH) ¶ 97,111 (D.D.C. 1979); SEC v. The Fundpack, Inc., [1979 Transfer Binder] FED. SEC. L. REP. (CCH) ¶ 96,951 (D.D.C. 1979).

190. 15 U.S.C. § 78o(c)(4) (1976).

ministrative process has obtained far-reaching forms of relief that affect internal corporate processes.[191] Another administrative technique that the Commission has employed in this regard is the issuance of Section 21(a) reports under the Exchange Act.[192]

It appears that the present Commission will continue, at least to a certain extent, its policy of seeking ancillary or other equitable relief in this context. For example, in recent actions, the Commission has obtained, through the consent process, court orders requiring that independent directors and special agents be appointed.[193] Moreover, the Commission in a Section 21(a) Report summarized the importance of timely disclosure by corporations of material developments where persons, having access to such nonpublic corporate information, may be trading in the subject company's securities.[194] Thus, the Commission's enforcement program, perhaps due in part to the widely accepted propriety of ancillary relief, will continue to affect corporate internal processes. Nonetheless, as will be discussed, the magnitude of this impact may well be smaller than it has in the past.

Respecting enforcement developments that affect internal corporate affairs and the Commission's perceived authority to address this subject, an interesting evolution appears to have taken place. The *Franchard* decision[195] in 1964 reflects the Commission's corporate governance philosophy at that

---

191. *See, e.g.,* SEC v. U.S. Steel Corp., [1979-1980 Transfer Binder] FED. SEC. L. REP. (CCH) ¶ 82,319 (1979). Pursuant to a Section 15(c)(4) proceeding settled by consent, the Commission found that the company made inadequate disclosure of environmental matters in its Exchange Act reports. As part of its offer of settlement, U.S. Steel undertook to appoint a task force to review its environmental disclosure and to prepare a report to its Audit Committee setting forth procedures to provide for timely and complete disclosure.

192. In pertinent part, Section 21(a) of the Exchange Act, 15 U.S.C. 78u(a), provides:

> The Commission is authorized in its discretion, to publish information concerning any such violations, and to investigate any facts, conditions, practices, or matters which it may deem necessary or proper to aid in the enforcement of such regulations under this title, or in securing information to serve as a basis for recommending further legislation concerning the matters to which this title relates.

The Commission has issued a number of Section 21(a) Reports that have affected corporate internal processes. *See, e.g., Staff Report on Proxy Solicitations in Connection with Compass Investment Group,* Securities Exchange Act Release No. 16343 (Nov. 15, 1979); Statement by State National Bank of Maryland, Securities Exchange Act Release No. 16321 (Nov. 5, 1979); In the Matter of Spartek, Inc., Securities Exchange Act Release No. 15567 (Feb. 14, 1979).

193. *See, e.g.,* SEC v. Petrowest, Inc., SEC Litigation Release No. 9604 (N.D. Tex. 1982), 24 SEC DOCKET 1522 (March 23, 1982); SEC v. Vornado, Inc., [1981-1982 Transfer Binder] FED. SEC. L. REP. (CCH) ¶ 98,377 (D.D.C. 1981); SEC v. Data Access Systems, Inc., SEC Litigation Release No. 9487 (D.N.J. 1981), 23 SEC DOCKET 1380, 1382 (Nov. 10, 1981).

194. *Report of Investigation in the Matter of Sharon Steel Corporation as It Relates to Prompt Corporate Disclosure,* Securities Exchange Act Release No. 18271 (Nov. 19, 1981).

195. 42 S.E.C. 163, [1964-1966 Transfer Binder] FED. SEC. L. REP. (CCH) ¶ 77,113 (1964).

time. In *Franchard*, the Commission asserted that the obligations and responsibilities of directors were subjects within the province of state law. The Commission also indicated that it did not have the desire to address this area.[196] A change in this philosophy, however, occurred in the 1970s. The staff report in the Penn Central matter[197] was a step in this direction. In that report, the staff—not the Commission—although not engaging in prescriptive standard setting, addressed what it perceived to be the directors' deficient conduct.[198]

The next significant development was the Stirling Homex report[199] in 1975. In the Commission's Section 21(a) report, this time the Commission—not the staff—commented upon the inadequate performance of the outside directors, stating that they "did not play any significant role in the direction of [the] company's affairs even though they possessed considerable business experience and sophistication."[200] This approach was adhered to in *SEC v. Shiell*,[201] where the Commission alleged that the subject directors violated the antifraud provisions by neglecting to perform their directorial duties. The Commission's complaint in *Shiell* along with the staff's affidavit in support of the motion for preliminary injunctive relief evidenced the evolutionary development since *Franchard*.[202]

In 1978, in *National Telephone*,[203] the Commission, rather than opining on the role of directors *qua* directors, identified structural deficiencies in what could be viewed as National Telephone's corporate governance machinery. For example, the audit committee, which consisted of three outside directors, never met.[204] At about the same time that *National Telephone* was handed down, the Commission brought an injunctive action against

---

196. *Id.* at 178, [1964-1966 Transfer Binder] Fed. Sec. L. Rep. (CCH) ¶ 77,113, at 82,046-48.

197. House Special Subcomm. on Investigations, 92d Cong., 2d Sess., Staff Report of the Securities and Exchange Commission, The Financial Collapse of the Penn Central Company (Subcomm. Print 1972).

198. *Id.* at 7-8.

199. Securities Exchange Act Release No. 11516, 7 SEC Docket 298 (July 2, 1975).

200. 7 SEC Docket at 300.

201. [1977-1978 Transfer Binder] Fed. Sec. L. Rep. (CCH) ¶ 96,190 (N.D. Fla. 1977).

202. *See* Litigation Release No. 7763, 11 SEC Docket 1664 (Jan. 31, 1978).

203. Securities Exchange Act Release No. 14380, 13 SEC Docket 1393, [1977-1978 Transfer Binder] Fed. Sec. L. Rep. (CCH) ¶ 81,410 (Jan. 16, 1978).

204. 13 SEC Docket at 1395. The Commission also stated: "The Commission is not saying that the directors of a company are responsible for approving every line of every press release and periodic filing made by the company; rather the Commission is saying that, at a time of distress in a company's existence, the directors have an affirmative duty to assure that the market place be provided accurate and full disclosure concerning the basic viability of the company and the continuity of its operations." *Id.* at 1393.

Killearn Properties.[205] There, in a consent judgment, the company was ordered to restructure its board of directors to consist of a majority of outside directors and to maintain an audit committee composed solely of outside directors.[206] More recently, the Commission, in the *Woods*[207] and *Spartek*[208] proceedings, embarked on the latest stage in this evolutionary process. In these cases, the Commission restructured specific transactions, finding that the companies' Exchange Act reports "were materially deficient in failing to disclose the full facts and circumstances surrounding the structure of the sale of assets transaction[s], including the purposes, and the determination of the price to be offered to shareholders."[209] To remedy these situations, the Commission ordered the respective companies to comply with the reporting requirements and to retain a "special review person" to negotiate on behalf of the public shareholders.[210]

From the above discussion, the conclusion emerges that the Commission through its enforcement actions, and the obtaining of ancillary or other equitable relief in such actions, has significantly affected corporate internal affairs. In so doing, however, it needs to be stressed that the Commission has not stretched its statutory mandates. Rather than being premised on breaches of fiduciary duty,[211] Commission actions in this context have been based principally on federal disclosure violations, and, hence, come well within the Commission's jurisdiction.[212]

Nonetheless, although it is premature to state with certainty, future SEC enforcement policies may have a narrower scope. One such area, as discussed before, may concern the duty to disclose qualitatively material information, including unadjudicated illegalities.[213] Moreover, present Enforcement Di-

---

205. SEC. v. Killearn Properties, Inc., [1979 Transfer Binder] FED. SEC. L. REP. (CCH) ¶ 96,256 (N.D. Fla. 1977).

206. *Id.* at 92,694-95.

207. In the Matter of Woods Corporation, Securities Exchange Act Release No. 15337, 16 SEC DOCKET 166 (Nov. 16, 1978).

208. In the Matter of Spartek, Inc., Securities Exchange Act Release No. 15567, 16 SEC DOCKET 1094 (Feb. 14, 1979).

209. 16 SEC DOCKET at 172. *See* 16 SEC DOCKET at 1099-1100.

210. 16 SEC DOCKET at 1100; 16 SEC DOCKET at 172. *See* Ferrara, *The Duty to Disclose Qualitative Material Information* in TWELFTH ANNUAL INSTITUTE ON SECURITIES REGULATION 145, 155-56 (Fleischer, Lipton, Mundheim & Santoni eds., 1980) (Practising Law Institute Transcript Series); Ferrara, note 118 *supra*, at 768-70. *See also* SEC v. Wej-It Corp., SEC Litigation Release No. 3299 (D.D.C. 1979) (in a consent judgment, the SEC alleged that Wej-It violated Section 14(e) of the Exchange Act by, *inter alia*, failing to disclose to its shareholders the full facts and circumstances regarding the manner and method by which the Wej-It board arrived at the offering price).

211. *See* note 110 *supra*.

212. *See generally* notes 77-114 and accompanying text *supra*.

213. *See* notes 115-27 and accompanying text *supra*.

rector John M. Fedders has announced a comprehensive review of the Commission's enforcement policies and practices.[214] He also has enumerated three specific areas for "renewed enforcement vigilance," namely, trading while in possession of material nonpublic information, manipulation of the securities markets, and fraudulent disclosure practices by reporting companies.[215] Undoubtedly, these three areas require vigorous SEC enforcement as they impact directly on the investing public and the securities markets. For better or worse, however, these areas of concern, although also part of the Sporkin era enforcement program, may well represent different "rhetoric and policies."[216] During the Sporkin era, it appeared that the Commission relied on the disclosure rationale underlying the federal securities laws as the basis for bringing enforcement actions that affected a wide range of corporate substantive conduct. In so doing, the Commission employed such policies as requiring disclosure of information because it bears on the integrity or competency of management, irrespective of the information's economic materiality,[217] holding that professionals, such as attorneys and accountants—those who act as the "passkey"[218] to securities offerings and other key corporate transactions—must be cognizant of, and responsible to,

---

214. Remarks by John M. Fedders, Director, Division of Enforcement, Securities and Exchange Commission, to the 1981 SEC Accounting Conference, Foundation for Accounting Education of the New York State Society of Certified Public Accountants at 4-8 (Nov. 16, 1981). Mr. Fedders announced that the initiation of this study was encouraged by Chairman Shad and the other Commissioners. *Id.* at 4. The study is intended to encompass such matters as the internal standards employed by the Commission when determining whether to litigate or settle cases, the internal standards utilized for authorizing formal orders of investigation, and whether such formal orders should automatically expire after a specified period, unless renewed by the Commission. *Id.* at 5. Mr. Fedders also initiated a study of the sanctions and remedies that are available to the Commission. This study will cover three areas: whether the present remedies and sanctions are adequate and, if not, whether the Commission should seek legislation; whether, in appropriate circumstances, the Commission should seek injunctions that expire after a specified period or upon the fulfillment of certain conditions; and whether the Commission should publish criteria that it would apply when deciding whether to consent to a request for modification or dissolution of an outstanding injunction. *Id.* at 6-7. The results of this study may portend a significant change in SEC enforcement policy. The Commission's position, at this time, apparently is consistent with prior policy, namely, that upon making a proper showing, it is entitled as a matter of statutory right to the ordering of a permanent injunction (Brief of the SEC at 10, SEC v. Associated Minerals, Inc., Nos. 79-1449, 79-1450 (6th Cir. 1980)), and that permanent injunctions should be difficult for subject parties to modify or dissolve. (SEC v. Clifton, [1981–1982 Transfer Binder] FED. SEC. L. REP. (CCH) ¶ 98,477 (D.D.C. 1982)), *aff'd*, [Current] FED. SEC. L. REP. (CCH) ¶ 99,100 (D.C. Cir. 1983).

215. Remarks of John M. Fedders, note 214 *supra*, at 8-11.

216. *See* Hudson, note 45 *supra*, at 18; Vilkin, note 123 *supra*.

217. *See* notes 115-27 and accompanying text *supra*. For further discussion herein on this subject, see pages 76-79 *infra*.

218. *See* Sommer, *The Emerging Responsibilities of the Securities Lawyer*, [1973-1974 Transfer Binder] FED. SEC. L. REP. (CCH) ¶ 79,631 (1974); note 248 and accompanying text *infra*.

the interests of the investing public,[219] and bringing enforcement actions on the basis of nondisclosure of management perquisites and for violation of the accounting provisions of the Foreign Corrupt Practices Act.[220] Whether the above policies will continue with full vigor under the present Commission appears unlikely, although a conclusive determination at this time cannot be made. In this regard, the present Commission's ultimate stance in pursuing these policies will significantly influence the extent to which corporate internal affairs will continue to be affected by the *in terrorem* impact of potential SEC enforcement action.[221]

VI. LEGISLATIVE PROGRAMS

With the exception of the Foreign Corrupt Practices Act of 1977 ("FCPA"), the Commission's recent legislative program has not directly impacted upon internal corporate affairs. Indeed, recent Commission policy has encouraged

---

219. *See, e.g.,* SEC v. Coven, 581 F.2d 1020 (2d Cir. 1978), *cert. denied,* 440 U.S. 950 (1979); SEC v. Spectrum Ltd., 489 F.2d 535 (2d Cir. 1973); SEC v. National Student Marketing Corp., 457 F. Supp. 682 (D.D.C. 1978); In re Arthur Andersen & Co., [1973-1974 Transfer Binder] FED. SEC. L. REP. (CCH) ¶ 79,900 (SEC 1974); *In re* Emanuel Fields, [1972-1973 Transfer Binder] FED. SEC. L. REP. (CCH) ¶ 79,407 (SEC 1973), *aff'd without opinion,* 495 F.2d 1075 (D.C. Cir. 1974). *But see* SEC v. Arthur Young & Co., 590 F.2d 785, 788 (9th Cir. 1979) (the court stated that acceptance of the Commission's position in that case would make the accountant "an insurer of his client's honesty and an enforcement arm of the SEC"). *See generally* Gruenbaum, *Clients' Frauds and Their Lawyers' Obligations: A Response to Professor Kramer,* 68 GEO. L.J. 191 (1979).

220. *See, e.g.,* SEC v. Page Airways, Inc., [1979-1980 Transfer Binder] FED. SEC. L. REP. (CCH) ¶ 97,341 (W.D.N.Y. 1980); SEC v. Joseph Schlitz Brewing Co., 452 F. Supp. 824 (E.D. Wis. 1978); SEC v. Kalvax, Inc., 425 F. Supp. 310 (S.D.N.Y. 1975); In re Playboy Enterprises, Inc., [1980 Transfer Binder] FED. SEC. L. REP. (CCH) ¶ 82,635 (SEC). *See generally* Vilkin, note 50 *supra,* at 8. The present Commission at times has brought suit for violations of the FCPA. *See, e.g.,* SEC v. Hermetite Corporation, 14 SEC. REG. & L. REP. (BNA) 1631 (Sept. 24, 1982); In the Matter of the Telex Corporation, Securities Exchange Act Release No. 18694 (April 29, 1982), 25 SEC DOCKET 275 (May 11, 1982); SEC v. Crown Cork & Seal Co., Inc., SEC Litigation Release No. 9437 (1981).

221. A recent article stated that "[s]ome securities lawyers say clients, sensing 'a new mood in Washington' favorable to business, are becoming more reluctant to disclose unflattering facts about their dealings. But other lawyers say they haven't detected any change in corporate attitudes." Hudson, note 45 *supra,* at 1. *See also SEC, Faced with Tight Budget, is Paring "Peripheral" Defendants from Complaints,* WALL ST. J., Oct. 20, 1982, p. 6, c. 2 (According to SEC Enforcement Director John Fedders, the SEC, due to budgetary restraints and a shrinking staff, "has for some time been paring 'peripheral' defendants from its court complaints. . . ." The article goes on to state: "Former SEC enforcement aides say privately that such 'peripheral' defendants have included big accounting firms, underwriters and others that are indirectly implicated in corporate securities fraud schemes, and cite as evidence a sharp drop in SEC cases against accountants.")

legislation to aid small issuers and capital formation.[222] And, as noted previously, in regard to the Metzenbaum Bill which called for the imposition of federal minimum standards upon internal corporate structures, former Chairman Williams testified in opposition to such government intervention.[223]

A graphic illustration, however, of how an SEC program can influence the effectuation of fundamental changes in corporate internal affairs is the experience in the area of questionable foreign payments. During the mid-1970s, the Commission became involved, on a programmatic basis, in investigations of companies that had channelled large sums of money to foreign officials in order to obtain business in those countries. The Commission discovered not only that such payments were being made on a widespread basis, but that in many instances they were occurring without the knowledge of top corporate officers and directors—in other words, that they reflected a more fundamental breakdown in the process of corporate accountability itself.[224] In May 1976, the Commission reported to Congress on the results of its investigations and enforcement actions, as well as data submitted by corporations pursuant to its voluntary disclosure program.[225]

Reacting to these and related developments, Congress enacted the Foreign Corrupt Practices Act of 1977. The FCPA outlaws "corrupt" payments to foreign officials or political parties that are designed to obtain or retain business for the company in question or to direct business to any other

---

222. *See, e.g.,* Small Business Investment Incentive Act of 1980. Generally the Act provides special, less burdensome treatment under the Investment Company Act of 1940 for certain venture capital companies, called "business development companies," provided they meet certain conditions. The legislation also added Section 4(6) to the Securities Act, generally providing an exemption from the registration provisions of that Act for transactions involving offers or sales of securities by an issuer solely to one or more "accredited investors" if the offering price does not exceed $5 million, the amount allowed under Section 3(b) of the Act. Also, the section precludes advertising or public solicitation and requires the issuer to file a notice of sales with the Commission.

223. *See* notes 39-42 and accompanying text *supra.*

224. *See* Securities Exchange Act Release No. 15570 (Feb. 15, 1979), 16 SEC DOCKET 1137, 1144-45 (March 6, 1979).

225. REPORT OF THE SECURITIES AND EXCHANGE COMMISSION ON QUESTIONABLE AND ILLEGAL CORPORATE PAYMENTS AND PRACTICES, SUBMITTED TO THE SENATE COMM. ON BANKING, HOUSING AND URBAN AFFAIRS, 94TH CONG., 2D SESS. (Comm. Print, 1976). Generally, a company participating in this program was encouraged to undertake a careful investigation of the facts under the auspices of persons not involved in the questionable conduct and to discuss the question of appropriate disclosure of the matters uncovered with the Commission's staff prior to filing any documents with the Commission. *Id.* at 6-13. As stated by the Commission in its Report, "[a]lthough participation in the voluntary program does not insulate a company from Commission enforcement action, it does diminish the possibility that the Commission will, in its discretion, institute an action." *Id.* at 8 n.7.

person. Further, in responding to the broader accountability concerns, Congress amended Section 13(b) of the Securities Exchange Act to require publicly held companies to (1) make and keep books, records and accounts that "in reasonable detail" accurately and fairly reflect the issuer's transactions and dispositions of assets and (2) devise and maintain systems of internal accounting controls sufficient to provide "reasonable assurances" that transactions are executed in accordance with management's authorization and recorded in conformity with generally accepted accounting principles, and that access to and accountability for assets are adequately controlled. While derived from investor protection and disclosure concerns, these accounting requirements have a direct substantive impact on day-to-day corporate management.[226]

A fairly recent study by the General Accounting Office showed that the FCPA's accounting provisions have forced publicly held companies to reevaluate and, in many cases, to improve their systems of internal accountability.[227] At the same time, the business community has expressed serious concerns about the law—particularly the vagueness of certain of its requirements—and the attendant costs of compliance.[228] During the last Congress,

---

226. Subsequently, the Commission adopted Regulation 13B-2 which affects record-keeping requirements, accountability over assets, and financial statement preparation. *See* [1979 Transfer Binder] FED. SEC. L. REP. (CCH) ¶ 82,063. Civil enforcement of the Act is currently divided between the SEC as to public companies and the Department of Justice as to others. For law review commentary on the FCPA, *see* Atkeson, *The Foreign Corrupt Practices Act of 1977: An International Application of SEC's Corporate Governance Reforms,* 12 INT'L LAW. 703 (1978); Baruch, *Foreign Corrupt Practices Act,* 57 HARV. BUS. REV. 32 (1979); Best, *The Foreign Corrupt Practices Act,* 11 REV. SEC. REG. 975 (1978); Goelzer, *The Accounting Provisions of the Foreign Corrupt Practices Act—The Federalization of Corporate Recordkeeping and Internal Control,* 5 J. CORP. L. 1 (1979); Herlihy & Levine, *Corporate Crisis: The Overseas Payment Problem,* 8 L. & POL'Y INT'L BUS. 547 (1976); Roth, *International Business—The Foreign Corrupt Practices Act of 1977: Background and Summary,* 1 CORP. L. REV. 347 (1978); Siegel, *The Implication Doctrine and the Foreign Corrupt Practices Act,* 79 COLUM. L. REV. 1085 (1979); Stevenson, *The SEC and Foreign Bribery,* 32 BUS. LAW. 53 (1976); Timmeny, *SEC Enforcement of the Foreign Corrupt Practices Act,* 2 LOY. L.A. INT'L & COMP. L. ANN. 25 (1979).

227. "Impact of Foreign Corrupt Practices Act on U.S. Business," Report to the Congress, General Accounting Office (March 4, 1981). The GAO did state, however, that the Commission should provide further guidance with respect to the concept of "reasonableness" contained in the FCPA's accounting provisions. In this respect, the GAO suggested that the "SEC must elicit the views and work closely with the corporate community and the accounting profession, in determining what additional guidance is needed and the format of the guidance." *Id.* at 25.

228. *See, e.g.,* Weisberg & Reichenberg, "The Price of Ambiguity: More Than Three Years Under the Foreign Corrupt Practices Act," at 26-27, Prepared for the International Division, Chamber of Commerce of the United States (1981).

the Senate passed a bill in an attempt to provide greater clarity to the Act.[229] The House of Representatives, however, declined to act.[230]

The Commission's position in response to these developments has remained basically the same during both the Williams and Shad chairmanships. For example, during the Williams era, the Commission issued a release designed to reassure the business community that minor or unintentional errors would not be the subject of enforcement action and that substantial deference would be accorded to reasonable business judgments by management as to what constitutes an appropriate accountability system for a given enterprise.[231] Expressing views consistent with the above policy statement, Chairman Shad during the past Congress testified in regard to the proposed legislation on the FCPA, recommending certain modifications believed necessary to clarify ambiguities in the Act which were detrimental to American business while preserving the FCPA's vitality.[232] A number of the

---

229. S. 708, 97th Cong., 1st Sess. (1981). Generally, the Senate-passed bill would have, *inter alia,* eliminated criminal liability premised on violation of the Act's accounting provisions; provided issuers, under the accounting provisions, with an affirmative "good faith" defense; adopted a mental state for individual liability under the accounting provisions similar to a scienter standard; adopted a definition of materiality to specify that the threshold standard for accuracy of corporate books and records and internal controls is that which a "prudent man would require in the management of his own affairs"; imposed liability under the anti-bribery provisions only if the culpable party "expressly or by course of conduct" authorized bribery; and transferred the SEC's responsibility for civil enforcement of the antibribery provisions to the Justice Department. *See* Sec. Reg. & L. Rep. (BNA) No. 630, AA-1 (Nov. 25, 1981). The Senate-passed bill represented a substantial modification from the bill as originally introduced by Senator Chafee. Also, the administration's approach has been rejected. In pertinent part, this approach would have deleted the Act's accounting provisions and replaced them with a provision that would have made it a criminal offense to conceal an instance of foreign bribery. *See* Taylor, *Move to Clarify, Soften Antibribery Law on Foreign Business Is Backed by Reagan,* Wall St. J., May 21, 1981, at 5, col. 1.

230. *See* Sec. Reg. & L. Rep. (BNA) No. 630, AA-1 (Nov. 25, 1981).

231. *Statement of Policy, Foreign Corrupt Practices Act of 1977,* Securities Exchange Act Release No. 17500 (Jan. 29, 1981), 21 SEC Docket 1466, 1466-72 (Feb. 10, 1981).

232. *See* Hearings on S. 708 Before the Joint Subcomms. of the Senate Banking, Housing and Urban Affairs Comm., 97th Cong., 1st Sess. (1981) (statement of SEC Chairman John S. R. Shad); *SEC Chairman Proposals for Change in Bribery Act,* Legal Times (Wash.), June 22, 1981, at 14, col. 1. Also of interest is former SEC Chairman Williams' testimony before the Committee. After discussing the FCPA's legislative history, Mr. Williams stated:

> I refer to the legislative history to show that the Act was a highly visible product of the political process. When Congress enacted the Act in 1977, it was well aware that many members of the business community thought bribery was essential to do business in certain parts of the world and that the Act's passage would result in loss of business for some American companies. Nevertheless, a consensus was reached that our government would not condone or ignore foreign bribery. And senior public officials in successive Republican and Democratic Administrations have stood firm behind that principle.

Hearings, *supra* (statement of former SEC Chairman Harold M. Williams). In his statement,

Commission's suggestions were incorporated in the Senate-passed bill.[233] Although it is premature to state with any certainty the ultimate results of these developments, it is nonetheless clear that the FCPA remains an important illustration of how Commission efforts geared toward effective corporate disclosure can have a direct impact on corporate internal affairs.

VII. SEC AS *AMICUS CURIAE*

The Commission not infrequently participates as *amicus curiae* in litigation between private parties under the federal securities laws, particularly in the federal appellate courts, to express its views with respect to the interpretation of the applicable provisions involved.[234] Sometimes the issue at bar may impact upon corporate internal processes. One such example is *Burks v. Lasker.*[235]

The issue in *Burks* was whether a quorum of four statutorily disinterested directors within the meaning of the Investment Company Act could terminate a nonfrivolous shareholders' derivative action against fellow directors on the basis that, in the exercise of their good faith business judgment, the continuation of the litigation was not in the company's best interests.[236] The district court, relying on the business judgment rule, held that such termination was proper.[237] The Second Circuit reversed, holding that "disinterested directors of an investment company do not have the power to foreclose the continuation of nonfrivolous litigation brought by shareholders against majority directors for breach of their fiduciary duties."[238]

Participating as *amicus curiae* before the Supreme Court, the Commission disagreed with the Second Circuit's position, reasoning that the court of appeals' approach neglected the vital statutory role served by disinterested directors as "watch-dogs" under the Investment Company Act.[239] To preserve this function yet ensure that the disinterested directors act in the best

---

Mr. Williams also expressed his general agreement with the views presented by Chairman Shad on behalf of the present Commission, which he believed were consistent with the Commission's 1981 policy statement.

233. *See* Sec. Reg. & L. Rep. (BNA) No. 630, AA-1 (Nov. 25, 1981) ("While several senators had pushed for a 'financial statement' materially standard, the Senate opted instead for a standard recommended by the SEC"). For further discussion herein on the FCPA, *see* pages 106-08 *infra*.

234. *See* SEC Litigation Release No. 9023 (Feb. 27, 1980), 19 SEC Docket 793 (March 11, 1980).

235. 441 U.S. 471 (1979).

236. *Id.* at 473-74.

237. 404 F. Supp. 1172 (S.D.N.Y. 1975).

238. 567 F.2d 1208, 1212 (2d Cir. 1978).

239. Brief for the SEC as *Amicus Curiae* at 12, Burks v. Lasker, 441 U.S. 471 (1979).

interests of the shareholders, the Commission asserted that the traditional business judgment rule should be applied within a framework of certain safeguards: that a determination by disinterested directors to terminate a nonfrivolous derivative suit should be given effect only where the court finds that the directors were independent, fully informed, and had acted reasonably.[240]

In its decision, the Supreme Court referred to the primary role of disinterested directors under the Investment Company Act to protect the interests of shareholders. The Court stated that "[t]here may well be situations in which the independent directors could reasonably believe that the best interests of the shareholders call for a decision not to sue."[241] Further, rather than directly answering the inquiry before it, the Court promulgated a two-step test which lower courts have elaborated upon:[242] (1) whether the applicable state law allows the disinterested directors to terminate a shareholders' derivative suit, and (2) whether such a state rule is consistent with the policies underlying the federal securities laws.[243]

After *Burks*, the Commission during both the Williams and Shad chairmanships has continued to appear as *amicus curiae* to set forth its position. For example, in *Maldonado v. Flynn*[244] and *Abramowitz v. Posner*,[245] the Commission argued that, in view of the important function served by private enforcement of the federal antifraud and proxy provisions, derivative actions against a corporation's directors for violation of these provisions "may be terminated by the board of directors only if the board's decision is an independent, fully informed, and reasonable business judgment."[246] Re-

---

240. *Id.* at 7.

241. 441 U.S. at 485.

242. *See, e.g.,* Lewis v. Anderson, 615 F.2d 778 (9th Cir. 1979), *cert. denied,* 101 S. Ct. 206 (1980); Galef v. Alexander, 615 F.2d 51 (2d Cir. 1980); Abbey v. Control Data Corp., 603 F.2d 724 (8th Cir. 1979), *cert. denied,* 444 U.S. 1017 (1980); Genzer v. Cunningham, 498 F. Supp. 682 (E.D. Mich. 1980); Maher v. Zapata Corp., 490 F. Supp. 348 (S.D. Tex. 1980). *See also* Maldonado v. Flynn, 430 A.2d 779 (Del. 1981); Auerbach v. Bennett, 47 N.Y.2d 619, 393 N.E.2d 994, 419 N.Y.S.2d 920 (1979). For further discussion herein on this subject, *see* pages 133-62 *infra*.

243. 441 U.S. at 480, 486.

244. 485 F. Supp. 274 (S.D.N.Y. 1980), *remanded,* [1981-1982 Transfer Binder] FED. SEC. L. REP. (CCH) ¶ 98,457 (2d Cir. 1982).

245. [1981 Transfer Binder] FED. SEC. L. REP. (CCH) ¶ 97,921, *remanded,* [1981-1982 Transfer Binder] FED. SEC. L. REP. (CCH) ¶ 98,458 (2d Cir. 1982).

246. *See* Brief for the SEC as *Amicus Curiae* at 11, Abramowitz v. Posner, No. 81-7320 (2d Cir.); Brief for the SEC as *Amicus Curiae* at 9, Maldonado v. Flynn, Nos. 80-7221, 80-7253 (2d Cir.). A rationale underlying the Commission's position may be seen from the following statement:

> The decision to terminate derivative suits against their fellow directors is peculiarly one which is fraught with conflicting interests. There is a substantial risk that directors may harbor a subconscious if not conscious bias in favor of their colleagues. . . .

gardless of whether this standard should ultimately prevail in the courts, the Commission's participation in these cases indicates that, even in its *amicus curiae* program, the positions advanced therein at times will continue to have a substantial effect on corporate internal affairs.[247]

VIII. ADVISERS TO CORPORATE MANAGEMENT— LAWYERS AND ACCOUNTANTS

The Commission does not take action against lawyers or accountants because it wishes to influence the internal affairs of their corporate clients. Nor, contrary to some unkind suggestions from members of these learned professions, does it do so for the sheer joy of the hunt. The Commission's concern with these professional groups stems from the important role they, together with professionals in the securities business itself, play in securities transactions. Indeed, it can be most difficult for an issuer of securities to raise money from the public without the assistance of a securities broker or dealer, an opinion from counsel, and a certificate from an auditor. These persons have been referred to as possessing the "passkeys" to the securities markets.[248]

Thus, in light of the essential functions performed by lawyers and accountants, it is scarcely surprising that, when things go wrong, and the Commission investigates the conduct of the promoters, officers, directors and other direct participants, the roles played by the broker, the lawyer and the accountant sometimes come into question. And just as the process by which corporations account to their investors was considered to be a legit-

---

Abramowitz Brief at 17. *See Maldonado* Brief at 14-15. The Second Circuit in both *Maldonado* and *Abramowitz* disagreed with the Commission's position, holding that Delaware law is consistent with the policies underlying Sections 10(b) and 14(a). *See* [1981-1982 Transfer Binder] FED. SEC. L. REP. (CCH) ¶ 98,458, at 92,691-95; [1981-1982 Transfer Binder] FED. SEC. L. REP. (CCH) ¶ 98,457, at 92,687. *See also* Brief for the SEC as *Amicus Curiae* at 12, Grossman v. Johnson, [1981-1982 Transfer Binder] FED. SEC. L. REP. (CCH) ¶ 98,619 (1st Cir. 1982) (although the First Circuit did not resolve the issue, the Commission argued that "[t]he congressional purpose in enacting Section 36(b) of the Investment Company Act, giving investment company shareholders an express right of action to recover on behalf of the investment company excessive advisory fees received by an investment adviser, precludes termination of such actions pursuant to the business judgment decision of the investment company's board of directors"). For further discussion herein on this subject, *see* pages 133-62 *infra*.

247. *See, e.g.,* Brief for the SEC as *Amicus Curiae*, General Steel Industries, Inc. v. Walco Corp., No. 81-2345 (8th Cir.) (taking the position that equitable relief such as rescission and divestiture may be granted, pursuant to the court's discretion, to remedy violations of Section 13(d) of the Exchange Act).

248. *See* Shipman, *The Need for SEC Rules to Govern the Duties and Civil Liabilities of Attorneys Under the Federal Securities Statutes*, 34 OHIO ST. L.J. 231 (1973); notes 218-19 and accompanying text *supra*.

imate subject of inquiry by the Corporate Accountability Staff Study and of regulation under the Foreign Corrupt Practices Act—because the individual cases studied showed that there needed to be a systemic approach—the relationship of the corporation to its legal and accounting advisers transcends particular cases and also warrants systemic study and comment.

A. Attorneys

Commission actions regarding the lawyer's relationship to the corporate client's internal processes are most often, though not always,[249] products of

---

249. Two such prior examples were the Commission's and staff's response to the "Georgetown Petition" and the discussion draft of the Model Rules of Professional Conduct. With respect to the Georgetown Petition, the Institute for Public Representation, affiliated with Georgetown University Law Center in Washington, D.C., submitted, pursuant to the Administrative Procedure Act, 5 U.S.C. § 553(e) (1976), a request that the Commission engage in rulemaking and adopt three proposed rules, which would have amended the Commission's disclosure forms to require disclosure by corporations of: (1) certification by the board of directors that it has instructed all attorneys employed or retained by the corporation to report to the board certain corporate activities discovered by the attorney which, in the attorney's opinion, violate or probably violate the law; (2) written agreements between corporations and outside counsel which specify, among other things, the frequency and nature of counsel's contacts with the board of directors; and (3) the circumstances of resignations or dismissals of general counsel or securities attorneys of the corporations. Securities Exchange Act Release No. 16045, 17 SEC Docket 1376 (July 25, 1979). On July 25, 1979, the Commission put out the request for public comment, without taking any position on the merits of the proposal. Id. The Commission received over 300 public comments regarding this proposal. On April 30, 1980, the Commission determined to deny the petition. Securities Exchange Act Release No. 16769, 19 SEC Docket 1300 (April 30, 1980).

In its release denying the petition, the Commission noted that one of the several reasons for denial urged by commentators was that many of the questions concerning "the nature of the obligations of attorneys to make appropriate disclosure of corporate illegalities they discover" were being addressed in the private sector. 19 SEC Docket at 1301. Thus, the Commission expressed the view that "it would be inappropriate, at this time, to consider further the rules proposed by the Institute" in light of the concerns expressed by the commentators, "particularly with respect to . . . the initiative in this area being taken by the legal profession. . . ." Id. at 1302. The Commission, however, stated that it would continue to monitor developments in this area. Id. at 1303. For further discussion herein on this subject, see pages 252-53 infra.

The Commission's reference to the "initiative in this area being taken by the legal profession" was addressed to the ongoing work of the Commission on Evaluation of Professional Standards of the American Bar Association ("Standards Commission"). On January 30, 1980, after more than two years of work, that group circulated for public discussion the discussion draft of the Model Rules of Professional Conduct, which comprehensively reformulated the ABA Model Code of Professional Responsibility for lawyers. Subsequently, the Standards Commission in May 1981 issued its proposed final draft.

On October 30, 1980, the Commission staff filed, in the name of the General Counsel, extensive comments on the draft Model Rules. Included were detailed staff views of the circumstances under which a lawyer representing a corporation may or should go over the head of the corporate official with whom he is dealing and refer the matter to higher authority, up to and including the board of directors. The staff also proffered recommendations on the

SEC enforcement[250] or disciplinary proceedings.[251] In these actions, the Commission has commented on the role that attorneys play in the disclosure process and, at times, has ordered the restructuring of internal procedures of law firms. For example, in *In the Matter of Emanuel Fields,*[252] the Commission asserted that securities lawyers occupy a strategic position in the investment process and that the SEC, with its limited resources, "is peculiarly dependent on the probity and diligence of the professionals who practice before it."[253] With respect to the lack of adequate internal procedures within law firms, the Commission has ordered that these procedures be revised and has made clear that "[a] law firm has a duty to make sure that disclosure documents filed with the Commission include all material facts about a

---

related question of when it would be appropriate for the lawyer to give unsolicited advice to his corporate client. Also of interest, the staff comments included discussion of situations which may arise when the board fails to act in the best interests of the shareholders of the corporation, such as when directors have conflicts of interests. Under such circumstances, according to the comments, counsel's responsibilities may run directly to the shareholders. Finally, although the staff stated that its comments were limited to professional responsibility questions and were not addressed to legal liability issues, it recognized the tension which often exists between the disclosure requirements inherent in the relationship between the corporation and its lawyer. Comments of the General Counsel at 48-75. Compare these views with those of the subsequent SEC General Counsel. *See* Remarks of Edward F. Greene to the New York County Lawyers' Association (Jan. 13, 1982), 14 Sec. Reg. & L. Rep. (BNA) 168 (Jan. 20, 1982). *See* note 268 *infra*.

It was noted in the staff document that the comments were not submitted to or reviewed by the Commission, formally or informally, and that the Commission, as a matter of policy, disclaimed responsibility for the private publication of its employees. The staff chose not to submit the comments to the Commission because they, in part, focused upon proposed rules concerning issues arguably present in the *Carter-Johnson* Rule 2(e) administrative disciplinary proceeding, which was then pending *sub judice* before the Commission. The staff wished to avoid even injecting the question of a possible *ex parte* contact or similar collateral issue in the proceeding. *Id.* For further discussion herein on this subject, *see* pages 260-67 *infra*.

250. *See, e.g.,* SEC v. Coven, 581 F.2d 1020 (2d Cir. 1978), *cert. denied,* 440 U.S. 950 (1979); SEC v. Spectrum, Ltd., 489 F.2d 535 (2d Cir. 1973); SEC v. National Student Marketing Corp., 457 F. Supp. 682 (D.D.C. 1978). For further discussion, see Gruenbaum, note 219 *supra*, at 204-11.

251. *See, e.g.,* In the Matter of Carter and Johnson, Securities Exchange Act Release No. 17597, [1981 Transfer Binder] Fed. Sec. L. Rep. (CCH) ¶ 82,847 (March 17, 1981); In the Matter of Keating, Muething & Klekamp, Securities Exchange Act Release No. 15982, [1979 Transfer Binder] Fed. Sec. L. Rep. (CCH) ¶ 82,124 (July 2, 1979); In the Matter of Emanuel Fields, Securities Act Release No. 5404, [1972-1973 Transfer Binder] Fed. Sec. L. Rep. (CCH) ¶ 79,407 (June 18, 1973), *aff'd without opinion,* 495 F.2d 1075 (D.C. Cir. 1974).

252. Securities Act Release No. 5404, [1972-1973 Transfer Binder] Fed. Sec. L. Rep. (CCH) ¶ 79,407 (June 18, 1973), *aff'd without opinion,* 495 F.2d 1075 (D.C. Cir. 1974).

253. [1972-1973 Transfer Binder] Fed. Sec. L. Rep. (CCH) ¶ 79,407, at 83,174-75 n.20. The Commission also stated that the securities lawyer "works in his office where he prepares prospectuses, proxy statements, opinions of counsel, and other documents that we, our staff, the financial community, and the investing public must take on faith." *Id.*

client of which it has knowledge as a result of its legal representation of that client."[254]

Undoubtedly, the most significant administrative disciplinary proceeding recently brought pursuant to Rule 2(e) of the SEC's Rules of Practice[255] is that of *In the Matter of Carter and Johnson*.[256] There, the Commission's Office of General Counsel (the division within the agency that prosecutes such proceedings) had argued, among other things, that when a lawyer's advice has been repeatedly rejected by management and when management persists in exposing the corporation to substantial risk of legal liability, the lawyer may have an obligation to go up the hierarchal structure within the corporation to the board of directors to prevent what the lawyer believes to be present or future violations of the law. The General Counsel also argued that this duty to go to the board may be necessary to fulfill the lawyer's obligation adequately to advise the corporate client.[257]

In February 1981, the Williams Commission handed down its opinion in the *Carter-Johnson* case.[258] It reversed the decision of the administrative law judge, who had found that Messrs. Carter and Johnson, lawyers who were experienced in corporate and securities matters, had violated the federal securities laws and had engaged in improper professional conduct.[259]

The Commission dismissed the proceedings against the two lawyers. While

---

254. In the Matter of Keating, Meuthing & Klekamp, Securities Exchange Act Release No. 15982, [1979 Transfer Binder] FED. SEC. L. REP. (CCH) ¶ 82,124 (July 2, 1979). *See* In the Matter of Plotkin, Yolles, Siegel & Turner, Securities Act Release No. 5841, 12 SEC DOCKET 263 (July 5, 1977); In the Matter of Jo M. Ferguson, Securities Act Release No. 5523, 5 SEC DOCKET 37 (Aug. 21, 1974).

255. Rule 2(e), 17 C.F.R. 201.2(e) (1982), provides that the Commission may temporarily suspend or permanently bar any person from practice before it if found (1) to lack the requisite qualifications to represent others, (2) to lack character or integrity or to have engaged in improper or unethical professional conduct, or (3) to have willfully violated or aided and abetted a violation of any provision of the federal securities law or a rule or regulation thereunder. An original proceeding pursuant to Rule 2(e), as was the *Carter-Johnson* proceeding, is conducted as an administrative proceeding before a federal administrative law judge with a right to review by the Commission and judicial review by a United States Court of Appeals. Some orders imposing restrictions on practice, however, are entered as a result of an injunction or felony conviction, or by consent in settlement of outstanding charges. These cases are disposed of summarily.

256. Securities Exchange Act Release No. 17597, [1981 Transfer Binder] FED. SEC. L. REP. (CCH) ¶ 82,847 (March 17, 1981), *reversing,* [1979 Transfer Binder] FED. SEC. L. REP. (CCH) ¶ 82,175.

257. Answering Brief of the Office of the General Counsel at 99-106, In the Matter of Carter and Johnson, File No. 3-5464 (Oct. 15, 1979).

258. Securities Exchange Act Release No. 17597, [1981 Transfer Binder] FED. SEC. L. REP. (CCH) ¶ 82,847 (March 17, 1971).

259. [1979 Transfer Binder] FED. SEC. L. REP. (CCH) ¶ 82,175.

reasserting its jurisdiction to conduct these kinds of proceedings,[260] it found that the lawyers were neither direct violators nor aiders and abettors of the violations of their client in this case;[261] moreover, the Commission found that they had not violated standards of professional responsibility because the Commission could not conclude that their conduct transgressed standards that were generally accepted at the time.[262] The Commission did, however, discuss the general standards of professional conduct that should guide lawyers in the future:

> [A] lawyer must, in order to discharge his professional responsibilities, make all efforts within reason to persuade his client to avoid or terminate proposed illegal action. Such efforts could include, where appropriate, notification to the board of directors of a corporate client.[263]

The Commission emphasized that the articulation of principles of professional conduct to the special role of the securities lawyer giving disclosure advice to a corporate client was not a simple task. The Commission pointed out that the lawyer is only an adviser and the final judgment and, indeed, responsibility as to what course of conduct is to be taken must lie with the client. The Commission acknowledged that disclosure issues often present difficult choices between multiple shades of gray and that the fact that the

---

260. [1981 Transfer Binder] FED. SEC. L. REP. (CCH) ¶ 82,847, at 84,146-50. *See* Touche Ross & Co. v. SEC, 609 F.2d 570 (2d Cir. 1979), where the Second Circuit concluded:

> To summarize: we reject appellant's assertion that the Commission acted without authority in promulgating Rule 2(e). Although there is no express statutory provision authorizing the Commission to discipline professionals appearing before it, Rule 2(e), promulgated pursuant to its statutory rulemaking authority, represents an attempt by the Commission to protect the integrity of its own processes. It provides the Commission with the means to ensure that those professionals, on whom the Commission relies heavily in the performance of its statutory duties, perform their tasks diligently and with a reasonable degree of competence. As such the Rule is "reasonably related" to the purposes of the securities laws. Moreover, we hold that the Rule does not violate, nor is it inconsistent with, any other provision of the securities laws. We therefore sustain the validity of the Rule as a necessary element adjunct to the Commission's power to protect the integrity of its administrative procedures and the public in general.

Id. at 582. *See generally* Downing & Miller, *The Distortion and Misuse of Rule 2(e)*, 54 NOTRE DAME LAW. 774 (1979); Gruenbaum, *The SEC's Use of Rule 2(e) to Discipline Accountants and Other Professionals*, 56 NOTRE DAME LAW. 820 (1981); Kramer, *Clients' Frauds and Their Lawyers' Obligations: A Study in Professional Irresponsibility*, 67 GEO. L.J. 991 (1979); Marsh, *Rule 2(e) Proceedings*, 35 BUS. LAW. 987 (1980); Comment, *Attorney Liability Under SEC Rule 2(e): A New Standard?* 11 TEXAS TECH. L. REV. 83 (1979).

261. [1981 Transfer Binder] FED. SEC. L. REP. (CCH) ¶ 82,847, at 84,167-69.
262. *Id.* at 84,169-70.
263. *Id.* at 84,170.

corporate client is pressing its lawyer hard for the minimum disclosure required by law is, by itself, not an appropriate basis for finding that a lawyer must resign or take some extraordinary action. It was emphasized in the opinion that the Commission would not seek to hold lawyers responsible for the exercise of professional judgment taken in good faith even if, in view of hindsight, the advice turned out to be wrong. The Commission was concerned that stiffer requirements might drive a wedge between reporting companies and their outside lawyers and that, under certain circumstances, management would soon realize there was nothing to be gained in consulting such lawyers.[264] The Commission stated:

> The Commission is of the view that the lawyer engages in "unethical or improper professional conduct" under the following circumstances: When a lawyer with significant responsibilities in the effectuation of a company's compliance with the disclosure requirements of the federal securities laws becomes aware that his client is engaged in a substantial and continuing failure to satisfy those disclosure requirements, his continued participation violates professional standards unless he takes prompt steps ["that lead to the conclusion that the lawyer is engaged in efforts to correct the underlying problem, rather than having capitulated to the desires of a strong-willed, but misguided client"] to end the client's non-compliance.

> . . . .

> Initially, counselling accurate disclosure is sufficient, even if [the lawyer's] advice is not accepted. But there comes a point at which a reasonable lawyer must conclude that his advice is not being followed, or even sought in good faith, and that his client is involved in the continuing course of violating the securities laws. At this critical juncture, the lawyer must take further, more affirmative steps in order to avoid the inference that he has been co-opted, willingly or unwillingly, into the scheme of nondisclosure.

> . . . .

> So long as a lawyer is acting in good faith in exerting reasonable efforts to prevent violations of the law by his client, his professional obligations have been met.[265]

---

264. *Id.* at 84,169-72.

265. *Id.* at 84,172-73. It should be made clear that there was no issue in the case as to whether the lawyer had a duty to make public disclosure of the confidences and secrets of the corporate client.

In that decision, the Commission also remarked that it intended to solicit public comment in regard to the standard adopted[266] which it subsequently did.[267] The SEC has not yet issued a release in response to the comments received. The content of such a release, if one were to be issued, could well portend the extent to which the present Commission intends to follow or depart from the principles of *Carter-Johnson*.[268]

B. Accountants

In the past several years, public and congressional concerns have been voiced regarding the extent to which the accounting profession has fulfilled its responsibility to promote public confidence in the integrity and credibility of financial reporting by publicly owned companies.[269] During the Williams chairmanship, the Commission responded both by intensifying its oversight of the accounting profession and by encouraging initiatives by the profession designed to increase public confidence (1) in the independence of accountants, (2) in the process by which accounting and auditing standards are established, and (3) in the profession's ability and resolve to develop and

---

266. *Id.* at 84,170.

267. Securities Act Release No. 6344, [1981-1982 Transfer Binder] FED. SEC. L. REP. (CCH) ¶ 83,026 (Sept. 21, 1981). For further discussion herein on *Carter-Johnson, see* pages 263-67 *infra.*

268. *See* Greene, note 249 *supra,* where the former SEC General Counsel presented his personal views on lawyer disciplinary proceedings before the Commission, stating: "My initial tentative view is that as a general matter the Commission should ordinarily only institute Rule 2(e) proceedings if the misconduct alleged is (i) a violation of established state law ethical or professional misconduct rules and (ii) has a direct impact on the Commission's internal processes, such as where the lawyer participates directly or indirectly in the preparation of disclosure documents filed with the Commission." *Id.* at 168.

269. *See generally* REPORT OF THE HOUSE OF REPRESENTATIVES SUBCOMM. ON OVERSIGHT AND INVESTIGATION OF THE COMMITTEE ON INTERSTATE AND FOREIGN COMMERCE, No. 95-134, 95th Cong., 1st Sess. (Oct. 1976) (hereinafter referred to as the MOSS REPORT); REPORT OF THE SENATE SUBCOMM. ON REPORTS, ACCOUNTING AND MANAGEMENT OF THE COMMITTEE ON GOVERNMENT RELATIONS, 94TH CONG., 2D SESS. (Committee Print, Dec. 1976) (hereinafter cited as the METCALF REPORT).

The Moss Report recommended, *inter alia,* that the SEC should prescribe by rule: a framework of uniform accounting principles, penalties for falsification of books and records, elimination of procedures that allow corporations to develop off-the-book accounts, that independent auditors should attest to the quality of internal controls and the quality of the enforcement of those controls in the annual report, a requirement that a majority of the board of directors be independent of management, and a requirement that the board's auditing and nominating committees be composed of a majority of independent directors. MOSS REPORT at 51-52.

The Metcalf Report recommended, *inter alia,* that "[t]he Federal Government should restore public confidence in the actual independence of auditors who certify the accuracy of corporate financial statements under the Federal securities laws by promulgating and enforcing strict standards of conduct for such auditors." METCALF REPORT at 22.

maintain a viable system of self-regulation.[270] The Commission's increased oversight resulted in significant and accelerated changes in the corporate structure for dealing with outside accountants and focused corporate attention on significant aspects of the company's relationship with its accountants.[271]

Many of the Commission's initiatives[272] were designed to assure the independence of outside accountants and to heighten corporate sensitivity to situations that may compromise such independence. One of the most successful efforts in this area related to the establishment of independent audit committees of the boards of directors of publicly held companies. The Commission has continued to urge companies to establish such audit committees, both to reinforce and ensure the independence of outside auditors by providing a buffer to insulate auditors from inordinate management pressures and to enhance the ability of the board of directors to monitor the issuer's accounting, financial reporting, and internal control systems.[273]

To date the response to the Commission's suggestions both by individual companies and the stock exchanges[274] has obviated the need for the Commission to exercise its authority to require publicly held companies to establish audit committees.[275] Thus, while the Commission reported to Congress on July 1, 1978, that "the concept of an independent audit committee . . . [had] begun to gain acceptance only recently, principally in the large companies,"[276] the Commission's recent analysis of 1981 proxy statements indicated that 86.4 percent of all of the companies maintained audit committees and, significantly, that 73.4 percent of the relatively small (under $50 million

---

270. *See, e.g., Securities and Exchange Commission (Second) Report to Congress on the Accounting Profession and the Commission's Oversight Role,* [1979 Transfer Binder] FED. SEC. L. REP. (CCH) ¶ 82,120.

271. *See* Address by Harold M. Williams, Chairman of the Securities and Exchange Commission, "The 1980s: The Future of the Accounting Profession" to the American Institute of Certified Public Accountants' Seventh National Conference on Current SEC Developments (Jan. 3, 1980).

272. This chapter does not address the several initiatives taken by the profession itself.

273. *See* note 34 and accompanying text *supra;* notes 276-78 and accompanying text *infra.*

274. *Id.*

275. Although the Commission does not require companies to maintain audit committees, registrants must state in their proxy materials whether they maintain an audit committee, and, if so, the composition of the committee in terms of membership, the number of meetings held during the latest fiscal year, and a brief description of the functions of the committee. Rule 14a-101 of the Proxy Rules (Item 6(d)(1), 17 C.F.R. 240.14a-101 (1982)).

Regarding the Commission's authority to require publicly held companies to maintain independent audit committees, *see* the June 10, 1977, and March 2, 1978, memoranda from Harvey L. Pitt, General Counsel of the Securities and Exchange Commission, to Chairman Harold M. Williams, which are reprinted in *Securities and Exchange Commission (First) Report to Congress on the Accounting Profession and the Commission's Oversight Role,* [1978 Transfer Binder] FED. SEC. L. REP. (CCH) ¶ 82,120.

276. [1978 Transfer Binder] FED. SEC. L. REP. (CCH) ¶ 82,120 at 81,954.

in assets) over-the-counter companies have audit committees.[277] The proxy statements further indicated that the new audit committees have assumed significant oversight responsibilities, with 70.4 percent engaging and discharging the outside auditors, 67.2 percent reviewing the audit plan, 84.5 percent reviewing the audit results, and 73.9 percent reviewing the adequacy of internal controls.[278] Clearly, the widespread emergence of audit committees, accelerated by the Commission's exhortations, has significantly altered the structure of corporate relationships with outside auditors.

A significant Commission retreat in this area, however, has emerged with respect to the disclosure of nonaudit services by auditors. The Williams Commission focused corporate attention on the potential negative impact on auditor independence when services of a nonaudit nature (*e.g.*, management advisory services, accounting and review services, and tax services) are also performed for the audit client. In 1978, Accounting Series Release No. 250[279] required that registrants disclose, *inter alia,* in their proxy statements the nature of nonaudit services performed by their independent auditors and the percentage relationships of fees incurred for such services to total fees incurred for audit services. This was followed in 1979 with Accounting Series Release No. 264,[280] in which the Commission discussed the primary factors that management, the audit committee, and the outside auditor should consider in determining whether the auditor's independence may be compromised if it provides management advisory services ("MAS") to an audit client. These factors included the relationship between revenues generated from MAS and from audit services, whether the MAS engagement improperly encompassed managerial and decision-making functions that were the client's responsibility, whether the services provided could ultimately result in auditor self-review, and whether audit quality might benefit from the performance of MAS which increased the auditor's understanding of the client's business. Viewing these Commission pronouncements as significant barriers to providing MAS, the accounting profession's response was highly negative.[281] Nonetheless, former Chairman Williams in a January 1980 address to the accounting profession stated that he was "somewhat disappointed at the tone and focus of the profession's response" and stressed that "there is significant public interest and concern surrounding this issue."[282]

---

277. *See Analysis of Results of 1981 Proxy Statement Disclosure Monitoring Program,* Securities Exchange Act Release No. 18532, 24 SEC DOCKET 1224, 1226, 1234 (March 16, 1982). *See also* SEC STAFF CORPORATE ACCOUNTABILITY REPORT, note 31 *supra,* at 28-29, 587; Securities Exchange Act Release No. 17518, 21 SEC DOCKET 1551 (Feb. 5, 1981).

278. 24 SEC DOCKET at 1235.

279. 6 FED. SEC. L. REP. (CCH) ¶ 72,272.

280. 6 FED. SEC. L. REP. (CCH) ¶ 72,286.

281. *See SEC Scuttles Rule Requiring Disclosure of Nonaudit Tasks Handled by Auditors,* Wall St. J., Jan. 29, 1982, at 8, col. 1.

282. Williams, note 271 *supra,* at 14.

Only two years later and less than five years after the Metcalf Report recommended that "[d]irect or indirect representation of clients' interests and performance of non-accounting management advisory services for public or private clients are two activities which are particularly incompatible with the responsibilities of independent auditors, and should be prohibited by Federal standards of conduct,"[283] the Commission rescinded ASRs 250 and 264.[284] In so doing, the Commission stated:

> Notwithstanding this action, the Commission believes it should continue to monitor the nonaudit service activity by accountants as a part of its oversight of the accounting profession. Other people may also want to monitor this activity. The Commission is satisfied with the information that will be available because of a recent revision of the membership requirements of the SEC Practice Section of the Division for Firms of the American Institute of Certified Public Accountants.[285]

Thus, the Commission relied in part upon the promulgation of self-regulatory standards which, although not nearly as extensive as its own pronouncements,[286] require member accounting firms in lieu of registrants to disclose information about their nonaudit management advisory services.[287]

---

283. METCALF REPORT, note 269 *supra,* at 22.

284. Accounting Series Release No. 304, 24 SEC DOCKET 938 (Feb. 16, 1982). The Commission rescinded the rule also because it believed that the disclosure requirement was "not generally of sufficient utility to investors to justify continuation of [this] requirement." *Id.*

285. *Id.* at 939.

286. *See* Wall Street Journal article, note 281 *supra* (stating that the AICPA's rule does not require as extensive disclosure as the SEC's pronouncements did, because, "[a]mong other things, the institute's rule requires auditors rather than companies, to disclose their nonaudit services, and doesn't require them to name the companies for which they provide the services").

287. The Commission stated:

> The SEC Practice Section responded promptly to the Commission's comment in ASR 296 that the accounting profession's self-regulatory mechanism should be able to generate sufficient information about nonaudit services performed by accountants to enable the Commission, the Public Oversight Board of the SEC Practice Section, and other interested persons to continue to monitor the nonaudit services performed by accountants. The SEC Practice Section revised its membership provisions to require member accounting firms to disclose additional information about their nonaudit service activity for clients that file with the Commission. . . .
>
> The Commission is satisfied that the additional disclosure required by the SEC Practice Section will enable it to adequately monitor trends in aggregate levels of nonaudit services performed by accountants for their registrant clients.

24 SEC DOCKET at 938.

IX. CONCLUSION

The Commission's role in influencing how corporations should be governed and how management should account to shareholders has been varied, controversial, and, at times, quite effective. We are in the midst of an ongoing process; whether we are at the beginning of it, in the middle, or at the end, we cannot yet tell. There are two variables, both of which are significantly changing: one is the membership of the Commission and certain of its senior staff and the other is the larger context of American political and corporate life. Although the author is reluctant to predict the stage of this process, it is probable that, with the exception of the American Law Institute's Tentative Draft Restatement on Corporate Governance,[288] the staff's Corporate Accountability Report represents the highwater mark. Nonetheless, as has been illustrated throughout this chapter, irrespective of the Commission's interest in promoting corporate accountability, the very nature of the SEC's processes signifies that corporate internal affairs will continue to be significantly affected.

---

288. *See* ALI Tentative Draft Restatement, note 61 *supra. See also American Law Institute Begins Debate on Corporate Governance Project,* 14 SEC. REG. & L. REP. (BNA) 1025 (June 4, 1982) (discussing provisions of and debate regarding the reporters' tentative draft).

2

Disclosure of Information Bearing on Management Integrity and Competency

I. INTRODUCTION

The duty to disclose information relating to the competency or integrity of management is an issue receiving considerable attention by the Securities and Exchange Commission ("Commission") and the courts. Although such information may not be *quantitatively* material because it does not impact significantly on an issuer's assets, it is often *qualitatively* material in that it reflects on the quality of corporate management. As the Commission succinctly stated over fifteen years ago, "[e]valuation of the quality of management—to whatever extent it is possible—is an essential ingredient of informed investment decisions."[1] The Commission more recently asserted that investors should be vitally concerned with the quality and integrity of management, stressing that disclosure of conflicts of interest and special perquisites to management underscores "the deeply held belief that the management of corporations are stewards acting on behalf of the shareholders. . . ."[2]

While the importance to investors of information bearing on the competency and integrity of management has been emphasized in recent judicial and Commission pronouncements, clear parameters for the disclosure obligations that attach to this type of information have yet to emerge.[3] As a

---

1. Franchard Corp., 42 S.E.C. 163, 170, [1964–1966 Transfer Binder] FED. SEC. L. REP. (CCH) ¶ 77,113, at 82,038, 82,042 (1964).

2. SENATE COMM. ON BANKING, HOUSING AND URBAN AFFAIRS, 94TH CONG., 2D SESS., REPORT OF THE SECURITIES AND EXCHANGE COMMISSION ON QUESTIONABLE AND ILLEGAL CORPORATE PAYMENTS PRACTICES 20 (Comm. Print, 1976) (hereinafter cited as SEC QUESTIONABLE PAYMENTS REPORT).

3. The Commission has promulgated rules explicating disclosure obligations with respect to this information. *See* notes 63, 179–83 and 207 and accompanying text *infra*.

result, the securities bar has been left, at times, in a quandary when attempting to advise clients when such information must be disclosed.

A brief analysis of the Commission's statutory mandate and disclosure policy lends some guidance in this area.[4] The general rulemaking provisions under the Securities Act of 1933 ("Securities Act")[5] and Securities Exchange Act of 1934 ("Exchange Act")[6] provide the Commission with authority to require information "necessary to carry out the provisions" of the securities acts.[7] Specific sections of the securities acts also empower the Commission to prescribe rules "as . . . necessary or appropriate in the public interest or for the protection of investors."[8]

Notwithstanding this broad statutory language, the Commission sometimes has interpreted its mandate more narrowly, and has suggested that the general thrust of its disclosure requirements is in the direction of providing information that is "economically significant" to a corporation's

---

4. This chapter will address only the disclosure obligations under the Securities Act of 1933, 15 U.S.C. §§ 77a–77aa (1976 & Supp. III 1979), and the Securities Exchange Act of 1934, 15 U.S.C. §§ 78a–78kk (1976 & Supp. III 1979), and will refer to these two statutes jointly as the "securities acts." The Commission, however, also is authorized to administer, *inter alia*, the Trust Indenture Act of 1939, 15 U.S.C. §§ 77aaa–77bbbb (1976 & Supp. III 1979), the Public Utility Holding Company Act of 1935, 15 U.S.C. §§ 79–79z–6 (1976 & Supp. III 1979), the Investment Company Act of 1940, 15 U.S.C. §§ 80a–1 to –52 (1976 & Supp. III 1979), and the Investment Advisors Act of 1940, 15 U.S.C. §§ 80b–1 to –21 (1976 & Supp. III 1979).

5. 15 U.S.C. §§ 77a–77aa (1976 & Supp. III 1979).

6. *Id.* §§ 78a–78kk.

7. Section 19(a) of the Securities Act, *id.* § 77s(a), expressly authorizes the Commission to promulgate rules "as may be necessary to carry out the provisions of this subchapter. . . ." Section 23(a) of the Exchange Act, *id.* § 78w(a)(1), provides that the Commission is authorized to promulgate rules "as may be necessary or appropriate to implement the provisions of this chapter for which [it is] responsible or for the execution of the functions vested in [it] by this chapter. . . ."

The preambles to the securities acts are also very broad, and do not suggest meaningful limitations to the Commission's disclosure authority. The preamble to the Securities Act states that its purpose is "[t]o provide full and fair disclosure of the character of securities sold in interstate and foreign commerce and through the mails, and to prevent frauds in the sale thereof, and for other purposes." Securities Act of 1933, Pub. L. No. 73–22, ch. 38, 48 Stat. 74 (1933). The preamble to the Exchange Act states that its purpose is "[t]o provide for the regulation of securities exchanges and of over-the-counter markets operating in interstate and foreign commerce and through the mails, to prevent inequitable and unfair practices on such exchanges and markets, and for other purposes." Securities Exchange Act of 1934, Pub. L. No. 73–291, ch. 404, 48 Stat. 881 (1934).

8. Securities Act of 1933, §§ 7, 10(c), 15 U.S.C. §§ 77g, 77j(c) (1976) (information requirements for, respectively, registration statements and prospectuses). Sections 12(b) (information requirements for issuers with securities registered on a national exchange), 13(a) (information requirements to keep registration statements current and for periodic reports), and 14(a) (information requirements for proxy statements) of the Exchange Act, *id.* §§ 78l(b), 78m(a), 78n(a), similarly limit the Commission's rulemaking authority to information "as necessary or appropriate for the proper protection of investors and to insure fair dealing in the security."

financial condition.[9] That point of view finds support in the legislative history of the securities acts,[10] the necessity to prescribe disclosure requirements that will not result in overly complex and unreadable documents for investors or unnecessary costs to issuers,[11] the difficulty in determining the relative materiality of different kinds of noneconomic information,[12] and, perhaps most importantly, the notion that investors are fundamentally interested in making money and thus are concerned with information that bears on the prospects of corporate gains and losses.[13]

---

9. *See* SEC Securities Act Release No. 5627, 8 SEC DOCKET 41, 43, [1975–1976 Transfer Binder] FED. SEC. L. REP. (CCH) ¶ 80,310, at 85,710 (Oct. 14, 1975) [hereinafter cited as SEC Release No. 5627], where the Commission stated that "[t]he Acts and the relevant legislative history also suggest that a prime expectation of the Congress was that the Commission's disclosure authority would be used to require the dissemination of information which is or may be economically significant."

This apparently narrow interpretation of the Commission's mandate has also been endorsed by a number of courts. *See, e.g.,* NAACP v. Federal Power Comm'n, 520 F.2d 432, 443 (D.C. Cir. 1975), *aff'd,* 425 U.S. 662 (1976), where the court, in commenting upon a Commission release addressing disclosure requirements pertaining to the pendency of civil rights proceedings, stated: "[i]n thus acting, however, the SEC appears to us merely to have been fulfilling its proper role of seeing that investors are fully informed of circumstances which bear on the financial prospects of securities-issuing corporations." *See also* Gaines v. Haughton, 645 F.2d 761 (9th Cir. 1981), *cert. denied,* 102 S. Ct. 1006 (1982).

10. The House Report accompanying the Securities Act stated that the information required to be disclosed in Schedule A registration statements "is of a character comparable to that demanded by competent bankers from their borrowers, and has been worked out in the light of these and other requirements." H.R. REP. NO. 85, 73d Cong., 1st Sess. 4 (1933). Likewise, referring to the type of information required under Sections 12(b) (registration statements) and 13 (periodic reports) of the Exchange Act, the Senate Report accompanying the Exchange Act stated that "[t]he bill provides that . . . a condition of such registration shall be the furnishing of complete information relative to the financial condition of the issuer, which information shall be kept up to date by adequate periodic reports." S. REP. NO. 792, 73d Cong., 2d Sess. 10 (1934) [hereinafter cited as SENATE REPORT NO. 792].

11. Indeed, it would be impracticable to require disclosure of all information that a small group of investors might find of interest. This would result in unmanageable detail, ultimately reducing the utility of disclosure documents. In addition, onerous costs to registrants, ultimately borne by shareholders, may outweigh the benefits investors would derive from certain disclosures. *See* SEC Release No. 5627, *supra* note 9, at 44, 51, [1975–1976 Transfer Binder] FED. SEC. L. REP. (CCH) at 85,712–13, 85,724–25.

12. *See* SENATE COMM. ON BANKING, HOUSING AND URBAN AFFAIRS, 96TH CONG., 2D SESS., SECURITIES AND EXCHANGE COMMISSION STAFF REPORT ON CORPORATE ACCOUNTABILITY 262–68, 274–76 (Comm. Print, 1980) [hereinafter cited as SEC CORPORATE ACCOUNTABILITY REPORT].

13. *See* SEC Release No. 5627, *supra* note 9, at 49, [1975–1976 Transfer Binder] FED. SEC. L. REP. (CCH) at 85,721, where it was stated:

> The Commission's experience over the years in proposing and framing disclosure requirements has not led it to question the basic decision of the Congress that, insofar as investing is concerned, the primary interest of investors is economic. After all, the principal, if not the only, reason why people invest their money in securities is to obtain a return. A variety of other motives is probably present in the investment decisions of numerous investors but the only common thread is the hope for a satisfactory return,

Nevertheless, three notable exceptions have developed to the accepted theology of limiting disclosure requirements to information that is significantly related to the financial condition of a corporation, *i.e.*, information deemed quantitatively material to investors. First, the Commission has required affirmative disclosure by registrants of certain information the Commission believes is "often of importance to investors generally."[14] Although this information may not be economically material, registrants are routinely required to disclose the called-for information in registration statements, periodic reports, and proxy solicitations,[15] unless the governing statute or specific rule expressly states that only material information need be disclosed.[16]

---

and it is to this that a disclosure scheme intended to be useful to all must be primarily addressed.

14. *Id.* at 41, [1975–1976 Transfer Binder] Fed. Sec. L. Rep. (CCH) at 85,707; *see* Brief for Appellee, Securities and Exchange Commission, at 27, SEC v. Falstaff Brewing Corp., 629 F.2d 62 (D.C. Cir. 1980), where the Commission argued that it is authorized to require disclosure of information called for in its rules, irrespective of economic materiality: "In addition, Rule 14a–3, 17 C.F.R. 240, 14a–3, and Schedule 14A, 17 C.F.R. 140, 14a–101, establish certain minimum disclosure requirements that must be met regardless of a finding of materiality." *See also* Brief for *Amicus Curiae*, Securities and Exchange Commission, Raybestos-Manhattan, Inc. v. Hi-Shear Indus., No. 80–9117 (2d Cir. 1981), where the Commission, arguing that Item 2(f) of Schedule 14D–1 required the disclosure of called-for information, regardless of its materiality, stated:

> Thus, in promulgating Item 2(f), the Commission determined that the information it calls for should be disclosed in *every* Schedule 14D–1. This determination reflects a Commission assessment of the likely importance of this type of information to shareholders in tender offers generally. Unlike the more general antifraud provisions set out in Section 14(e), however, it does not require or allow tender offerors—or courts—to determine the need for disclosure on the basis of case-by-case judgments of whether the specified information is actually important to shareholders in each particular tender offer. Accordingly, we urge this Court to reject any suggestion that materiality is required for a finding of a violation of Section 14(d).

Id. at 5–6.

15. *See, e.g.,* Item 402, Regulation S-K, 17 C.F.R. § 229.402 (1982). This item requires registrants to disclose affirmatively information about management remuneration in registration statements filed under the Securities Act, and in periodic reports and proxy solicitations regulated under the Exchange Act, irrespective of the economic materiality of the information. The Commission's rules also require information that is rarely, if ever, economically material. *See* Form 10-K, 4 Fed. Sec. L. Rep. ¶ 31,102 (Apr. 15, 1981), which calls for affirmative disclosure of a registrant's address, telephone number, and I.R.S. employer identification number.

16. *See* Sections 11, 12, and 17 of the Securities Act, 15 U.S.C. §§ 77k, 77l, 77q (1976). Rule 408 under the Securities Act, 17 C.F.R. § 230.408 (1982), and Rules 10b–5, 12b–12, 12b–20, and 14a–9 under the Exchange Act, *id.* §§ 240.10b–5, .12b–12, –20, .14a–9, all of which require the disclosure of material information. *See also* Item 401(f), Regulation S-K, *id.* § 229.401, *discussed in* text accompanying notes 179–83 *infra,* which calls for information only when materially related to the ability or integrity of management. The express materiality qualifications in some of the Commission's rules would be superfluous if the Commission believed that all disclosable information is material.

Second, the Commission has stated that, under Section 14(a) of the Exchange Act,[17] it may require proxy materials to include information that is not quantitatively material[18] in order to ensure that shareholders are adequately informed about issues to be voted upon at shareholder meetings.[19] This position is supported by the legislative history of Section 14(a), which suggests that Congress believed shareholders to be interested in, and entitled to be apprised of, more than merely economically significant information in exercising their corporate franchise.[20] In addition, both scholars[21] and the courts[22] have recognized the distinction between information important

---

17. 15 U.S.C. § 78n(a) (1976). Section 14(a) provides in pertinent part that proxies may be solicited only in conformity with "such rules and regulations as the Commission may prescribe as necessary or appropriate in the public interest or for the protection of investors." *Id.*

18. *See* SEC Release No. 5627, *supra* note 9, at 44, [1975-1976 Transfer Binder] FED. SEC. L. REP. at 85,711: "It is also evident, however, that, insofar as the Commission's rulemaking authority under Section 14(a) of the Securities Exchange Act is concerned, the primacy of economic matters, particularly with respect to shareholder proposals, is somewhat less." Rule 14a-9 under the Exchange Act, 17 C.F.R. § 240.14a-9 (1982), the general "antifraud" provision for proxy soliciting materials, limits actionable omissions or false statements to "material" information. Materiality, however, is not defined in the Exchange Act, and arguably, under the Commission's broad mandate with respect to Section 14(a), this term includes qualitative materiality. *See* SEC CORPORATE ACCOUNTABILITY REPORT, *supra* note 12, at 262.

19. *See* Mills v. Electric Auto-Lite Co., 396 U.S. 375 (1970), where the Court stated that the underlying purpose of Section 14(a) of the Exchange Act is to promote " 'the free exercise of the voting rights of stockholders' by ensuring that proxies [are] solicited in 'explanation to the stockholder of the real nature of the questions for which authority to cast his vote is sought.' " *Id.* at 381 (quoting H.R. REP. NO. 1383, 73d Cong., 2d Sess. 14 (1934) and S. REP. NO. 792, 73d Cong., 2d Sess. 12 (1934)). *See also* TSC Indus. v. Northway, Inc., 426 U.S. 438, 444 (1976); J.I. Case Co. v. Borak, 377 U.S. 426, 431 (1964).

20. *See* SENATE REPORT NO. 792, *supra* note 10, at 12:

> In order that the stockholder may have adequate knowledge as to the manner in which his interests are being served, it is essential that he be enlightened not only as to the financial condition of the corporation, but also as to the major questions of policy, which are decided at stockholders' meetings.

21. *See* 2 L. LOSS, SECURITIES REGULATION 918 (1961):

> In the context of election contests . . . the test of materiality which has been adopted has been the pragmatic one that the statement or omission claimed to be misleading must be such as would have influenced the stockholder's vote—just as the test of materiality . . . in the context of sales or purchases of securities is whether an "average prudent investor" ought reasonably to be informed of the particular fact before entering into the transaction.

22. *See* SEC v. Texas Gulf Sulphur Co., 401 F.2d 833 (2d Cir. 1968), *cert. denied*, 394 U.S. 976 (1969), where the court defined materiality, in the context of Rule 10b-5 and the purchase or sale of a security, as " 'whether a *reasonable* man would attach importance . . . in determining his choice of action in the transaction in question. . . .' This, of course, encompasses any fact '. . . which *might* affect the value of the corporation's stock or securities. . . .' " 401 F.2d at 849 (quoting List v. Fashion Park, Inc., 340 F.2d 457, 462 (2d Cir.), *cert. denied*,

to a *voting* decision and economically significant information deemed material to an *investment* decision.

Third, the Commission has departed from economic materiality as the basis for disclosure when other criteria are mandated by an independent federal statute. For example, the Commission has taken the view that the National Environmental Policy Act of 1969 ("NEPA"),[23] which directs all federal agencies to consider environmental values in formulating policies, rules, and statutes,[24] requires the Commission to consider the promotion of environmental protection as a factor in determining what information should be affirmatively disclosed by registrants. As the Commission stated, "while the disclosure of nonmaterial information is generally not required . . . adding the promotion of environmental protection to the other factors considered by the Commission in the administration of the disclosure process causes a different balance to be struck here."[25]

The Commission's policy with respect to disclosure of environmentally related information has provoked much controversy over the Commission's authority to use its disclosure mandate to deter socially undesirable behavior by corporate management which may have little connection to the securities markets. In this regard, it is significant that the Commission traditionally has taken the position that it is not authorized by Congress to utilize disclosure requirements solely to discourage undesirable corporate conduct, or to promote social goals unrelated to the objectives of the federal securities laws,[26] and that NEPA renders its position with respect to influencing a

---

382 U.S. 811 (1965)) (emphasis in original) (citations omitted). However, in TSC Indus. v. Northway, Inc., 426 U.S. 438, 449 (1976), the Court stated that information is material to a voting decision "if there is a substantial likelihood that a reasonable shareholder would consider it important in deciding how to vote."

23. 42 U.S.C. §§ 4321-4369 (1976 & Supp. III 1979).

24. Section 102(1) of NEPA provides that "to the fullest extent possible . . . the policies, regulations and public laws of the United States shall be interpreted and administered in accordance with the policies set forth in [NEPA]." *Id.* § 4332(1). Section 101(a) of NEPA provides that the "continuing policy" of the federal goverment is "to use all practicable means and measures" to protect environmental values. *Id.* § 4331(a).

25. *See* SEC Release No. 5627, *supra* note 9, at 48, [1975-1976 Transfer Binder] FED. SEC. L. REP. (CCH) at 85,718. Recently, the Commission adopted rules setting forth certain thresholds for disclosure under Regulation S-K of environmental legal proceedings. Securities Act Release No. 6383 (March 3, 1982).

26. The Commission has stated that

> the discretion vested in the Commission under the Securities Act and the Securities Exchange Act to require disclosure which is necessary or appropriate "in the public interest" does not generally permit the Commission to require disclosure for the sole purpose of promoting social goals unrelated to those underlying these Acts.

See SEC Release No. 5627, *supra* note 9, at 45, [1975-1976 Transfer Binder] FED. SEC. L. REP. at 85,713.

corporation's environmental policies *sui generis*.[27]

Yet a coherent disclosure policy for information bearing on management's competence or integrity is gradually emerging, based in some respects upon the traditional predicates for disclosure discussed above. For example, when qualitatively material information is also economically material—*e.g.*, where a director nominee's criminal conviction would jeopardize a corporate license to do business—conventional wisdom requires disclosure in both an investing and voting context. It is also evident that the competence or integrity of management is of direct and vital concern to shareholders when they exercise their corporate franchise, especially when confronted with a decision to vote for directors. Hence, much qualitatively material information, such as self-dealing by management, would predictably be disclosable in proxy soliciting materials for the election of directors.[28]

At the same time, however, it is difficult to explain the basis of disclosure requirements for other types of information bearing on management's competency or integrity. For example, one court has suggested that information about management's illegal bribes should be disclosed in connection with the sale of stock even when no proxy solicitation is involved, because the information, reflecting on the integrity of management, is material to investors.[29] Yet if the bribes do not engender significant economic repercussions to the corporation, requiring disclosure of such information in this context may be viewed as inconsistent with traditional notions of quantitative ma-

---

This does not mean, however, that affecting corporate conduct cannot be one of the desired goals of disclosure requirements. *See* SECURITIES AND EXCHANGE COMMISSION, THE WHEAT REPORT: DISCLOSURE TO INVESTORS—A REAPPRAISAL OF FEDERAL ADMINISTRATIVE POLICIES UNDER THE '33 AND '34 ACTS (1969):

> Although basically intended to inform, the disclosure provisions of the early Acts were expected to accomplish more. Their principal architects were disciples of Justice Brandeis who, in 1913, made the famous observation in *Other People's Money* that:
>
> > Publicity is justly commended as a remedy for social and industrial diseases. Sunlight is said to be the best of disinfectants. . . .
>
> The fact that there is a significant degree of truth in such observation is attested by all who have worked with the disclosure provisions of the '33 and '34 Acts. The registration process has sometimes been referred to as a housecleaning: one of its most valuable consequences is the elimination of conflicts of interest and questionable business practices which, exposed to public view, have what Justice Frankfurter once termed "a shrinking quality."

Id. at 50-51 (footnotes omitted).

27. *See* SEC CORPORATE ACCOUNTABILITY REPORT, *supra* note 12, at 257: "NEPA is unique in this respect. No other statute has a similar effect upon the Commission's substantive mandate embodied in the federal securities laws."

28. *See* notes 62-88 and accompanying text *infra*.

29. *See* SEC v. Jos. Schlitz Brewing Co., 452 F. Supp. 824, 830 (E.D. Wis. 1978).

teriality, articulated concerns of the average *investor*,[30] and the Commission's purported unwillingness to use disclosure requirements solely to influence undesirable corporate conduct.

Requiring disclosure of qualitatively material information is also fraught with inherent definitional problems. As a threshold matter, it is difficult to predict what information would objectively be considered important enough to be deemed qualitatively material from the vast amount of information that arguably bears on management's competence or integrity. This type of determination frequently requires subjective and moral judgments, and thus poses a more difficult task than deciding whether certain information is economically significant to a corporation's business.

Furthermore, it remains unclear in this context whether all qualitatively material information or only particular categories of information bearing on management's competence or integrity must be disclosed. For example, many courts have held that an adjudicated illegality committed by management must be disclosed in proxy solicitations because the information is material to management's integrity.[31] With the exception of self-dealing, however, some courts have been unwilling to require management to disclose improper conduct which has not been adjudicated to be unlawful, although such conduct may also be material to a director's integrity.[32] Indeed, at least one court has squarely held that, in the absence of affirmative statements by management stressing its integrity, management is not obligated to accuse itself of antisocial or illegal conduct.[33] Thus, it does not appear that qualitatively material information is *ipso facto* disclosable.[34]

---

30. This type of information arguably may be unimportant to shareholders *voting* for the election of directors who authorized or knew of the illegal payments. In this regard, a complementary relationship may exist between illegal or socially undesirable conduct by management, and the success of a corporate enterprise. For example, management's illegal bribes to foreign officials may result in greater corporate earnings. In such a case the average voter might find management's questionable practices immaterial in light of the corporation's profitable, albeit illegal, conduct.

31. *See* notes 179-94 and accompanying text *infra*.

32. *See, e.g.,* Gaines v. Haughton, 645 F.2d 761 (9th Cir. 1981), *cert. denied,* 102 S. Ct. 1006 (1982).

33. *See* Amalgamated Clothing & Textile Workers v. J. P. Stevens & Co., 475 F. Supp. 328 (S.D.N.Y. 1979), *vacated as moot per curiam,* 638 F.2d 7 (2d Cir. 1980).

34. This is in contradistinction to quantitatively material information, which is always disclosable subject to the limits of the Commission's rules—*i.e.,* generally such information must be called for by statute or Commission rule, or its omission must render misleading other statements made in Commission documents or materials disseminated to shareholders. *Cf.* State Teachers Retirement Bd. v. Fluor Corp., 500 F. Supp. 278, 291-92 (S.D.N.Y. 1980), *rev'd on other grounds,* [1981 Transfer Binder] FED. SEC. L. REP. (CCH) ¶ 98,005 (2d Cir. May 28, 1981) (district court suggested that, in some circumstances, there may be an affirmative duty to disclose economically material information not called for by a Commission rule). *See generally* Bauman, *Rule 10b-5 and the Corporation's Affirmative Duty to Disclose,* 67 GEO. L.J. 935 (1979); Comment, *Disclosure of Material Inside Information: An Affirmative Cor-*

Much of the uncertainty with respect to the disclosure obligations relating to management competence or integrity may be due to the inherently difficult nature of articulating sufficiently clear standards in determining how far to expand traditional notions of materiality. Although the Commission's statutory mandate appears to authorize disclosure requirements for qualitatively material information, the cornerstone of the disclosure process continues to be based on the concept of economic materiality.[35]

Courts have contributed to this uncertainty by engaging in perfunctory analysis and inadequate exposition of the bases underlying their decisions in determining whether to require disclosure of qualitatively material information. In this respect, courts may be having difficulty reconciling their jurisdiction over breaches of fiduciary duty and management misconduct— traditionally actionable under state law—with the disclosure obligation under the securities acts. Some of these courts may regard federal regulation of such state governed conduct as an encroachment on state judicial processes and a circumvention of the Supreme Court's decision in *Santa Fe Industries v. Green.*[36] Requiring adequate disclosure in appropriate circumstances, however, may be viewed as an acceptable jurisprudential accommodation between the federal interest in full disclosure and the state interest in redressing breaches of fiduciary duty.[37]

---

porate Duty? 1980 ARIZ. ST. L.J. 795. *See also* SEC CORPORATE ACCOUNTABILITY REPORT, *supra* note 12, at 230: "[t]he Commission has always been of the view that the securities laws require disclosure of any information, including environmental, political, and other social information, that is economically material."

35. *See* SEC CORPORATE ACCOUNTABILITY REPORT, *supra* note 12, at 277: "Proposals that the commission move away from primarily an economic test of materiality [to require disclosure of socially significant information] are troubling to the staff because there is no readily available alternative basis for determining the materiality of the information." *See generally* Stevenson, *The SEC and the New Disclosure,* 62 CORNELL L. REV. 50 (1976); *Disclosure of Regulatory Violations Under the Federal Securities Laws: Establishing the Limits of Materiality,* 30 AM. U.L. REV. 255 (1980).

36. 430 U.S. 462 (1977). *Santa Fe* held that mere breaches of fiduciary duty, not constituting deception or manipulation, do not violate Section 10(b) of the Exchange Act and Rule 10b-5 promulgated thereunder. *Id.* at 474-77. *See also* Cort v. Ash, 422 U.S. 66 (1975), where the Court stated: "Corporations are creatures of state law, and investors commit their funds to corporate directors on the understanding that, except where federal law *expressly* requires certain responsibilities of directors with respect to stockholders, state law will govern the internal affairs of the corporation." *Id.* at 84 (emphasis added). *See also* Burks v. Lasker, 441 U.S. 471, 478 (1979) ("the first place one must look to determine the powers of corporate directors is in the relevant State's corporation law"); Singer v. Magnavox Co., 380 A.2d 969, 976 n.6 (Del. 1977) (*Santa Fe* is a "current confirmation by the Supreme Court of the responsibility of a state to govern the internal affairs of corporate life").

37. Generally, federal and state courts, subsequent to *Santa Fe,* have reached such an accommodation regarding breaches of fiduciary duty where there is a material nondisclosure in the flow of information from management to shareholders. *See, e.g.,* Healey v. Catalyst Recovery, Inc., 616 F.2d 641 (3d Cir. 1980); Alabama Farm Bureau Mut. Cas. Co. v. American Fidelity Life Ins. Co., 606 F.2d 602 (5th Cir. 1979), *cert. denied,* 446 U.S. 933 (1980); Kidwell

The reticence of many courts in enunciating the basis for their decisions may also be due to a failure to identify a doctrine embodied in the securities acts which underlies the obligation to disclose information bearing on management's competency or integrity. Although the Commission stressed the importance to investors of this type of information several years ago in the seminal decision, *Franchard Corp.*,[38] the present disclosure obligation for qualitative information formulated by the courts has not been textured through a gradual evolutionary process over the past two decades. Rather, as evidenced by the dearth of judicial decisions in the late 1960s following *Franchard Corp.*, and the rash of cases that emerged in the mid and late 1970s pronouncing the need for investors and shareholders to be informed about the integrity of management,[39] the decisions requiring disclosure of qualitative information seem to be more a function of a reformist impulse, nurtured and shaped by the Watergate fallout and our society's ensuing obsession with openness, accountability, and integrity of public fiduciaries. If this disclosure requirement is a product of the socio-political atmosphere of the 1970s and a marked departure from traditional notions of materiality, courts in the 1980s may have to struggle to bring some consistency to bear on their decisions and the elusive obligation that has developed.

Notwithstanding the uncertainties and inconsistencies, it is possible to distill some common elements from Commission and judicial decisions holding that qualitatively material information is disclosable and to delineate some parameters for the emerging, and potentially boundless, disclosure obligation. The purpose of this chapter is to address the concept of qualitative materiality and the duty to disclose in the context of the securities acts. The chapter first will present an overview of relevant case law and Commission proceedings. Thereafter, the chapter will address management self-dealing (including the "true purpose" cases), questionable and illegal payments, unethical or unlawful company policies, adjudicated illegalities and pending

---

v. Meikle, 597 F.2d 1273 (9th Cir. 1979); Goldberg v. Meridor, 567 F.2d 209 (2d Cir. 1977), *cert. denied*, 434 U.S. 1069 (1978); Wright v. Heizer Corp., 560 F.2d 237 (7th Cir. 1977), *cert. denied*, 434 U.S. 1066 (1978); Roland Int'l Corp. v. Najjar, 407 A.2d 1032 (Del. 1979); Lynch v. Vickers Energy Corp., 383 A.2d 278 (Del. 1977); Singer v. Magnavox Co., 380 A.2d 969 (Del. 1977); Tanzer v. International Gen. Indus., 379 A.2d 1121 (Del. 1977); Young v. Valhi, Inc., 382 A.2d 1372 (Del. Ch. 1978); Kemp v. Angel, 381 A.2d 241 (Del. Ch. 1977). *See also* Perl v. IU Int'l Corp., 61 Hawaii 622, 607 P.2d 1036 (1980); Gabhart v. Gabhart, 267 Ind. 370, 370 N.E.2d 345 (1977); *In re* Jones & Laughlin Steel Corp., 448 Pa. 524, 412 A.2d 1099 (1980). For further discussion on this subject herein, *see* pages 163-98 *infra*.

38. 42 S.E.C. 163, [1964-1966 Transfer Binder] FED. SEC. L. REP. (CCH) ¶ 77,113 (1964). For a further discussion of this decision, see notes 66-69 and accompanying text *infra*.

39. *See, e.g.,* Maldonado v. Flynn, 597 F.2d 789 (2d Cir. 1979); Bertoglio v. Texas Int'l Co., 488 F. Supp. 630 (D. Del. 1980); Trans World Airlines v. Catalano, [1979-1980 Transfer Binder] FED. SEC. L. REP. (CCH) ¶ 97,159 (S.D.N.Y. Oct. 31, 1979); SEC v. Jos. Schlitz Brewing Co., 452 F. Supp. 824 (E.D. Wis. 1978); SEC v. Freeman, [1978 Transfer Binder] FED. SEC. L. REP. (CCH) ¶ 96,361 (N.D. Ill. Mar. 3, 1978); SEC v. Kalvex, Inc., 425 F. Supp. 310 (S.D.N.Y. 1975).

lawsuits against officers and directors, and business expertise and reputation of corporate officials. Finally, a standard for the disclosure of qualitatively material information—in both an investing and a voting context—will be proposed.

II. OVERVIEW OF CASE LAW

Upon examining relevant case law and Commission proceedings, a number of propositions can be proffered. First, when information relating to management competency or integrity is required to be disclosed pursuant to securities statutes or Commission rules, failure to disclose such information generally will result in liability.[40] For example, in *United States v. Fields*,[41] the United States Court of Appeals for the Second Circuit held that solicitation of proxies without disclosure of kickbacks contravened specific disclosure items mandated by Schedule 14A and thus constituted a violation of Section 14(a) of the Exchange Act.[42] Likewise, failure to disclose a director's or officer's prior adjudicated liability, if such liability relates to the "ability or integrity" of such person, violates the affirmative disclosure requirements of a number of Commission forms and schedules.[43] On this issue, the United States Court of Appeals for the District of Columbia, in finding a Section 13(d) violation, stated that "the fact of [the defendant's] participation, in view of his past troubles with the securities laws, is just the type of datum that is contemplated by the requirements of Schedule 13D."[44] Similarly, nondisclosures of significant management remuneration or instances of self-dealing contravene Commission disclosure requirements,[45] and, as held by several courts, constitute statutory violations.[46]

---

40. *See, e.g.,* United States v. Fields, 592 F.2d 638 (2d Cir. 1978), *cert. denied,* 442 U.S. 917 (1979); SEC v. Kalvex, Inc., 425 F. Supp. 310 (S.D.N.Y. 1975); Franchard Corp., 42 S.E.C. 163, [1964-1966 Transfer Binder] FED. SEC. L. REP. (CCH) ¶ 77,113 (1964).

41. 592 F.2d 638 (2d Cir. 1978), *cert. denied,* 442 U.S. 917 (1979).

42. 592 F.2d at 650 ("defendants' failure to disclose their interest in Westcalind kickbacks certainly would be a violation of Item 7(f) and consequently of Section 14(a)").

43. *See, e.g.,* Item 401(f), Regulation S-K, 17 C.F.R. § 229.401 (1982). *See* text accompanying notes 179-83 *infra.*

44. SEC v. Savoy Indus., 587 F.2d 1149, 1165 (D.C. Cir. 1978), *cert. denied,* 440 U.S. 913 (1979).

45. *See* Item 402(f), Regulation S-K, 17 C.F.R. § 229.402 (1982), which requires disclosure of

> any transaction since the beginning of the registrant's last fiscal year . . . to which the registrant or any of its subsidiaries was or is to be a party, in which any of the following persons had or is to have a direct or indirect material interest . . .
> (1) Any director or officer of the registrant;
> (2) Any nominee for election as a director. . . .

46. *See, e.g.,* SEC v. Kalvex, 425 F. Supp. 310 (S.D.N.Y. 1975) (defendant director siphoned off corporate funds for own use; kickback scheme also shown).

Second, making incomplete or misleading representations regarding management integrity or competency is frequently actionable, whether such statements are made voluntarily or in response to mandatory items of disclosure.[47] In one case, a defendant describing his prior occupations—as required by Schedule 14B—included his trading activities in commodities and precious metals without disclosing that a state court had found him liable for fraud in connection with trading in silver contracts.[48] Characterizing the defendant's description as "sheer puffery" and "misleading," the court entered an injunction.[49] Similarly, in another proceeding the Commission found that the "failure to disclose that management had never manufactured a product or run a business of that type was a material omission which rendered the offering circular misleading."[50]

Third, courts generally are inclined to hold that instances of self-dealing by corporate officers and directors are extremely important to shareholders. Accordingly, such information has been required to be disclosed—particularly in proxy solicitations for the election of directors—even if it is not specifically called for in Commission disclosure items[51] or does not render any specific statement in the proxy materials materially misleading.[52] As the United States Court of Appeals for the Second Circuit has stated, "going beyond [Rule 14a-9], it has been recognized that shareholders are entitled to truthful presentation of factual information "impugning the honesty, loyalty or competency of directors in their dealings with the corporation to which they owe a fiduciary duty."[53]

Fourth, although a number of courts have suggested that management's authorization of questionable or illegal payments must be disclosed in proxy solicitation materials if the payments are quantitatively material or result in kickbacks to corporate officials,[54] some courts have concluded that disclosure of such payments is required in any event because of their relation to the integrity of management.[55] In *SEC v. Joseph Schlitz Brewing Co.,*[56]

---

47. *See, e.g.,* Bertoglio v. Texas Int'l Co., 488 F. Supp. 630 (D. Del. 1980); SEC v. Century Mortgage Co., 470 F. Supp. 300 (D. Utah 1979); Berkman v. Rust Craft Greeting Cards, Inc., 454 F. Supp. 787 (S.D.N.Y. 1978).

48. Trans World Airlines v. Catalano, [1979-1980 Transfer Binder] FED. SEC. L. REP. (CCH) ¶ 97,159 (S.D.N.Y. Oct. 31, 1979).

49. *Id.* at 96,385-86.

50. Emer-Go Corp., SEC Securities Act Release No. 6066, 17 SEC DOCKET 500, 501 (May 7, 1979).

51. *See, e.g.,* Bertoglio v. Texas Int'l Co., 488 F. Supp. 630 (D. Del. 1980).

52. *See, e.g.,* Maldonado v. Flynn, 597 F.2d 789 (2d Cir. 1979).

53. *Id.* at 796.

54. *See, e.g.,* Weisberg v. Coastal States Gas Corp., 609 F.2d 650 (2d Cir. 1979), *cert. denied,* 445 U.S. 951 (1980); Kaplan v. Bennett, 465 F. Supp. 555 (S.D.N.Y. 1979).

55. *See, e.g.,* Berman v. Gerber Prods. Co., 454 F. Supp. 1310 (W.D. Mich. 1978); SEC v. Jos. Schlitz Brewing Co., 452 F. Supp. 824 (E.D. Wis. 1978). *But see* Gaines v. Haughton, 645 F.2d 761 (9th Cir. 1981), *cert. denied,* 102 S. Ct. 1006 (1982).

56. 452 F. Supp. 824 (E.D. Wis. 1978).

for example, the Commission alleged, *inter alia,* that Schlitz had failed to disclose improper payments. Denying Schlitz's motion to dismiss, the court stated that "the question of the integrity of management gives materiality to the matters the Commission claims should have been disclosed."[57]

Finally, courts often have required disclosure of specific facts concerning director nominees in proxy solicitation materials where such facts indicate that election of the nominees may imperil corporate assets or pose other substantial risks to the corporation.[58] As one court noted, "where a nominee's background is likely to adversely affect a profitable asset, such background should be disclosed to the shareholders."[59] In addition, courts have held that pending litigation against management alleging breaches of fiduciary duty must be disclosed.[60] Yet whether prior adjudicated illegalities and pending claims must be disclosed solely due to their relation to management's integrity is an issue that remains uncertain in the courts.[61]

While the foregoing discussion has delineated the development of qualitative materiality through case law and Commission proceedings, the following sections of this chapter will expand on the concepts raised. As will be seen, although some definitive conclusions can be reached, the courts' disparate approaches to a number of these issues make the slope of materiality a most slippery one.

III. SELF-DEALING BY CORPORATE DIRECTORS AND OFFICERS

Self-dealing by corporate directors and officers raises concerns regarding the integrity and competency of management. Accordingly, at least in proxy solicitations for the election of directors, the Commission and the courts have often required disclosure of perquisites, tax deductions, kickbacks, and other forms of self-dealing which redound to management's benefit.[62]

It is not as clear, however, whether courts would require disclosure of self-dealing in connection with the purchase or sale of securities if the conduct

---

57. *Id.* at 830.

58. *See, e.g.,* Chris-Craft Indus. v. Independent Stockholders Comm., 354 F. Supp. 895 (D. Del. 1973); Cooke v. Teleprompter Corp., 334 F. Supp. 467 (S.D.N.Y. 1971).

59. Kass v. Arden-Mayfair, Inc., 431 F. Supp. 1037, 1046 (C.D. Cal. 1977).

60. *See, e.g.,* Rafal v. Geneen, [1972-1973 Transfer Binder] FED. SEC. L. REP. (CCH) ¶ 93,505 (E.D. Pa. May 8, 1972); Robinson v. Penn Cent. Co., 336 F. Supp. 655 (E.D. Pa. 1971); Beatty v. Bright, 318 F. Supp. 169 (S.D. Iowa 1970).

61. *Compare* SEC v. Freeman, [1978 Transfer Binder] FED. SEC. L. REP. (CCH) ¶ 96,361 (N.D. Ill. Mar. 3, 1978) (disclosure based on qualitative materiality required) *with* Kass v. Arden-Mayfair, Inc., 431 F. Supp. 1037 (C.D. Cal. 1977) (disclosure required where nominee may jeopardize corporate asset).

62. Disclosure of such self-dealing is called for in Commission forms, including solicitations of proxies for the election of directors, periodic reports, and registration statements. *See* notes 63-79 and accompanying text *infra.*

did not pose the risk of significant economic losses to the corporation. Such information arguably is not material to investors because it does not relate to the financial soundness of the corporation. Yet if management's self-dealing is not a single incident, but rather a continuing scheme to bilk the corporation, it can be argued that the potential aggregate effect of this misconduct would be material to investors.

Self-dealing should also be deemed material to investors if a prospectus accompanying the sale of securities or an annual report filed with the Commission stressed management's competence or integrity as a selling point for the company's stock. In this situation, an investor could associate management's characterization of its ability or integrity with increased corporate earnings, and information dispelling this notion might very well be material to an investment decision.

A. Commission Disclosure Items and Affirmative Misrepresentations

Self-dealing by management is routinely required to be disclosed when the conduct comes within the Commission's disclosure items relating to remuneration and conflicts of interest,[63] or when management has made representations which are rendered misleading by the omission of such

---

63. *See* Item 402, Regulation S-K, 17 C.F.R. § 229.402 (1982), Item 404, Regulation S-K, *as adopted,* SEC Securities Exchange Act Release No. 19290 (Dec. 2, 1982). In part, Item 402 requires registrants to disclose the compensation of the five most highly paid executive officers receiving remuneration over $50,000, plus remuneration data for all officers and directors as a group, including all remuneration proposed to be made to the officers pursuant to any existing plans. Item 404 in part requires disclosure of transactions with the corporation by directors, director-nominees, executive officers, five percent shareholders, and members of the immediate family of the primary reporting persons involving more than $60,000 made within the past year in which such persons have a direct or indirect material interest. In addition, Item 402 provides, with certain limitations, for a specified tabular remuneration format which requires disclosure concerning remuneration paid to certain specified persons and groups "for services in all capacities to the registrant and its subsidiaries during the registrant's last fiscal year or, in specified instances, certain prior fiscal years." 17 C.F.R. § 229.402 (1982). The term "remuneration" includes, *inter alia,* salaries, fees, commissions, bonuses, securities, property, insurance benefits, and personal benefits not directly related to job performance, other than those provided to broad categories of employees and which do not discriminate in favor of officers and directors. *See* SEC Securities Act Release No. 6003, 16 SEC DOCKET 321, [1978 Transfer Binder] FED. SEC. L. REP. (CCH) ¶ 81,765 (Dec. 4, 1978). *See also* SEC Securities Act Release No. 6261, 21 SEC DOCKET 590, [1980 Transfer Binder] FED. SEC. L. REP. (CCH) ¶ 82,679, at 83,769 (Nov. 14, 1980) ("In general, the amendments pertain to various aspects of remuneration disclosure including: pension, option and stock appreciation right plans; the definition of an executive officer; compensation relating to the termination of employment; and indebtedness of management"). *See also* SEC Securities Exchange Act Release No. 19431 (Jan. 17, 1983) (proposing rule and schedule amendments to the disclosure of management remuneration, including proposed amendments to Item 402).

information.[64] In addition, some courts have apparently required disclosure of management self-dealing when the omitted information is deemed material, regardless of a pertinent Commission disclosure item or the existence of a misleading omission.[65]

When discussing management self-dealing in the qualitative materiality sense, the starting point is the Commission's opinion in *Franchard Corp.*,[66] written by former Chairman William Cary. In that case, a corporation's registration statement failed to disclose the diversion of company funds for the personal benefit of its chief executive officer. Holding that disclosure of such self-dealing was required, the Commission pointed to specific Commission disclosure items[67] and to information omitted from the registration statement which rendered the representations regarding the officer's reputation materially misleading.[68] Perhaps most significantly, the Commission found such self-dealing to be material to investors, even though the officer's withdrawals never exceeded 1.5 percent of the firm's total assets, because it was "germane to an evaluation of the integrity of management."[69]

Another important decision in this area is *SEC v. Kalvex, Inc.*[70] In that case, the defendant director participated in a scheme to funnel money through a dummy corporation for the purpose of secretly receiving kickback payments from a Kalvex supplier. In addition to the kickback scheme, the director siphoned off Kalvex funds for his personal use by submitting expense vouchers and obtaining reimbursement for expenses unrelated to any corporate purpose. The SEC alleged that the director had solicited proxies in violation of Section 14(a), Rules 14a-3 and 14a-9 thereunder, and specific disclosure requirements of Schedule 14A, because the director had failed to disclose his self-dealing in the proxy materials.[71] Although the proxies so-

---

64. *See, e.g.,* SEC v. Kalvex, Inc., 425 F. Supp. 310 (S.D.N.Y. 1975).

65. *See, e.g.,* Maldonado v. Flynn, 597 F.2d 789 (2d Cir. 1979).

66. 42 S.E.C. 163, [1964-1966 Transfer Binder] FED. SEC. L. REP. (CCH) ¶ 77,113 (1964).

67. The Commission stated that nondisclosure of the officer's self-dealing violated Item 20, Form S-1, 2 FED. SEC. L. REP. (CCH) ¶ 8215 (May 9, 1979), and Item 24, Form S-11, 2 FED. SEC. L. REP. (CCH) ¶ 7234 (Sept. 24, 1980), which require disclosure of material interests of management in transactions involving the corporation. Franchard Corp., 42 S.E.C. at 171 n.20, [1964-1966 Transfer Binder] FED. SEC. L. REP. (CCH) at 82,043 n.20.

68. In this regard, the Commission reflected that management's "quality" is of "cardinal importance" in judging any business. As such, "[d]isclosures relevant to an evaluation of management are particularly pertinent where . . . securities are sold largely on the personal reputation of a company's controlling person." Franchard Corp., 42 S.E.C. at 169, [1964-1966 Transfer Binder] FED. SEC. L. REP. (CCH) at 82,041.

69. *Id.* at 172, [1964-1966 Transfer Binder] FED. SEC. L. REP. (CCH) at 82,043. The Commission also asserted that the need to evaluate the quality of management "is an essential ingredient of informed investment decision [and comprises a] need so important [that it] cannot be ignored. . . ." *Id.* at 170, [1964-1966 Transfer Binder] FED. SEC. L. REP. (CCH) at 82,042.

70. 425 F. Supp. 310 (S.D.N.Y. 1975).

71. *Id.* at 312.

licited were "routine" in the sense that there was no contest for corporate control, the court nevertheless focused on shareholder concern over the integrity of management and asserted that "the undisclosed facts might have led a reasonable stockholder to question the integrity of [the director] and his ability to discharge his fiduciary obligations."[72] Finding violations of the federal proxy provisions, the court concluded that "[a]lthough obviously it was in his self-interest to conceal, as a director and officer of Kalvex, it was his duty to disclose his participation and that of others in the kickback scheme."[73]

The *Kalvex* court based its holding in part on the violation of specific disclosure requirements of Schedule 14A. In *United States v. Fields*,[74] which involved the receipt of kickbacks by corporate officers and directors, the United States Court of Appeals for the Second Circuit premised its holding on this aspect of the case *wholly* on the violation of specific disclosure items contained in Schedule 14A.[75]

Although courts have broadly construed Commission disclosure items in self-dealing cases, not all of management's pecuniary benefits are required to be disclosed. In *Lewis v. Dansker*,[76] for example, the court held that management need not disclose certain tax benefits received as a result of real estate transactions with the corporation.[77] Though the court's holding

---

72. *Id.* at 315. Speaking of the broad policies underlying the federal proxy provisions, the court stated:

> Section 14(a) of the Exchange Act was enacted by the Congress to ensure that full and fair disclosure would be made to stockholders whose proxies are being solicited so that an informed and meaningful consideration of the alternatives can be made. Thus, where a material statement is omitted from a proxy statement, or a statement contained in a proxy statement is false and misleading in light of the circumstances in which it is made, and where there is a likelihood that such an omission or representation will influence stockholder votes, the broad remedial purposes of Section 14(a) have been violated.

Id. at 314-15 (citations omitted).

73. *Id.* at 315. Without referring to any specific disclosure items or any specific misleading representations, the court also found a violation of Section 13(a) of the Exchange Act, reasoning that the annual and quarterly reports were false and misleading because they failed to disclose the kickbacks and other matters. *Id.* at 316.

74. 592 F.2d 638 (2d Cir. 1978), *cert. denied*, 442 U.S. 917 (1979).

75. 592 F.2d at 650 (defendants' "failure to disclose these kickbacks, if proven, would constitute a violation of Item 7(e)(4) and consequently of Section 14(a)").

76. 357 F. Supp. 636 (S.D.N.Y. 1973).

77. *Id.* at 642 ("While Item 7(f) appears to be a catch-all section, it would be expanding excessively the concept of an 'indirect material interest' to require merely potential tax benefits received in one's individual return to be reported under this section"). The court interpreted "indirect material interest" to signify that "something of positive value must pass from the corporation to the insider in order [for the benefit derived from the transaction] to come within the reporting requirements of the rule." *Id.* Although the defendants received what the court characterized as "incidental benefits" through transactions with the corporation, "they did not receive something of value passing either directly or indirectly from the corporation to

is subject to criticism,[78] it stands for the proposition that not all pecuniary benefits received by management in transactions with the issuer fall within the concept of "indirect material benefit" and, hence, must be disclosed.[79]

B. Disclosure Not Based on Line Items

Courts have had greater difficulty defining appropriate disclosure standards for management self-dealing practices not covered by the Commission's disclosure items relating to remuneration and conflicts of interest. Since most courts recognize that an election of directors is the only opportunity for shareholders to scrutinize management's qualifications and integrity, they generally have employed Rule 14a-9 as a means to require disclosure of self-dealing.[80] Nevertheless, to maintain consistency with the literal language of the rule, a number of courts have inquired whether the omission of such practices rendered misleading other specific statements or general impressions in the proxy materials.[81] It remains unclear whether some courts will find a violation of Rule 14a-9 where nondisclosure does not render any specific statement or general impression misleading.[82]

In this context, it is important to stress that Schedule 14A establishes only minimum disclosure standards. In other words, compliance with Schedule 14A "does not necessarily guarantee that a proxy statement satisfies Rule

---

them." *Id.* The court further noted that Item 7(f) expressly requires the reporting of only those indirect interests that are material. The court's opinion was that an investor deciding whether to approve the various transactions would not be influenced in any way by the amount of tax benefit the officers/directors received from their transactions with the corporation, as long as the transactions did not adversely affect the corporation or the investor's individual interest. The court concluded that the tax savings which the officers/directors received did not have any such effect. Note, however, that although finding inapplicable the specific disclosure item under the circumstances of that case, the court indicated that, if applicable, the violation of a disclosure item of Schedule 14A would constitute a violation of Section 14(a). *Id.* at 642-43.

78. *See, e.g.,* Maldonado v. Flynn, 597 F.2d 789 (2d Cir. 1979).

79. *See* notes 9, 26 and 45 *supra* for application of the concept of "indirect material benefit."

80. *See, e.g.,* Maldonado v. Flynn, 597 F.2d 789 (2d Cir. 1979); Bertoglio v. Texas Int'l Co., 488 F. Supp. 630 (D. Del. 1980); Berkman v. Rust Craft Greeting Cards, Inc., 454 F. Supp. 787 (S.D.N.Y. 1978). Rule 14a-9 provides in pertinent part that "[n]o solicitation subject to this regulation shall be made by means of any proxy statement . . . which omits to state any material fact necessary in order to make the statements therein not false or misleading. . . ." 17 C.F.R. § 240.14a-9 (1980).

81. *See, e.g.,* Cohen v. Ayers, 449 F. Supp. 298 (N.D. Ill. 1978), *aff'd,* 596 F.2d 733 (7th Cir. 1979); Perelman v. Pennsylvania Real Estate Inv. Trust, [1977-1978 Transfer Binder] FED. SEC. L. REP. (CCH) ¶ 96,202 (E.D. Pa. June 15, 1977); Ash v. Brunswick Corp., 405 F. Supp. 234 (D. Del. 1975).

82. *Compare* Maldonado v. Flynn, 597 F.2d 789 (2d Cir. 1979) *and* SEC v. Century Mortgage Co., 470 F. Supp. 300 (D. Utah 1979) *with* General Time Corp. v. Talley Indus., 403 F.2d 159 (2d Cir. 1968), *cert. denied,* 398 U.S. 1026 (1969) *and* Ash v. Brunswick Corp., 405 F. Supp. 234 (D. Del. 1975).

14a-9."[83] An example of this principle is *Maldonado v. Flynn*,[84] where a shareholder's derivative suit alleged violations of Sections 10(b) and 14(a) in management's administration of a stock option plan for key employees of Zapata Corporation and its subsidiaries. The Section 14(a) claim alleged that the proxy statements used to solicit votes for the election of Zapata's directors were materially false and misleading. In particular, the proxy statements did not disclose the interest-free loans extended to six optionees to enable them to exercise their stock options, the exercise date of such options being accelerated in light of an issuer tender offer. The plaintiffs contended that, by accelerating the exercise date and thus allowing the officers to exercise their options prior to the foreseen rise in the market price of Zapata stock, the board permitted the officers to reduce their tax liability and prevented the corporation from enjoying a correspondingly higher tax deduction.[85] Drawing upon Schedule 14A, Commission rules, and the misleading character of Zapata's proxy statement, the United States Court of Appeals for the Second Circuit concluded that a reasonable shareholder "could have considered" such information important in determining how to vote in director elections.[86] The court pointed out that "the alleged misleading statements and non-disclosures involve matters of direct and deep concern to shareholders in the exercise of their right to vote, which the Exchange Act expects to be fully disclosed in proxy solicitations for election of officers and directors."[87]

---

83. Maldonado v. Flynn, 597 F.2d 789, 796 n.9 (2d Cir. 1979) (citing Cohen v. Ayers, 449 F. Supp. 298, 317 (N.D. Ill. 1978), *aff'd*, 596 F.2d 733 (7th Cir. 1979)); Lyman v. Standard Brands, Inc., 364 F. Supp. 794, 796 (E.D. Pa. 1973). A recent decision stated:

> While [the SEC] regulations do not expressly require disclosure of the vesting provisions of stock options plans, it must be noted that Schedule 14A sets only minimum disclosure standards. Compliance with this schedule does not necessarily guarantee that a proxy statement satisfies Rule 14a-9. . . . Rather, the court must examine the materiality of the omitted information in the context of the proxy contest at issue.

Bertoglio v. Texas Int'l Co., 488 F. Supp. 630, 647 (D. Del. 1980).

84. 597 F.2d 789 (2d Cir. 1979).

85. *Id.* at 792.

86. The *Maldonado* court stated that

> a reasonable shareholder of Zapata Corporation could have considered it important, in deciding how to vote his proxy in 1976 and 1977, to know that the candidates for directorships had voted for, and in some cases benefited substantially from, the resolutions modifying the exercise date and removing the requirement of payment in cash so as to enable certain senior officers to avoid the adverse personal tax effect of the impending tender offer, known to them through inside information, while depriving the Corporation of a corresponding tax benefit.

Id. at 798. *Accord,* Bertoglio v. Texas Int'l Co., 488 F. Supp. 630, 648 (D. Del. 1980).

87. Maldonado v. Flynn, 597 F.2d at 796. The court also noted that the plaintiff's claim was not "merely another attempt to use § 14(a) and Rule 14a-9 as an avenue for access to

In a more general discussion of the relationship between self-dealing and director competency and integrity, the *Maldonado* court appeared to formulate a broad duty of disclosure, stating:

> Since self-dealing presents opportunities for abuse of a corporate position of trust, the circumstances surrounding corporate transactions in which directors have a personal interest are directly relevant to a determination of whether they are qualified to exercise stewardship of the company. . . . For this reason Rule 14a-9 specifically sets out minimum standards and, *going beyond the Rule,* it has been recognized that shareholders are entitled to truthful presentation of factual information "impugning the honesty, loyalty or competency of directors" in their dealings with the corporation to which they owe a fiduciary duty.[88]

Despite the above generalization, some courts have held that Section 14(a) imposes a duty to disclose information only if the information is required by specific disclosure items or if nondisclosure renders other statements made misleading. Thus, in order to violate Section 14(a), the omitted information must not only be material but also must be called for or must make other statements false or misleading.[89] For example, in *Perelman v.*

---

the federal courts in order to redress alleged mismanagement or breach of fiduciary duty on the part of the corporate executives." *Id.*

88. *Id.* (emphasis added) (quoting Cohen v. Ayers, 449 F. Supp. 298, 317 (N.D. Ill. 1978), *aff'd,* 596 F.2d 733 (7th Cir. 1979)); Berkman v. Rust Craft Greeting Cards, Inc., 454 F. Supp. 787 (S.D.N.Y. 1978); SEC v. Kalvex, Inc., 425 F. Supp. 310 (S.D.N.Y. 1977); Goldsholl v. Shapiro, 417 F. Supp. 1291, 1298-99 (S.D.N.Y. 1976); Rafal v. Geneen [1972-1973 Transfer Binder] FED. SEC. L. REP. (CCH) ¶ 93,505 (E.D. Pa. May 8, 1972); Robinson v. Penn Central Co., 336 F. Supp. 655 (E.D. Pa. 1971). Although the Second Circuit's expansive language suggests an affirmative duty to disclose information impugning management's integrity, the *Maldonado* court also relied on the omission of quantitatively material information called for by specific Commission disclosure items and affirmative misrepresentations contained in the proxy materials. *See* SEC v. Century Mortgage Co., 470 F. Supp. 300 (D. Utah 1979) (suggesting that certain information was required to be disclosed in a prospectus and registration statement solely because of its bearing on management's integrity).

89. *See, e.g.,* General Time Corp. v. Talley Indus., 403 F.2d 159, 162 (2d Cir. 1968), *cert. denied,* 393 U.S. 1026 (1969) (in holding that the nondisclosure of certain information was not actionable under Rule 14a-9, the court failed "to see how the details concerning the discussion between Industries and Fund that were omitted from the proxy statement were necessary in order to make the statements therein not false or misleading"); Ash v. Brunswick Corp., 405 F. Supp. 234, 245 (D. Del. 1975). In *Ash,* the court stated:

> As to the omissions, it may be assumed that at least some of these were material. Reference is made particularly to the failure of the statement to set forth the terms of the 1968 [stock option] plan, which, upon adoption of the 1974 [stock option] plan, was to cease to be effective. . . . An intelligent choice was impossible unless both plans were before them.

Pennsylvania Real Estate Investment Trust,[90] a proxy solicitation for the election of trustees did not disclose that the trust had formed a new partnership with a firm in which the sole stockholder was an existing trustee of the trust and which would receive a twenty percent greater share of income than one of the trust's previous partners. Although acknowledging that the nondisclosures probably would be material to voting shareholders because of the information's bearing on the "[t]rustee's sense of fiduciary responsibility in conflict of interest situations involving insider trustees,"[91] the court nonetheless held that the claim was not actionable, reasoning that the information was not called for in Schedule 14A and that the omission did not render the statements made false or misleading.[92]

A number of other courts, however, have not been as limited in their construction of Rule 14a-9. These courts have drawn on the general impressions conveyed by the proxy materials, rather than explicit statements rendered misleading, to hold such materials false and misleading under Section 14(a).[93] In *Berkman v. Rust Craft Greeting Cards, Inc.,*[94] for example, the

---

> Despite the desirability of Brunswick advising the stockholders of the terms of the 1968 plan, its disclosure was not necessary to make any of the statements in the proxy statement not false or misleading. Omissions constitute violations of the Act only if they are both material and make other statements false or misleading. Both Section 14(a) and Rule 14a-9(a) say as much, and authorities have given effect to their plain meaning.

Id.

90. [1977-1978 Transfer Binder] FED. SEC. L. REP. (CCH) ¶ 96,202 (E.D. Pa. June 15, 1977).

91. *Id.* at 92, 418.

92. The court stated:

> [I]f Schedule 14A, promulgated by the SEC, does not require the revelation of such information, failure to provide it cannot be regarded as a violation of the Act. . . .
>
> When all facts pertaining to the Cambridge Apartments project as recited in the proxy statement are considered, it is perfectly obvious that the omissions relied on do not make any of those statements false or misleading. Accordingly, Rule 14a-9(a) has not been violated. . . .

Id. at 92,412-20. *See* Cohen v. Ayers, 449 F. Supp. 298, 317 (N.D. Ill. 1978), *aff'd,* 596 F.2d 733 (7th Cir. 1979) ("The relevant inquiry is whether the omitted information was material and true, and whether it tended to make the proxy statement misleading").

93. *See, e.g.,* Berkman v. Rust Craft Greeting Cards, Inc., 454 F. Supp. 787 (S.D.N.Y. 1978). Although not as explicit as *Berkman,* the district court in Cohen v. Ayers, 449 F. Supp. 298, 317 (N.D. Ill. 1978), *aff'd,* 596 F.2d 733 (7th Cir. 1979), arguably relying on the general impressions conveyed by the proxy materials rather than express statements, stated that:

> Although tangential information need not be disclosed, the shareholders have an interest in knowing what compensation the directors received. In addition, they should not be precluded from learning facts impugning the honesty, loyalty or competency of directors, such as the existence of litigation against them, or self-dealing by them. The relevant inquiry is whether the omitted information was material and true, and whether it tended to make the proxy statement misleading.

94. 454 F. Supp. 787 (S.D.N.Y. 1978).

complaint challenged the sufficiency of proxy materials sent to the Rust Craft shareholders in connection with the reelection of the board of directors. The dispute arose from a friendly tender offer by another corporation for all outstanding Rust Craft shares. Unknown to certain of the directors, one of the investment banking firms hired by the company to prepare an appraisal opinion owned over five percent of its stock. Thereafter, at a board meeting held for the purpose of nominating directors, certain directors moved that those directors who knew of the conflict but failed to inform the others not be renominated. The motion failed, and a proxy statement was issued for the shareholders' annual meeting, where the election of directors would take place. Plaintiffs subsequently brought suit alleging that the proxy materials made inadequate disclosure of the facts surrounding the defendant directors' failure to disclose the investment banking firm's conflict of interest, as well as inadequate disclosure of the split board vote on the renomination question and the reasons behind the split vote.[95] The court stated that shareholders "in all probability" were entitled to be informed of the directors' failure to disclose the firm's conflict of interest.[96] Considering questions bearing on the "integrity and fitness" of the defendant directors, the court reasoned that, for purposes of preliminary injunctive relief, the defendant directors' failure to disclose the omitted information was qualitatively material:

> In the circumstances of this case, we think it probable that the facts surrounding the Kidder debenture purchase, the individual defendants' failure to disclose these facts, and the rift within the Rust Craft board

---

95. *Id.* at 789-90.
96. The court stated that

> [t]he shareholders, in turn, are, in all probability, entitled to know that certain candidates for reelection may well have breached their fiduciary obligations. Any reasonable shareholder would consider important the "track" record of a director whom he is asked to reelect. More likely than not, the failure to disclose a known conflict of interest would be regarded as a significant blot on such a track record, especially since the conflict centered upon the question of stock evaluation, a matter of direct importance to the shareholders. Of course, the individual defendants' failure to alert the remaining directors of the Kidder conflict may also have an adverse effect upon the shareholders' decision on the integrity and fitness of the individual defendants to hold office.

Id. at 791-92. Continuing on the theme that Rule 14a-9 vested shareholders with the right to receive the omitted information, the court commented:

> Likewise, the shareholders' judgment could well be influenced by the fact that two of the incumbent directors thought the defendants' failure to disclose serious enough to dissent on their fitness for renomination. It is by no means inconceivable that a shareholder would give substantial deference to the views of the plaintiffs, longtime shareholders of the company, who considered defendants' lack of candor a major failing in office. Indeed, plaintiffs' views find support in the board's action, also omitted from the proxy materials, retaining a third investment banking firm for a valuation opinion.

Id. at 792 (citation omitted).

over the renomination of the defendants, would give the shareholders pause when asked to entrust the stewardship of the company to these less than candid men. Plaintiffs have therefore demonstrated a likelihood of success on the issue of materiality.[97]

The above cases indicate that nondisclosure in contravention of specific disclosure items or omissions making other statements in the proxy materials false or misleading will certainly be actionable. Yet while a few courts have postulated a broad duty to disclose self-dealing that reflects on the integrity of management, others have imposed liability only where the omitted information made other statements false or misleading. Another group of courts seems to focus on general impressions, as opposed to explicit statements, conveyed by proxy materials to determine whether such materials are false and misleading under Section 14(a).

C. "True Purpose" Cases

The "true purpose" cases place a limitation on the disclosure requirements regarding management self-dealing and conflicts of interest. These cases generally provide that, although the objective aspects of management integrity may have to be disclosed, the subjective aspects do not. As aptly phrased by one authority: "It is not necessary to say, 'This is a grossly unfair transaction in which the board of directors is overreaching the minority stockholders.' You just have to give them the facts."[98] Management therefore

---

97. *Id.* The court also concluded that the plaintiffs had satisfied their burden of showing that the proxy materials were false and misleading:

> We further think it highly probable that plaintiffs will succeed in proving that the proxy materials, as they now stand, are false or misleading. The materials convey the aura of business as usual, despite the existence of a deep schism within the ranks of management. The entire slate of directors is proffered as that of "management," when in reality management is sharply divided over the qualifications of four of the nominees. What disclosure there is about the Kidder purchase is manifestly insufficient to apprise the shareholders of the fact that four nominees failed to advise the remainder of the board of the Kidder purchase in sufficient time to enable the board to evaluate the Kidder opinion in light of all the relevant facts. Thus, likelihood of success is demonstrated on this aspect of plaintiff's claim for relief.

Id.

98. Ratner, *Federal Corporation Law Before and After* Santa Fe Industries v. Green, in 9TH ANNUAL INSTITUTE ON SECURITIES REGULATION 305, 322 (Fleischer, Lipton & Vandegrift eds., 1977). *See also* Goldberg v. Meridor, 567 F.2d 209, 218 n.8 (2d Cir. 1977), *cert. denied,* 434 U.S. 1069 (1978). *Goldberg* is one of a number of post-*Santa Fe* federal appellate decisions which generally recognize a cause of action under Section 10(b) where the alleged misrepresentation or omission, if it had been disclosed, would have provided the aggrieved shareholder with the opportunity to enjoin the transaction in state court. *See* Healey v. Catalyst Recovery, Inc., 616 F.2d 641 (3rd Cir. 1980); Alabama Farm Bureau Mut. Cas. Co. v. American Fidelity

has no obligation under the federal securities laws to disclose its "true purpose" or "motivation."

The application of this principle can be seen in *Biesenbach v. Guenther*.[99] The plaintiffs in that case alleged that the defendant directors had recommended certain loan transactions as being in the corporation's and shareholders' best interests when, in actuality, the loans benefited the defendants personally. Rejecting the plaintiffs' claim, the United States Court of Appeals for the Third Circuit stated that

> it is bemusing, and ultimately pointless, to charge that directors perpetrated a "material omission" when they failed to (a) discover and adjudge faithless motives for their actions and (b) announce such a discovery in reporting the products of their managerial efforts and judgment. The securities laws, while their central insistence is upon disclosure, were never intended to attempt any such measures of psychoanalysis or reported self-analysis. The unclean heart of a director is not actionable, whether or not it is "disclosed," unless the impurities are translated into actionable deeds or omissions both objective and external.[100]

This "objective" approach to disclose has been adopted by several other courts.[101] For example, in *Rodman v. Grant Foundation,* the plaintiff argued

---

Life Ins. Co., 606 F.2d 602 (5th Cir. 1979), *cert. denied,* 446 U.S. 933 (1980); Kidwell v. Meikle, 597 F.2d 1273 (9th Cir. 1979); Wright v. Heizer Corp., 560 F.2d 237 (7th Cir. 1977), *cert. denied,* 434 U.S. 1066 (1978). These cases provide an exception to the Supreme Court's decision in Santa Fe Indus. v. Green, 430 U.S. 462, 474-77 (1977), which held that, absent deception or manipulation, there can be no actionable claim under Section 10(b) and Rule 10b-5 for breach of fiduciary duty. For an analysis of *Santa Fe* and subsequent developments in the federal and state courts herein, *see* pages 163-98 *infra.*

99. 588 F.2d 400 (3d Cir. 1978).

100. *Id.* at 402 (quoting Lavin v. Data Systems Analysis, Inc., 443 F. Supp. 107 (E.D. Pa. 1977)). In reaching its decision, the Third Circuit relied on the Supreme Court's decision in *Santa Fe. See* note 98 *supra.* In *Biesenbach,* the Third Circuit stated in this regard:

> *Santa Fe* made it clear that absent deception, misrepresentation, or nondisclosure a breach of fiduciary duty does not violate the statute or Rule. Appellants believe that the misrepresentations and omissions that occurred in this case were: (1) the misleading statements by defendants that the transactions were in the best interests of the shareholders and (2) the defendants' failure to disclose the true purpose behind the activities. In effect, appellants are stating that the failure to disclose the breach of fiduciary duty is a misrepresentation sufficient to constitute a violation of the Act. We refuse to adopt this approach which would clearly circumvent the Supreme Court's holding in *Santa Fe.*

Biesenbach v. Guenther, 588 F.2d at 402 (citation omitted).

101. *See, e.g.,* Selk v. St. Paul Ammonia Prods., Inc., 597 F.2d 635, 639 (8th Cir. 1979) (failure to disclose that purpose of merger was to freeze-out minority shareholders not actionable under Sections 10(b) and 14(a)); O'Brien v. Continental Ill. Nat'l Bank & Trust Co., 593 F.2d

that the defendants' desire to entrench their control was the principal, if not the sole, reason for a stock repurchase program and that this desire should have been disclosed to shareholders.[102] Rejecting the plaintiff's contention, the United States Court of Appeals for the Second Circuit concluded that, since "the proposed actions of the company and their effect on stockholdings were fully disclosed,"[103] there was no actionable claim under Section 14(a).[104] Similarly, the United States Court of Appeals for the Eighth Circuit, characterizing the plaintiff's allegations as seeking to require management to disclose its subjective motivations, commented that

> the plaintiffs are not complaining about any absence of facts in the proxy statement. Their complaint is that those who prepared the statement did not "disclose" what the plaintiffs say was the true motivation of Old PPD's management in selling the assets of the company, and did not characterize the bonus aspect of the transaction as plaintiffs would have it characterized. Under the Act and regulations plaintiffs were not entitled to have such a "disclosure" or such a characterization.[105]

In another recent case, *Bucher v. Shumway*,[106] the complaint alleged that the defendants had failed to disclose that the true purpose of separate tender

---

54, 60 (7th Cir. 1979) (failure to reveal that investment advice was self-serving not actionable under Section 10(b)); Gluck v. Agemian, 495 F. Supp. 1209, 1214 (S.D.N.Y. 1980) ("disclosure of subjective motive is not required under the federal securities laws"); Hundahl v. United Benefit Life Ins. Co., 465 F. Supp. 1349, 1364 (N.D. Tex. 1979) (failure to disclose breach of fiduciary duty or scheme to undervalue company not actionable under Section 10(b)).

102. 608 F.2d 64 (2d Cir. 1979).

103. *Id.* at 71.

104. *Id.* The court reasoned:

> The district court also held that corporate control is recognized to be of universal interest to corporate officers and directors and that the failure of proxy materials to disclose this subjective interest is not a violation of the securities laws. There is much support for this position. In Doyle v. Milton, 73 F. Supp. 281, 286 (S.D.N.Y. 1947), then Judge Rifkind asked, "assuming that data are supplied, is the proxy statement nevertheless false if it omits a confession of selfish motive." Pointing out that SEC regulation X-14, now Regulation 14A, 17 C.F.R. § 2440.14a-1 *et seq.*, does not require the inclusion of statements as to motive, he answered the question in the negative. Citing *Doyle* with approval, we stated in Crane Co. v. Westinghouse Air Brake Co., 419 F.2d 787, 803 (2d Cir. 1969), *cert. denied,* 400 U.S. 822, 91 S. Ct. 41, 27 L.Ed.2d 50 (1970) that "it is sufficient that the relevant facts were fairly stated in the proxy statement."

Id. The Second Circuit, however, has developed a limited exception to this principle. *See* notes 108 and 109 and accompanying text *infra.*

105. Golub v. PPD Corp., 576 F.2d 759, 765 (8th Cir. 1978). The Eighth Circuit subsequently reaffirmed the conclusion reached in *Golub.* Selk v. St. Paul Ammonia Prods., Inc., 597 F.2d 635, 639 (8th Cir. 1979) (failure to disclose that purpose of merger was to freeze-out minority shareholders not actionable under Sections 10(b) and 14(a)).

106. [1979-1980 Transfer Binder] FED. SEC. L. REP. (CCH) ¶ 97,142 (S.D.N.Y. Oct. 11, 1979), *aff'd,* 622 F.2d 572 (2d Cir.), *cert. denied,* 449 U.S. 841 (1980).

offers by the defendants was to consolidate Signal management's control, and thereby prevent competing offers. Relying on the "true purpose" cases, which preclude judicial examination of management's motivations, the court concluded that the required facts had been adequately disclosed.[107]

It nevertheless appears that management's "true purpose" may have to be disclosed under certain circumstances. Although recognizing in *Rodman* that "corporate control is of universal interest to corporate officers and directors and that failure of proxy materials to disclose this subjective interest is not a violation of the securities laws,"[108] the United States Court of Appeals for the Second Circuit indicated that retention of "some ulterior wrongful design hinging upon so-called 'entrenchment' " would be required to be disclosed.[109] Similarly, the United States Court of Appeals for the Fifth Circuit held as material management's failure to disclose its "program of maintaining control at the cost of inflating stock prices."[110] Although it is difficult to draw a clear conclusion, these two cases arguably stand for the proposition that when management embarks on a particular course of conduct for the purpose of perpetuating its control, disclosure of that design may be required.

The United States Court of Appeals for the Ninth Circuit has taken a possibly different approach. In *Vaughn v. Teledyne, Inc.,*[111] a shareholder alleged that a series of tender offers and acquisitions had been consummated as part of a management conspiracy to obtain greater control of the company, and that this scheme should have been disclosed. Although denying the shareholder's contention, the court enunciated a doctrine that may have broad implications: "Corporate officials are under no duty to disclose their precise motive or purpose for engaging in a particular course of corporate action, *so long as* the motive is not manipulative or deceptive and the nature and scope of any stock transaction are adequately disclosed to those involved."[112] The court's language implies that, if management intends to

---

107. [1979-1980 Transfer Binder] FED. SEC. L. REP. (CCH) at 96,299-300.

108. Rodman v. Grant Foundation, 608 F.2d at 71.

109. *Id.*

110. Alabama Farm Bureau Mut. Cas. Co. v. American Fidelity Life Ins. Co., 606 F.2d 602, 614 (5th Cir. 1979), *cert. denied,* 446 U.S. 933 (1980).

111. 628 F.2d 1214 (9th Cir. 1980).

112. *Id.* at 1221 (emphasis added). *See* SEC v. C & R Clothiers, Inc., [1980 Transfer Binder] FED SEC. L. REP. (CCH) ¶ 97,650 (D.D.C. Oct. 2, 1980) (consent decree), where the SEC alleged that, in structuring an issuer tender offer to benefit the two largest shareholders, the company had violated Sections 14(a) and 14(e). More particularly, the SEC alleged, *inter alia,* that the tender offer materials failed to disclose adequately "the true purposes and effects of the tender offer [and] that the tender offer is designed and structured to benefit and accommodate the interests of the largest shareholders. . . ." *Id.* at 98,475. Without admitting or denying the allegations in the Commission's complaint, the company consented to an injunction against future violations and to certain undertakings "reasonably designed to ensure compliance with the tender offer provisions of the Securities laws." *Id. See also* FSC Corp., SEC Securities Exchange Release No. 17892, 22 SEC DOCKET 1374, [1981 Transfer Binder] FED SEC. L. REP. (CCH) ¶ 82,886 (June 25, 1981). *See* note 116 *infra.*

manipulate the price of the issuer's stock or to deceive investors, disclosure of management's "true purpose" or motivation is required. Such a subjective approach would signify a marked departure from the objective disclosure rationale.[113] It appears, however, that in order to require disclosure of management's "subjective motive," the complainant must show that the motive was manipulative or deceptive, or that there was inadequate disclosure. In other words, under the court's approach, the complainant is in a quandary — to warrant disclosure of subjective motive, he apparently must first establish a successful cause of action. Thus, in all practicality, even if the court's approach represents a departure from the objective disclosure rationale, the extent of its substantive impact must await further judicial construction.[114]

It should be emphasized, however, that the same salutary result of adequate and fair disclosure frequently can be achieved by requiring the *effect* of management's course of conduct to be disclosed. For example, if management takes action to perpetuate its control, it should be required to disclose that the effect of such action is to solidify its position, rendering hostile takeover attempts less likely to occur, or at least less probable of succeeding.[115] If such disclosure is made, the shareholder generally will receive all the information needed to make an informed investment or voting decision. The shareholder normally will be able to deduce from this information whether it is in his best interest to sell or retain his stock, to seek the removal of incumbent management, or even to bring an action in state court alleging management's breach of fiduciary duty.[116]

---

113. *See* notes 98-107 and accompanying text *supra*.

114. The Ninth Circuit's potentially different approach may have an impact in some aspects. If the complainant does establish that management's motive was manipulative or deceptive, disclosure of subjective motive may enhance the recovery obtained. This is particularly true in SEC actions where procurement of injunctive relief requires a showing that there exists a reasonable likelihood that the defendant, absent an injunction, will again engage in violative conduct. Subjective motive is relevant to this determination. *See* Aaron v. SEC, 446 U.S. 680, 701 (1980); SEC v. Falstaff Brewing Corp., 629 F.2d 62, 77-78 (D.C. Cir. 1980); SEC v. Mize, 615 F.2d 1046, 1051 (5th Cir.), *cert. denied*, 449 U.S. 901 (1980); Steinberg, *SEC and Other Permanent Injunctions—Standards for Their Imposition, Modification and Dissolution,* 66 CORNELL L. REV. 27 (1980). In practice, however, the Ninth Circuit's language seems difficult to apply to any given case. Hopefully, that court will elaborate on the significance of this language in future decisions. At this point, it is premature to conclude that the Ninth Circuit has adopted a new rationale.

115. *See* SEC Securities Exchange Act Release No. 15230, 15 SEC DOCKET 1311, 1313, [1978 Transfer Binder] FED. SEC. L. REP. (CCH) ¶ 81,748, at 80,985 (Oct. 13, 1978), where the Commission's Division of Corporation Finance issued a statement regarding disclosure of antitakeover or similar proposals in proxy and information statements. In particular, the staff expressed its opinion that "the issuer's proxy material or information statements should disclose in a prominent place that the overall effect of the proposal is to render more difficult the accomplishment of mergers or the assumption of control by a principal stockholder, and thus to make difficult the removal of management."

116. *See* Steinberg, *Fiduciary Duties and Disclosure Obligations in Proxy and Tender Contests for Corporate Control,* 30 EMORY L.J. 167, 203-08 (1981). Moreover, regardless of case

IV. QUESTIONABLE AND ILLEGAL PAYMENTS

Cases involving questionable or illegal payments by corporations generally have not involved practices of self-dealing by management.[117] Yet to the extent that such payments involve substantial amounts of corporate funds or significant risk of expropriation or loss of business, they may be deemed quantitatively material. Nondisclosure or falsification of this information may violate specific disclosure items of the proxy, reporting, and registration provisions,[118] or generally accepted accounting principles requiring accrual or disclosure of contingent liabilities in the registrant's financial statements.[119] Moreover, the Commission in the past has taken the position that, even if questionable or illegal payments are not quantitatively material, disclosure of such payments may be required because of their bearing on management's competency or integrity.[120]

---

law, it is clear that certain Commission disclosure requirements provide that purpose must be revealed. *See* Schedule 13D, Item 4, 17 C.F.R. § 240.13d-101 (1982); Schedule 13E-3, Item 7(a), *id.* § 240.13e-100. With respect to case law regarding disclosure of purpose pursuant to Section 13(e)(1) and Rule 13e-1, *see, e.g.,* Crane Co. v. Harsco Corp., 511 F. Supp. 294, 301 (D. Del. 1981). *See also* SEC proceedings discussed, note 112 *supra*; Steinberg, *The "True Purpose" Cases,* 5 Corp. L. Rev. 249 (1982).

117. *See* notes 118-47 and accompanying text *infra.*

118. *See, e.g.,* Item 15, Schedule 14A, 17 C.F.R. § 240.14a-101 (1982).

119. *See Statement of Financial Accounting Standard No. 5: Accounting for Contingencies,* in Financial Accounting Standards Board, Financial Accounting Standards 732 (1975). FAS 5 requires accrual in the financial statements or disclosure in the notes to the financials of certain contingent liabilities. Paragraph 8 of FAS 5 requires *accrual* of "loss contigencies" as a charge to income if it is probable that an asset has been impaired or a liability incurred at the date of the issuance of financial statements, *and* the amount of the loss can be reasonably estimated. *Id.* at 734. If both of these tests are met, then disclosure of the loss contingency must be made in the notes to the financials if there is a reasonable possibility that a loss has occurred. The possibility of "unasserted claims" against the company must be disclosed if it is probable that a claim will be asserted and a reasonable possibility exists that the outcome will be unfavorable. *Id.* Some examples in FAS 5 of contingent liabilities include threat of expropriation, pending or threatened litigation, and actual or possible claims and assessments. *Id.* at 738-40. Therefore, illegal payments which might result in expropriation of assets, loss of contracts, or claims against the company may be required to be disclosed in the registrant's financials or notes to the financials if the above standards are satisfied.

120. This concern was stressed in the SEC Questionable Payments Report, note 2 *supra.* Stating that "investors should be vitally interested in the quality and integrity of management," the Commission emphasized that disclosure of conflicts of interest and special perquisites to management underscores

> the deeply held belief that the managements of corporations are stewards acting on behalf of the shareholders, who are entitled to honest use of, and accounting for, the funds entrusted to the corporation and to procedures necessary to assure accountability and disclosure of the manner in which management performs its stewardship.

Id. at 20.

The Commission, in an introduction to the report, pointed to illegal and questionable payments as proof that our system of corporate accountability had been frustrated. The system

In actions brought by the Commission alleging inadequate disclosure of questionable or illegal payments, the Commission usually has invoked Sections 10(b), 13(a), and 14(a) of the Exchange Act and various rules thereunder. Because practically all of the cases are settled pursuant to the consent negotiation process, where the defendant neither admits nor denies the Commission's allegations,[121] there is little judicial authority on whether such payments must be disclosed because they are qualitatively material. Two cases, however, lend support to the Commission's position.[122]

In *SEC v. Joseph Schlitz Brewing Co.*,[123] the Commission alleged that the defendant had failed to disclose a nationwide scheme of bribing retailers of beer and malt beverages to purchase Schlitz' products and also had failed to disclose its alleged violation of Spanish law in falsifying its books and records regarding payments and transactions with certain Spanish corporations described as affiliates. Denying Schlitz' motion to dismiss, the court concluded that "the question of the integrity of management gives materiality to the matters the Commission claims should be disclosed."[124]

In a second federal court case, *Berman v. Gerber Products Co.*,[125] the court held that the Williams Act[126] required a tender offeror to disclose

---

was designed to ensure that there is proper accounting for the use of corporate funds and that the documents presented to the Commission neither misstate nor misrepresent material facts. The Commission presented its basic approach to restore integrity to the system of corporate accountability by (1) ensuring that investors and shareholders receive material facts necessary to make informed investment decisions and to assess the quality of management; and (2) establishing a climate in which corporate management and the professionals that advise them become fully aware of accountability problems and deal with them in an effective and responsible manner. *Id.*

The Commission was of the view that questionable or illegal payments, if known to the board of directors, could be grounds for disclosure, regardless of the size of the payment itself or its impact on business. The Commission reasoned that situations involving corporate officials willing to make repeated illegal payments without board knowledge and without proper accounting raise questions regarding the proper exercise of corporate authority, which might be relevant to the "quality of management." Therefore, illegal payments are appropriate topics for disclosure to shareholders. *Id.* at 15.

121. *See, e.g.,* SEC v. Page Airways, Inc., [1979-1980 Transfer Binder] FED. SEC. L. REP. (CCH) ¶ 97,341 (W.D.N.Y. 1980).

122. Berman v. Gerber Prods. Co., 454 F. Supp. 1310 (W.D. Mich. 1978); SEC v. Jos. Schlitz Brewing Co., 452 F. Supp. 824 (E.D. Wis. 1978). *But see* Gaines v. Haughton, 645 F.2d 761 (9th Cir. 1981), *cert. denied*, 102 S. Ct. 1006 (1982); Lewis v. Valley, 476 F. Supp. 62 (S.D.N.Y. 1979).

123. 452 F. Supp. 824 (E.D. Wis. 1978).

124. *Id.* at 830 (citing SEC v. Kalvex, Inc., 425 F. Supp. 310 (S.D.N.Y. 1975) and Cooke v. Teleprompter Corp., 344 F. Supp. 467 (S.D.N.Y. 1971)).

125. 454 F. Supp. 1310 (W.D. Mich. 1978).

126. Pub. L. No. 90-439, 82 Stat. 454 (1968) (codified at 15 U.S.C. §§ 78m(d)-(e), 78n(d)-(f) (1976)). The Williams Act amended the Exchange Act by adding Sections 13(d)-(e) and 14(d)-(f). According to its sponsor, Senator Harrison Williams of New Jersey, the Act was designed to protect shareholders through full disclosure and "to avoid tipping the scales either

information relating to the competence and integrity of its management.[127] Under the circumstances of that case, the court concluded that this broad policy required the offeror to disclose which members of its management had taken part in a foreign payments scheme. The court reasoned that

> [i]n circumstances where actions by some members of corporate management have been challenged as being questionable, if not outright illegal, and such actions have indeed been acknowledged by the corporation itself, it is certainly necessary that stockholders have knowledge of the individuals involved and the activities which transpired in

---

in favor of management or in favor of the person making the takeover bids." 113 CONG. REC. 24664 (1967). *See* Rondeau v. Mosinee Paper Corp., 422 U.S. 49, 59 (1975) (Williams Act designed to protect shareholders without giving unfair advantage to target or bidder); Great W. United Corp. v. Kidwell, 577 F.2d 1256, 1276 (5th Cir. 1978) (underlying purpose of Williams Act is to protect investors through full disclosure by both sides), *rev'd on other grounds sub nom.* Leroy v. Great W. United Corp., 443 U.S. 173 (1979).

127. *But see* InterNorth, Inc. v. Cooper Indus., 80 Civ. 6724 (S.D.N.Y. Jan. 15, 1981), where the court held that a tender offeror, InterNorth, was not required to disclose to target company shareholders that InterNorth's management had acted improperly by threatening to terminate business relations with Cooper Industries, a competing tender offeror for Crouse-Hinds Company, if Cooper Industries did not withdraw its tender offer. The court assumed that InterNorth's threat to Cooper Industries was "legally defensible," but stated:

> Nor can we see how InterNorth can be faulted for not revealing its conduct to Crouse-Hinds stockholders. InterNorth's proposal to the stockholders is that they surrender their stock for cash. They could therefore have no real interest in InterNorth's moral character or business practices. If a stockholder decided to accept the cash he would have no further connection with InterNorth and could not be concerned with the question whether or not any deficiency in its moral character might someday lead into financial difficulties.
>
> The only relevance InterNorth's threat could have to Crouse-Hind's stockholders would be to alert them to the possibility that Cooper's stock might decline if the threat were carried out or that Cooper might withdraw its offer to prevent such a result. However, either of such considerations could only make the InterNorth offer more attractive.

Id. The court's holding in *InterNorth*, which acknowledges that the moral character of management may be quantitatively material, in the sense that it could create financial difficulties for a company in the future, appears to ignore situations in which a subject company shareholder, believing that the company will prosper under the bidder's management, chooses not to tender shares. These shareholders, whose financial interest in their company would continue after new management assumes control, would clearly have an interest in the moral character of management, assuming, as the court apparently did, that such character traits may engender financial difficulties for the company in the future.

Subsequently, the Commission suggested that the court modify its opinion asserting that the court's

> statement does not take into account those situations in which a subject company shareholder, perhaps believing that the company will prosper under the bidder's management, chooses not to tender or to tender only a portion of his or her shares; or

order that they may have a full opportunity to appraise those activities and the participants. Such activities bear the closest relationship to the integrity of management.[128]

Departing from the rationale of the above two cases, the United States Court of Appeals for the Ninth Circuit, in an action involving, *inter alia,* proxies solicited for elections of directors, distinguished between allegations of director misconduct involving self-dealing and allegations of breach of fiduciary duty. Based on this distinction, the court held that payment of "mere" bribes not involving kickbacks to directors is never material under Section 14(a). As a caveat, the court noted that instances of illegal conduct,

---

where, in the case of a tender offer made for less than all of the outstanding shares, only a portion of the tendered shares will be accepted.

Memorandum of the Securities and Exchange Commission at 2, InterNorth, Inc. v. Cooper Indus., 80 Civ. 6724 (S.D.N.Y. Jan. 15, 1981). The Commission concluded that in such situations, "the shareholders would have an acute interest in the 'moral character or business practices' of a bidder should it be successful because the shareholder's financial stake in the resulting company will continue after the tender offer is over and the bidder assumes control." *Id.* at 3. Because the case in question had been closed, the court denied the Commission's request. However, the court remarked that it had not considered these legal contentions in its earlier opinion. *See* InterNorth, Inc. v. Cooper Indus., 80 Civ. 6724 (S.D.N.Y. Jan. 29, 1981) (order denying motion to modify opinion).

Cf. Humana, Inc. v. American Medicorp. Inc., 77 Civ. 4809 (S.D.N.Y. Jan. 7, 1978) (bench opinion), *discussed in* M. LIPTON & E. STEINBERGER, TAKEOVERS AND FREEZEOUTS § 3.2.14 (1978) (court stated that a bidder's failure to disclose that its parent company had made $1,000,000 in questionable payments to foreign officials was not a material omission).

128. *See* Berman v. Gerber Prods. Co., 454 F. Supp. at 1322-23. Regarding disclosure of management competence and integrity under the Williams Act, the court stated:

As seen in the legislative history discussed above, Congress in enacting the Williams Act clearly intended that information with respect to the integrity of the tender offeror's management be disclosed. The Report of the House Committee which accompanied the Act stated: "The competence and integrity of a company's management, and of the persons who seek management positions, are of vital importance to the stockholder. Secrecy in this area is inconsistent with the expectations of the people who invest in the securities of publicly held corporations and impairs public confidence in securities as a medium of investment." H.R. No. 1711, 90th Cong., 2d Sess, *reprinted in U.S. Code Cong. & Admin. News,* 2811-12 (1968). The authors of the Act were similarly direct in expressing the crucial importance of exposing to public view the corporate activities of managing executives so that their competence and integrity can be evaluated.

Id. See Decker v. Massey-Ferguson, Limited, 681 F.2d 111, 118 (2d Cir. 1982) ("We believe that plaintiff's claim based upon the making of undisclosed, allegedly wrongful payments by a number of Massey's foreign subsidiaries was sufficient to get plaintiff by the pleading stage"). Ross v. Warner, [1980 Transfer Binder] FED. SEC. L. REP. (CCH) ¶ 97,735, at 98,861 (S.D.N.Y. 1980) (finding that GTE's nondisclosure of its questionable payments was material, the court stated that "[i]f nothing else, GTE's failure to disclose its practices left it susceptible to suits like this one—a prospect which investors are substantially likely to consider in making their investment decisions").

particularly criminal convictions, even though unrelated to self-dealing, must be disclosed. Accordingly, the court limited its holding to disclosure of noncriminal conduct in proxy solicitations involving an election of directors. The court premised its holding on the belief that reasonable investors are concerned with only financially significant information and that requiring disclosure in this context would usurp state corporation law.[129]

The Ninth Circuit's decision, in refusing to recognize in a voting context the materiality of noncriminal director misconduct other than self-dealing, fails to perceive that disclosure of questionable payments is within the purview of Section 14(a). Disclosure of such information, particularly in an election contest, is essential if shareholders are to evaluate the fitness of nominees to serve as fiduciaries of the corporate trust. Moreover, to assert, as the Ninth Circuit held, that requiring this type of disclosure impinges upon state corporation law is misplaced. The fundamental precept underlying the federal securities laws is that of adequate and fair disclosure. Far from being a subject within the province of state law, disclosure of such questionable payments, particularly in an election contest, lies at the very heart of the proxy provisions.

Further, the Ninth Circuit's implication that no reasonable shareholder would find the authorizing of such bribes material reflects a misunderstanding of shareholder suffrage. To be sure, shareholders are primarily interested in obtaining the maximum economic return on their investment. But many are also concerned that the corporations in which they invest and the nominees for whom they vote conduct themselves in accord with certain minimal ethical standards. Allegations that defendant directors authorized, employed, and affirmatively concealed corrupt business practices, including outright bribes to foreign government officials, if true, would be material to reasonable shareholders who are being asked to reelect these same directors. Thus, the Ninth Circuit's unduly restrictive conclusion, which threatens the sal-

---

129. Gaines v. Haughton, 645 F.2d 761, 776-79 (9th Cir. 1981), *cert denied*, 102 S. Ct. 1006 (1982). The court stated in part:

> Absent credible allegations of self-dealing by the directors or dishonesty or deceit which inures to the direct, personal benefit of the directors—a fact that demonstrates a betrayal of trust to the corporation and to shareholders and the director's essential unfitness for corporate stewardship—we hold that director misconduct of the type traditionally regulated by state corporate law need not be disclosed in proxy solicitations for director elections. This type of mismanagement, unadorned by self-dealing, is simply not material or otherwise within the ambit of the federal securities laws. A contrary holding would place an unwarranted premium on the form rather than the substance of a shareholder's complaint and, moreover, would represent a move toward the federalization of corporate law that the Supreme Court has repeatedly and emphatically rejected.

Id. at 779 (citations omitted).

utary disclosure mandate of the federal securities laws, hopefully will not be adopted by other courts.[130]

Turning next to the transactional causation requirement, in several derivative actions under Section 14(a), courts have dismissed suits seeking *damages* for management's nondisclosure of questionable foreign payments.[131] The rationale underlying these decisions is that there is not a sufficient causal nexus between the allegedly defective proxy materials and alleged damage to the corporation.[132] As noted by one commentator:

---

130. *See* Memorandum of *Amicus Curiae*, Securities and Exchange Commission, in Support of Petition for Rehearing and Rehearing *En Banc*, Gaines v. Haughton, No. 79-3336 (9th Cir. 1981). *See also* Johnson, *The Business Judgement Rule: A Review of Its Application to the Problem of Illegal Foreign Payments*, 6 J. Corp. L. 481, 508 (1981); *Concern for Issues Fills Some Investors*, Chi. Tribune, Sept. 15, 1981, § 3, at 3-4 ("a recent study by Georgeson & Co., an investor relations consultant, found that 20 per cent of a random sample of stock investors in seven companies rated corporate social responsibility performance as an important factor in their investment;" such investors range "from unions and pension funds to individuals").

131. *See, e.g.,* Gaines v. Haughton, 645 F.2d at 774-76; Abbey v. Control Data Corp., 603 F.2d 724, 732 (8th Cir. 1979), *cert denied,* 444 U.S. 1017 (1980); Zilker v. Klein, 510 F. Supp. 1070 (N.D. Ill. 1981); Nemo v. Allen, 466 F. Supp. 192 (S.D.N.Y. 1979); Herman v. Beretta, [1978 Transfer Binder] Fed. Sec. L. Rep. (CCH) ¶ 96,574 (S.D.N.Y. Oct. 10, 1978); *In re* Tenneco Sec. Litigation, [1978 Transfer Binder] Fed. Sec. L. Rep. (CCH) ¶ 96,492 (S.D. Tex. Apr. 28, 1978); Kammerman v. Pakco Cos. [1978 Transfer Binder] Fed. Sec. L. Rep. (CCH) ¶ 96,318 (S.D.N.Y. Feb 6, 1978); Lewis v. Elam, [1977-1978 Transfer Binder] Fed. Sec. L. Rep. (CCH) ¶ 96,013 (S.D.N.Y. Apr. 5, 1977); Levy v. Johnson, [1976-1977 Transfer Binder] Fed. Sec. L. Rep. (CCH) ¶ 95,899 (S.D.N.Y. Feb. 15, 1977).

132. As stated by one court,

> Plaintiff's argument, that "but for" the proxy violations the defendant directors would not have been re-elected and could not have authorized the alleged improper payments, does not meet the transaction causation standard. If the court were to adopt the plaintiff's standard, any suppression of a director's impropriety in proxy materials for re-election, followed by further impropriety after re-election, would state a claim under federal law. It was not intended that, by reasons of a proxy violation, a purely state claim might be transformed into a federal cause of action.

Levy v. Johnson, [1976-1977 Transfer Binder] Fed. Sec. L. Rep. (CCH) ¶ 95,899, at 91,324 (S.D.N.Y. Feb. 15, 1977); *Accord,* cases cited in note 131 *supra.*

The SEC is not required to show such a causal connection in its enforcement actions. As stated by the district court in *Schlitz:*

> Schlitz has cited no case in which an SEC complaint was dismissed for failure to plead or prove an injury proximately caused by a Section 14(a) violation. . . .
>
> The Commission cogently argues that to accept Schlitz' argument would emasculate the Commission's powers under section 21(d) of the Securities Exchange Act . . . to enjoin violations before they occur or reoccur. To establish a claim under § 14(a), the Commission need only to allege a material violation of the proxy rules.

SEC v. Jos. Schlitz Brewing Co., 452 F. Supp. at 832.

where a complaint alleges that the election of directors pursuant to allegedly deficient proxy materials results in a continuation of allegedly improper and undisclosed business practices, several courts have held that the subsequent acts are too remote from the election to provide the requisite causal nexus between the proxy solicitation and the alleged damage.[133]

Although the transactional causation requirement may act as a bar to shareholder derivative suits seeking monetary damages, it appears that non-disclosure of questionable payments may be actionable if the suit seeks to set aside the election of directors procured through allegedly misleading proxy materials, particularly when a management cover-up or kickback scheme is alleged. The leading decision in this area is *Weisberg v. Coastal States Gas Corp.*[134] In that case the plaintiff shareholder sought to have the election of officers set aside, claiming that the proxy statements were inadequate because they did not disclose that the company had paid eight million dollars in bribes and that the directors thereafter had concealed the wrongful activity.[135] Distinguishing cases which had dismissed claims for failure to meet the transactional causation requirement, the United States Court of Appeals for the Second Circuit concluded that the plaintiff had satisfied this requirement. The court reasoned that the proxy solicitation was an essential link in the accomplishment of the challenged transaction, *i.e.,* the election of the directors.[136] Accordingly, the court stated that the plaintiff should have an opportunity to prove the materiality of the questionable payment information omitted from the proxy materials.[137] The court commented further that if the payment of bribes were coupled with a cover-up or kickbacks, such "a cover-up of massive bribes and of kickbacks to the directors . . . would be material to the shareholders in deciding whether to reelect directors. . . ."[138] In conclusion, the court emphasized that share-

---

133. Block & Barton, *The Business Judgment Rule as Applied to Stockholder Proxy Derivative Suits Under the Securities Exchange Act,* 8 SEC. REG. L.J. 99, 115 (1980).

134. 609 F.2d 650 (2d Cir. 1979), *cert denied,* 445 U.S. 951 (1980). *See also* Gaines v. Haughton, 645 F.2d at 778-79 (credible allegations of bribes coupled with kickbacks essential to maintain action); Herman v. Beretta, [1980 Transfer Binder] FED. SEC. L. REP. (CCH) ¶ 97,685 (S.D.N.Y. Nov. 7, 1980) (*Weisberg* distinguished on basis that shareholder's suit to void the election of directors was moot).

135. Weisberg v. Coastal States Gas Corp., 609 F.2d at 651.

136. *Id.* at 654 (following Mills v. Electric Auto-Lite Co., 396 U.S. 375, 385-88 (1970)).

137. Weisberg v. Coastal States Gas Corp., 609 F.2d at 654-55.

138. *Id.* at 655. *See also* Gaines v. Haughton, 645 F.2d 761, 778 (9th Cir. 1981) ("The distinction between 'mere' bribes and bribes coupled with kickbacks to the directors makes a great deal of sense, indeed, is fundamental to a meaningful concept of materiality under § 14(a) and the preservation of state corporate law").

holders are entitled "to truthful presentation of factual information concerning the honesty of directors in their dealings with the corporation."[139]

In addition to these cases, the Foreign Corrupt Practices Act ("FCPA")[140] lends additional authority for requiring disclosure of illegal foreign payments based on a qualitative materiality rationale. The FCPA, *inter alia,* amended Section 13(b) of and added Section 30A to the Exchange Act. Generally, Section 30A prohibits public companies, and others acting on their behalf, from bribing foreign government officials or foreign political parties for the purpose of obtaining or retaining business, or of directing business to any other person.[141] The amendment to Section 13(b) is found in Subsection 13(b)(2). Part A of Subsection 13(b)(2) requires publicly held companies to "make and keep books, records, and accounts, which, in reasonable detail, accurately and fairly reflect the transactions and dispositions of the[ir] assets."[142] Part B of Subsection 13(b)(2) requires these companies to "devise and maintain a system of internal accounting controls sufficient to provide reasonable assurances that" transactions are executed in compliance with management's authorization and recorded in accordance with generally accepted accounting principles, and that access to and accountability for assets are adequately controlled.[143] To promote compliance with Subsection 13(b)(2), the Commission has adopted rules which proscribe the falsification of any book, record, or account, and the making of any materially false, misleading, or incomplete statement to an accountant in connection with any audit or

---

139. Weisberg v. Coastal States Gas Corp., 609 F.2d at 655 (following Maldonado v. Flynn, 597 F.2d 789, 796 (2d Cir. 1979)). The court stated that "[b]ecause plaintiff's allegations of a cover-up of massive bribes and of kickbacks to the directors, if true, would be material to the shareholders in deciding whether to reelect directors, we conclude that plaintiff's complaint was prematurely dismissed." Weisberg v. Coastal States Gas Corp., 609 F.2d at 655. *See* Kaplan v. Bennett, 465 F. Supp. 555, 565-66 (S.D.N.Y. 1979), where the court implied that nondisclosure of illegal or questionable payments may be actionable under Section 10(b) and Rule 10b-5.

140. Pub. L. No. 95-213, title I, 91 Stat. 1494 (1977).

141. 15 U.S.C. § 78dd-1 (Supp. III 1979). *See Impact of the Antibribery Prohibitions in Section 30A of the Securities Exchange Act of 1934,* SEC Securities Exchange Act Release No. 16593, 19 SEC DOCKET 691, [1979-1980 Transfer Binder] FED. SEC. L. REP. (CCH) ¶ 82,454 (Feb. 21, 1980). Enforcement of the FCPA is divided between the SEC as to public companies and the Justice Department as to all others. *See generally* Gruenbaum & Steinberg, *Accountants' Liability and Responsibility: Securities, Criminal and Common Law,* 13 LOY. L.A.L. REV. 247, 287 n.216 (1980); Timmeny, *SEC Enforcement of the Foreign Corrupt Practices Act,* 2 LOY. L.A. INT'L & COMP. L. ANN. 25 (1979).

142. 15 U.S.C. § 78m(b)(2)(A) (Supp. III 1979). *See generally* American Bar Association, Committee on Corporate Law and Accounting, *A Guide to the New Section 13(b)(2) Accounting Provisions of the Securities Exchange Act of 1934,* 34 BUS. LAW. 307, 313-16 (1978).

143. 15 U.S.C. § 78m(b)(2)(B) (Supp. III 1979). *See generally* American Bar Association Committee on Corporate Law and Accounting, *supra* note 142, at 316-20.

examination of the registrant's financial statements or the filing of required reports.[144]

There can be little question that the FCPA and the rules promulgated thereunder will have a deterrent effect on questionable and illegal payments.[145] The FCPA may also provide the SEC with a potent enforcement tool to require corporate *recording* of information relating to management's integrity, possibly without the application of traditional standards of materiality.[146] The FCPA's effect on *disclosure* of such information to investors,

---

144. SEC Securities Exchange Act Release No. 15570, 16 SEC DOCKET 1143, [1979 Transfer Binder] FED. SEC. L. REP. (CCH) ¶ 81,959 (Feb. 15, 1979) (hereinafter cited as SEC Release No. 15570). On the other hand, the Commission has declined to adopt proposed rules which would have required a public company's management to render its opinion on the effectiveness of the company's internal controls, and also would have mandated that the company's independent accountants examine and report on management's opinion. *See* SEC Securities Exchange Act Release No. 15772, 17 SEC DOCKET 421, [1979 Transfer Binder] FED. SEC. L. REP. (CCH) ¶ 82,063 (Apr. 30, 1979). *See also* Gruenbaum & Steinberg, *supra* note 141, at 291-92.

145. As stated in the Senate Report on the FCPA, "[t]he affirmative duties [contained in the accounting provisions] will go a long way to prevent the use of corporate assets for corrupt purposes." S. REP. NO. 114, 95th Cong., 1st Sess. 7 (1977). The Commission has instituted a number of injunctive suits to enforce the provisions of the FCPA. *See, e.g.,* SEC v. Katy Indus., SEC Litigation Release No. 8519, 15 SEC DOCKET 891 (N.D. Ill. Aug. 30, 1978); SEC v. Sisco, SEC Litigation Release No. 8483, 15 SEC DOCKET 536 (S.D.N.Y. July 28, 1978); SEC v. Page Airways, Inc., [1978 Transfer Binder] FED. SEC. L. REP. (CCH) ¶ 96,393 (D.D.C. Apr. 12, 1978), *settled,* [1979-1980 Transfer Binder] FED. SEC. L. REP. (CCH) ¶ 97,341 (W.D.N.Y. Apr. 8, 1980); SEC v. Aminex Res. Corp., [1978 Transfer Binder] FED. SEC. L. REP. (CCH) ¶ 96,352 (D.D.C. Mar. 9, 1978). *See also* Timmeny, *supra* note 141, at 38-39. In addition, Playboy Enterprises consented to the first administrative proceeding brought by the SEC under Section 15(c)(4) to enforce the accounting control requirements of the FCPA. Playboy Enterprises, [1980 Transfer Binder] FED. SEC. L. REP. (CCH) ¶ 82,635 (Aug. 13, 1980).

146. *See* SEC Release No. 15770, *supra* note 144, at 1148 n.25, [1979 Transfer Binder] FED. SEC. L. REP. (CCH) at 81,395 n.25. The apparent lack of a traditional materiality requirement in Section 13(b)(2) has generated much debate. The Commission has stated that the new requirements of Section 13(b)(2)(A) are "qualified by the phrase 'in reasonable detail' rather than by the concept of 'materiality.' " *Id.* at 1150-51, [1979 Transfer Binder] FED. SEC. L. REP. (CCH) at 81,396. "The statute does not require perfection but only that books, records and accounts '*in reasonable detail* accurately and fairly reflect the transactions and dispositions of the assets of the issuer.' " *Id.* at 1151, [1979 Transfer Binder] FED. SEC. L. REP. (CCH) at 81,398. For a discussion of whether a materiality requirement exists under Section 13(b)(2), see American Bar Association, Committee on Corporate Law and Accounting, *Practical Implications of the Accounting Provisions of Foreign Corrupt Practices Act of 1977, and Recent Developments,* 35 BUS. LAW. 1713 (1980).

The FCPA has generated much confusion and controversy. The Commission has reassured the business community that minor or unintentional errors will not be the subject of enforcement action under the FCPA's accounting provisions and that substantial deference will be accorded to reasonable business judgments as to what constitutes an appropriate accountability system for a given enterprise. *See* SEC Securities Exchange Act Release No. 17500, 21 SEC DOCKET 1466, (Jan. 29, 1981). Most recently, the Senate passed a bill which would have amended the FCPA. S. 708, 97th Cong., 1st Sess. (1981). The House of Representatives, however, declined

however, remains uncertain. Although the FCPA's provisions do not specifically mandate disclosure to investors, as a practical matter such disclosure may well result. For example, violations of the FCPA's provisions may be required to be disclosed in Commission filings, particularly if a conviction or injunction ensues from the violation.[147] Thus, although the degree of the FCPA's salutary effect on disclosure practices cannot be ascertained at this time, it appears that the FCPA will have such an effect.

V. ANTISOCIAL, UNLAWFUL OR UNETHICAL COMPANY POLICIES

A. Overview of Case Law

Although antisocial, unlawful or unethical company policies may have a significant bearing on the integrity and competency of management, courts generally have been reluctant to require disclosure of such practices absent an adjudicated illegality, a pending claim, or an instance of self-dealing. It must be emphasized, however, that this subject has been addressed by only a few courts.

The leading decision in this area, although subsequently vacated as moot, is *Amalgamated Clothing & Textile Workers v. J. P. Stevens & Co.*[148] In that case, the plaintiff alleged that Stevens had violated federal proxy law by falsely stating that all nominees for the board of directors were qualified to serve as fiduciaries and omitting to state that the nominees either knowingly and willfully participated in a concerted effort to "thwart" the labor laws or failed to perform their responsibilities by insuring that management did not engage in such practices. The plaintiff sought to set aside Stevens' most recent election of directors and invalidate the elections of Stevens' directors from 1972 through 1978.[149] The district court granted the defendant's motion to dismiss, concluding that the proxy provisions do not require such disclosures for at least two reasons.

---

to act. For a discussion herein of the pertinent provisions of the Senate-passed bill, see page 58, n.229 *supra*.

147. *See, e.g.*, Item 401(f), Regulation S-K, 17 C.F.R. § 229.20 (1982). *See also* note 183 *infra*. Whether an implied private right of action exists to enforce the provisions of the FCPA remains an open question. The SEC has taken the position that such a right of action should be implied. *See Notification of Enactment of Foreign Corrupt Practices Act of 1977,* SEC Accounting Series Release No. 242, 14 SEC DOCKET 180, 182, 6 FED. SEC. L. REP. (CCH) ¶ 72,264 at 62,701 (Feb. 16, 1978). There is also legislative support for this proposition. *See* H.R. REP. No. 640, 95th Cong., 1st Sess. 10 (1977).

148. 475 F. Supp. 328 (S.D.N.Y. 1979), *vacated as moot per curiam*, 638 F.2d 7 (2d Cir. 1980).

149. 475 F. Supp. at 329.

First, the court distinguished the United States Court of Appeals for the Second Circuit's decision in *Maldonado v. Flynn*[150] on the ground that it involved a matter "impugning the loyalty and honesty of directors '*in their dealings with the corporation to which they owe a fiduciary duty.*' "[151] Disclosure is required in such a situation because of the stockholders' interest in director loyalty. Relying on *Maldonado,* the court reasoned that the case at bar involved only a question of management's business judgment, a matter beyond the purview of the federal disclosure provisions. In short, according to the court, mere shareholder disagreement with the efficacy or wisdom of management's course of action does not give rise to a federal claim.[152]

Second, the court held that the federal proxy provisions "do not require management to accuse itself of antisocial or illegal policies."[153] The court commented that, even if the complaint were amended to substitute an intention to "violate" the federal labor laws rather than an intention to "thwart" them, its holding would remain unchanged.[154] As a caveat, the court re-

---

150. 597 F.2d 789 (2d Cir. 1979).

151. Amalgamated Clothing & Textile Workers v. J. P. Stevens & Co., 475 F. Supp. at 330 (emphasis in original) (quoting Maldonado v. Flynn, 597 F.2d 789, 796 (2d Cir. 1979)).

152. The court stated in pertinent part:

> I do not read *Maldonado v. Flynn* as meaning that instances of illegal or immoral conduct are never required to be included in proxy materials unless they relate to self-dealing; nor do I mean to imply so rigid a rule. There are clearly instances of illegal conduct by director-nominees, unrelated to self-dealing, which would have to be disclosed, especially where they involved criminal convictions.
>
> I find rather that the present allegations fall into a category recognized by *Maldonado,* relating to a question of management's business judgment, as to which omissions from proxy materials soliciting re-election of directors are not actionable even if claims of illegality of the sort alleged here are involved. As to plaintiffs' allegation that Stevens' labor policy has resulted in significant expenses, management is clearly not required to submit in proxy statements seeking re-election of directors all business judgments whenever it would be possible for shareholders to disagree with their efficacy or wisdom.

Amalgamated Clothing & Textile Workers v. J. P. Stevens & Co., 475 F. Supp. at 331 (citations omitted).

153. Amalgamated Clothing & Textile Workers v. J. P. Stevens & Co., 475 F. Supp. at 331. Although recognizing that a reasonable shareholder might consider such information important in deciding how to vote, the court characterized such a disclosure requirement as "contrary to human nature" and a "silly, unworkable rule." *Id.* at 332.

154. *Id.* at 331. The court reasoned:

> No matter how the proxy rule is construed, indeed even if it explicitly stated such a duty, corporate management would not announce in proxy literature an intention to violate laws. It is simply contrary to human nature. The rule, if it were construed to require this, would never succeed in its purpose of bringing such disclosure to the shareholders. It would do nothing more than license retrospective litigation, casting doubts on the results of shareholder elections and the legitimacy of management. Such an interpretation would not enhance the accomplishment of the purposes of other proxy rules, but would only create litigation and insecurity in the tenure of management. I

marked that if management sets forth facts to shareholders to establish its innocence, it may well be required to disclose any additional facts necessary to make the statements made, or the general impressions conveyed, not misleading. The court concluded, however, that mere "protestations of innocence of mind . . . do not give rise to an unrealistic obligation to declare guilt."[155]

An earlier decision, inconsistent with *J. P. Stevens,* is *Natural Resources Defense Council, Inc. v. SEC,*[156] in which the court alluded to the qualitative nature of information relating to a corporation's environmental policy. The plaintiffs in that case, desiring broader SEC disclosure rules, sought to require the Commission to modify its corporate disclosure regulations so that each reporting company had to "provide to the SEC for public disclosure information concerning the effect of its corporate activities on the environment and statistics about its equal employment practices."[157] With regard to the environmental portion of the claim, the court discussed the concept of materiality in the context of the relationship between the ethical investor and management:

> There are so many so-called "ethical investors" in this country who want to invest their assets in firms which are concerned about acting on environmental problems of the nation. This attitude may be based purely upon a concern for the environment; but it may also proceed from the recognition that awareness of and sensitivity to environmental problems *is the mark of intelligent management.* Whatever their motive, this court is not prepared to say that they are not rational investors and that the information they seek is not material information within the meaning of the securities laws.[158]

---

conclude that the rule cannot be reasonably interpreted to require reporting of illegal intentions.

Id. at 332.

155. *Id.* at 333. *See* 14 SEC. REG. & L. REP. (BNA) 419 (March 10, 1982) (SEC statement, in declining to bring an enforcement action against Citicorp for alleged foreign tax law violations, reasoned in part that the law regarding disclosure of unadjudicated illegalities is unclear); SEC v. Chicago Helicopter Indus., Civ. No. 79C0469 (N.D. Ill. 1980)("It is unlikely that the materiality requirement of § 10(b) was ever intended to require management to accuse itself of antisocial behavior"), *discussed in* SEC. REG. & L. REP. (BNA) § A, at 4 (Mar. 18, 1981) (remarks of W. Timmeny). *See also* Gaines v. Haughton, 645 F.2d at 776-77 (9th Cir. 1981) ("We draw a sharp distinction . . . between allegations of director misconduct involving breach of trust or self-dealing—the nondisclosure of which is presumptively material—and allegations of simple breach of fiduciary duty/waste of corporate assets—the nondisclosure of which is never material for § 14(a) purposes").

156. 389 F. Supp. 689 (D.D.C. 1974). *See also* Natural Resources Defense Council, Inc. v. SEC, 432 F. Supp. 1190 (D.D.C. 1977), *rev'd,* 606 F.2d 1031 (D.C. Cir. 1979).

157. Natural Resources Defense Council, Inc. v. SEC, 389 F. Supp. at 692.

158. *Id.* at 700 (emphasis added). *See* Stevenson, *supra* note 35, at 58-66.

This indicates that some courts may require disclosure of certain corporate policies bearing on management's competence or integrity, even if no illegality or self-dealing has been alleged. Arguably, under traditional notions of materiality concerning the interests of voting shareholders, such disclosure should sometimes be required. In a number of situations, and particularly in an election for directors,[159] a reasonable shareholder is likely to consider information regarding a company's antisocial or unethical policies important in deciding how to vote. Although a number of shareholders wish solely to maximize their investments, others have a strong concern that the companies in which they have an equity interest comply with certain minimal ethical and legal standards.[160] Labeling such shareholders "unreasonable" or such information "unimportant" discounts a corporation's accountability to its shareholders and to society in general.[161] Further, permitting nondisclosure on the sweeping rationale that it would be contrary to management's interests to disclose such information[162] ignores the fact that, under well-established

---

159. *See generally* TSC Indus. v. Northway, Inc., 426 U.S. 449 (1976).

160. *See generally* Curzan & Pelesh, *Revitalizing Corporate Democracy: Control of Investment Managers' Voting on Social Responsibility Proxy Issues*, 93 HARV. L. REV. 670 (1980); Steinberg, note 116 *supra*.

161. The responsibility of corporations to their shareholders and noninvestor interests is a hotly debated topic. Noninvestor interests may include the corporation's employees, the communities in which it transacts business, and the corporation's responsibility to the environment. For example, in a shareholder derivative suit, the United States Court of Appeals for the Tenth Circuit remarked that

> [a] corporation publishing a newspaper such as the Denver Post certainly has other obligations besides the making of a profit. It has an obligation to the public, that is, the thousands of people who buy the paper, read it, and rely upon its contents. . . .
>
> Such a newspaper corporation, not unlike other corporations, also has an obligation to those people who make its daily publication possible. A great number of the employees are either members of a profession or highly skilled and specialized in their crafts. Many of them have dedicated their lives to this one endeavor. The appellants' sincere interest in their employees also refutes the allegation of illegal design.

Herald Co. v. Seawell, 472 F.2d 1081, 1094-95 (10th Cir. 1972) (interpreting Colorado law). *See* Ferrara & Steinberg, *The Role of Inside Counsel in the Corporate Accountability Process*, 4 CORP. L. REV. 3 (1981); Mace, *Directors: Myth and Reality—Ten Years Later*, 32 RUTGERS L. REV. 293 (1979); Werner, *Management, Stock Market and Corporate Reform: Berle and Means Reconsidered*, 77 COLUM. L. REV. 388 (1977); As recently stated by Irving Shapiro:

> In the past businessmen wore blinders. After hours they would run to their club, play golf with other businessmen, have a martini—and that was about it. They did not see their role as being concerned with public policy issues. In a world where government simply took taxes from you and did not interfere with your corporations, maybe that idea was sensible. In today's world it is not.

Loeb, *The Corporate Chiefs' New Class*, TIME, Apr. 14, 1980, at 87.

162. *See* Amalgamated Clothing & Textile Workers v. J. P. Stevens & Co., 475 F. Supp. at 331-33; note 153 *supra*.

disclosure standards, management must reveal much that is not in its interests.[163]

The *NRDC* opinion may be somewhat problematic in that it suggests a potentially limitless expansion of traditional disclosure principles with respect to information material to the average investor. The court's view that an investor might find a corporation's sensitivity to environmental problems a mark of intelligent management is, at first blush, a logical extension of quantitative materiality, because the intelligence of management would enhance its ability to operate a corporation profitably. Given its logical extension, however, such a materiality concept could encompass innumerable types of information that might have some subjective nexus to the intelligence or competence of management. Faced with such a boundless concept of materiality, registrants would be hard pressed to determine the parameters of the disclosure requirement.[164]

The potential scope of *NRDC*, however, has been narrowed considerably by the Commission's subsequent interpretation of its disclosure mandate and the unique role NEPA plays in the disclosure scheme. The Commission has stated that NEPA requires it to consider the promotion of environmental values in its disclosure process, irrespective of the information's economic materiality.[165] At the same time, however, the Commission has stressed that it is not generally authorized under its broad mandate concerning the public interest "to require disclosure for the sole purpose of promoting social goals unrelated to those underlying [the Securities] Acts."[166]

---

163. *See, e.g.,* Item 402, Regulation S-K, 17 C.F.R. § 229.402 (1982). Unethical or unlawful company policies may be quantitatively material because they may produce substantial contingent liabilities, such as the payment of attorneys' fees, fines, and damages. *See* discussion of FAS 5, note 119 *supra.*

164. Apparently, the Commission thus far has not expressly embraced the theory that a registrant's environmental policies must be disclosed because they reflect upon management's competence or integrity. In one recent administrative proceeding against United States Steel Corporation, the Commission stated that its disclosure approach in the environmental area "reflects the Commission's belief that omissions of *material* environmental information would render misleading the required disclosures concerning financial matters and the nature of a registrant's business." United States Steel Corp., SEC Securities Exchange Act Release No. 16223, 18 SEC DOCKET 497, 504 n.30, [1979-1980 Transfer Binder] FED. SEC. L. REP. (CCH) ¶ 82,319, at 82,382 n.30 (Sept. 27, 1979) (emphasis in original). No suggestion was made that a company's environmental policies are material in terms of their reflection upon the competency or integrity of management. *See* SEC Securities Act Release No. 6130, 18 SEC DOCKET 453, 2 FED. SEC. L. REP. (CCH) ¶ 23.507B (Sept. 27, 1979), where the Commission simultaneously interpreted its environmental disclosure rules.

165. *See* SEC Release No. 5627, *supra* note 9, at 47, [1975-1976 Transfer Binder] FED. SEC. L. REP. (CCH) at 85,716-17: "Accordingly, we believe that NEPA authorizes and requires the Commission to consider the promotion of environmental protection 'along with other considerations' in determining whether to require affirmative disclosures by registrants under the Securities Act and the Securities Exchange Act...."

166. *Id.* at 45, [1975-1976 Transfer Binder] FED. SEC. L. REP. (CCH) at 85,713, where, in defining its disclosure mandate, the Commission stated that

The Commission's apparent position is that socially significant information outside the environmental area that is not deemed material to the reasonable investor generally will not be required to be disclosed. For example, consistent with this position, the Commission has stated that it will not require disclosure of economically immaterial information concerning a registrant's compliance with the Equal Employment Opportunity Act because such information reflects the concerns of only a small group of investors whose interests in equal opportunity employment are indistinguishable from many other categories of investors intent upon ameliorating comparable social conditions.[167]

B. Public Citizen's "Cross-Town Hypocrisy" Petition

In May 1980, Public Citizen filed a rulemaking petition with the Commission alleging that several publicly held corporations failed to disclose to their shareholders material statements made to federal agencies or courts concerning the effects of proposed or implemented regulations.[168] The petition, seeking requirements to ensure consistent disclosure, has been hailed by its proponents as necessary to put an end to "cross-town hypocrisy."[169] This hypocrisy, according to the petition, enables "numerous corporations [to] inform agencies and courts that regulations will have serious impacts

---

although the Commission's discretion to require disclosure is broad, its exercise of authority is limited to contexts related to the objectives of the federal securities laws. Specifically, insofar as it is relevant here, the Commission may require disclosure by registrants under the Securities Act and the Securities Exchange Act if it believes that the information would be necessary or appropriate for the protection of the investors or the furtherance of fair, orderly and informed securities markets or for fair opportunity for corporate suffrage. Although disclosure requirements may have some indirect effect on corporate conduct, the Commission may not require disclosure solely for this purpose.

167. *See id.* at 51, [1975-1976 Transfer Binder] FED. SEC. L. REP. (CCH) at 85,724-25, where the Commission stated that

there is no distinguishing feature which would justify the singling out of equal employment from among the myriad of other social matters in which investors may be interested in the absence of a specific mandate comparable to that of NEPA. Disclosure of comparable nonmaterial information regarding each of these would in the aggregate make disclosure wholly unmanageable and would significantly increase the costs to all involved without, in our view, corresponding benefits to investors generally.

See generally Gaines v. Haughton, 645 F.2d at 778 n.29 (9th Cir. 1981) (referring to *J. P. Stevens,* the Ninth Circuit stated that the case "is perhaps the quintessential example of stockholders' creative—and inappropriate—use of the federal securities laws to attempt to regulate the normative content of corporate policies and management business decisions").

168. Public Citizen Litigation Group, Petition to Require Consistent Disclosure, *filed with* Securities and Exchange Commission (May 5, 1980) (hereinafter cited as Public Citizen Petition).

169. *See* Statement of Ralph Nader, *quoted in* SEC. REG. & L. REP. (BNA) § A, at 15 (May 7, 1980).

on their ability to do business while not disclosing, or not fully disclosing, this information to shareholders or the Commission."[170]

To remedy this perceived problem, Public Citizen petitioned the Commission to propose three rules: (1) that corporations be required to disclose to shareholders any material information on the impact or cost of regulations submitted to agencies or the courts; (2) that such information in all circumstances be deemed material if the cost of the regulation exceeds 2 percent of the corporation's average net income; and (3) that corporations be required to file with the SEC, but not necessarily include in disclosure documents, all submissions to other agencies on the cost of regulations regardless of their materiality.[171]

Predictably, the petition met with mixed reaction. In support of the petition, one respected authority asserted that "[t]he instances of inconsistent disclosure cited in the petition are evidence that a significant number of corporations are misleading either their stockholders or the government, or both, in their statements on the matter."[172] Not surprisingly, a number of corporations opposed the petition.[173] One such corporation pointed to Public Citizen's "inaccurate and misleading presentation" as "underscor[ing] the dubious wisdom" of any such proposed rules.[174]

The Commission subsequently denied the rulemaking petition.[175] In so doing, the Commission reasoned that existing rules and regulations currently

---

170. Public Citizen Petition, *supra* note 168, at 1. According to the petition,

> [t]he reason for this "crosstown hypocrisy" is clear: corporations wish to delay or prevent the adoption of regulations that may increase costs or decrease profits. At the same time they wish to keep their stock prices high and their shareholders happy by not disclosing the possible impact of these proposed regulations.

Id.

171. *Id.* at 10-15. The first proposed rule would not establish any new requirements. Rather, the proposed rule "would indicate that the Commission is aware that corporations have not been making material disclosures in this area, and would be a clear signal that in the future the Commission will not tolerate this type of inconsistent disclosure." *Id.* at 10-11. According to Ralph Nader, the proposed rules would not be burdensome. "In fact, [they] may cut down on the fees of the lawyers and the experts [the corporations] have been paying to come up with these inconsistent statements." Statement of Ralph Nader, *quoted in* SEC. REG. & L. REP. (BNA) § A, at 15-16 (May 7, 1980).

172. Letter from Professor David L. Ratner to Edward F. Greene, Director, Division of Corporation Finance, Securities and Exchange Commission (June 19, 1980).

173. *See, e.g.,* letters from Exxon Co., Mead Corp., Union Carbide Corp. to the Securities and Exchange Commission and United States Congress (May 12 & June 9, 1980). *See also* Kast, *Members of House Panel Hit Nader Proposal to SEC,* Wash. Star, May 6, 1980, § A, at 10.

174. *See* letter of Mead Corp. to the Securities and Exchange Commission, at 1-2 (May 12, 1980).

175. SEC Securities Exchange Act Release No.17390, 21 SEC DOCKET 1117, [1980 Transfer Binder] FED. SEC. L. REP. (CCH) ¶ 82,711 (Dec. 18, 1981).

mandate disclosure of all material information bearing on the impact of proposed or implemented regulations. If a registered company makes inconsistent disclosures of material facts, the Commission currently has recourse to pursue whatever measures it deems appropriate under the circumstances. In addition, the Commission concluded that adoption of a rigid, percentage-based materiality standard was undesirable. As to the third proposed rule, the Commission found that acting as central depository for all agency cost submissions was inconsistent with its statutory obligations.[176]

Although the Commission denied Public Citizen's rulemaking petition, some observations may be proffered in this area. First, if material misstatements in the form of inconsistent disclosures are made in Commission and other agency filings, such conduct may well give rise to liability under the federal securities laws.[177] Inconsistent disclosures in this setting create the impression that statements made in Commission filings are misleading, either by containing affirmative misrepresentations or omissions rendering the statements made suspect. Failure to disclose, even without any affirmative misrepresentations, may also result in liability. The underlying rationale is

---

176. *Id.* at 1118, [1980 Transfer Binder] FED. SEC. L. REP. (CCH) at 83,890. According to one source, the SEC has already begun taking action in this area:

> The SEC . . . is already looking at the conflicting filings of at least one company that was called to its attention by the EPA. Sharon Steel Corp., controlled by financier Victor Posner, had a history of air pollution violations at its Farrell Works in Sharon, Pa. But the company protested last November when EPA moved to place it on a list of those barred from receiving government contracts. Sharon contended that the penalty was "so severe that its imposition may destroy a going business." Yet in a prospectus filed with the SEC less than a month earlier for a $60 million debenture offering, Sharon said that, if it were blacklisted, it "does not anticipate that the resulting loss of business, if any, would have a material adverse effect on its consolidated sales or results of operations."

A U.S. Drive to Curb Corporate Doubletalk, BUS. WEEK, May 12, 1980, at 35.

177. *See* notes 63-97 and accompanying text *supra.* Enforcement efforts to combat inconsistent disclosure may depend, at least in part, on the Commission's requirement that corporations report financial liabilities stemming from government regulations. In United States Steel Corp., SEC Securities Exchange Act Release No. 16223, 18 SEC DOCKET 497, 502, [1979-1980 Transfer Binder] FED. SEC. L. REP. (CCH) ¶ 82,319, at 82,381 (Sept. 27, 1979) (footnote omitted), the Commission stated:

> In its filings with the Commission on Form 10-K and Form S-7 for the years 1973 to 1976, USSC set forth what the Company had spent or authorized in the past and what it expected to spend or authorize in the ensuing two or three years in order to comply with the pollution control requirements of environmental statutes. However, USSC engineers had also developed various estimates of the Company's costs to meet environmental standards for additional years, some of which involved material capital expenditures. These estimates were not disclosed to shareholders or to the investing public.

See note 164 *supra.*

that, by disclosing the proposed regulation's impact in certain agencies' filings but not in Commission filings, the general impressions conveyed in the Commission filings may be rendered misleading.[178] Even if the information is not quantitatively material, such inconsistent disclosures may be actionable on a qualitative materiality basis. Along with such misconduct as self-dealing, adjudicated illegality, and kickback schemes, the intentional filing of inconsistent disclosures directly reflects on management's integrity. Because in such cases management deliberately intends to mislead the corporation's shareholders, the investing public, and perhaps regulatory agencies, Congress, and the courts as well, the significance of such misbehavior is fairly evident. To the shareholder vested with authority to elect directors, who in turn exercise stewardship over the corporation and discharge fiduciary responsibilities, the intentional practice of inconsistent disclosure may well be deemed qualitatively material.

VI. ADJUDICATED ILLEGAL ACTIVITIES BY OFFICERS AND DIRECTORS

Generally, both Commission forms and the courts have required disclosure of adjudicated illegal activities by officers and directors, provided such violations are material to an evaluation of the ability or integrity of such persons. With respect to Commission forms, the pertinent guideline is Item 401(f) of Regulation S-K,[179] which is incorporated into Item 11, Form S-1,[180] Item 10, Form 10-K,[181] and Item 6(a), Schedule 14A.[182] Item 401(f) requires disclosure of certain "events" transpiring during the previous five years which are material to an evaluation of the competency or integrity of any director, director-nominee, or executive officer.[183]

---

178. See notes 93-97 supra.
179. 17 C.F.R. § 229.401 (1982).
180. 2 FED. SEC. L. REP. (CCH) ¶ 8215 (Sept. 8, 1982).
181. 4 id. ¶ 31,105 (Dec. 13, 1982).
182. 17 C.F.R. § 240.14a-101 (1982).
183. Id. § 229.401. Such "events" include:

   (1) A petition under the Bankruptcy Act or any State insolvency law was filed by or against, or a receiver, fiscal agent or similar officer was appointed by a court for the business or property of such person, or any partnership in which he was a general partner at or within two years before the time of such filing, or any corporation or business association of which he was an executive officer at or within two years before the time of such filing;

   (2) Such person was convicted in a criminal proceeding or is a named subject of a pending criminal proceeding (excluding traffic violations and other minor offenses);

   (3) Such person was the subject of any order, judgment, or decree, not subsequently reversed, suspended or vacated, of any court of competent jurisdiction permanently or temporarily enjoining him from, or otherwise limiting the following activities:

Courts have required disclosure of adjudicated illegal activity because of specific disclosure requirements,[184] because the omitted information rendered the statements made misleading, or because the omitted information was quantitatively material.[185] Although this discussion will not address cases focusing on the quantitative materiality of such omissions, these cases generally stand for the principle that "where a nominee's background is likely to adversely affect a profitable company asset, such background should be disclosed to the shareholders."[186]

With respect to the failure to disclose adjudicated illegalities rendering the statements made misleading, the opinion in *Trans World Airlines v. Catalano*[187] is instructive. In that case, the defendant described his occupation as including trading in commodities and precious metals without disclosing

---

    (i) Acting as an investment adviser, underwriter, broker, or dealer in securities, or as an affiliated person, director or employee of any investment company, bank, savings and loan association, or insurance company, or engaging in or continuing any conduct or practice in connection with such activity;

    (ii) Engaging in any type of business practice; or

    (iii) Engaging in any activity in connection with the purchase or sale of any security or in connection with any violation of Federal or State securities laws;

(4) Such person was the subject of any order, judgment, or decree, not subsequently reversed, suspended or vacated, of any Federal or State authority barring, suspending or otherwise limiting for more than 60 days the right of such person to engage in any activity described in paragraph (f)(3) of this section, or to be associated with persons engaged in any such activity;

(5) Such person was found by a court of competent jurisdiction in a civil action or by the Commission to have violated any Federal or State securities laws, and the judgment in such civil action or finding by the Commission has not been subsequently reversed, suspended, or vacated.

184. *See, e.g.,* SEC v. Savoy Indus., 587 F.2d 1149, 1165 (D.C. Cir. 1978), *cert. denied,* 440 U.S. 913 (1979)("the fact of [the defendant's] participation, in view of his past troubles with the securities laws, is just the type of datum that is contemplated by the requirements of Schedule 13D"). *See also* text accompanying notes 63-79 *supra.*

185. *See, e.g.,* Kass v. Arden-Mayfair, Inc., 431 F. Supp. 1037, 1046 (C.D. Cal. 1977) ("there is authority for the proposition that where a nominee's background is likely to adversely affect a profitable company asset, such background should be disclosed to the shareholders"); Chris-Craft Indus. v. Independent Stockholders Comm., 354 F. Supp. 895, 924 (D. Del. 1973) ("information [of director's past illegal conduct that could result in FCC revocation of the corporation's television license] directly affecting a profitable asset would have a significant propensity to affect a shareholder's vote"); Cooke v. Teleprompter Corp., 334 F. Supp. 467, 470-71 (S.D.N.Y. 1971) (independent shareholders may conclude that it "is inappropriate for a publicly held corporation, which must deal on an almost daily basis with municipal officers in connection with the awarding and administration of franchises for cable television, to be controlled directly or indirectly by a person who a jury has found guilty of bribing such officials").

186. Kass v. Arden-Mayfair, Inc., 431 F. Supp. 1037, 1046 (C.D. Cal. 1977).

187. [1979-1980 Transfer Binder] Fed. Sec. L. Rep. (CCH) ¶ 97,159 (S.D.N.Y. Oct. 31, 1979).

that a state court had found him liable for fraud in connection with trading in silver contracts. Describing the defendant's characterization as "sheer puffery" and "misleading," the court issued an injunction prohibiting him from engaging in further fraudulent practices in connection with his proxy activities in TWA.[188] In another case, *Cooke v. Teleprompter Corp.*,[189] the court stated that the defendant director's failure to disclose that he had been found guilty of bribery rendered "[t]he exposition of facts [in the proxy solicitation materials], while not untruthful *per se*, somewhat slanted and one-sided,"[190] even though no judgment of conviction had yet been entered.

Nevertheless, disclosure of such illegality may not be required if the prior adjudication of illegality is sufficiently stale or does not bear on the director's integrity or competency. For example, the United States Court of Appeals for the First Circuit declined to find a disclosure violation where one of the defendant corporate officers had failed to reveal a prior conviction, reasoning that

> [t]he district court's finding that the omission from the memo of Laura's past criminal record was not material was a judgment call and, in our opinion, correct. Laura's character and integrity were not involved; it was his idea that attracted the investors. Calling attention to a youthful misstep, if it was that, would in no way have alerted potential investors to a possibility of material misrepresentations and omissions in the debenture circular.[191]

Although most courts have not required disclosure based on the pure qualitative materiality of such information, at least one court apparently has adhered to this doctrine. In *SEC v. Freeman*,[192] the defendant was charged with failing to disclose prior judicial proceedings in which he had been found guilty of misrepresentation in connection with the sale of franchises and had been indicted for securities fraud. The defendant's counsel argued that disclosure of such civil violations would "brand as unfit to do business" any unsuccessful defendant and that disclosure of the prior indictment (which was dismissed after a mistrial) would run counter to the presumption of

---

188. *Id.* at 96,385-86.

189. 334 F. Supp. 467 (S.D.N.Y. 1971).

190. *Id.* at 470. The court also concluded that the nondisclosure was material in a quantitative sense.

191. Hoffman v. Estabrook & Co., 587 F.2d 509, 517 (1st Cir. 1978). *See* Raybestos-Manhattan, Inc. v. Hi-Shear Industries, Inc., 503 F. Supp. 1122 (E.D.N.Y. 1980) ("The existence of past securities violations and injunctions may be important to stockholders in deciding whether to tender their shares [because] it may put into question the integrity of offeror's management and indirectly raise doubts about the honesty and fairness of the tender offer itself"). *See also* note 185 *supra*.

192. [1978 Transfer Binder] FED. SEC. L. REP. (CCH) ¶ 96,361 (N.D. Ill. Mar. 3, 1978).

innocence.[193] Holding that such information was disclosable in an offering of securities by virtue of Section 17(a) of the Securities Act and Section 10(b) of the Exchange Act, the court implied that the bearing such information had on management's integrity was the relevant criterion.[194]

VII. PENDING LAWSUITS AGAINST OFFICERS AND DIRECTORS

Courts have required disclosure, especially in proxy solicitation materials, of pending lawsuits against officers and directors, particularly when self-dealing or fraud is alleged, even if the information is not expressly required by Commission disclosure items.[195] The rationale of these cases is that the partial disclosure or omission of such information renders the representations made in the proxy materials misleading. In this regard, the courts generally have not based their decisions on finding a specific misleading statement. Rather, general discussions regarding director nominees have been held misleading when inadequate or no disclosure of pending lawsuits has been made. Further, courts are inclined to require disclosure of such litigation upon a qualitative materiality rationale, reasoning that these types

---

193. *Id.* at 93,244.

194. *Id.* The court stated:

> If Mr. Freeman feels that he has been the victim of injustice in these past proceedings, nothing prevents him from explaining his side of each controversy to potential investors. But the policy of the securities laws is protection of the investor through full disclosure, not protection of the reputation of promoters. Thus we cannot accept counsel's argument for a rule which would permit sellers of securities to remain silent when facts exist which might turn buyers away. Such information must be considered material by any sensible standard.

Id. See also SEC Securities Act Release No. 5466, 3 SEC Docket 647, 648, [1973-1974 Transfer Binder] Fed. Sec. L. Rep. (CCH) ¶ 79,699 (Mar. 8, 1974), in which the Division of Corporation Finance opined that the conviction of a corporation or its officers or directors for making illegal campaign contributions, and pending indictments alleging such violations, should be disclosed to shareholders. Such convictions, the Division reasoned, impact on an evaluation of management's integrity, particularly as such conduct relates to the use of corporate funds.

195. *See* notes 202-09 and accompanying text *infra.* In these decisions, courts have not relied upon Commission disclosure items. The Commission's items generally require disclosure of pending legal proceedings to which the registrant or any of its subsidiaries is a party, other than incidental routine litigation. *See* Item 103, Regulation S-K, 17 C.F.R. § 229.103 (1982). *See generally* Zell v. Intercapital Income Securities, Inc., 675 F.2d 1041 (9th Cir. 1982) (failure to disclose company's pending lawsuits in proxy statement held to be material information); SEC v. Falstaff Brewing Corp., 629 F.2d 62, 72 (D.C. Cir. 1980) (Section 13(a) violation affirmed when corporation did not adequately describe pending litigation on Form 10-K). Note, however, that Item 401(f), Regulation S-K, 17 C.F.R. § 229.401 (1982), calls for disclosure of pending criminal proceedings against officers and directors. *See* note 183 *supra.*

of allegations directly impact on management's ability to discharge fiduciary obligations and are therefore important to shareholders when they elect director-nominees.

For example, in *Beatty v. Bright*,[196] the plaintiffs contended that proxy solicitation materials were false and misleading for failure to describe adequately two pending lawsuits against certain officers and directors.[197] In granting the plaintiffs' motion for summary judgment, the court noted the large "discrepancies in basic data" and the important nature of "the facts misrepresented and withheld" when it compared the allegations in the pending lawsuits with the disclosures made in the proxy statement.[198]

Similarly, in *Robinson v. Penn Central Co.*,[199] the court held that a plan for refinancing, which was one of the major items of business at the shareholder meeting, had not been adequately explained. Further, the court held that the proxy material, which also solicited for the reelection of the board, was misleading because it did not reveal the connection between two candidates and several past members of the board who had negotiated the plan and who were also defendants in lawsuits charging them with fraud against the company and breach of fiduciary duty. The court's rationale was premised on an affirmative duty of disclosure under such circumstances.[200]

In yet another case, a court found that implied representations about management's honest and fiduciary conduct in the proxy materials sent to shareholders before the proposed election of directors were rendered misleading because the proxies failed to disclose that there were lawsuits alleging insider trading violations pending against three of the nominees.[201] The district court stated that

---

196. 318 F. Supp. 169 (S.D. Iowa 1970).

197. *Id.* at 171.

198. The court stated that

> [t]he complaints in the state court actions are replete with allegations of fraud, self-dealing, conflict of interest and mismanagement on the part of the officers and directors of Gains. The proxy statement, prepared by these very same officers and directors, discloses only that three shareholders instituted two suits in Polk County District Court against certain directors and officers claiming that certain payments made by them on behalf of Gains for property acquisition, insurance commissions and property management were made in excess of the amount due for the fair and reasonable value thereof.

Id. at 173.

199. 336 F. Supp. 655 (E.D. Pa. 1971).

200. *Id.* at 658. The court stated that "[t]he facts must be fully and explicitly disclosed. It is not inconceivable that a stockholder would look with jaundiced eye upon a plan and proposed director bearing such an imprimatur." *Id.*

201. Rafal v. Geneen, [1972-1973 Transfer Binder] FED. SEC. L. REP. (CCH) ¶ 93,505 (E.D. Pa. May 8, 1972).

in their proxy statements [defendants] have elegant pictures of the directors and precise notations of their academic background and corporate experience. In short, these qualifications suggest an imprimatur of extraordinary excellence, responsibility and good judgment— on the basis of their past positions in the corporate world and in the nation. Certainly the fact that these individuals who are being asked to guide the destiny of IT&T have been charged (though admittedly not proven) with insider trading violations of the Securities Exchange Act of 1934 may be sufficient to cause some stockholders to pause before granting these individuals the important fiduciary responsibility of managing one of the world's largest corporations.[202]

In *SEC v. Century Mortgage Co.,*[203] the court seemed to go farther than previous decisions on this subject. In particular, the court held that failure to disclose pending criminal charges against a director-controlling person was a material omission from a prospectus accompanying the sale of stock. The court evidently based its decision solely on the qualitative materiality of the information, irrespective of whether such information was required to be disclosed pursuant to Commission rule or whether a specific statement or implication was rendered misleading by the omission of such information.[204]

---

202. *Id.* at 92,442. *See* Bertoglio v. Texas Int'l Co., 488 F. Supp. 630, 661 (D. Del. 1980) ("[e]ven should [the director-nominee] ultimately be successful in defending against these [pending securities fraud] claims, [shareholders] were entitled to know that serious allegations, arguably bearing on his fitness for the office he sought, had been lodged against him").

203. 470 F. Supp. 300 (D. Utah 1979).

204. *Id.* at 304-06. The court stated:

> [W]hen the amended prospectus was issued on June 15, Gilliland [author of the prospectus] knew that Century's sole shareholder, director and controlling person [Kearney] had been criminally indicted. The financial statement in the prospectus included Med-Idents as an asset of Century, yet Gilliland failed to disclose the material fact that criminal charges were pending against Kearney based on his activities in connection with Med-Idents in Arizona.

Id. at 306.

See Treadway Cos. v. Care Corp., [1980 Transfer Binder] FED. SEC. L. REP. (CCH) ¶ 97,603 (2d Cir. Aug. 12, 1980), where the court set aside an election of directors because the proxy contest was conducted at a time when the district court, in a case *sub judice* involving proxy contestants, issued, and ordered not to be disclosed, tentative findings of fact relating to the "responsibility, diligence and integrity" of director-nominees. The Second Circuit stated that

> [t]his information [bearing on the nominees' integrity] about the conduct of two of the nominees must be considered material to the shareholders' voting decision. The district court's order thus squarely conflicted with the spirit of § 14(a) of the 1934 Act . . . which section embodies a strong policy in favor of full disclosure of all material facts to the voting shareholders.

Id. at 98,213.

One possible limitation to the rule requiring disclosure of pending litigation against officers and directors is that disclosure may not be required if the pending lawsuit does not involve either self-dealing or fraud. In denying the plaintiff's request for a preliminary injunction to enjoin a stockholders' meeting at the "eleventh hour," the district court in *Seibert v. Abbott*[205] considered, *inter alia,* the fact that, with the exception of one claim alleging insider trading, none of the pending litigation involved self-dealing or fraud against the company or violations of law bearing upon the integrity of the candidates for election. The court commented, however, that the denial of preliminary injunctive relief had no bearing upon the ultimate determination of the plaintiff's proxy claims.[206]

VIII. BUSINESS EXPERTISE AND REPUTATION OF OFFICERS AND DIRECTORS

Information bearing on management's business expertise and reputation can be highly material to shareholder decision making, primarily because such information reflects upon the potential for corporate profitability. It thus is somewhat surprising that the Commission's disclosure items in this area are not very extensive.[207] Yet the Commission and the courts, recognizing the material nature of this type of information, have readily found antifraud violations when management engages in "puffing" or makes af-

---

205. [1973 Transfer Binder] FED. SEC. L. REP (CCH) ¶ 93,939 (E.D. Pa. Dec. 7, 1973).
206. The court stated that

> [a]part from the charge of insider dealing . . . none of the litigation adverted to by the plaintiff involves charges of self-dealing or fraud against the company or violations of law bearing on the integrity of the candidates for election. Whether that is a distinction without a difference is one of the questions which must await more careful study of the issues, both legal and factual.
>
> Nothing I have said here is intended as a final determination as to whether the defendant has complied or failed to comply in its proxy statement with the requirements of Rule 14(a)-9 when the case has been further developed by discovery or otherwise and when the matter has been presented to the Court with fuller opportunity for study and reflection.

Id. at 93,742.
207. *See* Item 401(e), Regulation S-K, 17 C.F.R. § 229.401 (1982), which requires a brief account of the business experience of management and nominees during the prior five years. In pertinent part, Item 401(e) requires

> a brief account of the business experience during the past five years of each director, person nominated or chosen to become a director or executive officer . . . including his principal occupations and employment during that period and the name and principal business of any corporation or other organization in which such occupations and employment were carried on. . . .

Id.

firmative representations regarding business expertise and reputation that render other statements made or the general impressions conveyed misleading.[208]

Nevertheless, the failure by management to disclose poor business judgment or lack of skill in making decisions intended to benefit the corporation generally is not actionable under the federal securities laws. The courts have reasoned that these types of claims are in reality based on breaches of fiduciary duty or corporate mismanagement, and are properly within the province of state law.[209] A federal claim may be asserted, however, if management engages in misrepresentations or nondisclosures that render other statements made in regard to business expertise and reputation misleading.[210] In addition, repeated incidents of mismanagement, demonstrating a clear lack of ability to operate a corporation successfully, might be the type of information courts would require to be disclosed.

In *Trans World Airlines v. Catalano*,[211] the court enjoined the defendant when, in listing his material occupations as required by Schedule 14B, he failed to disclose his prior involvement in an unsuccessful health food business.[212] In another recent case, *Bertoglio v. Texas International Co.*,[213] the court rendered two significant holdings with respect to disclosure of management expertise and reputation. First, the court held that information concerning first-quarter losses was material to a shareholder's evaluation assessing the wisdom of management's opinion on the company's prospects of achieving its objectives.[214] Second, and perhaps more significant, the court

---

208. *See* notes 211-17 and accompanying text *infra*.

209. *See, e.g.,* Santa Fe Indus. v. Green, 430 U.S. 462, 478 (1977); Maldonado v. Flynn, 597 F.2d 789, 798 (2d Cir. 1979); Amalgamated Clothing & Textile Workers v. J. P. Stevens & Co., 475 F. Supp. 328, 331-32 (S.D.N.Y. 1979), *vacated as moot per curiam*, 638 F.2d 7 (2d Cir. 1980); Levy v. Johnson, [1976-1977 Transfer Binder] Fed. Sec. L. Rep. (CCH) ¶ 95,899 (S.D.N.Y. Feb. 15, 1977). *See also* note 98 *supra*.

210. *See* note 98 *supra*.

211. [1979-1980 Transfer Binder] Fed. Sec. L. Rep. (CCH) ¶ 97,159 (S.D.N.Y. Oct. 31, 1979).

212. *Id.* at 96,385. *See* Kammerman v. Pakco Cos., [1978 Transfer Binder] Fed. Sec. L. Rep. (CCH) ¶ 96,318, at 93,066 (S.D.N.Y. 1978) ("True it is, of course, that the annual failure to reveal such thievery [by the *de facto* director] from the corporation's till constitutes material omissions, . . . and that the appointments to corporate office effected thereby would be voidable as a result").

213. 488 F. Supp. 630 (D. Del. 1980).

214. *Id.* at 644-45. Discussing the materiality of this omitted information, the court stated that

> The . . . proxy contest centered around the election of three members of a ten-person Board of Directors. As in any case involving election of directors, shareholders are entitled to receive information bearing on the competence of those exercising stewardship over the corporation. In evaluating the performance of incumbent directors, profits realized or losses sustained by a corporation are universally accorded a high priority.

Id. at 644 (citation omitted).

held that a nominee's proxy solicitation materials were defective in not disclosing his "questionable involvement" with a bankrupt company, even though that conduct had occurred more than five years earlier. Noting that Schedule 14A establishes only minimum disclosure requirements and that compliance with the schedule does not necessarily guarantee that a proxy statement satisfies Rule 14a-9, the court stated that

> [t]he policy considerations underlying the SEC's adoption of a rule imposing a period of only five years for disclosure of business experience most likely revolve around the diminishing relevance of "ancient history." This is particularly true where a ten or fifteen-year old incident mars an otherwise unblemished record. Such a rationale is far less compelling in a case like the one at bar, where the ESI consent order in 1964 was the first in a series of securities law and business difficulties for Mr. Ling that continue until the present time. If TI shareholders had been informed of Ling's departure from ESI and the accompanying consent agreement, they would have been more likely to view him as a "recidivist" securities law violator. The Court is reluctant to conclude that this fact was not material to a shareholder's assessment of Ling's qualifications to serve as a director.[215]

In addition to the judicial activity in this area, the SEC has brought administrative actions for failure to disclose adequately management's expertise and reputation. For example, in *Emer-Go Corp.*,[216] the Commission commented that the "failure to disclose that management had never manufactured a product or run a business of that type was a material omission which rendered the offering circular misleading."[217]

IX. A PROPOSED FRAMEWORK

The Commission and judicial decisions discussed above demonstrate that certain information bearing on management's competence or integrity must be disclosed in documents filed with the Commission, proxy materials disseminated to shareholders, and prospectuses furnished to investors. However, as is evident by the often inconsistent, and sometimes irreconcilable, holdings of these decisions, neither the Commission nor the courts have established a clear doctrinal basis or systematic methodology in requiring

---

215. *Id.* at 661.

216. SEC Securities Act Release No. 6066, 17 SEC DOCKET 500 (May 7, 1979).

217. *Id.* at 501. *See* Lasar Nucleonics, Inc., 44 S.E.C. 206, 207-08 (1970) (failure to disclose accurate and sufficient information regarding the background and expertise of the company president).

the disclosure of qualitatively material information. As a result, the parameters of the disclosure obligation remain elusive.

One approach to alleviate this problem might be for the Commission to promulgate or the courts to adopt a sweeping rule paralleling the line of cases suggesting that all qualitatively material information, similar to economically material information, must be disclosed to investors and shareholders. However, while such a disclosure obligation has some initial appeal in eliminating the process of line drawing between disclosable and nondisclosable categories of qualitatively material information, some important considerations militate against prescribing such a broad rule.

First, the subjective nature of the determination makes it difficult to identify the information that materially bears on the competence or integrity of management. Thus, requiring the disclosure of all qualitatively material information would not enhance predictability. Instead, such a requirement could engender the disclosure of excessive and immaterial information, thereby resulting in unreadable or unmanageable disclosure documents, unnecessarily burdensome costs to registrants, and possible vexatious litigation.

Second, while most investors and shareholders are interested in information that materially bears on the profitability of their investment, thereby justifying economic materiality as a threshold disclosure requirement, it is questionable whether all information that materially bears on the integrity or competence of management is of equal importance. Especially in this era of deregulation, requiring disclosure of all qualitatively material information would appear to be an overbroad exercise of rulemaking power, not essential to investor protection.

Finally, fairness problems inhere in a pervasive disclosure requirement based upon qualitative materiality. For example, it might be unfair to require management to disclose unlawful acts during the period it is unaware that its conduct is illegal. Moreover, it may be unrealistic as well as inequitable to require management to accuse itself of unlawful conduct at a time when directors and officers may have a constitutional or statutory right[218] to keep this information private or when management denies any such wrongdoing.

As an alternative to a broad rule requiring disclosure of all qualitatively material information, the Commission, if it decides to act in this area, should reject administrative convenience and prescribe a narrower disclosure requirement that is sensitive to the interests of investors and shareholders, the burdens visited upon registrants and management, and the practical problems encountered in attempting to construct a workable standard that di-

---

218. Under such circumstances, officers and directors may exercise their fifth amendment right against self-incrimination. *See* Statement of Wallace Timmeny, *quoted in* SEC. REG. & L. REP. (BNA) § A, at 3-4 (March 18, 1981). It also appears that disclosure ordinarily would not be required in the context of private investigations initiated by the Commission. *See* 17 C.F.R. § 203.5 (1982).

verges from the traditional economic materiality rationale. In this regard, the Commission could issue a release describing the evolution of qualitative materiality and redefining the contextual framework that gives rise to disclosure obligations respecting management's competence or integrity.[219] In such a release, the Commission could provide the analytical tools necessary to craft disclosure requirements in terms of workable, if not totally familiar, standards. Such a release would enable courts to proceed in this area on a case-by-case basis with greater consistency and predictability.

The threshold question in a systematic approach to determine the disclosure obligation for qualitatively material information would be whether the subject information has a reasonable nexus to management's competence or integrity. While a director's recent conviction for securities fraud would invariably be deemed material to a director's integrity, other situations would require more fact-finding and judgment by a court. For example, a criminal conviction more than ten years past, with no subsequent misconduct, may have little bearing on a director's integrity. Likewise, nonadjudicative conduct by a "white-hearted" officer for short-swing profits in violation of Section 16(b)[220] of the Exchange Act arguably may reveal little about his integrity or the quality of his stewardship over corporate assets.[221]

Upon finding a reasonable nexus to competency or integrity, the next determination should be whether there is a likelihood that the subject information would be important to an investor or shareholder in making an investment or voting decision. Since most investors are interested primarily in making money and maintaining accountability for corporate assets, qualitatively material information would usually assume importance in an investment decision when management's dishonesty or incompetence has a realistic potential of significantly impairing the economic performance or prospects of a company. The potential to cause either significant short- or long-term economic harm therefore should be the touchstone for the disclosure of qualitative information in an investment context.

For example, where instances of self-dealing do not result in significant short-term losses to a company, such conduct might nonetheless be required to be disclosed in a selling document because of the aggregate economic

---

219. See SEC Release No. 5627, note 9 supra, where the Commission issued a similar release with respect to the evolution of economic materiality as a disclosure standard.

220. Section 16 of the Exchange Act, 15 U.S.C. § 78p (1976), prohibits an officer or director, as well as any person owning 10 percent of an issuer's stock, from purchasing and selling, or selling and purchasing, any equity security of the issuer within a period of six months. Any profits are recoverable by the issuer, irrespective of the intention of the shareholder, director, or officer.

221. In this situation, a court may examine the evidence to determine whether the officer traded in his company's stock with reason to know that he was violating Section 16(b) of the Exchange Act, or whether the violation was due to innocent inadvertence, and thus had little bearing on the officer's competence or integrity.

impact the misconduct may have over a period of time. Likewise, a criminal conviction might be required to be disclosed because of its potential for jeopardizing an important corporate license or contract. In the same vein, illegal payments might be required to be disclosed because of their potential to materially distort financial statements over time, or due to contingent liability possibly resulting in damage to the corporation's reputation and loss of good will.

Some factors that are relevant to determining whether qualitatively material information significantly bears on the economic prospects of a company include the centrality of a particular director or officer whose competence or integrity is at issue,[222] management's possession of scienter in prior misconduct,[223] the relationship of past problems to management's present responsibilities,[224] the continuous nature of management's misconduct,[225] and the extent to which management placed its competence or integrity at issue in selling a security.[226] On the other hand, qualitatively material information which does not bear on the economic prospects of a company often may not be deemed important in an investment context. This type of information, however, should be disclosable where management has reason to know that a particularly important investor or group of investors would consider certain managerial qualities or policies significant in deciding whether to enter into a particular transaction.[227]

Since most shareholders, like investors, are interested in the profitability of their investment, qualitatively material information deemed significant in an investment context would also be important to shareholders voting in an election of directors.[228] Moreover, qualitative information may be even more important in the voting context because shareholders, in exercising

---

222. A history of bankruptcies or acts of corporate disloyalty by the chief executive officer or other dominant figure might be more relevant to determining potential losses of a company than the track record or integrity of an outside director with less influence over the corporation.

223. For discussion of the meaning of "scienter," *see* note 232 *infra.*

224. For example, an officer's intentional violation of the securities laws would be a better indication of management's inability to handle corporate assets responsibly than an officer's conviction for drunk driving.

225. One poor business decision standing alone may have no bearing on management's ability, but a series of failures might indicate a deficiency in management's judgment which could lead to substantial losses for the company.

226. Besides the notion that management should be accountable for the accuracy of information it provides investors, there is a greater chance that investors will be influenced by this information if management stresses its competence or integrity in a selling document.

227. *See, e.g.,* Natural Resources Defense Council, Inc. v. SEC, 389 F. Supp. 689 (D.D.C. 1974). *See generally* notes 117-67 and accompanying text *supra.*

228. *See, e.g.,* Gladwin v. Medfield Corp., [1974-1975 Transfer Binder] FED. SEC. L. REP. (CCH) ¶ 95,013, at 97,535 (M.D. Fla. 1975), *aff'd,* 540 F.2d 1266 (5th Cir. 1976), where the court stated "[i]t is clear that a contest for the election of directors places in issue the financial condition and earnings of the company...."

their corporate franchise, must decide which director-nominees should be selected to assume stewardship of the corporation and influence its direction, and therefore must assess the qualities of a nominee such as loyalty, credibility, integrity, judgment, and even social and political policies.[229] Thus, although a director's questionable or unethical conduct may not be considered important in an investment context due to the remote chance that economic repercussions would result from such action, this conduct may be deemed important to shareholders voting for the election of directors because it reflects upon a director's ability to assume a corporate position of trust.

After determining that qualitatively material information would likely be important to an investing or voting decision, policies such as prevention of vexatious litigation, fairness to management, and practical application should be considered before a disclosure obligation arises. For example, information concerning pending litigation in state court against a director for breach of fiduciary duty may well be qualitatively material to shareholders in voting for a director in a proxy election. Yet an absolute obligation to disclose this information could provide hostile shareholders with a mechanism to delay an election by filing a derivative suit only a few days prior to a shareholder meeting. In such situations, a court should consider circumstances such as the suit's proximity to the election, the plaintiffs' motives, and the probability of the plaintiffs' success on the merits before enjoining an election of directors for failure to disclose pending suits.

Problems may also arise in requiring management to disclose possibly unlawful activity when such conduct is neither alleged nor adjudicated to be illegal until after the consummation of a proxy contest or other disclosure event.[230] In this situation, it would be unfair retrospectively to require disclosure if management did not know or proceed in reckless disregard of whether its conduct was unlawful, even though such information might be important to investors or shareholders.

Similarly, it may be significant to shareholders or investors that the Commission has issued a formal order of private investigation concerning possible securities laws violations by management. However, requiring management

---

229. *See* Rafal v. Geneen, [1972-1973 Transfer Binder] Fed. Sec. L. Rep. (CCH) ¶ 93,505, at 92,441 (E.D. Pa. May 8, 1977):

> The election of a board of directors may be the most important, and in some cases the only, transaction in which the stockholder has any significant voice in determining the company's destiny. For the directors collectively are the captains of the [corporate] ship. Presumably, after evaluating the rolling seas of competition and the swings of public policy and corporate ethics, the directors then chart the course. . . .

230. In situations where a director or officer has been convicted or sued, requiring disclosure of the information would not be fundamentally unfair because the director or officer is apprised of the conduct which may be of interest to shareholders or investors.

to disclose the Commission's investigation before any violation is alleged would seem to undercut the purpose of a private investigation.[231]

Therefore, in this context, requiring proof of facts which establish that management or a director-nominee was at least reckless in failing to ascertain the legality of its conduct[232] will imbue the disclosure obligation with a degree of fairness, prevent much retrospective, vexatious litigation, and will create a less burdensome and indefinite disclosure requirement. Moreover, if a director or officer did not realize at the time that his conduct might be illegal, such conduct has less relevance to the evaluation of his integrity.[233]

---

231. *See* 17 C.F.R. § 203.5 (1982): "Unless otherwise ordered by the Commission, all formal investigative proceedings shall be non-public."

232. This standard should encompass both intentional and "highly reckless" misconduct. In Ernst & Ernst v. Hochfelder, 425 U.S. 185 (1976), the Supreme Court held that scienter must be shown in private damage actions brought for violations of Section 10(b) and Rule 10b-5. The Court left open the question of whether reckless conduct constitutes scienter under the statute and rule. *Id.* at 194 n.12. Similarly, in Aaron v. SEC, 446 U.S. 680 (1980), the Court held that the Commission must prove scienter as an element in a civil enforcement action to enjoin violations of Section 10-b, Rule 10b-5, and Section 17(a)(1), but need not prove scienter for violations of Section 17(a)(2) and 17(a)(3). The recklessness issue was left unresolved. *Id.* at 686 n.5.

Subsequent to *Hochfelder,* the overwhelming majority of courts have held that recklessness constitutes sufficient scienter. *See, e.g.,* G. A. Thompson & Co. v. Partridge, 636 F.2d 945, 961-62 (5th Cir. 1981); Healey v. Catalyst Recovery, Inc., 616 F.2d 641, 649-50 (3d Cir. 1980); Mansbach v. Prescott, Ball & Turben, 598 F.2d 1017, 1023-25 (6th Cir. 1979); Mawood & Co. v. SEC, 591 F.2d 588, 595-97 (10th Cir. 1979); Nelson v. Serwold, 576 F.2d 1332, 1337 (9th Cir.), *cert. denied,* 439 U.S. 970 (1978); Rolf v. Blyth, Eastman Dillon & Co., 570 F.2d 38, 44 (2d Cir.), *cert. denied,* 439 U.S. 1039 (1978); Sundstrand Corp. v. Sun Chem. Corp., 553 F.2d 1033, 1039-40 (7th Cir.), *cert. denied,* 434 U.S. 875 (1977). *See also* Cook v. Avien, Inc., 573 F.2d 685, 692 (1st Cir. 1978) (court reserved judgment on this issue); Nassar & Co. v. SEC, 566 F.2d 790, 796 (D.D.C. 1977) (Leventhal, J., concurring) ("[t]he concept that recklessness may serve as surrogate for subjective intent is not new to the law").

Although the courts have generally agreed that recklessness constitutes scienter, they have disagreed on the proper definition of the term. A number of courts define recklessness very strictly as conduct which represents "an extreme departure from the standards of ordinary care . . . to the extent that the danger was either known to the defendant or so obvious that the defendant must have been aware of it." Sundstrand Corp. v. Sun Chem. Corp., 553 F.2d 1033, 1045 (7th Cir.), *cert. denied,* 434 U.S. 875 (1977) (citations omitted). *See, e.g.,* Healey v. Catalyst Recovery, Inc., 616 F.2d 641, 649-50 (3d Cir. 1980); Mansbach v. Prescott, Ball & Turben, 598 F.2d 1017, 1025 (6th Cir. 1979); Rolf v. Blyth, Eastman Dillon & Co., 570 F.2d 38, 47 (2d Cir.), *cert. denied,* 439 U.S. 1039 (1978); Franke v. Midwestern Okla. Dev. Auth., 428 F. Supp. 719, 725 (W.D. Okla. 1976), *vacated,* 619 F.2d 856 (10th Cir. 1980).

For a recent article addressing the concept of recklessness and the various definitions accorded to the term, see Steinberg & Gruenbaum, *Variations of "Recklessness" After* Hochfelder *and* Aaron, 8 SEC. REG. L.J. 179 (1980).

233. The language of the Commission's rules presents an important limitation on the disclosure obligations for qualitatively material information. For example, a director's conviction for securities fraud—information clearly important to investors and shareholders—is required to be included in a registration statement. *See* 17 C.F.R. § 229.401 (1982). Yet this information arguably may not be required to be disclosed in a prospectus sent to shareholders in an offering

X. CONCLUSION

In an attempt to construct a workable framework for predicting disclosure obligations that attach to qualitatively material information, this chapter has analyzed a large number of Commission and judicial decisions addressing disclosure of information bearing on management's competence and integrity. While clearly delineated parameters do not emerge from the decisions, some useful guidelines may be offered.

First, courts often defer to the Commission's expertise by requiring disclosure of qualitatively material information specifically called for by Commission rules. Thus, if the fruits of management's self-dealing can be characterized as remuneration, indebtedness to, or a product of transactions with the corporation, such information may be disclosable in registration statements and annual reports filed with the Commission and in proxy statements sent to shareholders. Other qualitatively material information required by Commission rules includes management's convictions, civil injunctions related to business practices, violations of the securities laws, and business experience within the past five years.

Courts also have frequently required disclosure of qualitatively material information when omission of this information renders misleading representations made by management in documents filed with the Commission or in proxy materials disseminated to shareholders. Courts thus have found actionable the omission of qualitatively material information that rendered misleading specific statements concerning, for example, management's business expertise, adjudicated illegal activities, pending claims involving fiduciary breaches of duty, and illegal corporate payments authorized by management.

A number of courts have also held that qualitatively material information must be disclosed in proxy solicitations for the election of directors if omission of this information renders misleading general impressions or implied representations regarding the competency or integrity of management. In this connection, some courts have found in proxy solicitations an implied

---

unregistered under the Securities Act unless statements in the prospectus are rendered misleading by omission of the information. *See* Section 17(a)(2) of the Securities Act, 15 U.S.C. § 77q(a)(2) (1976); Rule 10b-5 under the Exchange Act, 17 C.F.R. § 240.10b-5 (1982). In this regard, courts could find in a selling document an implication that at least the major officers of a company are honest and competent, and that this representation is rendered misleading by omission of qualitatively material information such as convictions and repeated injunctions for violation of the antifraud provisions of the securities acts. Courts might also find omission of this information violative of Rule 10b-5(c), which prohibits any person from engaging "in any act, practice, or course of business which operates or could operate as a fraud or deceit upon any person in the purchase or sale of a security." *Id.* In addition, such omission may also violate Section 17(a)(3) of the Securities Act. *See generally* Aaron v. SEC, 446 U.S. 680, 695-700 (1980).

statement that director-nominees are honest and competent, and have held these implied representations to be misleading by omission of information which indicates a lack of integrity or competency.

In a final category of cases, some courts have held that information bearing on management's competence or integrity must be disclosed if it is qualitatively material, even though the information neither is required by a Commission line item nor, if omitted, would render an explicit or implicit representation misleading. This type of disclosure requirement generally has been limited to information concerning management self-dealing, illegal foreign payments, and adjudicated violations of law.

The cases therefore indicate that, although the slope of materiality may be a slippery one, it is not necessarily impossible to traverse. In undertaking this journey, however, many apparently conflicting and irreconcilable principles must be harmonized into a compatible framework. At one end of the spectrum is the effectuation of corporate accountability and meaningful shareholder suffrage. At the other end is the difficulty of formulating and applying sufficiently objective and comprehensible materiality standards so that management can implement them without engendering the disclosure of superfluous information and without fear of vexatious litigation. In between are a multitude of materiality-related issues that give rise to puzzling disclosure questions and, perhaps, concomitant obligations. In addition, the federal courts' concern over accommodating the federal interest in adequate and fair disclosure with the state interest in redressing breaches of fiduciary duty may appear on the spectrum. In an effort to delineate and reconcile these issues, this chapter has attempted to identify a doctrinal basis for requiring the disclosure of qualitatively material information.

3

The Use of Special Litigation Committees to Terminate Shareholder Derivative Suits

I. INTRODUCTION

What may be viewed as a fairly new defensive strategy in response to shareholders' derivative suits against corporate directors is the appointment of a special litigation committee by the defendant corporation's board of directors. The committee, usually composed of nondefendant directors, retains outside counsel of unimpeachable integrity. After calling witnesses, examining documentary evidence, and issuing a detailed report, the committee, with the concurrence of the special counsel, concludes that the suit is contrary to the corporation's best interests because of the litigation's improbability of success, its high costs, the disruption to the company's business, and the adverse impact on employee morale. Relying on the special litigation committee's report, the corporation seeks to dismiss the complaint.[1]

The extent to which a special litigation committee appointed by a corporation's board of directors can exercise its business judgment to cause the dismissal of such a shareholders' derivative suit remains somewhat un-

---

1. *See, e.g.,* Abramowitz v. Posner, [1981-1982 Transfer Binder] Fed. Sec. L. Rep. (CCH) ¶ 98,458 (2d Cir. 1982); Maldonado v. Flynn, [1981-1982 Transfer Binder] Fed. Sec. L. Rep. (CCH) ¶ 98,457 (2d Cir. 1982); Gaines v. Haughton, 645 F.2d 761 (9th Cir. 1981), *cert. denied,* 102 S. Ct. 1006 (1982); Galef v. Alexander, 615 F.2d 51 (2d Cir. 1980); Lewis v. Anderson, 615 F.2d 778 (9th Cir. 1979), *cert. denied,* 101 S. Ct. 206 (1980); Abbey v. Control Data Corp., 603 F.2d 724 (8th Cir. 1979), *cert. denied,* 444 U.S. 1017 (1980); Genzer v. Cunningham, 498 F. Supp. 682 (E.D. Mich. 1980); Maher v. Zapata Corp., 490 F. Supp. 348 (S.D. Tex. 1980); Zapata Corp. v. Maldonado, 430 A.2d 779 (Del. 1981); Auerbach v. Bennett, 47 N.Y.2d 619, 393 N.E.2d 994, 419 N.Y.S.2d 920 (1979). *See also* Bishop, *Derivative Suits Against Bank Directors: New Problems, New Strategies,* 97 Banking L.J. 158 (1980).

settled.[2] This chapter will address that issue in the context of the applicable federal and state law, analyze the discerning trends in the case law, and focus on the use of procedures that may help protect the best interests of the corporation and its shareholders.

One of the more important decisions in this context is the Supreme Court's opinion in *Burks v. Lasker*.[3] Also significant are the post-*Burks* lower federal court holdings that scrutinize crucial issues not raised before the Supreme Court. Moreover, state court decisions must be fully digested, particularly in light of the recent decision by the Delaware Supreme Court in *Zapata Corporation v. Maldonado*.[4]

II. THE BUSINESS JUDGMENT RULE AND *BURKS V. LASKER*

As a general proposition, modern corporation laws vest responsibility for the monitoring of a corporation in the board of directors, which stands in a fiduciary relationship to both the shareholders and the corporation. These fiduciary responsibilities require directors to act in good faith and in the corporation's best interests.[5] The business judgment rule complements this standard by generally providing that directors, absent self-dealing or other personal interest,[6] shall be insulated from liability for injury to the corpo-

---

2. *Compare, e.g.,* Abbey v. Control Data Corp., 603 F.2d 724 (8th Cir. 1979), *and* Maldonado v. Flynn, 485 F. Supp. 274 (S.D.N.Y. 1980), *with* Maher v. Zapata Corp., 490 F. Supp. 348 (S.D. Tex. 1980), *and* Maldonado v. Flynn, 413 A.2d 1251 (Del. Ch. 1980).

3. 441 U.S. 471 (1979).

4. 430 A.2d 779 (Del. 1981).

5. *See, e.g.,* DEL. CODE ANN. tit. 8, §§ 141(a), 145(a) (1974 & Supp. 1978); N.Y. BUS. CORP. LAW § 717 (McKinney 1963). *See also* Arsht, *The Business Judgment Rule Revisited,* 8 HOFSTRA L. REV. 93 (1980); Block & Barton, *The Business Judgment Rule as Applied to Stockholder Proxy Derivative Suits Under the Securities Exchange Act,* 8 SEC. REG. L.J. 99 (1980); Carney, *Fundamental Corporate Changes, Minority Shareholders, and Business Purposes,* 1980 AM. B. FOUNDATION J. 69, 69-77; Gorman, *Federalism and the* Burks *Factors: When Can Directors Dismiss Derivative Suits?* 5 CORP. L. REV. 120 (1982). *See generally* AMERICAN LAW INSTITUTE, PRINCIPLES OF CORPORATE GOVERNANCE AND STRUCTURE: RESTATEMENT AND RECOMMENDATIONS § 4.01 (Tentative Draft No. 1 1982).

6. As stated by one commentator:

> [W]here a director or controlling stockholder has a material personal interest in the outcome of a transaction or is engaged in self-dealing, it will fall to that individual to prove that the transaction he or she authorized is intrinsically fair to the corporation and its stockholders. Otherwise stated, where such a personal interest or self-dealing is shown to exist, a presumption of overreaching arises that can be overcome only by proof of intrinsic fairness. This has been denominated the intrinsic fairness rule.

Arsht, *supra* note 5, at 115-16 (citations and footnotes omitted); *see* Lewis v. S.L. & E., Inc., 629 F.2d 764, 768-70 (2d Cir. 1980); Blake v. National Research Assocs., Inc., 466 F.2d 570, 572 (4th Cir. 1972); Trans World Airlines, Inc. v. Summa Corp., 374 A.2d 5, 9 (Del. Ch. 1977). *See also* Johnson v. Trueblood, 629 F.2d 287, 292-93 (3d Cir. 1980).

ration resulting from their decisions if those decisions "lie within the powers of the corporation and the authority of management and were reasonably made in good faith and with loyalty and due care."[7] In other words, under the business judgment rule, directors are not liable for mere errors in judgment not constituting breaches of their fiduciary duty.[8]

Included within the authority to monitor the corporation is the directors' determination of whether the corporation shall bring suit for redress of

---

7. Dent, *The Power of Directors to Terminate Shareholder Litigation: The Death of the Derivative Suit*, 75 Nw. U.L. Rev. 96, 101 (1980). As defined by Fletcher:

> It is too well settled to admit of controversy that ordinarily neither the directors nor other officers of a corporation are liable for mere mistake or errors of judgment, either of law or fact. In other words, directors of a commercial corporation may take chances, the same kind of chances that a man would take in his own business. Because they are given this wide latitude, the law will not hold directors liable for honest errors, for mistakes of judgment, when they act without corrupt motive and in good faith, that is, for mistakes which may properly be classified under the head of honest mistakes. And that is true even though the errors may be so gross that they may demonstrate the unfitness of the directors to manage the corporate affairs. The rule is commonly referred to as the "business judgment rule," which generally applies to decisions of executive officers as well as those of directors. The basis of this rule is the wide latitude that directors of a corporation are given in the management of the affairs of a corporation provided always that judgment, and that means an honest, unbiased judgment, is reasonably exercised by them.

3A W. FLETCHER, CYCLOPEDIA OF THE LAW OF PRIVATE CORPORATIONS § 1039 at 37-38 (rev. perm. ed. 1975). Recently, one commentator has proffered the following definition of the business judgment rule:

> A corporate transaction that involves no self-dealing by, or other personal interest of, the directors who authorized the transaction will not be enjoined or set aside for the directors' failure to satisfy the standards that govern a director's performance of his or her duties, and directors who authorized the transaction will not be held personally liable for resultant damages, unless:
> (1) the directors did not exercise due care to ascertain the relevant and available facts before voting to authorize the transaction; or
> (2) the directors voted to authorize the transaction even though they did not reasonably believe or could not have reasonably believed the transaction to be for the best interest of the corporation; or
> (3) in some other way the directors' authorization of the transaction was not in good faith.

Arsht, *supra* note 5, at 111-12.

8. *See* authorities cited in notes 5-7 *supra*. In Auerbach v. Bennett, 47 N.Y.2d 619, 629, 393 N.E.2d 994, 1000, 419 N.Y.S.2d 920, 926 (1979), the New York Court of Appeals gave its rationale for the applicability of the business judgment doctrine:

> It appears to us that the business judgment doctrine, at least in part, is grounded in the prudent recognition that courts are ill equipped and infrequently called on to evaluate what are and must be essentially business judgments. The authority and responsibilities

vested in corporate directors both by statute and decisional law proceed on the as-

wrongs it allegedly has suffered.[9] Invocation of the business judgment rule as a ground for the directors' refusal to bring suit or their active opposition to a derivative action will warrant, under some circumstances, dismissal of the action.[10] Until recently, this principle was primarily applied when the alleged wrongdoers were not affiliated with the corporation. Under such circumstances, directors could be expected to judge impartially the benefits and detriments of bringing suit.[11] For example, Mr. Justice Brandeis, addressing the decision by the board of directors of a corporation not to bring an antitrust action against a third party, remarked:

> Whether or not a corporation shall seek to enforce in the courts a cause of action for damages is, like other business questions, ordinarily a matter of internal management and is left to the discretion of the directors, in the absence of instruction by vote of the shareholders. Courts interfere seldom to control such discretion *intra vires* the corporation, *except where the directors are guilty of misconduct equivalent to a breach of trust, or where they stand in a dual relation which prevents an unprejudiced exercise of judgment.* . . .[12]

As Mr. Justice Brandeis implied, the rule generally has not been invoked if the directors are implicated in the alleged wrong.[13] Recently, however,

---

sumption that inescapably there can be no available objective standard by which the correctness of every corporate decision may be measured, by the courts or otherwise. Even if that were not the case, by definition the responsibility for business judgments must rest with the corporate directors; their individual capabilities and experience peculiarly qualify them for the discharge of that responsibility. Thus, absent evidence of bad faith or fraud (of which there is none here) the courts must and properly should respect their determinations.

9. *See* United Copper Sec. Co. v. Amalgamated Copper Co., 244 U.S. 261 (1917).

10. *See, e.g., id.;* Gall v. Exxon Corp., 418 F. Supp. 508, 515 (S.D.N.Y. 1976); Steinberg v. Hardy, 90 F. Supp. 167, 169 (D. Conn. 1950); Babcock v. Farwell, 245 Ill. 14, 46, 91 N.E. 683, 694 (1910); Barr v. Wackman, 36 N.Y.2d 371, 378, 329 N.E.2d 180, 185-86, 368 N.Y.S.2d 497, 504-05 (1975); Passmore v. Allentown & Reading Traction Co., 267 Pa. 356, 358-59, 110 A. 240, 241 (1920); 13 W. FLETCHER, CYCLOPEDIA OF THE LAW OF PRIVATE CORPORATIONS § 5822 at 145 (rev. perm. ed. 1975); Dent, *supra* note 7, at 98.

11. *See* Dent, *supra* note 7, at 98.

12. United Copper Sec. Co. v. Amalgamated Copper Co., 244 U.S. at 263-64 (emphasis added).

13. *Id.; see* Hawes v. City of Oakland, 104 U.S. 450, 460 (1881); Ash v. International Business Machs., Inc., 353 F.2d 491, 493 (3d Cir. 1965), *cert. denied,* 384 U.S. 927 (1966); Stadin v. Union Elec. Co., 309 F.2d 912, 921-22 (8th Cir. 1962), *cert. denied,* 373 U.S. 915 (1963); Findley v. Garrett, 109 Cal. App. 2d 166, 176, 240 P.2d 421, 427 (1952); Swenson v. Thibaut, 39 N.C. App. 77, 106-07, 250 S.E.2d 279, 298 (1978).

As an analogy, before commencing suit, a shareholder must make a demand on the board of directors that it bring suit to seek redress, unless such a demand would be futile. *See* FED. R. CIV. P. 23.1:

several courts have applied the rule when a duly appointed special litigation committee composed of directors not involved in the alleged wrong has elected not to bring suit.[14] The starting point in this analysis is the Supreme Court's fairly recent decision in *Burks v. Lasker*.[15]

The issue in *Burks* was whether a quorum of four statutorily disinterested directors within the meaning of the Investment Company Act[16] could terminate a shareholders' derivative suit against fellow directors on the basis that, in the exercise of their good faith business judgment, the continuation of the litigation was not in the company's best interests.[17] Rather than directly answering this inquiry, the Supreme Court promulgated a two-prong test: (1) whether the applicable state law allows the disinterested directors to terminate a shareholders' derivative suit, and (2) whether such a state rule is consistent with the policies underlying the federal securities laws.[18]

In a derivative action brought by one or more shareholders or members to enforce a right of a corporation or of an unincorporated association, the corporation or association having failed to enforce a right which may properly be asserted by it, the complaint shall be verified and shall allege ... with particularity the efforts, if any, made by the plaintiff to obtain the action he desires from the directors or comparable authority and, if necessary, from the shareholders or members, and the reasons for his failure to obtain the action or for not making the effort.

Such a demand on the board has been held to be futile if the alleged wrongdoers constitute a majority of the board. *See, e.g.,* Meltzer v. Atlantic Research Corp., 330 F.2d 946 (4th Cir.), *cert. denied,* 379 U.S. 841 (1964) (applying Virginia law); Orlando Orange Groves Co. v. Hale, 107 Fla. 304, 316, 144 So. 674, 678 (1932); Robb v. Eastgate Hotel, Inc., 347 Ill. App. 261, 279, 106 N.E.2d 848, 856 (1952); Eston v. Argus, 328 Mich. 554, 556, 44 N.W.2d 154, 155 (1950); Caldwell v. Eubanks, 326 Mo. 185, 192, 30 S.W.2d 976, 979 (1930); Barr v. Wackman, 36 N.Y.2d 371, 379, 329 N.E.2d 180, 186, 368 N.Y.S.2d 497, 505 (1975); H. Henn, Handbook of the Law of Corporations and Other Business Enterprises § 365 (2d ed. 1970); N. Lattin, The Law of Corporations § 105 (2d ed. 1971); Dent, *supra* note 7, at 99. For further discussion on this subject, *see* notes 97-108 and accompanying text *infra*.

14. *See, e.g.,* Lewis v. Anderson, 615 F.2d 778 (9th Cir. 1979); Abbey v. Control Data Corp., 603 F.2d 724 (8th Cir. 1979); Auerbach v. Bennett, 47 N.Y.2d 619, 393 N.E.2d 994, 419 N.Y.S.2d 920 (1979).

15. 441 U.S. 471 (1979).

16. 15 U.S.C. §§ 80a-2(a)(19), -10 (1976).

17. 441 U.S. at 473-74. The disinterested directors were appointed by the board of directors of the defendant fund and were not named as defendants.

18. *Id.* at 480, 486. Although the Court's decision promulgated this standard within the context of the Investment Company Act, subsequent lower court decisions have applied it irrespective of the federal securities act alleged to have been violated. *See* cases cited in note 1 *supra*. Unlike the other securities acts, however, the Investment Company Act requires that at least 40 percent of the directors of such companies be disinterested. *See* 15 U.S.C. §§ 80a-2(a)(19), -10 (1976); 441 U.S. at 482. As noted by the *Burks* Court: "Congress' purpose in structuring the Act as it did is clear. It was 'designed to place the unaffiliated directors in the role of "independent watchdogs." ' " *Id.* at 484 (quoting Tannenbaum v. Zeller, 552 F.2d 402, 406 (2d Cir.), *cert. denied,* 434 U.S. 934 (1977)). Nevertheless, the Second Circuit in *Burks* held that "disinterested directors of an investment company do not have the power to

The Court's opinion, however, left unresolved a number of issues. For example, what constitutes, for purposes other than the Investment Company Act, a "disinterested" director? Will courts inquire into the "reasonableness" of the directors' determination to bar a shareholders' derivative suit? May less than a quorum of directors properly act for the corporate entity for these purposes?

Of course, prior to the Court's opinion in *Burks,* a number of lower federal courts rendered decisions on this subject, generally holding that a good faith decision by a special litigation committee to bar a shareholders' derivative suit against fellow directors is permitted under the business judgment rule. Decisions reflecting this rationale include *Rosengarten v. International Telephone & Telegraph Corp.*[19] and *Gall v. Exxon Corp.*[20] In both of these decisions, it is interesting to note that the plaintiffs were granted limited discovery to test the bona fides and independence of the special litigation committee members.[21] In subsequent cases, if the plaintiff has pleaded bad faith or lack of independence on the part of the members of the committee, a number of courts have similarly permitted limited discovery.[22]

Although the result reached in cases like *Rosengarten* and *Gall* may well be the same after *Burks,* it is clear that *Burks'* two-prong analysis must now be employed. One pre-*Burks* decision, however, may still remain good law. In *Miller v. American Telephone and Telegraph Co.,*[23] the complaint in a shareholders' derivative action alleged that the company had neglected to collect a $1.5 million debt owed by the Democratic National Committee.[24]

---

foreclose the continuation of nonfrivolous litigation brought by shareholders against majority directors for breach of their fiduciary duties." Lasker v. Burks, 567 F.2d 1208, 1212 (2d Cir. 1978), *rev'd,* 441 U.S. 471 (1979).

19. 466 F. Supp. 817 (S.D.N.Y. 1979).

20. 418 F. Supp. 508 (S.D.N.Y. 1976). As stated by the court in *Gall:*

> It is clear that absent allegations of fraud, collusion, self-interest, dishonesty or other misconduct of a breach of trust nature, and absent allegations that the business judgment exercised was grossly unsound, the court should not at the instigation of a single shareholder interfere with the judgment of the Corporate officers.

Id. at 516. *But see* Nussbacher v. Chase Manhattan Bank, 444 F. Supp. 973, 977 (S.D.N.Y. 1977) ("It is inconceivable that directors who participated in and allegedly approved of the transaction under attack can be said to have exercised unbiased business judgment in declining suit based on that very transaction"); Swenson v. Thibaut, 39 N.C. App. 77, 250 S.E.2d 279 (1978) (court refused to apply business judgment rule to determination made by special litigation committee when defendant directors influenced members of the committee).

21. *See* 466 F. Supp. at 823; 418 F. Supp. at 520 ("Plaintiff must be given an opportunity to test the bona fides and independence of the Special Committee through discovery and, if necessary, at a plenary hearing").

22. *See, e.g.,* Galef v. Alexander, 615 F.2d 51, 56 (2d Cir. 1980); Lewis v. Anderson, 615 F.2d 778 (9th Cir. 1979); Genzer v. Cunningham, 498 F. Supp. 682, 687 (E.D. Mich. 1980).

23. 507 F.2d 759 (3d Cir. 1974).

24. *Id.* at 761.

Holding that the business judgment rule was unavailable under New York law, the court rested its decision on the premise that, as alleged in the complaint, the failure of the directors to collect the debt may itself have constituted a continuing illegal act. Atypical of the *Burks* scenario was the presence in *Miller* of an allegation that the directors' decision not to prosecute the claim was *itself* an illegal act.[25]

III. *BURKS'* PROGENY IN THE FEDERAL AND STATE COURTS

The following discussion analyzes the relevant federal and state court decisions on the authority of special litigation committees to dismiss shareholder derivative suits against fellow directors. Note that the first prong of *Burks'* two-prong analysis may require a federal court, in essence, to sit as a state court.[26] Only if relevant state law permits director dismissal of the derivative suit will a federal court turn to the second prong.[27] If, however, dismissal is sought in state court, the only inquiry is whether applicable state law authorizes such dismissal.[28]

A. Federal Court Decisions

After *Burks,* a number of federal courts have considered the authority of special litigation committees to dismiss shareholder derivative suits. For example, in *Abbey v. Control Data Corp.,*[29] shareholders brought a derivative action to recover $1.3 million from seven senior officers and directors after the corporation pled guilty to making illegal payments to certain foreign entities. In particular, the suit charged violations of sections 13(a) and 14(a) of the Securities Exchange Act[30] by the corporation's failure to disclose the illegal payments.[31] After conducting its investigation, a special litigation

---

25. *Id.* at 762. The district courts in *Gall* and *Rosengarten* expressly distinguished *Miller* on this basis. *See* 466 F. Supp. at 824 n.8; 418 F. Supp. at 518.

26. *E.g.,* Lewis v. Anderson, 615 F.2d 778, 781 (9th Cir. 1979).

27. *See* Burks v. Lasker, 441 U.S. at 480-81. *Burks* signified, as have other recent cases, that the degree of investor protection under the federal securities law will depend in large part on state law. Thus, the Court remarked: "Congress has never indicated that the entire corpus of state corporate law is to be replaced simply because a plaintiff's cause of action is based upon a federal statute." *Id.* at 478. *See* Santa Fe Indus., Inc. v. Green, 430 U.S. 462, 479 (1977); Cort v. Ash, 422 U.S. 66, 84 (1975).

28. *See* Zapata Corp. v. Maldonado, 430 A.2d 779 (Del. 1981); Auerbach v. Bennett, 47 N.Y.2d 619, 393 N.E.2d 994, 419 N.Y.S.2d 920 (1979).

29. 603 F.2d 724 (8th Cir. 1979), *cert. denied,* 444 U.S. 1017 (1980).

30. 15 U.S.C. §§ 78a-78h (1976).

31. 603 F.2d at 726.

committee composed of seven outside directors, who were appointed by their fellow directors, concluded that the derivative suit was not in the corporation's best interests.[32] The district court subsequently granted summary judgment for the corporation.[33] Employing *Burks'* two-prong analysis, the Eighth Circuit affirmed, concluding that Delaware law authorizes dismissal of a shareholders' derivative suit if the determination by the outside directors was reasonable and in good faith,[34] and that, in this case, the plaintiff's federal law claims were at best weak.[35] In an accompanying footnote, however, the court implied that, in certain instances, the strength of the federal policy involved may preclude committee dismissal of the plaintiff's federal claims.[36]

Relying on both *Burks* and *Abbey,* the Ninth Circuit reached a like result in *Lewis v. Anderson,*[37] with the exception that the *Lewis* court reserved for trial the issue whether the committee did, in fact, exercise good faith business judgment.[38] Interestingly, one claim of the plaintiffs alleged that the defendants violated Section 10(b) of the Securities Exchange Act[39] by trading on inside information.[40] The court's dismissal of this claim raises important policy considerations. Even in light of the Supreme Court's restrictive decisions in the securities law area,[41] including *Chiarella v. United*

---

32. *Id.* at 727.

33. *Id.*

34. "As a matter of Delaware law, we agree with the district court that the rule apparently applies to any reasonable good faith determination by an independent board of directors that the derivative action is not in the best interests of the corporation." *Id.* at 730.

35. *Id.* at 731-32. *See* Maldonado v. Flynn, [1981-1982 Transfer Binder] FED. SEC. L. REP. (CCH) ¶ 98,457 (2d Cir. 1982); Gaines v. Haughton, 645 F.2d 761 (9th Cir. 1981), *cert. denied,* 102 S. Ct. 1006 (1982); Stein v. Bailey, [1981-1982 Transfer Binder] FED. SEC. L. REP. (CCH) ¶ 98,470 (S.D.N.Y. 1982). The *Abbey* court observed that the plaintiff had failed to show "transactional causation." *See* notes 57-60 and accompanying text *infra.*

36. *See* 603 F.2d at 728 n.4. *See also* Burks v. Lasker, 441 U.S. at 487 (Blackmun, J., concurring) ("[I]t seems to me that a situation could very well exist where state law conflicts with federal policy"); Genzer v. Cunningham, 498 F. Supp. 682, 690 (E.D. Mich. 1980) ([T]here may be cases in which a business judgment dismissal of claims that directors have violated the proxy solicitation rules is not consistent with the policy of full disclosure which is necessary for the ultimate goal of shareholder protection. . .."). *But see* 441 U.S. at 487 (Stewart, J., concurring in the judgment) ("I cannot agree with the implications in the Court's opinion . . . that there is any danger that state law will conflict with federal policy").

37. 615 F.2d 778 (9th Cir. 1979), *cert denied,* 101 S. Ct. 206 (1980).

38. *Id.* at 780.

39. 15 U.S.C. § 78j(b) (1976).

40. 615 F.2d at 783-84. *See also* Abramowitz v. Posner, [1981-1982 Transfer Binder] FED. SEC. L. REP (CCH) ¶ 98,458 (2d Cir. 1982).

41. *See, e.g.,* Aaron v. SEC, 100 S. Ct. 1945 (1980) (scienter required in SEC injunctive actions under § 10(b) of Exchange Act, Rule 10b-5 thereunder, and § 17(a)(1) of Securities Act); Chiarella v. United States, 100 S. Ct. 1108 (1980) (no duty to disclose under Section 10(b) from mere possession of nonpublic market information); Transamerica Mortgage Advisors, Inc. v. Lewis, 100 S. Ct. 242 (1979) (no implied private right of action under § 206 of

States,[42] there can be little question that the proscription against trading on inside information by those who owe a fiduciary duty to shareholders and the corporation remains a fundamental tenet underlying the objectives of the federal securities acts of protecting the investing public and the integrity of the marketplace.[43] To allow dismissal of such claims without permitting

the Investment Advisers Act; limited implied private right of action under § 215); Touche Ross & Co. v. Redington, 99 S. Ct. 2479 (1979) (no implied private right of action under § 17(a) of the Exchange Act); International Bhd. of Teamsters v. Daniel, 439 U.S. 551, 559 (1979) (interest in noncontributory, compulsory pension plan not "security" subject to regulation under Securities Acts); SEC v. Sloan, 436 U.S. 103, 111-12 (1978) (limiting SEC's right to suspend summarily trading in registered securities for successive ten-day periods); Santa Fe Indus., Inc. v. Green, 430 U.S. 462, 473-74 (1977) (breach of fiduciary duty, without manipulation or deception, not actionable under § 10(b) of Exchange Act and Rule 10b–5); Piper v. Chris-Craft Indus., Inc., 430 U.S. 1, 28 (1977) (defeated tender offeror has no standing to bring implied private right of action for damages under § 14(e) of Exchange Act); Ernst & Ernst v. Hochfelder, 425 U.S. 185, 199 (1976) (scienter required in private damage actions under § 10(b) and Rule 10b-5); Blue Chip Stamps v. Manor Drug Stores, 421 U.S. 723, 749 (1975) (only purchasers and sellers have standing to bring implied private cause of action for damages under § 10(b) and Rule 10b-5). *See generally* Lowenfels, *Recent Supreme Court Decisions Under the Federal Securities Laws: The Pendulum Swings,* 65 GEO. L.J. 891 (1977); Steinberg, *Implied Private Rights of Action Under Federal Law,* 55 NOTRE DAME LAW. 33 (1979). With respect to § 10(b), Justice Blackmun, dissenting in *Chiarella,* stated: "The Court continues to pursue a course, chartered in certain recent decisions, designed to transform § 10(b) from an internationally elastic 'catchall' provision to one that catches relatively little of the misbehavior that all too often makes investment in securities a needlessly risky business for the uninitiated investor." 100 S. Ct. at 1123-24 (Blackmun, J., dissenting).

On occasions, however, the Court has departed from this restrictive approach. *See, e.g.,* Herman & MacLean v. Huddleston, [Current] FED. SEC. L. REP. (CCH) ¶ 99,058 (U.S. 1983) (cumulative remedies between Section 11 of the Securities Act and Section 10(b) of the Securities Exchange Act recognized; preponderance of the evidence test held to be appropriate standard in private actions for damages under Section 10(b)); Steadman v. SEC, 101 S. Ct. 999 (1981) (SEC correctly employed preponderance of the evidence standard in administrative proceeding); Rubin v. United States, 101 S. Ct. 698 (1981) (pledge of stock as collateral for a loan is an "offer or sale" of a security under § 17(a) of the Securities Act); Aaron v. SEC, 100 S. Ct. 1945 (1980) (scienter not required in SEC injunctive actions under § 17(a)(2) or § 17(a)(3) of Securities Act); United States v. Naftalin, 441 U.S. 768 (1979) (reach of § 17(a) of Securities Act extends beyond actual purchasers and sellers and encompasses aftermarket trading frauds). *See generally* Cannon v. University of Chicago, 441 U.S. 677 (1979) (implication of private right of action under Title IX of the Education Amendments of 1972). For a discussion of the possible ramifications of *Aaron, Naftalin,* and *Steadman,* see Steinberg, *SEC and Other Permanent Injunctions—Standards for Their Imposition, Modification, and Dissolution,* 66 CORNELL L. REV. 27 (1980); Steinberg, *Steadman v. SEC—Its Implications and Significance,* 6 DEL. J. CORP. L. 1 (1981); Steinberg, *Section 17(a) of the Securities Act of 1933 After Naftalin and Redington,* 68 GEO. L.J. 163 (1979).

42. 100 S. Ct. 1108 (1980).

43. The *Chiarella* Court recognized:

Thus, administrative and judicial interpretations have established that silence in connection with the purchase or sale of securities may operate as a fraud actionable under § 10(b) despite the absence of statutory language or legislative history specifically

the opportunity for redress arguably runs contrary to these objectives.[44]

Equally disconcerting is the *Lewis* court's implicit approval of the special litigation committee's composition, which consisted of two outside directors and one director who was a *named defendant* but who did not personally benefit from the challenged transaction.[45] The potential danger of using named defendants to dismiss shareholder derivative suits is illustrated by the Second Circuit's decision in *Galef v. Alexander.*[46] In *Galef,* the derivative action alleged that all fifteen directors had violated the proxy prohibitions

---

addressing the legality of nondisclosure. But such liability is premised upon a duty to disclose arising from a relationship of trust and confidence between parties to a transaction. Application of a duty to disclose prior to trading guarantees that corporate insiders, who have an obligation to place the shareholder's welfare before their own, will not benefit personally through fraudulent use of material nonpublic information.

Id. at 1115.

44. Quoting approvingly from Cady, Roberts & Co., 40 S.E.C. 907 (1961), the Supreme Court in *Chiarella* stated that the obligation to disclose or abstain from trading derives from

[a]n affirmative duty to disclose material information[,] [which] has been traditionally imposed on corporate "insiders," particularly officers, directors, or controlling stockholders. We, and the courts have consistently held that insiders must disclose material facts which are known to them by virtue of their position but which are not known to persons with whom they deal and which, if known, would affect their investment judgment.

100 S. Ct. at 1114 (quoting 40 S.E.C. at 911).

Another important question is whether a special litigation committee may, consistently with federal policy, terminate a derivative action alleging violations of § 16(b) of the Securities Exchange Act or § 36(b) of the Investment Company Act. By its terms, § 16(b) authorizes shareholders, under certain circumstances, to sue derivatively to enforce the corporation's right to recover insiders' short-swing profits. 15 U.S.C. § 78p(b) (1976); *see* Genzer v. Cunningham, 498 F. Supp. 682, 689 (E.D. Mich. 1980) (In ordering dismissal under § 14(a), the court noted that "[t]his is in sharp contrast to § 16(b) . . . [which] specifically authorizes shareholder suits to be instituted if the board of directors fails or refuses to bring the suit. . ."); Grynberg v. Farmer, [1980 Transfer Binder] FED. SEC. L. REP. (CCH) ¶ 97,683 (D. Colo. Oct. 8, 1980) (Federal district court rejected the special litigation committee's determination and denied a motion for summary judgment in a suit based on violations of § 16(b) on the grounds that the members of the committee were biased, that the committee failed to engage independent counsel, and that one member of the committee was counsel to a defendant-director). Section 36(b) empowers shareholders to bring derivative actions to recover excessive advisory fees. *See* Blatt v. Dean Witter InterCapital, Inc., [1981-1982 Transfer Binder] FED. SEC. L. REP. (CCH) ¶ 98,406, at 92,431 (S.D.N.Y. 1982) (in a § 36(b) action, "unlike the ordinary derivative suit, the directors have no power to terminate the suit"). *See also* Burks v. Lasker, 441 U.S. 471, 484 (1979) (dismissal precluded under § 36(b)) (*dicta*); Grossman v. Johnson, [1981-1982 Transfer Binder] FED. SEC. L. REP. (CCH) ¶ 98,619 (1st Cir. 1982) (requiring demand in § 36(b) action). *But see* Fox v. Reich & Tang, Inc., [1982 Transfer Binder] FED. SEC. L. Rep. (CCH) ¶ 98,845 (2d Cir.) (excusing demand in a § 36(b) action as an "empty, unfruitful, and dilatory exercise").

45. 615 F.2d 778, 782 (9th Cir. 1979).

46. 615 F.2d 51 (2d Cir. 1980).

of the Securities Exchange Act. Those defendant directors who did not benefit from the transaction[47] determined that the suit was not in the corporation's best interests and sought dismissal. In holding that dismissal of the suit was inappropriate, the Second Circuit concluded that the defendant directors who sought dismissal stood in a "dual relation" which prevented an unbiased exercise of judgment.[48] In reaching this conclusion, the court seemed to imply that "disinterested" within the "dual relation" context must signify, at a minimum, that the disinterested directors did not authorize or approve the challenged transaction and were not named as defendants in the lawsuit.[49] Thus, the court asserted, one could not expect that directors who had participated in or approved of the transaction, or who were themselves subject to personal liability, would determine impartially whether the shareholders' derivative suit was warranted.[50]

Viewing *Lewis* and *Galef* in conjunction, one can reconcile the two decisions only on the basis that the defendant director in *Lewis* composed only a minority of the special litigation committee. Hence, dismissal of the derivative suit would have occurred regardless of the defendant director's appointment to the committee. Whether this distinction between these two cases is viable remains to be seen. Unfortunately, the court in *Lewis* never focused on the issue.[51]

In *Galef,* the Second Circuit also relied on the strong federal policies underlying claims based on the federal proxy provisions and on the defendant directors' participation in the alleged proxy violation.[52] Turning to this point, the court observed that management's role in adequately educating the shareholder to enable him to vote intelligently is unique. Because directors are fiduciaries, have the greatest access to factual corporate information, and are most knowledgeable about the corporation's long-range plans, shareholders naturally rely heavily on their representations. Because of such reliance, the objective of Section 14(a),[53] that communications from management

---

47. The complaint alleged that proxy statements, seeking shareholder approval of stock option plans benefiting various directors, failed to meet the disclosure requirements of § 14(a) of the Securities Exchange Act. *Id.* at 53.

48. *Id.* at 60 (quoting United Copper Sec. Co. v. Amalgamated Copper Co., 244 U.S. 261, 264 (1917)). Distinguishing *United Copper* from the case at bar, the *Galef* court noted that "[i]n each case, the court has indeed allowed directors to preclude pursuit of a corporate claim, but in each the directors who made such a determination were not alleged to have authorized or approved the challenged transaction, and they were not made defendants in the lawsuit." 615 F.2d at 60.

49. 615 F.2d at 60, 61.

50. *Id.* at 61.

51. *See* 615 F.2d at 783.

52. 615 F.2d at 62-66.

53. 15 U.S.C. § 78n(a) (1976).

be full and fair as to all material facts, is a crucial one.[54] According to the court, the achievement of this goal:

> would quite clearly be frustrated if a director who was made a defendant in a derivative action for providing inadequate information in connection with a proxy solicitation were permitted to cause the dismissal of that action simply on the basis of his judgment that its pursuit was not in the best interests of the corporation. The very premises which give life to a derivative right of action to enforce § 14(a) must save it from a premature death. In short, we conclude that to the extent that a complaint states claims against directors under § 14(a) upon which relief may be granted, federal policy prevents the summary dismissal of those claims pursuant to the business judgment of those defendant directors.[55]

At first glance, it may appear that the court's rationale in *Galef* extends to any shareholders' derivative suit alleging Section 14(a) violations by defendant directors. In other words, the federal policies in favor of disclosure are so vital that any state rule that allows dismissal in such circumstances necessarily conflicts with such policies.[56] An important limitation in the court's language, however, is that a claim under Section 14(a) must be one "upon which relief may be granted."[57] As interpreted by the courts, "transactional causation" is an essential element of a Section 14(a) cause of action,[58] signifying that "[t]he harm to plaintiff-shareholders must have resulted from

---

54. *Id.* at 63-64; *see* J. I. Case Co. v. Borak, 377 U.S. 426, 431-32 (1964). *See also* Steinberg, *Fiduciary Duties and Disclosure Obligations in Proxy and Tender Contests for Corporate Control*, 30 EMORY L.J. 169, 200-05 (1981).

55. 615 F.2d at 63-64. In making this statement, the court pointed out that its holding did not mean that a plaintiff could evade an otherwise available business judgment dismissal merely by asserting claims against all of the directors under § 14(a). The court opined that, depending on the facts of each particular case, a motion to dismiss under FED. R. CIV. P. 12(b)(6) or a motion for summary judgment under *id.* 56, would be appropriate. 615 F.2d at 66. *But see* Gaines v. Haughton, 645 F.2d 761 (9th Cir. 1981).

The *Galef* court also analogized to the demand requirement, noting that the type of cases "in which the plaintiff stockholder has made a demand on the directors which has been rejected, are structurally closer to the case at hand, because the business decision not to have the corporation's claim pursued has been made and is known, and the question is whether that decision will be treated as definitive." *Id.* at 60.

56. *See* 615 F.2d at 63, 64.

57. *Id.* at 64; *see* note 55 *supra*.

58. *See, e.g.,* Abbey v. Control Data Corp., 603 F.2d 724, 732 (8th Cir. 1979); Weisberg v. Coastal States Gas Corp., 609 F.2d 650 (2d Cir. 1979), *cert. denied*, 100 S. Ct. 1600 (1980); *In re* Tenneco Sec. Litigation, 449 F. Supp. 528 (S.D. Tex. 1978); Limmer v. General Tel. & Elecs. Corp., [1977-1978 Transfer Binder] FED. SEC. L. REP. (CCH) ¶ 96,111 (S.D.N.Y. 1977); Lewis v. Elam, [1977-1978 Transfer Binder] FED. SEC. L. REP. (CCH) ¶ 96,013 (S.D.N.Y. 1977).

the corporate transactions which were authorized as a result of the false or misleading proxy solicitations."[59] As applied to the facts in *Galef,* the defendant directors allegedly failed to disclose material facts when securing shareholder approval of stock option plans that inured to the direct benefit of certain recipient-directors, and when subsequently seeking the election of those directors. In this context, *Galef* may stand for the proposition that when there is a direct link between the alleged nondisclosures and the shareholder vote, the federal policies embodied in Section 14(a)[60] preclude dismissal of the derivative suit by defendant directors.

In *Galef,* the Second Circuit left unresolved the question whether it would contravene federal policy for (1) nondefendant directors or (2) a committee composed of disinterested nondirectors to authorize, if state law allowed, the termination of a shareholders' derivative suit alleging violations of the proxy provisions.[61] The federal district court's opinion in *Maldonado v. Flynn,*[62] affirmed in relevant part by the Second Circuit,[63] sheds some light on the question. In that case, the plaintiff alleged that the proxy materials used to secure the election of Zapata Corporation's board of directors were false and misleading in failing to disclose the circumstances surrounding modification of a stock option plan.[64] In response to this suit and two related

---

59. Abbey v. Control Data Corp., 603 F.2d at 732; *accord,* cases cited in note 58 *supra.*

60. *See* 615 F.2d at 63-64. In *Galef,* the shareholders also sought to void the 1974-1976 election of directors, alleging inadequate disclosure of certain directors' remuneration from the stock option grants. Because the suit sought, *inter alia,* to set aside the elections on account of the alleged nondisclosures, the court deemed the causation requirement satisfied. *Id.* at 65-66 (relying on Weisberg v. Coastal States Gas Corp., 609 F.2d 650 (2d Cir. 1979), *cert. denied,* 100 S. Ct. 1600 (1980)).

61. 615 F.2d at 64 n.20.

62. 485 F. Supp. 274 (S.D.N.Y. 1980).

63. [1981-82 Transfer Binder] Fed. Sec. L. Rep. (CCH) ¶ 98,457 (2d Cir. 1982).

64. 485 F. Supp. at 278. For an additional recital of the facts, *see* Maldonado v. Flynn, 430 A.2d 779 (Del. 1981).

The first *Maldonado* case, Maldonado v. Flynn, 597 F.2d 789 (2d Cir. 1979), also a shareholder's derivative suit, involved allegations that §§ 10(b) and 14(a) of the Securities Exchange Act were violated in the administration of the corporation's stock option plan for key employees of Zapata and its subsidiaries. The Second Circuit found the claim under § 10(b) to be without merit, reasoning that "[s]ince the amendments [modifying the stock option plan] were thus validly enacted by a vote of disinterested board members who had been fully informed of all material facts, their knowledge was attributable to the Corporation and no 'deception' occurred within the meaning of Rule 10b-5." *Id.* at 795. For a more extensive discussion herein on this aspect of *Maldonado, see* pages 90-91 *supra.* With respect to the Section 14(a) claim, which alleged that the proxy statements soliciting votes for the election of Zapata's directors were materially false and misleading, the Second Circuit remanded, reasoning that a reasonable shareholder could have considered the information important. 597 F.2d at 796-98. Thereafter, the corporation formed a special litigation committee consisting of two newly appointed directors who, after conducting an investigation, recommended that the derivative action be terminated. 485 F. Supp. at 278.

actions, Zapata's board formed an "independent investigation committee" composed of two nondefendant directors who were appointed to the board after the derivative suits had commenced. After retaining special counsel to assist it, the committee conducted a three-month investigation, which included examining thousands of documents and conducting numerous interviews. In its report, the committee ultimately determined that the three actions were not in the corporation's best interest, for twelve specified reasons. Zapata thereupon moved to dismiss Maldonado's complaint.[65]

Applying *Burks*, the district court held that an independent committee of disinterested nondefendant directors could foreclose the bringing of a shareholder's derivative suit against corporate directors based on federal proxy claims if the applicable state law permitted such termination and if such dismissal was not inconsistent with the policies underlying the federal proxy provisions.[66] Answering both questions in the affirmative, the court concluded that "if a committee of independent, personally disinterested directors of Zapata has determined in good faith that in its business judgment the continuation of this action is not in the best interests of the corporation, the action must be dismissed."[67]

It is significant that the district court reached its decision notwithstanding that the directors comprising the special investigation committee (1) were not elected by the shareholders, but were appointed by the defendant directors, (2) were appointed for the sole purpose of serving on the committee, *i.e.*, to exercise their business judgment about the derivative litigation, and (3) had some prior, although not substantial, contacts with certain of the defendant directors. In sum, the logic of the court's decision may well have been based on such factors as the thorough investigative and procedural record developed by the committee, the apparent disinterestedness of the committee's members in the activities they investigated, and the board's delegation of binding authority (not subject to the board's review) to the committee to investigate and ultimately to determine whether the litigation was in the corporation's best interests.[68]

---

65. *See* authorities cited in note 64 *supra*.

66. 485 F. Supp. at 278.

67. *Id.* at 282.

68. *Id.* at 282-86. The law firm of one of the newly appointed directors was hired by the corporation as independent counsel for purposes of the investigation. The plaintiff argued that this appointment showed a lack of independence. The court disposed of this contention as "a non sequitur and hardly worthy of comment." *Id.* at 283. As pointed out later in this chapter, however, the meaning of independence should be fairly narrowly construed. Contrary to the court's holding, a plausible argument can be made that there exists, at the least, an appearance of impropriety when the newly appointed director, who is selected by the defendant directors, uses his law firm as independent counsel. The generation of fees induced by such business may prompt, albeit unintentionally, a disposition in favor of the defendants. Further, if the director and his law firm recommend termination, this may well prompt other corporate director defendants to seek their services. *See* text accompanying notes 150-53 *infra*.

On appeal, in view of the Delaware Supreme Court's subsequent decision in *Zapata Corporation v. Maldonado*,[69] the Second Circuit remanded the case.[70] The Second Circuit, however, affirmed in relevant part the district court's rationale. Most significantly, the appellate court held that Delaware law is consistent with the policies underlying Section 14(a).[71] Accordingly, provided that Delaware law authorizes dismissal under the circumstances of that case, then such dismissal is also consistent with the policies underlying the federal proxy provisions.[72]

B. State Court Decisions

Under the first prong of the *Burks* standard, a federal court is to determine whether the applicable state law permits the disinterested directors to terminate a shareholder's derivative suit against their fellow directors.[73] In many situations, however, the applicable state law may be unresolved, often because no decision of a high court of the state is squarely on point.[74] In such instances, the federal court, in effect, will be "sitting as a state court."[75] Assuming this role, both the federal district court in *Maldonado* and the Eighth Circuit in *Abbey* construed Delaware law to allow such dismissal.[76] Furthermore, until the decision by the Delaware Court of Chancery in *Maldonado v. Flynn*,[77] no federal court had decided that any state law

---

69. 430 A.2d 779 (Del. 1981).

70. Maldonado v. Flynn, [1981-1982 Transfer Binder] FED. SEC. L. REP. (CCH) ¶ 98,457 (2d Cir. 1982).

71. *Id.* at 92,687. *Accord*, Stein v. Bailey [1981-1982 Transfer Binder] FED. SEC. L. REP. (CCH) ¶ 98,470 (S.D.N.Y. 1982). *See also* Abramowitz v. Posner, [1981-1982 Transfer Binder] FED. SEC. L. REP. (CCH) ¶ 98,458 (2d Cir. 1982) (Delaware law is consistent with the policies underlying Section 10(b)).

72. [1981-1982 Transfer Binder] FED. SEC. L. REP. (CCH) ¶ 98,457, at 92,687. The Second Circuit also remanded for the district court to determine whether the suit is barred by *res judicata*. *See also* Joy v. North, [1982 Transfer Binder] FED. SEC. L. REP. (CCH) ¶ 98,860 (2d Cir.).

73. *See* Burks v. Lasker, 441 U.S. at 480, 486; notes 19-20 and accompanying text *supra*.

74. *See, e.g.*, Galef v. Alexander, 615 F.2d 51, 61 (2d Cir. 1980); Lewis v. Anderson, 615 F.2d 778, 781 (9th Cir. 1979).

75. *See* Lewis v. Anderson, 615 F.2d at 781. *See generally* Commissioner v. Estate of Bosch, 387 U.S. 456 (1967), in which the Court stated:

> [T]he State's highest court is the best authority on its own law. If there be no decision by that court then federal authorities must apply what they find to be the state law after giving "proper regard" to relevant rulings of other courts of the State. In this respect, it may be said to be in effect, sitting as a state court.

Id. at 465. *See also* Berhardt v. Polygraphic Co. of America, 350 U.S. 198, 205 (1956).

76. *See Abbey*, 603 F.2d at 729; *Maldonado*, 485 F. Supp. at 278-80.

77. 413 A.2d 1251 (Del. Ch. 1980), *rev'd and remanded*, 430 A.2d 779 (Del. 1981).

precluded disinterested nondefendant directors from barring a shareholders' derivative action against fellow directors.[78]

Apparently, however, these federal court interpretations misconstrued the position of some state courts. For example, the plaintiffs in *Maldonado v. Flynn*, in addition to their federal claims, brought suit in the Delaware Chancery Court on various state law claims.[79] The defendants argued, as they did in the federal district court, that the business judgment rule required dismissal of the state law claims. Noting the spate of recent federal court decisions permitting disinterested directors to bar derivative suits, the Delaware Chancery Court stated:

> All of these cited federal cases . . . incorrectly assume that State law necessarily enables the corporate directors (or a committee thereof) to compel the dismissal of a pending stockholder's derivative suit by invoking the business judgment rule. . . . It is clear, however, that under well settled Delaware law, the directors cannot compel the dismissal of a pending stockholder's derivative suit which seeks redress for an apparent breach of fiduciary duty, by merely reviewing the suit and making a business judgment that it is not in the best interests of the corporation.[80]

Thus, the court reasoned that the business judgment rule provides only a "shield" with which directors may protect their decisions from shareholder attack; nothing in the rule grants a corporate board of directors any independent power to bar a derivative suit against fellow directors.[81] Contrary to the corporation's assertion that a shareholder's right to bring suit is always subordinate to that of the corporation and therefore subject to a corporate decision to bar its continuance, the court asserted that "[a]ggrieved shareholders of Delaware corporations ought to be able to expect that an impartial tribunal, and not a committee appointed by the alleged wrongdoers, will decide whether a stockholder's derivative suit alleging breach of fiduciary duty has any merit."[82] In summary, the court concluded:

> [A]n analysis of the business judgment rule shows that while it is a limitation on liability and ordinarily protects corporate directors when

---

78. *See, e.g.,* Galef v. Alexander, 615 F.2d 51 (2d Cir. 1980) (result unclear under Ohio law); Lewis v. Anderson, 615 F.2d 778 (9th Cir. 1979) (dismissal proper under California law); Abbey v. Control Data Corp., 603 F.2d 724 (8th Cir. 1979) (dismissal proper under Delaware law); Genzer v. Cunningham, 498 F. Supp. 682 (E.D. Mich. 1980) (dismissal proper under Michigan law).
79. 413 A.2d 1251 (Del. Ch. 1980).
80. *Id.* at 1257.
81. *Id.*
82. *Id.* at 1263, *citing,* Galef v. Alexander, 615 F.2d 51 (2d Cir. 1980).

they, in good faith, decide not to pursue a remedy on behalf of the corporation, it is not an independent grant of authority to the directors to dismiss derivative suits. Under settled Delaware law the directors do not have the right to compel the dismissal of a derivative suit brought by a stockholder to rectify an apparent breach of fiduciary duty by the directors to the corporation and its stockholders after the directors have refused to institute legal proceedings, because the stockholder then possesses an independent right to redress the wrong.[83]

Subsequent to the Delaware Chancery Court's decision in *Maldonado*, two federal courts applied that decision's rationale to preclude dismissal under the applicable state law.[84] Thus, in *Abella v. Universal Leaf Tobacco, Inc.*, Judge Merhige held that dismissal was improper under Virginia law.[85] Also, in *Maher v. Zapata Corporation*, the district court, relying on the court of chancery's opinion, held that Delaware law precludes directors or a committee thereof from dismissing shareholder derivative suits brought against fellow directors for alleged breaches of fiduciary duty.[86] Although the court was not bound by the decision of the court of chancery, it was "convinced" that the Delaware Supreme Court would adopt that tribunal's "thorough well-reasoned analysis."[87]

It is in this context that the Delaware Court of Chancery's decision in *Maldonado* had assumed such great significance. If the chancery court's rationale had been adopted by the Delaware Supreme Court, director dismissal of such shareholder derivative suits would have been effectively precluded. In view of the number of conflicting federal and state court decisions, however, it was difficult to perceive what was the "real" Delaware law on this subject. The stage was therefore set for the Delaware Supreme Court to clarify this important, yet uncertain, area of corporate law.

Reversing and remanding the chancery court's decision, the Delaware Supreme Court in *Zapata Corporation v. Maldonado*[88] stated that "when stockholders, after making demand and having their suit rejected, attack the board's decision as improper, the board's decision falls under the 'busi-

---

83. 413 A.2d at 1262.

84. Abella v. Universal Leaf Tobacco Co., 495 F. Supp. 713 (E.D. Va. 1980) (Virginia law); Maher v. Zapata Corp., 490 F. Supp. 348 (S.D. Tex. 1980) (Delaware law).

85. 495 F. Supp. 713, 717 (E.D. Va. 1980) ("Virginia law does not permit directors, interested or disinterested, to effect the dismissal of a derivative suit against a corporation and its directors, based simply on their business judgment that the suit is contrary to the corporation's best interests"). Subsequently, applying the Delaware Supreme Court's decision in *Maldonado*, the district court reversed itself and dismissed the action. *See* 546 F. Supp. 795 (E.D. Va. 1982).

86. 490 F. Supp. 348, 351-53 (S.D. Tex. 1980).

87. *Id.* at 353.

88. 430 A.2d 779 (Del. 1981).

ness judgment' rule and will be respected if the requirements of the rule are met."[89] However, the case at bar involved an instance where demand was properly excused.[90] In such a situation, the court, balancing the corporation's interest to rid itself of vexatious litigation against the shareholders' interest to utilize the derivative suit as an effective intracorporate means to police boards of directors, held that a two-step test should be employed in the chancery court's exercise of "independent discretion" in determining whether to grant dismissal:[91] First, with the corporation bearing the burden of proof, the court should inquire into the special litigation committee's independence and good faith and the bases supporting its conclusions.[92] Second, providing that the first step is satisfied, the court should apply "its own independent business judgment" and "should, when appropriate, give special consideration to matters of law and public policy in addition to the corporation's best interests."[93]

It is somewhat unclear from the Delaware high court's decision whether a tribunal may deny the corporation's dismissal motion even if the first step has been satisfied, without ever reaching the second step.[94] A number of commentators, however, have apparently concluded that if the first step is

---

89. *Id.* at 784 n.10.

90. *Id.* at 784-85. *See* Clark v. Lomas & Nettleton Financial Corp., 625 F.2d 49, 53 (5th Cir. 1980), *cert. denied*, 101 S. Ct. 1738 (1981); Cramer v. GTE Corp., 582 F.2d 259, 276-77 (3d Cir. 1978), *cert. denied*, 439 U.S. 1029 (1979); Buxbaum, *Conflict-of-Interest Statutes and the Need for a Demand on Directors in Derivative Suits*, 68 CALIF. L. REV. 1122 (1980); Comment, *The Demand and Standing Requirements in Stockholder Derivative Actions*, 44 U. CHI. L. REV. 168 (1976); Note, *Demand on Directors and Shareholders as a Prerequisite to a Derivative Suit*, 73 HARV. L. REV. 729 (1960).

91. 430 A.2d at 788-89.

92. *Id.* Further, limited discovery may be ordered to facilitate these inquiries. In sum, regarding this first step: "If the Court determines either that the committee is not independent or has not shown reasonable bases for its conclusions, or, if the Court is not satisfied for other reasons relating to the process, including but not limited to the good faith of the committee, the Court shall deny the corporation's motion." *Id.* at 789.

93. *Id.* at 789. In addition, two Texas state court decisions rejected attempts by defendants to dismiss derivative suits on the basis of recommendations of the board of directors. Sonics Int'l, Inc. v. Dorchester Enterprises, Inc., 593 S.W.2d 390 (Tex. Civ. App. 1980); Zauber v. Murray Sav. Ass'n, 591 S.W.2d 932 (Tex. Civ. App. 1980). *See also* Nussbacher v. Chase Manhattan Bank, 444 F. Supp. 973, 977 (S.D.N.Y. 1977) ("It is inconceivable that directors who participated in and allegedly approved of the transaction under attack can be said to have exercised unbiased business judgment in declining to bring suit based on that very transaction"); Swenson v. Thibaut, 39 N.C. App. 77, 250 S.E.2d 279 (1978) (court refused to apply business judgment rule to determination made by special litigation committee when defendant directors influenced members of the committee).

94. 430 A.2d at 789 ("If . . . the Court is satisfied . . . that the committee was independent and showed reasonable bases for good faith findings and recommendations, the Court *may* proceed, *in its discretion*, to the next step") (emphasis added).

satisfied, a court *must* proceed to the second step.[95] In any event, it appears clear that a court cannot grant the corporation's motion only on the basis of the first step without reaching the second step because the Delaware Supreme Court placed great emphasis on the latter step. Thus, in regard to the second step, the court asserted that this step provides "the *essential* key in striking the balance between legitimate corporate claims as expressed in a derivative stockholder suit and a corporation's best interests as expressed by an independent investigating committee."[96]

The Delaware Supreme Court's decision will undoubtedly have a significant impact on the ability of special litigation committees to terminate shareholder derivative suits against fellow directors when demand on the board is excused. Yet, when demand must be made, the Delaware high court authorizes committee dismissal pursuant to the business judgment rule. In other words, the court seems to have drawn a distinction between shareholder derivative suits naming an "acquiescent" or "interested" majority of directors as defendants and suits naming only a minority of such directors.[97] The apparent drawing of such a distinction signifies that the court impliedly concluded that the impartiality of and judgments reached by a special litigation committee depend on the number of "acquiescent" or "interested" directors named as defendants. Such a conclusion is misplaced. The inherent problems of "structural bias"[98] remain, regardless of whether the complaint accuses a majority or a minority of such directors of wrongdoing.[99] More-

---

95. *See* Brodsky, *Terminating Derivative Suits Under Business Judgment Rule*, N.Y.L.J., May 20, 1981, at 1, col. 1; DeMott, *Defending the Quiet Life: The Role of Special Counsel in Director Termination of Derivative Suits*, 56 NOTRE DAME LAW. 850, 853-54 (1981); Hinsey & Dreizen, *Delaware Court Addresses Business Judgment Rule*, Legal Times (Wash.) June 8, 1981, at 15, col. 3; Olson, *Delaware Court Addresses Business Judgment Rule*, Legal Times (Wash.), June 8, 1981, at 15, col. 1. *But see* Coffee & Schwartz, *The Survival of the Derivative Suit: An Evaluation and a Proposal for Legislative Reform*, 81 COLUM. L. REV. 261 (1981).

96. 430 A.2d at 789 (emphasis added).

97. *See id.* at 786-89. *See generally* Comment, 44 U. CHI. L. REV., note 90 *supra*:

> When a majority of the directors have engaged in fraud or self-dealing, such as appropriating a corporate opportunity, courts have generally not required demand. But when a majority of the directors are accused of approving or passively acquiescing in an allegedly injurious transaction, courts are split on whether demand should be required.

Id. at 176. *See* Note, *A Procedural Treatment of Derivative Suit Dismissals by Minority Directors*, 69 CALIF. L. REV. 885, 889-90 (1981).

98. "Structural bias" may be defined as "inherent prejudice against any derivative action resulting from the composition and character of the board of directors." Note, *The Business Judgment Rule in Derivative Suits Against Directors*, 65 CORNELL L. REV. 600, 601 n.14 (1980). In a recent decision, the Fifth Circuit recognized the problem of structural bias, holding that, because of conflicts of interest, a corporation's board of directors was incompetent to compromise the plaintiff shareholders' derivative claims. Clark v. Lomas & Nettleton Financial Corp., 625 F.2d 49 (5th Cir. 1980), *cert. denied*, 101 S. Ct. 1738 (1981).

99. *See* Coffee & Schwartz, note 95 *supra*, at 329-30; Note, note 98 *supra*, at 629.

over, the court's holding in this regard, although arguably *dicta,* seems to assure that shareholders will attempt to excuse the demand requirement by naming at least a majority of "acquiescent" or "interested" directors as defendants whenever practicable in order to avoid application of the business judgment rule.[100] Thus, the next key issue to surface in this context may well entail the circumstances under which demand on the board is excused. Depending on how this issue is resolved, the Delaware Supreme Court's distinction between suits when demand must be made and when it is excused at best may have limited practical effect and, at worse, may spell the death knell to shareholder derivative suits against directors whenever demand must arguably be made.

In order to preserve the vitality of the shareholder derivative suit in this context, the Delaware courts should excuse the demand requirement whenever a majority of "acquiescent" as well as "interested" directors are named as defendants.[101] Moreover, demand should be excused if a majority of the board is disabled, such as being under the domination of a controlling shareholder.[102] In the above settings, the board should be deemed as "stand[ing] in a dual relation which prevents an unprejudiced exercise of judgment."[103] The reason for this conclusion is fairly clear: If a majority of such directors (including directors who approved the challenged transaction) are given authority to determine whether the suit should proceed, they will necessarily make a judgment, perhaps implicitly, on the propriety of their own conduct. To expect such directors who have authorized or benefited from a challenged transaction (that has perhaps benefited fellow directors as well) to judge in good faith whether the suit naming them as defendants is in the corporation's best interests is futile.[104] By the very nature of their

---

100. *See* authorities *supra* notes 90, 97. In certain situations, demand may be excused even if a majority of the directors are not named as defendants. *See* Clark v. Lomas & Nettleton Financial Corp., 625 F.2d 49, 53 (5th Cir. 1980), *cert. denied,* 101 S. Ct. 1738 (1981); Abbe v. Goss, 411 F. Supp. 923, 924–25 (S.D.N.Y. 1975); *In re* Penn Central Securities Litigation, 367 F. Supp. 1158, 1164–65 (E.D. Pa. 1973).

101. *See* Kim, *The Demand on Directors Requirement and the Business Judgment Rule in the Shareholder Derivative Suit: An Alternative Framework,* 6 J. CORP L. 511, 513 (1981) ("Futility may be shown . . . when a majority of the board of directors actually participated or acquiesced in the alleged wrongdoing"); authorities cited in notes 97-98 *supra.*

102. In this regard, however, "a bare allegation of control without factual support cannot excuse demand since the required particularity in pleading is absent." Stepak v. Dean, 434 A.2d 388, 391 (Del. Ch. 1981), *citing,* Greenspun v. Del. E. Webb Corp., 634 F.2d 1204, 1208 (9th Cir. 1980); *In re* Varnars v. Young, 539 F.2d 966 (3d Cir. 1976); *In re* Kauffman Mutual Fund Actions, 479 F.2d 257, 263 (1st Cir. 1973).

103. United Copper Sec. Co. v. Amalgamated Copper Co., 244 U.S. 261, 264 (1917) (Brandeis, J.). *See also* Clark v. Lomas & Nettleton Financial Corp., 625 F.2d 49, 52-54 (5th Cir. 1980), *cert. denied,* 101 S. Ct. 1738 (1981); Sohland v. Baker, 141 A.2d 277, 281-82 (Del. 1927); Ainscow v. Sanitary Co., 180 A.2d 614, 615 (Del. Ch. 1935).

104. This conclusion holds true regardless whether self-dealing (*e.g.,* remuneration benefits) or other types of misconduct (*e.g.,* illegal foreign payments) are involved. The crucial criterion is that the majority of directors in this context are incapable of exercising good faith judgment.

participation in the alleged illegal conduct, such directors are incapable of rendering impartial judgment. A contrary holding discounts the realities of the corporate decision-making process and fundamental principles of corporate accountability.[105]

Returning to *Maldonado*, the Delaware high court's promulgation of the two-step test in instances where demand is excused represents an innovative approach. In regard to the first step, the court correctly placed the burden on the corporation to show independence, good faith, and reasons supporting its determination.[106] Placing the burden on the party who selected the committee members, as the court implicitly noted, helps to remedy the appearance (and, indeed, perhaps the presence) of impropriety. Moreover, the court properly ordered inquiry into the reasonableness of the committee's investigation and bases for its conclusions. Although some courts have concluded that such an assessment is outside the province of the business judgment rule,[107] the better view is that the use of such committees to bar shareholder derivative suits against fellow directors reflects different policies than those present in the ordinary corporate decision clearly protected by the doctrine.[108] In such a situation, the pressure on the disinterested directors to disregard the corporation's best interests is so great that only a court's careful assessment of the reasonableness of the committee's investigation and conclusions will ensure the protection of the entity's welfare.

Turning to the second step, some commentators assert that, by requiring a court to exercise its own independent business judgment in determining whether to order dismissal, such courts are left with unduly broad and vague guidelines.[109] While this assertion has some merit, it bears emphasis that the Delaware Supreme Court correctly recognized that committee members pass judgment on fellow directors, thereby providing the need to implement "sufficient safeguard against abuse, perhaps subconscious abuse."[110] To help

---

105. *See generally* ALI Draft Restatement, note 5 *supra*, at § 7.03. Steinberg, *Application of the Business Judgment Rule and Related Judicial Principles—Reflections from a Corporate Accountability Perspective*, 56 NOTRE DAME LAW. 903, 915 (1981) ("although courts should apply the business judgment rule and related judicial principles in appropriate situations to shield management's conduct, they should be careful to ensure that their processes are not used as a sword by recalcitrant management to pierce legitimate shareholder interests"); Steinberg, *The ALI Draft Restatement on Corporate Governance—The Business Judgment Rule, Related Principles and Some General Observations*, 37 U. MIAMI L. REV. (Special Issue 1983).

106. 430 A.2d at 788.

107. *See, e.g.*, Gaines v. Haughton, 645 F.2d 761 (9th Cir. 1981); Auerbach v. Bennett, 47 N.Y.S.2d 619, 633-35, 393 N.E.2d 994, 1002-02, 419 N.Y.S.2d 920, 928-29 (1979).

108. *See* Cramer v. GTE Corp. 582 F.2d 259, 275 (3d Cir. 1978), *cert. denied*, 439 U.S. 1029 (1979); Genzer v. Cunningham, 498 F. Supp. 682, 689 (E.D. Mich. 1980); Maher v. Zapata Corp., 490 F. Supp. 348, 351-54 (S.D. Tex 1980).

109. *See, e.g.*, Brodsky, note 95 *supra*; Kinzey & Dreizer, note 95 *supra*. *See generally* Block & Prussin, *The Business Judgment Rule and Shareholder Derivative Actions: Viva Zapata?* 37 BUS. LAW. 27 (1981).

110. 430 A.2d at 787.

alleviate this deficiency, the court placed upon the movants the burden of proving independence, good faith, and reasonableness. Moreover, the court implicitly acknowledged that, even if this burden were met, to the shareholder seeking redress on the corporation's behalf, judicial deference to a special litigation committee's determination to bar the suit smacks of unfairness.[111] To counteract this effect as much as practicable, yet retain the committee's authority to terminate such actions, the Delaware high court expressly authorized the chancery court to exercise its own business judgment and, "when appropriate, [to] give special consideration to matters of law and public policy. . . ."[112]

Such a standard, although perhaps not subject to uniform application, may well be susceptible to practical implementation. The Delaware Supreme Court simply assured that the chancery court would independently consider the relevant factors and circumstances rather than relying on the committee's subjective assessment. Viewed another way, the chancery court's exercise of independent judgment may be another means by which to scrutinize the reasonableness of the committee's judgment. In this vein, such "reasonableness" transcends the sometimes narrow economic interests of the corporation and encompasses principles of shareholder welfare, public policy and, in essence, corporate accountability.

In summation, rather than being criticized, the Delaware Supreme Court should be applauded for its insightful approach to the issue of litigation termination when demand is excused. Although it is far too premature to venture whether the court's two-step test will lend itself to practical and equitable application, the Delaware high court innovatively sought a solution to a difficult conflict which was in dire need of clarification. By recognizing and attempting to reconcile these opposing interests—the need of a board to rid itself of unwanted, even if not frivolous, litigation and the accompanying problem of giving too much power to dissident shareholders *against* the need to provide an equitable resolution to legitimate corporate claims as expressed in a shareholder derivative action in light of serious problems of conflicts of interest and "structural bias"—the Delaware Supreme Court offered a refreshing approach. In this regard, although regrettably distinguishing between actions where demand is required as opposed to those where demand is excused, the court's decision in the latter area should be

---

111. *Id.* at 787-89.

112. *Id.* at 789. The court drew "some analogy to a settlement in that there is a request to terminate litigation without a judicial determination on the merits." *Id.* at 787-88, *citing,* Neponsit Investment Co. v. Abramson, 405 A.2d 97, 100 (Del. 1979) (and cases therein). The Delaware Supreme Court's rationale in *Maldonado* was adopted in Joy v. North, [1982 Transfer Binder] FED. SEC. L. REP. (CCH) ¶ 98,860 (2d Cir.) (applying Connecticut law); Watts v. Des Moines Register and Tribune, 525 F. Supp. 1311 (S.D. Iowa 1981) (applying Iowa law).

viewed as a welcome and needed judicial response addressing a fundamental concern in corporate accountability.

A New York Court of Appeals decision, *Auerbach v. Bennett*,[113] indicates that New York law apparently conflicts with the decision by the Delaware Supreme Court in *Maldonado*. Decided before *Maldonado*, *Auerbach* recognizes the propriety of a committee composed of disinterested directors, appointed by the board, to exercise its business judgment in terminating a shareholders' derivative action seeking damages against fellow directors.[114] In such a situation, the court must confine its inquiry to assessing the "independence" of the members of the committee and the appropriateness and adequacy of the investigative procedures selected and pursued by the committee.[115] In so holding, the court concluded that the substantive aspects of the committee's decision to bar a shareholders' derivative suit "is beyond judicial inquiry under the business judgment doctrine."[116]

Two recent New York lower court decisions have applied *Auerbach*. In *Falkenberg v. Baldwin*,[117] the Supreme Court of New York County held that a committee composed of outside directors of Uniroyal Corporation exercised its business judgment in recommending dismissal of a shareholders' derivative suit alleging violations of Title VII of the Civil Rights Act of 1964

---

113. 47 N.Y.2d 619, 393 N.E.2d 994, 419 N.Y.S.2d 920 (1979).

114. *Id.* at 630-34, 393 N.E.2d at 1000-02, 419 N.Y.S.2d at 926-28.

115. *Id.* at 634-35, 393 N.E.2d at 1002-03, 419 N.Y.S.2d at 929.

116. *Id.* at 623, 633, 393 N.E.2d at 926, 1002, 419 N.Y.S.2d at 922, 928. The court also expressly rejected the intervenor's contention that any committee appointed by the directors, some of whom were defendants, were legally infirm and thus had no authority to bar a derivative suit. The court stated:

> To accept the assertions of the intervenor and to disqualify the entire board would be to render the corporation powerless to make an effective business judgment with respect to prosecution of the derivative action. The possible risk of hesitancy on the part of the members of any committee, even if composed of outside, independent, disinterested directors, to investigate the activities of fellow members of the board where personal liability is at stake is an inherent, inescapable, given aspect of the corporation's predicament. To assign responsibility of the dimension here involved to individuals wholly separate and apart from the board of directors would, except in the most extraordinary circumstances, itself be an act of default and breach of the non-delegable fiduciary duty owed by the members of the board to the corporation and to its shareholders, employees and creditors. For the courts to preside over such determinations would similarly work an ouster of the board's fundamental responsibility and authority for corporate management.

Id. at 633, 393 N.E.2d at 1002, 419 N.Y.S.2d at 928. *But see* Chief Judge Cooke's dissent in *Auerbach*, where he asserted that "[s]ince the continuation of the suit is dependent, in large measure, upon the motives and actions of the defendants and the special litigation committee, and since knowledge of the matters 'is peculiarly in the possession of the defendants themselves,' summary judgment should not be granted prior to disclosure proceedings." *Id.* at 637, 393 N.E.2d at 1004, 419 N.Y.S.2d at 931 (Cooke, C. J., dissenting) (citation omitted).

117. SEC. REG. & L. REP. (BNA) No. 545, at A-14 (N.Y. Sup. Ct. Mar. 3, 1980).

(discrimination against female employees) by corporate officers and directors.[118] In so holding, the court placed the burden on the plaintiffs to show
lack of independence or insufficient investigative procedures by the committee.[119] The second case, *Parkoff v. General Telephone and Electronics
Corp.*,[120] relying directly on *Auerbach*, held that a decision to terminate a
shareholders' derivative action against the defendant directors for alleged
waste of corporate assets and breach of fiduciary duties in connection with
questionable foreign payments lay within the business judgment of a special
litigation committee composed of three outside directors, who were not
directors at the time of the transactions at issue.[121]

Although subsequently reversed by the New York Court of Appeals, the
lower appellate court's opinion in *Auerbach*[122] may be deemed relevant by
courts in other jurisdictions. In holding that the business judgment rule
could not be invoked to allow summary dismissal of a shareholders' derivative suit alleging breach of fiduciary duty, the lower court approved the
propriety of inquiring into the reasonableness of the investigative committee's decision.[123] Factors that such a committee must consider in an improper
payments case, and which a court presumably must assess, include "the
reasons for the payments, the advantages or disadvantages accruing to the
corporation by reason of the transactions, the extent of the participation
or profit by the respondent directors and the loss, if any, of public confidence
in the corporation which might be incurred."[124] In addition, the court emphasized that the hesitancy that outside directors may have in investigating
the activities of their fellow directors, particularly when personal liability
is at stake, "is a consideration of moment."[125]

---

118. *Id.* (relying on *Auerbach*).
119. *Id.*
120. 74 A.D.2d 762, 425 N.Y.S.2d 599 (1980).
121. *Id.* at 764, 425 N.Y.S.2d at 601.
122. Auerbach v. Bennett, 64 A.D.2d 98, 408 N.Y.S.2d 83 (1978).
123. *Id.* at 106-08, 408 N.Y.S.2d at 87-88; *see* Cramer v. General Tel. & Elecs. Corp., 582
F.2d 259, 275 (3d Cir. 1978); Maher v. Zapata Corp., 490 F. Supp. 348 (S.D. Tex. 1980).
124. 64 A.D.2d at 107, 408 N.Y.S.2d at 87-88.
125. *Id.* at 107, 408 N.Y.S.2d at 88. Speaking of the business judgment rule in this context,
the court asserted:

> The business judgment doctrine should not be interpreted to stifle legitimate scrutiny
> by stockholders of decisions of management which, concededly, require investigation
> by outside directors and present ostensible situations of conflict of interest. Nor should
> the report of the outside directors be immune from scrutiny by an interpretation of the
> doctrine which compels the acceptance of the findings of the report on their face. In
> particular, summary judgment which ends a derivative action at the threshold, before
> the plaintiff has been afforded the opportunity of pretrial discovery and examination
> before trial, should not be the means of foreclosing a nonfrivolous action.

Id. at 107-08, 408 N.Y.S.2d at 88.

As a final caveat, it should be mentioned that although both *Auerbach* and *Maldonado* contained allegations of breaches of fiduciary duty, *Auerbach* involved questionable foreign payments whereas *Maldonado* concerned a stock option plan.[126] Thus distinguished, the decisions in *Auerbach* and *Maldonado* arguably may be compatible. Unlike a number of shareholder derivative actions,[127] including the *Auerbach* suit, the situation in *Maldonado* involved direct self-dealing on the part of the defendant directors.[128] In such a situation, even assuming that the directors composing the special litigation committee do not "stand in a dual relation which prevents an unprejudiced exercise of judgment,"[129] the appearance of impropriety may be so great in certain cases as to preclude the committee from terminating the shareholders' suit. On the other hand, it is possible that when the alleged actions by the defendant directors have not inured to their direct benefit or do not involve conflicts of interest or fraudulent conduct, courts will be more receptive in permitting a special litigation committee to bar a shareholders' derivative suit.

IV. FURTHER REFLECTIONS ON THE USE OF SPECIAL LITIGATION COMMITTEES TO BAR SHAREHOLDER DERIVATIVE SUITS

To find a proper solution to this issue is a difficult proposition. As pointed out by the Ninth Circuit, to permit one stockholder to incapacitate an entire board of directors merely by alleging their having breached a fiduciary duty gives too much power to dissident shareholders.[130] Further, to disable the board from terminating derivative actions could well saddle the corporation with expensive and vexatious litigation.[131] On the other hand, to allow directors to bar lawsuits against their fellow directors raises serious questions

---

126. *Compare* 47 N.Y.2d at 623-25, 393 N.E.2d at 996-97, 419 N.Y.S.2d at 922-23, *with* 413 A.2d at 1254.

127. *See, e.g.,* Lewis v. Anderson, 615 F.2d 778, 780 (9th Cir. 1979); Abbey v. Control Data Corp., 603 F.2d 724, 726-27 (8th Cir. 1979).

128. *See* 413 A.2d at 1254-55. *See also* 430 A.2d at 780-81.

129. United Copper Sec. Co. v. Amalgamated Copper Co., 244 U.S. 261, 264 (1917).

130. *See* Lewis v. Anderson, 615 F.2d at 783. The court also stated that "[t]here is no reason to believe that a minority shareholder is more likely to act in the best interest of the corporation than are directors who are elected by a majority of the stockholders." *Id.* Although this assertion is certainly true in the ordinary management of the corporation, it clearly is not when management is alleged to have engaged in conflicts of interest, self-dealing, or fraud.

131. *See* Dent, *supra* note 7, at 98.

of conflicts of interest and ignores the inherent problem of "structural bias."[132] In this vein, there is certainly something to be said for the observation that aggrieved shareholders, when suing directors of their corporation for alleged breaches of fiduciary duty, are entitled to receive judgment from an impartial tribunal rather than from a committee appointed by the alleged wrongdoers.[133]

As noted earlier, the appearance of impartiality may be as important as impartiality in fact. To the shareholder seeking redress on behalf of the corporation, judicial deference to a special litigation committee's decision to terminate the suit smacks of unfairness. To counteract this effect as much as practicable, yet retain the board's authority to bar such suits, a court in this situation should scrutinize the committee's composition and decision to assure that the committee is, in fact, independent and disinterested, and that its determination is reasonable under all of the circumstances.[134]

---

132. In an interesting and provocative article, one commentator argues that the courts have largely ignored the structural bias problem in shareholder derivative suits. In so doing, the commentator contends that courts have effectively insulated corporate malfeasants from liability. In conclusion, the commentator asserts:

> Current judicial treatment of derivative actions against directors threatens to eliminate the utility of such suits. By applying the business judgment and demand rules originally designed for derivative suits against third parties to suits against directors, most courts have failed to recognize the inherent structural bias that corporate boards exhibit toward actions against directors. The use of special litigation committees has magnified the problem. Courts should only allow directors accused of wrongdoing to raise the business judgment rule as a defense to the alleged violation at a trial on the merits. They should retain the demand rule as a procedural requisite for derivative plaintiffs to give the corporation an opportunity to conduct the litigation. If the corporation declines that invitation, courts should allow the shareholder-plaintiff to pursue the claim.

Note 98 supra, at 632-33.

133. See Maldonado v. Flynn, 413 A.2d at 1262-63, rev'd and remanded, 430 A.2d 779 (Del. 1981). Note also that the issue remains whether a board of directors can validly delegate its authority to a special litigation committee, since a number of state statutes provide that committees serve "at the pleasure of the board." See, e.g., CAL. CORP. CODE § 311 (West 1977); MICH. COMP. LAWS ANN. § 450.1527 (1973); N.Y. BUS. CORP. LAW § 712(c) (McKinney Supp. 1979). Such statutes raise questions about the validity of the board's delegation of "binding" authority to the special litigation committee. See Note, supra note 98, at 618, 619.

134. See generally Cramer v. General Tel. & Elecs. Corp., 582 F.2d 259 (3d Cir. 1978):

> [W]e do not think that the business judgment of the directors should be totally insulated from judicial review. In order for the directors' judgment to merit judicial deference, that judgment must have been made in good faith and independently of any influence of those persons suspected of wrongdoing. In addition, where the shareholder contends that the directors' judgment is so unwise or unreasonable as to fall outside the permissible bounds of the directors' sound discretion, a court should, we think, be able to conduct its own analysis of the reasonableness of that business judgment.

Id. at 275. See Galef v. Alexander, 615 F.2d 51, 57-64 (2d Cir. 1980); Maher v. Zapata Corp., 490 F. Supp. 348, 351-54 (S.D. Tex. 1980); Maldonado v. Flynn, 413 A.2d 1251 (Del. Ch. 1980), rev'd and remanded, 430 A.2d 779 (Del. 1981).

Some courts and commentators have concluded that assessing the "reasonableness" of the committee's judgment is outside the purview of the business judgment rule.[135] Even assuming arguendo that such a position is technically correct, one should recognize that the use of special litigation committees to bar shareholder derivative suits against fellow directors is extraordinary. Indeed, three courts interpreting state law have placed this determination outside the province of the business judgment rule.[136] Even if viewed within the rule, such a determination nevertheless reflects different policies from those present in the ordinary corporate decision clearly protected by the doctrine.[137] A relevant analogy can be drawn from derivative suits challenging "interested transactions" between a corporation and its officers or directors. In these situations, even if a majority of disinterested directors approve such a transaction, a prevailing view is that the transaction's fairness to the corporation will be rigorously scrutinized.[138] The rationale for this approach equally applies to the issue of litigation termination: even if disinterested directors make that decision, the pressure to disregard the corporation's best interests is so great that only a court's careful scrutiny of the directors' conduct will ensure the protection of the entity's welfare.[139]

In addition, the members who compose the special litigation committee should be both disinterested and independent. At the very least, "disinterested" should signify that the directors did not authorize or approve the challenged transaction and are not named as defendants in the law suit.[140]

---

135. *See, e.g.,* Auerbach v. Bennett, 47 N.Y.2d 619, 633-35, 393 N.E.2d 994, 1002-03, 419 N.Y.S.2d 920, 928-29 (1979); Olson, *Courts Firm Against Creation of U.S. Corporation Law,* Legal Times (Wash.), April 2, 1980, at 42.

136. Abella v. Universal Leaf Tobacco Co., 495 F. Supp. 713 (E.D. Va. 1980) (Virginia law); Maher v. Zapata Corp., 490 F. Supp. at 351 (Delaware law); Maldonado v. Flynn, 413 A.2d 1251 (Del. Ch. 1980), *rev'd and remanded,* 430 A.2d 779 (Del. 1981).

137. *See* Genzer v. Cunningham, 498 F. Supp. 682, 689 (E.D. Mich. 1980) ("The court is aware that application of the business judgment rule to circumstances where a committee is charged with the responsibility of determining whether shareholder litigation should continue is an expansion of the traditional rule").

138. *See, e.g.,* Pepper v. Litton, 308 U.S. 295, 306 (1939); Gottlieb v. Heyden Chem. Corp., 33 Del. Ch. 82, 88, 90 A.2d 660, 663 (1952); Abeles v. Adams Eng'r Co., 35 N.J. 411, 428-29, 173 A.2d 246, 255 (1961); Marsh, *Are Directors Trustees? Conflict of Interest and Corporate Morality,* 22 Bus. Law. 35, 43 (1966). Additionally, it is important to emphasize that the business judgment rule does not apply to the scrutiny of such transactions. *See* notes 5-8 *supra.*

139. *See* Dent, *supra* note 7, at 121, 122, 137. Note that under this standard, the court scrutinizes the "reasonableness" of the special litigation committee's determination, avoiding the result that "almost any decision to terminate a derivative action will appear 'reasonable' to a 'reasonable' special litigation committee." Note, *supra* note 98, at 626.

140. *See* Galef v. Alexander, 615 F.2d 51, 59-61 (2d Cir. 1980); Abbey v. Control Data Corp., 603 F.2d 724, 727 (8th Cir. 1979); Nussbacher v. Chase Manhattan Bank, 444 F. Supp. 973, 977 (S.D.N.Y. 1977).

Further, the term "independent" should signify that the members of the committee are not subject to the defendants' influence and can exercise independent judgment on behalf of the corporation. The "independence" of the members, particularly if selected by the defendants, should be subject to rigorous scrutiny. *Any* prior contacts or relationships between the members and the defendants should be examined with care. Particularly if a member stands to gain financially or otherwise by determining that the derivative suit should be terminated, his "independent" status should be inherently suspect.[141] Further, although some courts have placed the burden on the shareholders,[142] such burden of establishing independence should be placed on the parties seeking dismissal. When the defendants have selected the committee members, the appearance of impropriety (indeed, perhaps the presence of it) can be remedied only if the persons who made that selection satisfy the court on the issue of independence.[143]

Because the pleadings are usually inadequate for the court to assess the reasonableness of the special litigation committee's judgment, including such issues as whether the members were fully informed of the facts material to their decision[144] and whether the particular members were in fact independent, it is appropriate for the court to permit limited discovery.[145] Despite entailing some expense and inconvenience to the corporation, discovery is necessary for the court to rule in an informed manner on the defendants' motion to dismiss the complaint.[146]

As a final comment, *Maldonado* in Delaware may have as its benchmark the theme of corporate accountability. Although corporations are ordinarily managed under the direction of their boards of directors,[147] *Maldonado* suggests that at least some courts are showing less tolerance for self-dealing and conflicts of interest by directors that cause hardship to shareholders of

---

141. *See* Galef v. Alexander, 615 F.2d at 60-61; Maher v. Zapata Corp., 490 F. Supp. 348, 353-54 (S.D. Tex. 1980).

142. *See* Lewis v. Anderson, 615 F.2d at 783; Auerbach v. Bennett, 47 N.Y.2d at 633-35, 393 N.E.2d at 1002-03, 419 N.Y.S.2d at 928-29; Falkenberg v. Baldwin, Sec. Reg. & L. Rep. (BNA) No. 545, at A-14 (N.Y. Sup. Ct. March 3, 1980).

143. "Plaintiffs' allegation that the Committee merely conducted a 'rationalization' of the claims instead of an investigation since the exculpation of Defendants' conduct was foreordained is not totally incomprehensible in view of the fact that the Committee was appointed by the alleged wrongdoers." Maher v. Zapata Corp., 490 F. Supp. at 354. *See* Maldonado v. Flynn, 430 A.2d at 788-89.

144. *See* Auerbach v. Bennett, 64 A.D.2d 98, 106-07, 408 N.Y.S.2d 83, 87-88 (1978). *See* Brief for the SEC as *Amicus Curiae* at 18, Burks v. Lasker, 441 U.S. 471 (1979).

145. *See, e.g.,* Lewis v. Anderson, 615 F.2d at 783; Maldonado v. Flynn, 485 F. Supp. 274, 285-86 (S.D.N.Y. 1980); Rosengarten v. International Tel. & Tel. Corp., 466 F. Supp. 817, 823 (S.D.N.Y. 1979); Gall v. Exxon Corp., 418 F. Supp. 508, 520 (S.D.N.Y. 1976).

146. *See* Brief for the SEC, *supra* note 144, at 16.

147. *See* authorities cited in note 5 *supra.*

publicly held corporations.[148] Viewed from this perspective, the Delaware Supreme Court's decision is refreshing. Regardless of whether other tribunals follow *Maldonado's* rationale on the applicability of the business judgment rule in this context, one can only hope that they will respect and heed its concern for corporate accountability.

V. CONCLUSION

Although the complexities intertwined with director dismissal of shareholder derivative suits against fellow directors may sometimes appear incapable of resolution, certain criteria may be set forth to guide the conduct of special litigation committees. First, from decisions thus far, less than a quorum of directors can properly act for the corporation in seeking the termination of a shareholders' derivative action.[149] Second, although the decisions arguably are conflicting,[150] the wisest course of action would be to name only nondefendant, disinterested, and independent persons to the special litigation committee. Third, the board should delegate binding, nonreviewable authority to the committee to investigate and determine whether the suit is in the corporation's best interests.[151] Fourth, the committee should employ thorough investigative procedures, including the appointment of a reputable special counsel and law firm to assist in the investigation.[152] Fifth, the directors and other relevant parties should inform committee members of all facts material to the committee's decision.[153] And, as a final caveat, the special litigation committee should conduct itself so as to withstand strict judicial scrutiny.

---

148. The Goldberg v. Meridor line of Rule 10b-5 cases provides another example of this judicial scrutiny. *See, e.g.,* Healey v. Catalyst Recovery, Inc., 616 F.2d 641 (3d Cir. 1980); Alabama Farm Bureau Mut. Cas. Co. v. Alabama Fidelity Life Ins. Co., 606 F.2d 602 (5th Cir. 1979), *cert. denied,* 100 S. Ct. 77 (1980); Kidwell *ex rel.* Penfold v. Meikle, 597 F.2d 1273 (9th Cir. 1979); Goldberg v. Meridor, 567 F.2d 209 (2d Cir. 1977), *cert. denied,* 434 U.S. 1069 (1978); Wright v. Heizer Corp., 560 F.2d 236 (7th Cir. 1977), *cert. denied,* 434 U.S. 1066 (1978). For an analysis of this trend, herein, *see* pages 163-98 *infra.*

149. *See, e.g.* Lewis v. Anderson, 615 F.2d at 782 n.1; Maldonado v. Flynn, 485 F. Supp. at 286, *remanded,* [1981-1982 Transfer Binder] FED. SEC. L. REP. (CCH) ¶ 98,457 (2d Cir. 1982).

150. *Compare* Lewis v. Anderson, 615 F.2d at 783, *with* Galef v. Alexander, 615 F.2d at 60-61, 63-64.

151. *See, e.g.,* Maldonado v. Flynn, 485 F. Supp. at 283, *remanded,* [1981-1982 Transfer Binder] FED. SEC. L. REP. (CCH) ¶ 98,457 (2d Cir. 1982).

152. *See, e.g.,* Auerbach v. Bennett, 47 N.Y.2d at 634-35, 393 N.E.2d at 1002-03, 419 N.Y.S.2d at 929.

153. *See generally* Cramer v. General Tel. & Elecs. Corp., 582 F.2d 259, 275 (3d Cir. 1978).

Although the principles outlined above and throughout this chapter may not guarantee vindication of the shareholders' and corporation's grievances, they will help ensure, if diligently applied by the courts, increased accountability for directors' conduct. In a world where corporations fear "strike suits," sometimes with good reason,[154] and where the business judgment rule protects directors as the monitors of our corporations,[155] perhaps this approach is most practicable. On the other hand, when directors' alleged actions involve conflicts of interests, fraud, or self-dealing, which inure to their direct benefit, there is much to be said for the approaches adopted by the Delaware Chancery and Supreme Courts in *Maldonado*.[156] Whichever approach ultimately prevails, the courts should strive to implement the principle of corporate accountability in an attempt "to find a balancing point where bona fide stockholder power to bring corporate causes of action cannot be unfairly trampled on by the board of directors, [while allowing] the corporation [to] rid itself of detrimental litigation."[157]

---

154. *See* Blue Chip Stamps v. Manor Drug Stores, 421 U.S. 723, 737-48 (1975). With regard to strike suits, the Supreme Court has stated:

> [I]n the field of federal securities laws governing disclosure of information even a complaint which by objective standards may have very little chance of success at trial has a settlement value to the plaintiff out of any proportion to its prospect of success at trial so long as he may prevent the suit from being resolved against him by dismissal or summary judgment. The very pendency of the lawsuit may frustrate or delay normal business activity of the defendant which is totally unrelated to the lawsuit.

Id. at 740 (citations omitted). Arguably, however, the courts may combat the potential of vexatious litigation by measures such as requiring plaintiffs to post security for expenses, requiring judicial review of derivative settlements, and granting summary judgment motions. See Note, *supra* note 98, at 632. A number of states now require the posting of security for expenses. *See, e.g.,* CAL. CORP. CODE § 800(d) (West 1976); N.J. STAT. ANN. § 14A:3-6(3) (West Supp. 1976); N.Y. BUS. CORP. LAW § 627 (McKinney Supp. 1979); MODEL BUS. CORP. ACT § 59, ¶ 2 (1976). In one case, the Second Circuit held that, pursuant to New York law, the trial court properly dismissed a shareholder's derivative suit for failure to post the required security. The court concluded that the shareholder's acquisition of stock after the commencement of the action was not sufficient to obviate the security requirement. Haberman v. Tobin, 626 F.2d 1101 (2d Cir. 1980).

155. *See* notes 5-13 and accompanying text *supra*.

156. *See also* Genzer v. Cunningham, 498 F. Supp. 682, 688 (E.D. Mich. 1980) ("[U]nlike in *Maldonado,* there is no allegation of personal gain by the directors. . .").

157. Maldonado v. Flynn, 430 A.2d 779, 787 (Del. 1981).

4

The Corporate Mismanagement-
Nondisclosure Cases

I. INTRODUCTION

In *Santa Fe Industries, Inc. v. Green,*[1] the Supreme Court refused to recognize an actionable claim under Section 10(b) of the Securities Exchange Act of 1934[2] and Rule 10b-5 thereunder[3] for alleged breaches of fiduciary duty in

---

1. 430 U.S. 462 (1977).
2. 15 U.S.C. § 78j(b) (1976). Section 10(b) provides:

> Section 10. It shall be unlawful for any person, directly or indirectly, by the use of any means or instrumentality of interstate commerce or of the mails, or of any facility of any national securities exchange—
>
> . . .
>
> (b) To use or employ, in connection with the purchase or sale of any security registered on a national securities exchange or any security not so registered, any manipulative or deceptive device or contrivance in contravention of such rules and regulations as the Commission may prescribe as necessary or appropriate in the public interest or for the protection of investors.

3. 17 C.F.R. § 240.10b-5 (1981). Rule 10b-5 provides:

> It shall be unlawful for any person, directly or indirectly, by the use of any means or instrumentality of interstate commerce, or of the mails, or of any facility of any national securities exchange,
>
> (1) to employ any device, scheme, or artifice to defraud,
>
> (2) to make any untrue statement of a material fact or to omit to state a material fact necessary in order to make the statements made, in the light of the circumstances under which they were made, not misleading, or
>
> (3) to engage in any act, practice, or course of business which operates or would operate as a fraud or deceit upon any person, in connection with the purchase or sale of any security.

connection with a corporate merger.[4] The *Santa Fe* Court concluded that, absent "manipulation" or "deception," the statute and rule do not reach breaches of fiduciary duty.[5] The Supreme Court's decision was widely regarded as sharply curtailing the scope of Rule 10b-5.[6] In what has become an important caveat to the *Santa Fe* holding, however, the Court reasoned in footnote fourteen:

> [The plaintiffs'] major contention in this respect is that the majority stockholder's failure to give the minority advance notice of the merger was a material nondisclosure, even though the Delaware short-form merger statute does not require such notice. But respondents do not indicate how they might have acted differently had they had prior notice of the merger. Indeed, they accept the conclusion of both courts below that under Delaware law they could not have enjoined the merger because an appraisal proceeding is their sole remedy in the Delaware courts for any alleged unfairness in the terms of the merger. Thus, the failure to give advance notice was not a material nondisclosure within the meaning of the statute or the Rule.[7]

Today, however, no plaintiff would concede that appraisal is his sole remedy under Delaware law in a *Santa Fe*-type situation. Shortly after *Santa Fe*, the Delaware Supreme Court reexamined its traditional merger doctrines and adopted a new approach to the subject.[8] This approach has proved significantly more sensitive than prior state law to the interests of minority shareholders.[9] Concomitantly, federal courts have contributed to the protection of investor interests: noting that shareholders may bring state law

---

4. 430 U.S. at 471. In *Santa Fe,* minority shareholders objected to the terms of a short-form merger pursuant to a Delaware state statute. In lieu of pursuing their appraisal remedies, the shareholders commenced an action on behalf of the corporation and other minority shareholders seeking to set aside the merger or to recover the alleged full value of their shares. *Id.* 466-67.

5. *Id.* 473-74.

6. *E.g.,* Campbell, Santa Fe Industries, Inc. v. Green: *An Analysis Two Years Later,* 30 MAINE L. REV. 187 (1979); Jacobs, *Rule 10b-5 and Self Dealing by Corporate Fiduciaries: An Analysis,* 48 U. CIN. L. REV. 643 (1979); Ratner, *"Federal Corporation Law" Before and After Santa Fe Industries v. Green,* in NINTH ANNUAL INSTITUTE ON SECURITIES REGULATION—CORPORATE TRANSCRIPT SERIES 305, 322 (Fleischer, Lipton, & Vandegrift eds., 1978); Note, *Suits for Breach of Fiduciary Duty Under Rule 10b-5 After Santa Fe Industries, Inc. v. Green,* 91 HARV. L. REV. 1874 (1978).

7. 430 U.S. at 474 n.14 (citations omitted).

8. *See, e.g.,* Weinberger v. UOP, Inc., 15 SEC. REG. & L. REP. (BNA) 327 (Del. 1983); Roland Int'l Corp. v. Najjar, 407 A.2d 1032 (Del. 1979); Tanzer v. International Gen. Indus., Inc., 379 A.2d 1121 (Del. 1977); Singer v. Magnavox Co., 380 A.2d 969 (Del. 1977).

9. *See* notes 85-90 *infra* and text accompanying notes 75-90 *infra.*

claims based on breaches of fiduciary duty, a number of federal courts have concluded that, in certain circumstances, the nondisclosure of facts needed in order to bring such claims constitutes "deception" within the meaning of Section 10(b) and Rule 10b-5.[10]

The evolution of *Santa Fe* and its progeny in the federal and state courts can be seen as an experiment in American federalism.[11] Prior to *Santa Fe,* it was widely felt that state corporation laws inadequately protected shareholders from overreaching by management. Indeed, the trend towards "flexible" and "modern" corporation statutes was frequently characterized as a "race to the bottom" that ignored all interests except management's.[12] The remedies proposed for the perceived abuses were often some form of federal regulation. A number of commentators urged a system of federal chartering of corporations,[13] while others advocated statutory adoption of federal standards of corporate responsibility[14] or an expansion of existing federal securities law remedies.[15] Indeed, federal regulation of various aspects of corporation law became increasingly common. Both courts[16] and

---

10. *See, e.g.,* Healey v. Catalyst Recovery, Inc., 616 F.2d 641 (3d Cir. 1980); Alabama Farm Bureau Mut. Cas. Co. v. Alabama Fidelity Life Ins. Co., 606 F.2d 602 (5th Cir. 1979), *cert. denied,* 101 S. Ct. 77 (1980); Kidwell *ex rel.* Penfold v. Meikle, 597 F.2d 1273 (9th Cir. 1979); Goldberg v. Meridor, 567 F.2d 209 (2d Cir. 1977), *cert. denied,* 434 U.S. 1069 (1978); Wright v. Heizer Corp., 560 F.2d 236 (7th Cir. 1977), *cert. denied,* 434 U.S. 1066 (1978).

11. It is important to emphasize that the term "federalism" is used in this chapter in a colloquial sense only, without implicating constitutional overtones.

12 *E.g.,* Cary, *Federalism and Corporate Law: Reflections Upon Delaware,* 83 YALE L.J 663 (1974); Folk, *Corporation Statutes: 1959-1966,* 1966 DUKE L.J. 875; Jennings, *Federalization of Corporation Law: Part Way or All the Way,* 31 BUS. LAW. 991 (1976); Kaplan, *Fiduciary Responsibility in the Management of the Corporation,* 31 BUS. LAW. 883 (1976); Schwartz, *Federal Chartering of Corporations: An Introduction,* 61 GEO. L.J. 71 (1972); Note, *Federal Chartering of Corporations: A Proposal,* 61 GEO. L.J. 89 (1972).

13. *E.g.,* R. Nader, *The Case for Federal Chartering,* in CORPORATE POWER IN AMERICA 67 (R. Nader & M. Green eds., 1973); Henning, *Federal Corporate Chartering for Big Business: An Idea Whose Time Has Come?* 21 DEPAUL L. REV. 915 (1972); Reuschlein, *Federalization—Design for Corporate Reform in a National Economy,* 91 U. PA. L. REV. 91 (1942); Schwartz, *supra* note 12; Note, *supra* note 12; Note, *Federal Chartering of Corporations: Constitutional Challenges,* 61 GEO. L.J. 123 (1972); Comment, *Law for Sale: A Study of the Delaware Corporation Law of 1967,* 117 U. PA. L. REV. 861, 898 (1969).

14. *E.g.,* Cary, *supra* note 12; Ruder, *Pitfalls in the Development of a Federal Law of Corporations by Implication Through Rule 10b-5,* 59 NW. U.L. REV. 185 (1964); Vagts, *The Governance of the Corporation: The Options Available and the Power to Prescribe,* 31 BUS. LAW. 929 (1976).

15. *E.g.,* Fleischer, *"Federal Corporation Law": An Assessment,* 78 HARV. L. REV. 1146 (1965); Folk, *Corporation Law Developments—1969,* 56 VA. L. REV. 755 (1970). *Cf.* Kaplan, *supra* note 12 (discussing possibilities for expansion of Rule 10b-5); Jennings, *supra* note 12 (discussing recent expansion of Rule 10b-5).

16. *E.g.,* McClure v. Borne Chem. Co., 292 F.2d 824 (3d Cir.), *cert. denied,* 368 U.S. 939 (1961).

commentators[17] spoke of an emerging "federal corporation law." Interestingly, after *Santa Fe,* the roles have been somewhat reversed, particularly in the Delaware courts.[18] Generally, it is now the state courts that scrutinize alleged breaches of fiduciary duty while the lower federal courts apply footnote fourteen of *Santa Fe* to extend federal protection to shareholders in such cases.[19]

The following discussion shall examine *Santa Fe* and its progeny from the preceding perspective. First, for historical purposes, it will describe the chartering states' "race for the bottom" in the pre-*Santa Fe* period. Second,

---

17. Fleischer, *supra* note 15; Friendly, *In Praise of Erie—And of the New Federal Common Law,* 39 N.Y.U.L. REV. 383, 413-14.

18. *See* note 8 *supra* and accompanying text.

19. *See* note 10 *supra* and accompanying text. There appears to be little question that recent Supreme Court decisions have restricted the reach, scope and effect of the federal securities laws. *See, e.g.,* Aaron v. SEC, 100 S. Ct. 1945 (1980) (scienter required in SEC injunctive actions under § 10(b) of Securities Exchange Act, Rule 10b-5 thereunder, and § 17(a)(1) of Securities Act); Chiarella v. United States, 100 S. Ct. 1108 (1980) (no duty to disclose under § 10(b) of Securities Exchange Act arises from mere possession of nonpublic market information); Transamerica Mortgage Advisors, Inc. v. Lewis, 444 U.S. 11 (1979) (no implied private right of action under § 206 of the Investment Advisers Act; limited implied private right of action under § 215); Touche Ross & Co. v. Redington, 442 U.S. 560 (1979) (no implied private right of action under § 17(a) of the Exchange Act); International Bhd. of Teamsters v. Daniel, 439 U.S. 551 (1979) (interest in noncontributory, compulsory pension plan not "security" subject to regulation under Securities Acts); SEC v. Sloan, 436 U.S. 103 (1978) (limiting SEC's right to suspend summarily for successive ten-day periods trading in registered securities); Santa Fe Indus., Inc. v. Green, 430 U.S. 462 (1977) (breach of fiduciary duty, without manipulation or deception, not actionable under § 10(b) of Exchange Act and Rule 10b-5); Piper v. Chris-Craft Indus., Inc., 430 U.S. 1 (1977) (defeated tender offeror has no standing to bring implied private right of action for damages under § 14(e) of Exchange Act); Ernst & Ernst v. Hochfelder, 425 U.S. 185 (1976) (scienter required in private damage actions under § 10(b) and Rule 10b-5); Blue Chip Stamps v. Manor Drug Store, 421 U.S. 723 (1975) (only purchasers and sellers have standing to bring implied private cause of action for damages under § 10(b) and Rule 10b-5). This trend is particularly evident when the recent cases are contrasted with expansive decisions of the past. *See, e.g.,* Superintendent of Ins. v. Bankers Life & Cas Co., 404 U.S. 6 (1971). *See generally* Lowenfels, *Recent Supreme Court Decisions Under the Federal Securities Laws: The Pendulum Swings,* 65 GEO. L.J. 891 (1977); Steinberg, *Implied Private Rights of Action Under Federal Law,* 55 NOTRE DAME LAW. 33 (1979). With respect to § 10(b), Justice Blackmun, dissenting in *Chiarella,* stated: "The Court continues to pursue a course, charted in certain recent decisions, designed to transform § 10(b) from an intentionally elastic 'catchall' provision to one that catches relatively little of the misbehavior that all too often makes investment in securities a needlessly risky business for the uninitiated investor." 100 S. Ct. at 1123-24 (Blackmun, J., dissenting).

On some specific issues, however, the Court has departed from this restrictive approach. *See, e.g.,* Herman and MacLean v. Huddleston, [Current] FED. SEC. L. REP. (CCH) ¶ 99,058 (U.S. 1983) (cumulative remedy approach as well as preponderance of the evidence standard in private actions adopted); Merrill Lynch, Pierce, Fenner & Smith, Inc. v. Curran, 102 S. Ct. 1825 (1982) (implied right of action for damages under Commodity Exchange Act); Steadman v. SEC, 101 S. Ct. 999 (1981) (preponderance of the evidence is the proper standard to be

the discussion will turn to the *Santa Fe* line of cases in both the federal and state courts. As hopefully will be seen, the respective positions taken by the federal and state tribunals represent a surprising and delicate experiment in federalism.

II. "THE RACE FOR THE BOTTOM"—
A BRIEF OVERVIEW

Shortly after the passage of the Delaware Corporation Law of 1967,[20] a critical commentator observed:

The sovereign state of Delaware is in the business of selling its corporation law. This is profitable business, for corporation law is a

---

applied in SEC administrative actions based on fraud); Rubin v. United States, 101 S. Ct. 698 (1981) (pledge of stock as collateral for a loan is an "offer or sale" of a security under § 17(a) of the Securities Act); Aaron v. SEC, 100 S. Ct. 1945 (1980) (scienter not required in SEC injunctive actions under § 17(a)(2) and (3) of Securities Act); United States v. Naftalin, 441 U.S. 768 (1979) (reach of § 17(a) of Securities Act extends beyond actual purchasers and sellers and encompasses aftermarket trading frauds).

If the Supreme Court ultimately rejects the imposition of liability under § 10(b) and Rule 10b-5 in cases relying on footnote fourteen of *Santa Fe,* a possible remedy under the federal securities laws for alleged violations of this sort may be § 17(a) of the Securities Act. In light of recent Supreme Court decisions, plaintiffs may be forced to argue under that section that a private right of action exists, that aggrieved offerees have standing, and that there is no scienter requirement. After *Aaron,* it is clear that the SEC is not required to prove scienter in Commission injunctive actions based on violations of § 17(a)(2) and (3). 100 S. Ct. at 1956-57. For scholarly comment on § 17(a), *see, e.g.,* Hazen, *A Look Beyond the Pruning of Rule 10b-5: Implied Remedies and Section 17(a) of the Securities Act of 1933,* 64 VA. L. REV. 641 (1978); Horton, *Section 17(a) of the 1933 Securities Act—The Wrong Place for a Private Right,* 68 NW. U.L. REV. 44 (1973); Steinberg, *Section 17(a) of the Securities Act of 1933 After Naftalin and Redington,* 68 GEO. L.J. 163 (1979).

Another possible remedy in *Santa Fe* footnote fourteen-type cases is § 14(a) of the Securities Exchange Act and Rule 14a-9 promulgated thereunder. Organic corporate changes, such as mergers or consolidations, require a shareholder vote, and hence, solicitation of proxies. In these types of situations, shareholders may be able to seek relief under both § 10(b) and § 14(a). Because the standards underlying a § 14(a)/14a-9 remedy may differ from those in a § 10(b)/10b-5 cause of action, the implied remedy under § 14(a) may sometimes give relief where the § 10(b) remedy may fail. Moreover, because mergers may involve the *Santa Fe*-type situation, in which dissenting shareholders are frozen out, actions brought pursuant to § 14(a) will bring the *Santa Fe* state law analysis into sharp focus. Indeed, the federal-state tension that underlies much of *Santa Fe* may attach to any proxy-related claim in which the minority does not receive fair share for its stock. In contrast to *Santa Fe,* however, the proxy provisions do not contain a requirement of "manipulative" or "deceptive" conduct. Thus, § 14(a) may arguably be used to avoid the strictures of *Santa Fe. See* Hazen, *Corporate Mismanagement in the Federal Securities Act's Anti-Fraud Provisions: A Familiar Path with Some New Detours,* 20 B.C.L. REV. 819, 850 (1979); Steinberg, *Fiduciary Duties and Disclosure Obligations in Proxy and Tender Contests for Corporate Control,* 30 EMORY L.J. 169, 193-95 (1981).

20. DEL. CODE ANN. tit. 8, §§ 101-398 (1974 & Supps. 1978 & 1979).

good commodity to sell. The market is large, and relatively few producers compete on a national scale. The consumers of this commodity are corporations, and as we shall see, Delaware, like any other good businessman, tries to give the consumer what he wants. In fact, those who will buy the product are not only consulted about their preferences, but are also allowed to design the product and run the factory.[21]

Although this statement may appear somewhat exaggerated and unfair, a number of observers have found it reasonably accurate.[22] For example, Professor William L. Cary, who was a former Chairman of the Securities and Exchange Commission, described state corporation law as a "race for the bottom" that Delaware had won.[23]

Delaware, however, was not alone in enacting a corporation law designed to encourage corporate chartering in the state. New Jersey, for example, eager for the revenues derived from corporate chartering, enacted in 1896 what has been viewed as the first of the modern liberal corporation statutes.[24] The Act attracted the incorporation of the New Jersey trusts, including the old Standard Oil Company.[25] At the insistence of then Governor Woodrow Wilson, New Jersey eventually tightened its corporation law in 1913,[26] but

---

21. Comment, *supra* note 13, at 861-62.

22. *See, e.g.,* authorities cited in note 12 *supra*. Professor Manning has characterized state corporation statutes as "towering skyscrapers of rusted girders, internally welded together and containing nothing but wind." Manning, *supra* note 12, at 245 n.37. Another distinguished scholar, Professor Folk, who served as reporter to the Delaware Corporation Law Revision Committee, has said of corporation law generally:

> Almost without exception, the key movement in corporation law revisions is toward ever greater permissiveness. . . . Explicitly positing an objective of "flexibility," statutory revisers . . . have usually sought to enlarge the ambit of freedom of corporate management to take whatever action it may wish. . . . Indeed the new statutes seem to be exclusively concerned with only one constituent of the corporate community—management—and have disregarded the interests of shareholders and creditors, let alone more tangentially interested parties, such as employees, customers, and the general public. . . . [I]t appears that these trends are irreversible, absent some presently unforeseeable changes in the basic structure of the American economy. State efforts to go against such deep-seated dispositions, even if desired, would be futile.

Folk, *Some Reflections of a Corporation Law Draftsman,* 42 CONN. B.J. 409, 410 (1968). *See generally, Symposium on Federal and State Roles in Establishing Standards of Conduct for Corporate Management,* 31 BUS. LAW. 856 (1976), in which the inadequacies of state corporation law were debated, discussed, and documented at great length (and in which Delaware and other prominent states had their ardent supporters).

23. Cary, *supra* note 12, at 705.

24. E. DODD & R. BAKER, CASES AND MATERIALS ON CORPORATIONS 38 (2d ed. 1951); Cary, *supra* note 12, at 664.

25. Cary, *supra* note 12, at 664.

26. *Id. See also* E. DODD & R. BAKER, *supra* note 24, at 38.

the tone of permissiveness resurfaced in the state's Corporation Law Revision Commission's Report of 1968:

> Since World War I, however, it is clear that the trend has been steadily toward Delaware incorporation as New Jersey has fallen further behind in modernizing its corporation act to meet current needs and practices. The Commission trusts that this trend will now be reversed, in light of the revision of the New Jersey corporation laws herewith submitted.[27]

Despite New Jersey's efforts, Delaware has emerged as the clear victor in this race.[28] As Professor Cary pointed out, however, if Delaware had elected not to retain its lead, other states would have hastened to assume its lucrative position.[29]

Due to this perverse competition, the adequacy of the protections that state corporation law provides investors has long been questioned.[30] As alluded to above, this competition rewards the state that can be most permissive. All too often the competition is sadly one-sided. Frequently, entrenched management's viewpoint is dominant in the state capitals,[31] and little attention is given to traditional fiduciary standards or to the investor's claim to fair treatment.[32]

In response to this situation, many commentators have advocated the application of federal standards of corporate responsibility.[33] Some observers believed that Rule 10b-5 should have been expansively interpreted to act as the watchdog for all corporate activity.[34] Indeed, the impetus for this approach may have been provided by the federal judiciary itself.[35] For ex-

---

27. N.J. STAT. ANN. § 14A, at x (West 1968).

28. See Cary, supra note 12, at 668:

> Delaware understandably does not wish to surrender its lead. Amending its law in 1969, and again in 1970 and 1971, it is setting the pace. It likes to be number one. With some justification Delaware corporate counsel take pride in their role and enjoy the fees that flow from it. The system "engenders a volume of business for the bar which tends to be regarded as a vested interest, so that any attempt to retrace steps would encounter opposition in powerful quarters." Most important, the raison d'etre behind the whole system has been achieved—revenue for the state of Delaware.

Id. (citations omitted).

29. Id. 665. Apparently, Nevada has attempted to become the western Delaware but has not had comparable success. Id. See also Comment, supra note 13, at 871-72.

30. See authorities cited in note 12 supra.

31. Cf. Cary, supra note 12, at 690-92 (discussing links between Delaware Law Revision Commission of 1967 and the corporate bar); Comment, supra note 13 (same).

32. Cary, supra note 14; Folk, supra note 22; Comment, supra note 13.

33. See authorities cited in notes 14 and 15 supra.

34. See authorities cited in note 15 supra.

35. McClure v. Borne Chem. Co., 292 F.2d 824, 834 (3d Cir.), cert. denied, 368 U.S. 939 (1961) (Securities Exchange Act termed "far reaching Federal substantive corporation law"). See also cases cited in notes 36-38 infra.

ample, the federal courts interpreted Rule 10b-5 in various cases to protect purchasers and sellers from persons who improperly traded on the basis of inside information,[36] to provide relief to participants in transactions involving misleading corporate publicity,[37] and to relax the reliance requirement in cases of nondisclosure.[38]

Expansion of Rule 10b-5 to encompass the "corporate universe" was not the only method proposed by commentators to advance the application of federal standards of corporate responsibility. One alternative, federal incorporation, was far from novel. Indeed, from 1903 to 1914, no less than twenty bills were introduced in Congress to provide for the incorporation of companies conducting interstate business or to require such companies to obtain federal licenses.[39] Although never successful, the concept continues to attract the attention of reformers.[40]

A third alternative, proposed by Professor Cary, recommended the adoption of a federal statute that would provide for, *inter alia,* the implementation of federal fiduciary standards, a requirement that all "interested directors" transactions be fair, and greater shareholder participation in the corporate

---

36. *See, e.g.,* SEC v. Geon Indus., Inc., 531 F.2d 39 (2d Cir. 1976); SEC v. Shapiro, 494 F.2d 1301 (2d Cir. 1974); SEC v. Great Am. Indus., Inc., 407 F.2d 453, 462 (2d Cir. 1968) (Kaufman, J., concurring), *cert. denied,* 395 U.S. 920 (1969) ("[a]ny claim that material facts were withheld in a transaction in connection with the sale or purchase of securities must be scrutinized with care, whether or not there would have been liability at common law for such a deed"). *But see* Chiarella v. United States, 100 S. Ct. 1108 (1980) (no duty to disclose under § 10(b) arises from mere possession of nonpublic market information). This prohibition against insider trading extends as well to tippees. *See, e.g.,* SEC v. Geon Indus., Inc., 531 F.2d 39 (2d Cir. 1976).

37. *See, e.g.,* SEC v. Texas Gulf Sulphur Co., 401 F.2d 833 (2d Cir. 1968) (*en banc*), *cert. denied,* 394 U.S. 976 (1969):

> [A]nyone in possession of material inside information must either disclose it to the investing public, or, if he is disabled from disclosing it in order to protect a corporate confidence, or he chooses not to do so, must abstain from trading in or recommending the securities concerned while such inside information remains undisclosed.

Id. 848.

38. *See, e.g.,* Affiliated Ute Citizens v. United States, 406 U.S. 128 (1972). In another case, although there was no holding that reliance is unnecessary, the Court applied § 10(b) where there was a somewhat tenuous connection between the securities transaction and the fraudulent activity. *See* Superintendent of Ins. v. Bankers Life & Cas. Co., 404 U.S. 6 (1971).

39. FEDERAL TRADE COMMISSION, COMPILATION OF PROPOSALS AND VIEWS FOR AND AGAINST INCORPORATION OR LICENSING OF CORPORATIONS, S. DOC. NO. 92, 70th Cong., 1st Sess., pt. 69-A, at 44 (1934) (quoted in Schwartz, *supra* note 12, at 71). Indeed, "[t]he advisability of such congressional charters was debated in the Constitutional Convention, and federal incorporation was recommended by Presidents Theodore Roosevelt, Taft, and Wilson." Reuschlein, *supra* note 13, at 106-07 (citations omitted).

40. *See* authorities cited in note 13 *supra.*

governance area.[41] Recent bills introduced in Congress, somewhat resembling Professor Cary's concept, may be viewed as akin to proposals seeking a federal corporation law. One such bill, the Corporation Democracy Act of 1980,[42] would have applied to the country's 800 largest corporations and would have addressed the composition and duties of boards of directors, the public disclosure of corporate operations and activities, the rights of employees, the impact of plant closings on affected communities, the regulation of interlocking directorates, and the accountability of corporate officers for violations of federal law by the corporate entity.[43]

The preceding discussion illustrates the considerable appeal of *federal* solutions to problems of corporation law. Ironically, however, several commentators have suggested that the chartering states' "race for the bottom" was, at least in part, a result of federal regulation in the area of corporation law.[44] One commentator has written:

---

41. Cary, *supra* note 12, at 701-03. As outlined by Cary:

> To illustrate, some of the major provisions of such a federal statute might include (1) federal fiduciary standards with respect to directors and officers and controlling shareholders; (2) an "interested directors" provision prescribing fairness as a prerequisite to any transaction; (3) a requirement of certain uniform provisions to be incorporated in the certificate of incorporation: for example, authority to amend by-laws, initiate corporate action, or draw up the agenda of shareholders' meetings shall not be vested exclusively in management; (4) a more frequent requirement of shareholder approval of corporate transactions, with limits placed upon the number of shares authorized at any one time; (5) abolition of nonvoting shares; (6) the scope of indemnification of directors specifically prescribed and made exclusive; (7) adoption of a long-arm provision comparable to § 27 of the Securities Exchange Act to apply to all transactions within the corporate structure involving shareholders, directors and officers.

Id. 702 (citations omitted).

42. H.R. 7010, 96th Cong., 2d Sess. (1980).

43. *Id.* Another such bill, the Protection of Shareholders' Rights Act of 1980, S. 2567, 96th Cong., 2d Sess. (1980), introduced by Senator Metzenbaum, had comparable provisions. *See* 550 SEC. REG. & L. REP. (BNA) F-1 (April 23, 1980). Pertinent provisions of these bills, if enacted, would have required that a majority of a corporation's board be composed of independent directors, that the audit and nominating committees be composed solely of independent directors, that each director owes a "duty of loyalty" and a "duty of care" to the corporation and its shareholders, that cumulative voting be used in directors' elections, that a shareholder vote be conducted on major corporate transactions, and that extensive disclosure be provided in regard to such matters as employment discrimination, compliance with environmental controls, tax rates, cost of legal and accounting fees, and planned plant closings.

44. *See, e.g.,* Latty, *Why Are Business Corporation Laws Largely "Enabling"?* 50 CORNELL L.Q. 599 (1965); Sowards & Mofsky, *Factors Affecting the Development of Corporation Law,* 23 U. MIAMI L. REV. 746 (1969) (quoting authorities); Comment, *supra* note 13, at 896. *Cf.* Folk, *supra* note 12, at 958 ("Thus the overall balance is between increasing state law permissiveness and widening federal regulation—a development not without parallel in other areas of life and law").

In any event, all this federal legislation and activity has gone far to create the belief that the "bad" parts of the old corporate machinery have been pretty well replaced, to the further complacency of the draftsmen of state corporation laws, to which complacency is perhaps also added the uncomfortable suspicion that what they are doing is not so important anyhow.[45]

It may be an oversimplification to emphasize the causal relation between federal regulation and state permissiveness—numerous other considerations were important in the "race for the bottom."[46] Nonetheless, the development of a "federal corporation law" provided a plausible justification for state corporation laws and judicial decisions to discount the interests of investors and the public. For example, the New Jersey Corporation Law Revision Commission argued that "it is clear that the major protections to investors, creditors, employees, customers, and the general public have come, and must continue to come, from Federal legislation and not from state corporation acts. . . . [T]he means of assuring such protections must be provided by the Federal Government."[47] The relationship between increasing federal regulation and state permissiveness was a curious one; as will be discussed below, its curiosity was heightened by some state courts' responses to the Supreme Court's decision in *Santa Fe.*

III. *SANTA FE INDUSTRIES, INC. V. GREEN*— AN OVERVIEW

Santa Fe Industries, Inc. v. Green[48] involved the merger[49] of the Kirby Lumber Corporation into its parent, Santa Fe Industries, Inc., which owned 95 percent of Kirby's stock. Santa Fe availed itself of a simplified Delaware

---

45. Latty, *supra* note 44, at 617.

46. *See id.* at 611-19.

47. N.J. STAT. ANN. § 14A, at xi (West 1968).

48. 430 U.S. 462 (1977).

49. The type of merger involved in *Santa Fe* is only one of a variety of ways that majority shareholders can squeeze out minority shareholders. Another, spawned by the depressed markets of recent years, is the "going private" transaction in which the controlling persons of a corporation eliminate public shareholders while retaining their control and ownership of the business. In 1979, the SEC adopted Rules 13e-3 and 13e-4 relating to going-private transactions by public companies or their affiliates. *See* Securities Act Release Nos. 6100, 6109 (August 1979). In general, the rules prohibit fraudulent, deceptive, and manipulative acts or practices in connection with going-private transactions and prescribe new filing, disclosure, and dissemination requirements as a means reasonably designed to prevent such acts or practices. Of particular interest, the original proposal for Rule 13e-3 included the requirement that a going-private transaction must be both substantively and procedurally fair to unaffiliated security

procedure known as a "short-form" merger, under which a parent that owns at least 90 percent of a subsidiary's outstanding stock can absorb the subsidiary without being required to obtain approval by the shareholders of either corporation.[50] The day after the merger became effective, Kirby's minority shareholders were informed that they would receive $150 in cash

holders. Securities Exchange Act Release No. 14185 (Nov. 17, 1977). Many commentators expressed the view that the Commission should not attempt to regulate the fairness of going-private transactions because such regulation was more properly within the province of the states. The Commission, in adopting Rule 13e-3 and Schedule 13E-3, required the issuer to state whether it reasonably believes that the going-private transaction is fair or unfair to unaffiliated security holders. While the Commission deferred its decision on the promulgation of a "federal fairness requirement" until it could review the efficacy of the Rule 13e-3 adopted, it nevertheless continued to adhere to the position that "the views expressed in the 1977 release are sound and therefore specifically affirms those views."

A second situation, similar to the going-private scenario, is the "buy-out." In this transaction, a controlling group causes "its" corporation to sell its assets for cash, which is frequently then invested in tax-exempt securities. The members of the controlling group derive substantial benefits from this arrangement. The insiders, who are often in high tax brackets, are frequently motivated by tax avoidance considerations. The buy-out generally results in no realization of gain or loss for tax purposes, and thus allows insiders to defer their tax liabilities. Additionally, highly remunerative employment contracts are often involved. The SEC's Division of Corporation Finance has expressed concern that past disclosure in buy-out situations has not "adequately highlighted the actual and potential conflicts of interest presented to management or its affiliates in transactions such as these, which are structured in part to accommodate their tax or estate needs and in which the purchaser also retains the management under long term employment arrangements." Securities Exchange Act Release No. 15572 (February 1979).

The public shareholder's assessment of the "buy-out" is quite different from that of the controlling group. The public shareholder receives no employment contract. Further, the switch from taxable dividends to tax-exemption may frustrate his expectations. Indeed, had he wanted a tax-exempt investment, rather than an investment in a going business that offered a prospect of increased income and capital appreciation, he no doubt would have purchased tax-exempt securities in the first place. Thus, in a buy-out situation, the public shareholder is confronted with a choice between an interest in a new investment company or cash for his stock at a price somewhat above its market price. Perhaps largely for this reason, the SEC staff has taken the position that adequate disclosure must be made regarding, *inter alia*, the reasons for and the effect of the contemplated "buy-out" transaction, the terms of financing, the fairness of the price offered, and the rights of stockholders under state law. *See* Securities Exchange Act Release No. 15572.

It should be added that frequently the entity that buys the business does so with borrowed money—hence the term "leveraged buy-out." An investor caught in such a transaction may well question the fairness of being divested of his interest and foreclosed from any further participation in an enterprise that sophisticated investment bankers find attractive enough to warrant both heavy borrowing at today's high interest rates and agreement to onerous employment contracts with the controlling group. The SEC has initiated administrative actions in response to certain leveraged buy-out transactions. *See in re* Spartek Inc., Securities Exchange Act Release No. 15567, FED. SEC. L. REP. (CCH) ¶ 81,961 (Feb. 14, 1979); *In re* Woods Corp., Securities Exchange Act Release No. 15337 (Nov. 16, 1978).

For additional discussion herein on this subject, *see* pages 35-36 *supra*.

50. DEL. CODE ANN. tit. 8, § 253 (1974).

for each of their shares, and that, if dissatisfied, they could seek appraisal[51] in the Delaware courts.[52]

Santa Fe also provided the Kirby shareholders with an information statement containing facts and figures that convinced S. William Green, one of the recipients, that Kirby stock was actually worth at least $772 a share.[53] Green did not claim that these materials were deceptive. Indeed, he built his case on them.[54] Green's basic premise was that the gross undervaluation of his shares was itself a "fraud" within the meaning of Rule 10b-5.[55]

The district court found Green's argument unpersuasive.[56] A majority of the Second Circuit, however, accepted it. The prevailing opinion held:

> Whether full disclosure has been made is not the crucial inquiry since it is the merger and the undervaluation which constitute the fraud, and not whether or not the majority determines to lay bare their real motives. If there is no valid corporate purpose for the merger, then even the most brazen disclosure of that fact to the minority shareholders in no way mitigates the fraudulent conduct.[57]

The Supreme Court reversed. Citing a commentator's observation that *Santa Fe* and the Second Circuit's decision in a contemporaneous going private case[58] were the first appellate decisions to permit "a 10b-5 claim without some element of misrepresentation or nondisclosure,"[59] the Court held "that the transaction . . . was neither deceptive nor manipulative and

---

51. The inadequacy of an exclusive appraisal right has been forcefully demonstrated elsewhere. *E.g.*, Brudney & Chirelstein, *Fair Shares in Corporate Mergers and Takeovers*, 88 HARV. L. REV. 297, 307 (1974) ("[Appraisal] neither serves nor is designed to serve as a remedy for the fiduciary misbehavior at which the fairness challenge is directed"); Manning, *The Shareholder's Appraisal Remedy: An Essay for Frank Coker*, 72 YALE L.J. 223 (1962). *But see* Weinberger v. UOP, Inc., 15 SEC. REG. & L. REP. (BNA) 327 (Del. 1983).

52. 430 U.S. at 466.

53. *Id.* 466-67.

54. *Id.* 474.

55. Green v. Santa Fe Indus., Inc., 533 F.2d 1283, 1285 (2d Cir. 1976).

56. Green v. Santa Fe Indus., Inc., 391 F. Supp. 849 (S.D.N.Y. 1975).

57. 533 F.2d 1283, 1292 (2d Cir. 1976).

58. Marshel v. AFW Fabric Corp., 533 F.2d 1277 (2d Cir.), *vacated and remanded for a determination of mootness*, 429 U.S. 881 (1976), *dismissed*, [1977-1978 Transfer Binder] FED. SEC. L. REP. (CCH) ¶ 96,243 (S.D.N.Y. 1977). In *Marshel*, the Second Circuit held that

> when controlling stockholders and directors of a publicly-held corporation cause it to expend corporate funds to force elimination of minority stockholders' equity participation for reasons not benefiting the corporation but rather serving only the interest of the controlling stockholders such conduct will be enjoined pursuant to Section 10(b) and Rule 10b-5.

Id. 1281.

59. 89 HARV. L. REV. 1917, 1926 (1976), *quoted in Santa Fe*, 430 U.S. at 475-76 n.15.

therefore did not violate either § 10(b) of the [Exchange] Act or Rule 10b-5."[60]

The plaintiffs also argued that a material nondisclosure had occurred because they had not received the information regarding the merger until after it had been consummated. The Court brushed this "timing" argument aside in what has become, due to lower court application,[61] a most significant footnote.[62]

Santa Fe was scarcely a surprise after the Court's previous decisions in *Ernst & Ernst v. Hochfelder*[63] and *Cort v. Ash.*[64] *Hochfelder* held that there can be no implied private right of action for damages under Section 10(b) and Rule 10b-5, absent an allegation of scienter.[65] The decision was predicated on a strict construction of Rule 10b-5 and its statutory source, Section 10(b).[66] This approach to the language of the statute and rule was expressly affirmed and adopted by the *Santa Fe* court.[67] In *Cort,* the Court demonstrated its reluctance to imply federal causes of action in areas traditionally left to state law.[68] The Court observed that "corporations are creatures of

---

60. 430 U.S. at 474.

61. *See* note 10 *supra* and accompanying text.

62. 430 U.S. at 474 n.14. *See* notes 76-97 *infra* and accompanying text. For the language of footnote 14, see text accompanying note 6 *supra*.

63. 425 U.S. 185 (1976).

64. 422 U.S. 66 (1975).

65. 425 U.S. at 214.

66. *Id.* 197, 200. Similarly, the Court has recently noted that its conclusion in *Hochfelder* rested on several grounds, the "most important" of which was

> the plain meaning of the language of § 10(b). It was the view of the Court that the terms "manipulative," "device," and "contrivance"—whether given their commonly accepted meaning or read as terms of art—quite clearly evinced a congressional intent to proscribe only "knowing or intentional misconduct." This meaning, in fact, was thought to be so unambiguous as to suggest that "further inquiry may be unnecessary."

Aaron v. SEC, 100 S. Ct. 1945, 1952 (1980) (citation omitted).

67. 430 U.S. at 472.

68. 422 U.S. at 80. The Court enunciated a four-prong test for determining the existence of an implied private right of action under a federal statute:

> First, is the plaintiff "one of the class for whose *especial* benefit the statute was enacted. . . . " Second, is there any indication of legislative intent, explicit or implicit, either to create such a remedy or to deny one? Third, is it consistent with the underlying purposes of the legislative scheme to imply such a remedy for the plaintiff? And finally, is the cause of action one traditionally relegated to state law, in an area basically the concern of the States, so that it would be inappropriate to infer a cause of action based solely on federal law?

Id. 78 (citations omitted) (emphasis in original). Recently, the Court evidently modified the four-prong *Cort* test. Under the new standard, the primary, if not controlling, criterion appears to be whether Congress intended, either expressly or by implication, to create a private remedy. *See, e.g.,* Transamerica Mortgage Advisors, Inc. v. Lewis, 444 U.S. 11 (1979); Touche Ross & Co. v. Redington, 442 U.S. 560 (1979); Cannon v. University of Chicago, 441 U.S. 677

state law, and investors commit their funds to corporate directors on the understanding that, except where federal law *expressly* requires certain responsibilities of directors with respect to stockholders, state law will govern the internal affairs of the corporation."[69] Both cases evidence the Court's recent contraction of the scope of the federal securities laws.[70] According to one commentator, *Hochfelder,* taken with *Cort,* "unequivocally reverses the trend toward expanding plaintiff's rights under the federal securities law."[71] *Santa Fe* combined the approaches of *Hochfelder* and *Cort,* employing a narrow approach to construction and stressing that the regulation of the internal management of corporations is within the ambit of state corporation law.

Santa Fe is undeniably significant. Had the Court upheld the Second Circuit's "new fraud" or "equitable fraud" concept,[72] minority shareholders would have obtained the federal shield of protection from overreaching that many have argued they need.[73] Justice White acknowledged this concern at the close of his majority opinion in *Santa Fe:* "There may well be a need for uniform federal fiduciary standards to govern mergers such as that challenged in this complaint. But those standards should not be supplied by judicial extension of § 10(b) and Rule 10b-5 to 'cover the corporate universe.' "[74]

(1979) (Powell, J., dissenting) ("[T]he 'four factor' analysis of [*Cort*] is an open invitation to federal courts to legislate causes of action not authorized by Congress. It is an analysis not faithful to constitutional principles and should be rejected . . ."). *See generally* Steinberg, *Implied Private Rights of Action Under Federal Law,* 55 NOTRE DAME LAW. 33 (1979). The Court recently issued, however, what may properly be viewed as an expansive decision in the implied rights area. Merrill Lynch, Pierce, Fenner & Smith, Inc. v. Curran, 102 S. Ct. 1825 (1982) (implied right of action for damages under Commodity Exchange Act). *See* Steinberg, *The Propriety and Scope of Cumulative Remedies Under the Federal Securities Laws,* 67 CORNELL L. REV. 557 (1982).

69. 422 U.S. at 84, *quoted in Santa Fe,* 430 U.S. at 479 (emphasis in *Santa Fe*). *See also* Burks v. Lasker, 441 U.S. 471, 478 (1979) ("As we have said in the past, the first place one must look to determine the powers of corporate directors is in the relevant State's corporation law").

70. *See* note 19 *supra.*

71. Lowenfels, *supra* note 19, at 900.

72. The Second Circuit, followed by a number of other federal courts, permitted Rule 10b-5 actions even in situations not involving deception. Under the "new fraud" approach, Rule 10b-5 liability could be premised on a wide range of corporate mismanagement. *See generally* Jacobs, *supra* note 6, at 57-61.

73. *See* note 12 *supra.*

74. 430 U.S. at 479-80 (footnotes omitted). Referring to Professor Cary's article, Mr. Justice White commented: "Professor Cary argues vigorously for comprehensive federal fiduciary standards, but urges a 'frontal' attack by a new federal statute rather than an extension of Rule 10b-5." *Id.* 480 n.17.

Santa Fe makes it clear that a federal claim cannot be stated under Rule 10b-5 without alleging manipulation or deception.[75] As noted at the outset of this discussion, however, *Santa Fe* had a second aspect, arising from the Court's comment that failure to provide the minority with advance notice was not a material nondisclosure because, as the plaintiffs conceded, "under Delaware law [the plaintiffs] could not have enjoined the merger because an appraisal proceeding [was] their sole remedy in the Delaware courts for any alleged unfairness in the terms of the merger."[76] Today no plaintiff would make this concession in a *Santa Fe* situation. Six months after *Santa Fe*, in *Singer v. Magnavox Co.*,[77] the Delaware Supreme Court took a fresh look at its merger doctrines and embarked on a new course.

IV. POST-*SANTA FE* DECISIONS IN THE STATE COURTS

Perhaps influenced by the Supreme Court's decision in *Santa Fe*, and the consequent likelihood of reduced federal regulation in the area of management malfeasance,[78] the Delaware Supreme Court apparently has assumed this protective role.[79] In *Singer*,[80] minority shareholders frozen out by a merger sought nullification of the merger and compensatory damages. The plaintiffs alleged that the sole purpose of the merger was removal of the minority, and that the majority had offered grossly inadequate compensation for stock held by the minority.[81] In reversing the lower court's dismissal of the complaint on the ground that appraisal was the exclusive remedy,[82] the Delaware high court stated that "a § 251 merger, made for the sole purpose of freezing out minority stockholders, is an abuse of the corporate process;

---

75. *Id.* 473-74. *See also* Mobil Corp. v. Marathon Oil Co., 669 F.2d 366 (6th Cir. 1981) (option agreements entered into between target corporation and white knight held to be "manipulative" practices under § 14(e) of the Securities Exchange Act).

76. 430 U.S. at 474 n.14. Interestingly, prior to *Santa Fe*, there was some authority that, under relevant state law, minority shareholders could not be eliminated in a cash-out merger transaction unless a valid business purpose could be shown. *See, e.g.*, Bryan v. Brock & Blevins Co., Inc., 490 F.2d 563, 571 (5th Cir.), *cert. denied*, 419 U.S. 844 (1974) (interpreting Georgia law). *But see* Stauffer v. Standard Brands, Inc., 187 A.2d 78, 80 (Del. 1962) (appraisal remedy exclusive absent fraud or illegality).

77. 380 A.2d 969 (Del. 1977).

78. *See* notes 44-47 *supra* and accompanying text.

79. It is noteworthy that the *Singer* court viewed *Santa Fe* as a "current confirmation by the Supreme Court of the responsibility of a state to govern the internal affairs of corporate life." 380 A.2d at 976 n.6.

80. Singer v. Magnavox, 380 A.2d 969 (Del. 1977).

81. *Id.* 972.

82. Singer v. Magnovox [sic] Co., 367 A.2d 1349 (Del. Ch. 1976). A number of commentators have addressed the inadequacy of the appraisal remedy. *See* note 51 *supra*.

and . . . states a cause of action for violation of a fiduciary duty."[83] Moreover, the court emphasized that even the existence of a valid business purpose would not preclude relief to the minority shareholders:

> On the contrary, the fiduciary obligation of the majority to the minority stockholders remains and proof of a purpose, other than such freeze-out, without more, will not necessarily discharge it. In such case the Court will scrutinize the circumstances for compliance with the *Sterling* rule of *"entire fairness"* and, if it finds a violation thereof, will grant such relief as equity may require.[84]

Hence, under *Singer*, if it is alleged that the purpose of the merger is improper, the majority shareholders must prove a proper business purpose. Further, even if there is proof of a proper business purpose, a court must scrutinize the transaction for its entire fairness and award appropriate relief if a violation is found.

Singer was the harbinger of a new era in Delaware. Subsequent Delaware cases have confirmed and extended the viability of *Singer*'s principles. From these decisions, a number of general principles can be proffered: a majority shareholder's fiduciary duty is not fulfilled simply by relegating the minority stockholders to their statutory appraisal remedy;[85] majority shareholders

---

83. 380 A.2d at 980.

84. *Id.* (emphasis added). In so holding, the court relied on the *Sterling* rule, Sterling v. Mayflower Hotel Corp., 33 Del. Ch. 293, 298, 93 A.2d 107, 110 (1952), that the majority must "bear the burden of establishing [the transaction's] entire fairness . . . [which must] pass the test of careful scrutiny by the courts." *See Singer*, 380 A.2d at 976.

For further discussion of *Singer, see, e.g.*, Brudney & Chirelstein, *A Restatement of Corporate Freezeouts*, 87 YALE L.J. 1354 (1978); Elfin, *Changing Standards and the Future Course of Freezeout Mergers*, 5 J. CORP. LAW 261 (1980); Rothschild, *Going Private, Singer, and Rule 13e-3: What Are the Standards for Fiduciaries*, 7 SEC. REG. L.J. 195 (1979); Comment, *Delaware Reverses Its Trend in Going Private Transactions: The Forgotten Majority*, 11 LOY. L.A.L. REV. 567 (1978); Comment, Singer v. Magnavox *and Cash Take-Out Mergers*, 64 VA. L. REV. 1101 (1978).

85. 380 A.2d at 978. *But see* Weinberger v. UOP, Inc., 426 A.2d 1333 (Del. Ch. 1981), *rev'd and remanded*, 15 SEC. REG. & L. REP. (BNA) 327 (Del. 1983), where the chancery court stated that "*Sterling* . . . is the bedrock on which *Singer, Tanzer*, and *Roland International* are built." 426 A.2d at 1344, *citing*, Sterling v. Mayflower Hotel Corp., 93 A.2d 107 (Del. 1952). However, as recognized by one recent commentator, "[l]eft open after *Sterling* was the question whether appraisal was the exclusive remedy in an action challenging a completed interested merger and whether a majority stockholder had an absolute right to use his majority control to bring about a merger for whatever reason he chose, subject only to the duty to pay a fair price." Sparks, *State Regulation of Conflict Transactions* 235, 248 in STANDARDS FOR REGULATING CORPORATE INTERNAL AFFAIRS (The Ray Garrett, Jr., Corporate and Securities Law Institute, 1981).

cannot effect a merger solely for the purpose of eliminating the minority;[86] such a merger must be for a proper purpose and must be entirely fair to the minority;[87] a merger made primarily to advance the business purpose of a majority stockholder is proper so long as it has a bona fide purpose and is entirely fair to the minority;[88] and where a complaint alleges that the purpose of the merger was to eliminate minority shareholders, such a complaint may often be immune from a motion to dismiss.[89] The foregoing

---

86. *Id.* 978-80. *See* Young v. Valhi, Inc., 382 A.2d 1372 (Del. Ch. 1978). In *Young*, the chancery court issued a preliminary injunction barring the merger and held that, notwithstanding management's assertion that the merger would result in tax savings and the avoidance of future conflicts of interest, "the basic purpose behind the merger now before the Court is effectuation of a long standing decision on the part of Contran to eliminate the minority shares of Valhi by whatever means as might be found to be workable." *Id.* 1378.

87. Tanzer v. International Gen. Indus., Inc., 379 A.2d 1121, 1124-25 (Del. 1977). The "entire fairness" test applies not only to the price offered for the stock but to "all aspects of the transaction." *Id.* 1125. *See also* Securities Act Release Nos. 6100, 6109 (Aug. 1979), in which the SEC adopted Rules 13e-3 and 13e-4 relating to going-private transactions by public companies or their affiliates. For a discussion of the fairness aspects of the rules, *see* note 49 *supra*.

88. *Tanzer*, 379 A.2d at 1124-25. Thus, the *Tanzer* court held:

> As a stockholder, IGI [the common parent] need not sacrifice its own interest in dealing with a subsidiary; but that interest must not be suspect as a subterfuge, the real purpose of which is to rid itself of unwanted minority shareholders in the subsidiary. That would be a violation of *Singer* and any subterfuge or effort to escape its mandate must be scrutinized with care and dealt with by the Trial Court. And, of course, in any event, a *bona fide* purpose notwithstanding, IGI must be prepared to show that it has met its duty, imposed by *Singer* and *Sterling v. Mayflower Hotel Corp.* of "entire fairness" to the minority.

Id. 1124 (citation omitted). *See also* Fins v. Pearlman, 424 A.2d 305 (Del. 1980) (intrinsic fairness of terms of the settlement, not proper purpose for the merger, is the standard to be applied to the settlement of an action challenging the merger); Bell v. Kirby Lumber Corp., 413 A.2d 137 (Del. 1980) (distinguishing entire fairness under appraisal statute from that of entire fairness standard under *Singer*). One commentator remarks that the recent Delaware cases suggest that a cash-out merger, even though serving no corporate purpose, may, nonetheless, pass scrutiny if it serves a purpose of the fiduciary. Rothschild, *supra* note 84, at 215.

89. *See* Kemp v. Angel, 381 A.2d 241 (Del. Ch. 1977), in which the chancery court held that where there is a reasonable probability that the minority shareholders might prevail because the merger was unfair, the case must proceed to trial:

> [I]t being only at trial that the Court can give the required careful scrutiny to the testimony adduced subject to objection and cross examination as well as to other evidence offered in an orderly fashion and also test the credibility of witnesses before reaching a determination as to whether or not the transaction under attack is in fact entirely fair to minority stockholders. ...

Id. 245.

In a recent decision, Harman v. Masoneilan Int'l., Inc., 442 A.2d 487 (Del. 1982), the Delaware Supreme Court held that approval of a squeeze-out merger by the minority stockholders will generally immunize the transaction from challenge, unless these are allegations

principles are applicable to short-form as well as long-form mergers.[90]

It remains to be seen whether other states will follow Delaware's lead. For example, the Indiana Supreme Court, relying on *Singer,* held that the effectuation of a merger that eliminated a minority shareholder, even though in compliance with the technical requirements of the state's merger statute, must advance a corporate purpose in order to withstand attack under Indiana law.[91] Similarly, the Supreme Court of Hawaii recently followed the *Singer* decision, stating that "a merger effected for the sole purpose of freezing out

---

that the majority obtained the minority's "independent approval" in order to eliminate such shareholders or used its controlling influence to "coerce" the minority's approval. *See* 14 SEC. REG. & L. REP. (BNA) 353-54 (Feb. 24, 1982). *Compare* Michaelson v. Duncan, 407 A.2d 211 (Del. 1979).

90. Roland Int'l Corp. v. Najjar, 407 A.2d 1032 (Del. 1979). Applying the *Singer* principles, the court reasoned that "the need to recognize and enforce such equitable principles is probably greater when the size of the minority is smaller." *Id.* 1036. The *Roland* court's holding signifies that an acquiror, in engaging in an integrated two-step transaction for cash of 100 percent of the subject company, must show that both steps had a bona fide purpose and treated minority shareholders fairly. Note that this principle creates an apparent inconsistency with SEC Rule 13e-3 which "excepts a second-step transaction effected by an offeror who became an affiliate by virtue of an earlier tender offer, provided that the second-step (clean-up) transaction is effected within a year of the earlier offer on terms at least as favorable to the minority as those in the earlier offer." Rothschild, *supra* note 84, at 213. *See generally* Coleman v. Taub, 638 F.2d 628 (3d Cir. 1981) (applying Delaware law); Lynch v. Vickers Energy Corp., 429 A.2d 497 (Del. 1981); Lynch v. Vickers Energy Corp., 383 A.2d 278 (Del. 1977); Gabelli & Co., Inc., Profit Sharing Plan v. Liggett Group, Inc., 444 A.2d 261 (Del. Ch. 1982).

91. Gabhart v. Gabhart, 267 Ind. 370, 388, 370 N.E.2d 345, 356 (1977). The Indiana Supreme Court apparently stopped short of adopting the *Singer* two-step rationale. The *Gabhart* court stated:

> The case before us is similar to the case of *Singer v. Magnavox Co.* . . . In that case, the Supreme Court of Delaware . . . relied upon agency principles of fiduciary duty to hold that a corporate merger is subject to judicial scrutiny concerning its "entire fairness" to minority shareholders. We see no need to go that far in deciding the question before us. Under the Delaware view, it appears that every proposed merger would be subject to having its bona fides determined by judicial review. We do not believe the judiciary should intrude into corporate management to that extent.

267 Ind. at 388, 370 N.E.2d at 356. *See* Rothschild, *supra* note 84, at 215-16. *See also* Jones v. H. F. Ahmanson & Co., 1 Cal. 3d 93, 108, 81 CAL. RPTR. 592, 599, 460 P.2d 464, 471 (1969) ("[a]ny use to which [majority shareholders] put the corporation or their power to control the corporation must benefit all shareholders proportionately and must not conflict with the proper conduct of the corporation's business"). As interpreted by the Hawaii Supreme Court, "[a]lthough *Ahmanson* did not involve a merger, it appears clear from the language of the opinion that the California Supreme Court would apply the fiduciary duty of good faith and inherent fairness to such a situation." Perl v. IU Int'l Corp., 607 P.2d 1036, 1047 n.12 (Hawaii 1980). *See also* Twenty-Seven Trust v. Realty Growth Investors, 533 F. Supp. 1027 (D. Md. 1982) (appraisal not exclusive remedy in freeze-out merger under Maryland law); Masinter v. Webco Co., 262 S.E.2d 433 (W. Va. 1980) (adopting *Singer* rationale).

the minority interest is a violation of fiduciary principles."[92] In contrast, the Pennsylvania Supreme Court recently held that appraisal is the sole *post-merger* remedy under that state's law for aggrieved minority shareholders.[93] Although the court was "not unmindful of the grave unfairness and fraud frequently present in mergers of this type, especially where there is a 'cash-out' of the minority stockholders,"[94] it concluded that the state legislature intended that the appraisal statute serve as the sole postmerger remedy. The court recognized, however, the minority's right in the *premerger* period to seek injunctive relief to prevent the merger's consummation.[95] The majority's holding occasioned a vigorous dissent that relied on Delaware case law to assert that "stockholders who allege that a merger is 'fraught with fraud or fundamental unfairness' should be permitted to challenge the validity of said merger *at any time,* including post-merger."[96] Importantly, however, the Pennsylvania, Delaware, and other decisions indicate that aggrieved shareholders may bring suit in state court to enjoin a merger that has not been consummated. Based on the rebirth of these fiduciary principles, *Santa Fe* might have been decided differently today.[97]

---

92. Perl v. IU Int'l Corp., 607 P.2d 1036, 1046 (Hawaii 1980). The Hawaii Supreme Court acknowledged that the situation in *Perl* was arguably different from the Delaware cases in that the minority shareholders were not literally squeezed out. The court refused to distinguish the Delaware cases on this basis, reasoning that

> [i]t makes little sense ... to condemn cash out mergers on the one hand, and yet to permit mergers using preferred securities redeemable at the option of the majority on the other if the minority may be just as effectively eliminated from the corporation by the redemption of the stock as by the straight cash out method.

Id. 1047-48. *See generally* Gillerman, *The Corporate Fiduciary Under State Law,* 3 CORP. L. REV. 299 (1980); Note, *Partial and Selective Reacquisitions of Corporate Securities,* 15 CAL. WEST. L. REV. 264 (1979).

93. *In re* Jones & Laughlin Steel Corp., 412 A.2d 1099 (1980). For a discussion of this case, *see* 549 SEC. REG. & L. REP. (BNA) A-6 (April 16, 1980).

94. 412 A.2d at 1104.

95. *Id.* 1103-04. *See also* Dower v. Mosser Indus., Inc., 648 F.2d 183, 188-89 (3d Cir. 1981) (applying Pennsylvania law) ("A merger intended solely to 'freeze out' or 'cash out' minority equity holders from their positions may be enjoined as an attempted breach of that fiduciary duty"). *But see* Yanow v. Teal Industries, Inc., 178 Conn. 262, 422 A.2d 311 (1979) (appraisal exclusive remedy).

96. 412 A.2d at 1105 (Larsen, J., dissenting) (emphasis in original) (citing as persuasive Roland Int'l Corp. v. Najjar, 407 A.2d 1032 (Del. 1979)). *See* note 90 *supra.*

97. *See* Roland Int'l Corp. v. Najjar, 407 A.2d 1032 (Del. 1979), which involved a short-form merger. Applying the "bona fide purpose" and "entire fairness" principles of *Singer,* the court upheld a minority shareholder's complaint because appraisal was no longer the sole remedy. *See* note 90 *supra* and accompanying text. Also, some states have elected to regulate such freeze-out mergers by statute or rule. *See, e.g.,* CAL. CORP. CODES § 1312(b) (1977); IND. CODE ANN. §§ 23-1-5-7, 23-1-12-4 (Burns 1972); 8 WISC. ADM. CODE § 5.05 (1976). For further discussion on state legislation, *see* Roberts, *The Status of Minority Shareholders' Rem-*

V. POST-*SANTA FE* DECISIONS IN THE FEDERAL COURTS

A. Federal Disclosure Requirements Based on State Law Claims—The *Goldberg* Rationale

After the *Singer* line of cases, and similar developments in other jurisdictions, minority shareholders in situations like *Santa Fe* not only can enforce their right to seek redress under state law, but can obtain under federal law, subject to certain limitations, information needed to determine whether management has breached its fiduciary duty under state law.[98] Failure to provide this information, according to a number of courts,[99] may be a material deception actionable under Section 10(b). This federal right to information extends well beyond the freeze-out merger situation. Indeed, subject to certain caveats, it encompasses every corporate transaction in securities that shareholders could have attacked under state law, had they known the facts. Since *Santa Fe,* five appellate decisions—in the Second, Third, Fifth, Seventh, and Ninth Circuits—have recognized such a right.[100] These five cases warrant closer examination. Although involving a variety of factual settings, the decisions represent a coherent and consistent approach to *Santa Fe*'s footnote fourteen.

---

edies for Oppression After Santa Fe *and* Singer *and the Question of "Reasonable Investment Expectation" Valuation,* 6 DEL. J. CORP. LAW 16, 36-37 (1981).

As this book was in the proofing process, the Delaware Supreme Court decided Weinberger v. UOP, Inc., 15 SEC. REG. & L. REP. (BNA) 327 (Del. 1983). There, the court expressed its preference for the appraisal remedy for minority shareholders in a cash-out merger, stating that "a plaintiff's monetary remedy ordinarily should be confined to the more liberalized appraisal proceeding herein established," and that "in a non-fraudulent transaction . . . price may be the preponderant consideration outweighing other features of the merger." *Id.* at 332, 334. Moreover, the Delaware high court expressly held that defendants are no longer required to show a legitimate business purpose for the merger. *Id.* at 334. Significantly, however, the court's decision is consistent with its prior holdings in *Singer, Tanzer* and *Najjar,* in that a minority shareholder's remedies are not, in certain circumstances, limited solely to appraisal rights. Although expressing a preference for the appraisal remedy, the court made clear that such a remedy may not be adequate where "fraud, misrepresentation, self-dealing, deliberate waste of corporate assets, or gross and palpable overreaching are involved." *Id.* In such circumstances, the Chancellor may "fashion any form of equitable and monetary relief as may be appropriate, including rescissory damages." *Id.*

98. This federal right, however, is subject to certain caveats. *See* notes 126–63 *infra* and accompanying text.

99. *See* notes 100-26 *infra* and accompanying text.

100. *See* Healey v. Catalyst Recovery, Inc., 616 F.2d 641 (3d Cir. 1980); Alabama Farm Bureau Mut. Cas. Co. v. American Fidelity Life Ins. Co., 606 F.2d 602 (5th Cir. 1979), *cert. denied,* 101 S. Ct. 77 (1980); Kidwell *ex rel.* Penfold v. Meikle, 597 F.2d 1273 (9th Cir. 1979); Goldberg v. Meridor, 567 F.2d 209 (2d Cir. 1977), *cert. denied,* 434 U.S. 1069 (1978); Wright v. Heizer Corp., 560 F.2d 237 (7th Cir. 1977), *cert. denied,* 434 U.S. 1066 (1978).

Goldberg v. Meridor[101] involved a subsidiary's sale of part of its stock to its parent in exchange for certain assets. The plaintiff, a minority shareholder of the subsidiary, alleged that the parent's assets had been grossly overvalued and that the subsidiary had been looted.[102] The plaintiff filed his derivative action prior to *Santa Fe* and, after amending his complaint in response to the Supreme Court's decision, based his claim of deception on the failure of the interested parent and its management to reveal facts that, if disclosed, would have enabled the minority stockholders to enjoin the transaction in a New York state court. The plaintiff also claimed that allegedly false press releases issued by the parent when the transaction was consummated had lulled the minority shareholders into inaction.[103]

The Second Circuit held that the plaintiff's complaint properly stated a cause of action under Rule 10b-5. The court observed that "[t]he problem with the application of § 10(b) and Rule 10b-5 to derivative actions has lain in the degree to which the knowledge of officers and directors must be attributed to the corporation, thereby negating the element of deception."[104] The court found the deception requirement satisfied by refusing to attribute the knowledge of management to the corporation because management was not disinterested—a theory of deception based on a long line of pre-*Santa Fe* cases.[105] The court went on to find that if the facts were as the plaintiff alleged, and if timely disclosure of these facts had been made, then the minority shareholders could have brought suit to enjoin the transaction under New York law.[106] Consequently, the case was distinguishable from

---

101. 567 F.2d 209 (2d Cir. 1977), *cert. denied*, 434 U.S. 1069 (1978).

102. *Id.* 211.

103. *Id.*

104. *Id.* 215.

105. *Id.* For this theory of deception, the Second Circuit relied on several of its earlier decisions: Schlick v. Penn-Dixie Cement Corp., 507 F.2d 374 (2d Cir. 1974), *cert. denied*, 421 U.S. 976 (1975); Drachman v. Harvey, 453 F.2d 722 (2d Cir. 1972) (en banc); Schoenbaum v. Firstbrook, 405 F.2d 215 (2d Cir. 1968) (en banc), *cert. denied*, 395 U.S. 906 (1969); Ruckle v. Roto Am. Corp., 339 F.2d 24 (2d Cir. 1964). *See also* Shell v. Hensley, 430 F.2d 819 (5th Cir. 1970); Pappas v. Moss, 393 F.2d 865 (3d Cir. 1968); Dasho v. Susquehanna Corp., 380 F.2d 262 (7th Cir.) (concurring opinion), *cert. denied*, 389 U.S. 977 (1967).

106. *Id.* 219. *See also* the Second Circuit's statement in SEC v. Parklane Hosiery Co., Inc., 558 F.2d 1083 (2d Cir. 1977). There, the court asserted that

> had the shareholders of Parklane been aware of Somekh's reasons for the going private transaction, they, or others, might well have been able to enjoin the merger under New York law as having been undertaken for no valid corporate purpose. . . . This case involves a failure to disclose when the non-disclosed information could have been used by the minority shareholders to attempt to enjoin the merger.

Id. 1088.

The *Goldberg* majority evoked a strong dissent from Judge Meskill, who argued that "the majority has neatly undone the holdings of *Green, Piper* and *Cort* by creating a federal cause of action for a breach of fiduciary duty that will apply in all cases, save for those rare instances

Santa Fe, and the plaintiff's complaint stated a cause of action under Rule 10b-5.

Recently, the Second Circuit reaffirmed the *Goldberg* rationale in *IIT v. Cornfeld,*[107] in which the court held actionable under Rule 10b-5 an alleged deception of a foreign mutual fund through misleading disclosure of material facts. Quoting from *Goldberg,* the court stated that "an action under Rule 10b-5 can lie if 'there is deception of the corporation (in effect, of its minority shareholders) when the corporation is influenced by its controlling shareholder to engage in a transaction adverse to the corporation's interests (in effect, the minority shareholders' interests) and there is nondisclosure or misleading disclosures as to the material facts of the transaction.' "[108]

The Seventh Circuit case, *Wright v. Heizer Corp.,*[109] also involved an action by minority shareholders of a subsidiary against the parent corporation. The plaintiffs sought to set aside the subsidiary's pledge of its most valuable asset, stock in a third corporation, as collateral for a loan procured by the subsidiary from the parent. The evidence indicated that the transaction had been arranged in order to allow the parent to foreclose on the pledged stock, an action the parent intended to take if minority shareholders were successful in related litigation involving the subsidiary.[110]

---

where the fiduciary denounces himself in advance." *Id.* 225 (Meskill, J., dissenting). Reflecting on *Goldberg*'s significance, one commentator opined:

> [G]eneral application of the standard will allow a large number of suits involving breach of fiduciary duties against corporate directors into federal court under rule 10b-5. . . . A federal cause of action will thus arise whenever a fiduciary opts not to disclose facts that the minority could use to enjoin him.

Note, 46 GEO. WASH. L. REV. 861, 875 (1978). For other law review articles discussing *Goldberg, see* Block & Schwarzfeld, *Corporate Mismanagement and Breach of Fiduciary Duty After* Santa Fe v. Green, 2 CORP. L. REV. 91 (1979); Campbell, Santa Fe Industries, Inc. v. Green: *An Analysis Two Years Later,* 30 MAINE L. REV. 187 (1979); Hazen, *supra* note 19; Jacobs, *Rule 10b-5 and Self Dealing by Corporate Fiduciaries: An Analysis,* 48 U. CIN. L. REV. 643 (1979); Sherrard, *Federal Judicial and Regulatory Responses to* Santa Fe Industries, Inc. v. Green, 35 WASH. AND LEE L. REV. 695 (1978); Comment, Santa Fe Industries v. Green *Revisited: A Critique of Circuit Court Application of Rule 10b-5 to Breaches of Fiduciary Duty to Minority Shareholders,* 28 UCLA L. REV. 564 (1981); Note, *Suits for Breach of Fiduciary Duty Under Rule 10b-5 After* Santa Fe Industries, Inc. v. Green, 91 HARV. L. REV. 1874 (1978); Note, Goldberg v. Meridor: *The Second Circuit's Resurrection of Rule 10b-5 Liability for Breaches of Corporate Fiduciary Duties to Minority Shareholders,* 64 VA. L. REV. 765 (1978); Note, *Liability for Corporate Mismanagement Under Rule 10b-5 After* Santa Fe v. Green, 27 WAYNE L. REV. 269 (1980). *See also* Borden, *Predict* Sue 'Fact' *Doctrine Demise: A Threat to Corporate Management,* N.Y.L.J., Dec. 15, 1980, at 29, col. 2.

107. 619 F.2d 909 (2d Cir. 1980).
108. *Id.* 917.
109. 560 F.2d 236 (7th Cir. 1977), *cert. denied,* 434 U.S. 1066 (1978).
110. *Id.* 244-45, 248-49.

The district court, writing before the Supreme Court's decision in *Santa Fe,* held the pledge invalid under Rule 10b-5 because of overreaching and unfairness.[111] The Seventh Circuit, faced with *Santa Fe,* adopted another rationale. The court first observed that under applicable Delaware law pledges do not require shareholder approval.[112] It therefore found that "under rule 10b-5 disclosure to . . . [the pledgor-subsidiary's] board of directors would be sufficient, unless Heizer [the parent] controlled the board to such an extent that only the independent shareholders were able to safeguard the corporation's interests."[113] Concluding that there was such control, and that under Delaware law Heizer had a fiduciary duty to deal fairly with the subsidiary—a duty that the minority shareholders could have enforced in a state court[114]—the court reasoned: "Under these circumstances, Heizer was obliged to disclose the material facts concerning the transaction to the independent shareholders *prior to its consummation.* This obligation was not fulfilled: the shareholders were first informed of the general terms of the pledge and the reasons therefor two months after the transaction."[115]

Sweeping relief was granted. The subsidiary's wrongfully obtained pledge was nullified, reducing Heizer to the position of a general, unsecured creditor.[116] Moreover, Heizer was enjoined from entering into any securities transaction with its subsidiary without first complying with several court-ordered restrictions.[117]

The Ninth Circuit's decision in *Kidwell ex rel. Penfold v. Meikle,* following *Goldberg* and *Wright,* held that inadequate disclosure by interested directors may give rise to a federal claim under Rule 10b-5.[118] The court, noting the apparent availability of state court injunctive relief, reasoned that "[i]nadequate disclosures lull into security those shareholders who might bring derivative actions under state law to enjoin the securities transactions if all material facts were revealed."[119]

In *Alabama Farm Bureau Mutual Casualty Co. v. American Fidelity Life Insurance Co.,*[120] the Fifth Circuit became the fourth federal appellate court

---

111. Wright v. Heizer Corp., 411 F. Supp. 23 (N.D. Ill. 1975).

112. 560 F.2d at 248.

113. *Id.* (citations omitted). The court also stated as a general principle: "When an entire board of directors is controlled by a self-dealing director or shareholder the corporation can only be represented by the independent shareholders, to whom full disclosure must be made. Conversely, where disinterested directors constitute a majority of the board of directors, disclosure to the board is sufficient." *Id.* 249 (citations omitted).

114. *Id.* 251.

115. *Id.* 249 (emphasis added).

116. *Id.* 253.

117. *Id.* 255-56.

118. 597 F.2d 1273, 1290-97 (9th Cir. 1979). *See* 14 U. RICH. L. REV. 588 (1980).

119. *Id.* 1292.

120. *Id.* 606 F.2d 602 (5th Cir. 1979), *cert. denied,* 101 S. Ct. 77 (1980).

to distinguish *Santa Fe*'s prohibition against employing Rule 10b-5 to redress claims based essentially on breaches of fiduciary duty. The case involved a corporation's repurchase of its own stock as part of management's alleged attempt to perpetuate its control of the company by artificially raising the market price of its stock, thereby discouraging takeover attempts. The defendants allegedly failed to disclose this inflationary effect of the stock repurchase plan on the market price of the corporation's outstanding shares.[121] Adopting the *Goldberg* rationale, the Fifth Circuit held that this nondisclosure, coupled with the possible availability of injunctive relief from a state court, provided the basis for a derivative action based on deception under Rule 10b-5.[122]

In another recent decision, *Healey v. Catalyst Recovery, Inc.,*[123] the defendants, controlling shareholders, sought to merge the subject company into a second corporation that they also controlled. Their plans were opposed by a 20 percent minority shareholder of the subject company who requested and was refused information regarding the second corporation. After the merger was effected, the minority shareholder brought suit under Rule 10b-5.[124] Plaintiff successfully argued that he was a "seller" of securities and had been deceived by defendants' nondisclosure.[125] *Healey* is therefore distinguishable from the four cases discussed above because they involved derivative actions claiming that a corporation had been deceived. Despite this altered fact pattern, the Third Circuit adopted the *Goldberg* rationale and held that "where a misrepresentation or omission of material information deprives a proper plaintiff minority shareholder of an opportunity under state law to enjoin a merger, there is a cause of action under Rule 10b-5."[126]

Given a broad reading, these cases may appear to hold that a breach of fiduciary duty, coupled with misrepresentation or nondisclosure, that would have entitled the complainant to seek state court relief to enjoin the contemplated transaction is a sufficient basis upon which a post-*Santa Fe* federal claim may be predicated. The ensuing discussion reveals, however, that this general principle is subject to a number of caveats.

Before turning to these caveats, however, the point should be made that a Section 10(b) claim in this context may be premised on grounds other

---

121. *Id.* 606-07.

122. *Id.* 614-15. Dissenting, Judge Skelton asserted that the case did not involve deception. Indeed, it was "much ado about nothing and border[ed] on being frivolous." *Id.* 618 n.1.

123. 616 F.2d 641 (3d Cir. 1980).

124. *Id.* 645.

125. *Id.* 647.

126. *Id.* Judge Aldisbert dissented, arguing that *Santa Fe*'s reasoning applied to the case at bar. He concluded, "[b]ecause I cannot justify the majority's bold action in 'federaliz[ing] [a] substantial portion of the law of corporations that deals with transactions in securities,' . . . I dissent." *Id.* 661 (quoting Santa Fe Indus., Inc. v. Green, 430 U.S. 462, 479 (1977)).

than those which would support a successful state court action for injunctive relief. As recently stated by the Ninth Circuit, a fact is material if a reasonable investor "could respond to the fact's disclosure by protecting himself from possible financial loss."[127] In this regard, the *Goldberg* line of cases "simply recognizes that facts can be useful and, consequently, material when an investor can obtain a state injunction against the proposed transaction."[128] This rationale aptly protects the substantial federal disclosure interests at issue, including the beneficial "sunlight" effect of such disclosure.[129]

B. Caveats to the *Goldberg* Rationale

For the lawyer who counsels management, the post-*Santa Fe* cases present the dilemma of whether his client will be served best by full *advance* disclosure to minority stockholders whenever management is involved in a conflict of interest situation without the input of an independent and disinterested board of directors. Advance disclosure may result, of course, in a state law action for breach of fiduciary duty;[130] absent such disclosure, however, a Rule 10b-5 violation may ensue. In any event, advance disclosure does not require that management indict itself.[131] As one authority has observed: "It is not necessary to say, 'This is a grossly unfair transaction

---

127. United States v. Margala, [1981-1982 Transfer Binder] FED. SEC. L. REP. (CCH) ¶ 98,363, at 92,221 (9th Cir. 1981). *See* SEC v. Blatt, 583 F.2d 1325, 1331-32 (5th Cir. 1978) ("*Santa Fe* does not control a case in which information that would prove useful to investors is withheld"). *See also* Wright v. Heizer Corp., 560 F.2d 236, 250 (7th Cir. 1977), *cert. denied,* 434 U.S. 1066 (1978).

128. [1981-1982 Transfer Binder] FED. SEC. L. REP. (CCH) ¶ 98,363, at 92,221. The Ninth Circuit also stated that "[t]he importance of the fact to the state is not relevant in itself and is a poor measure of the importance of the fact to the investor." *Id.*

129. BRANDEIS, OTHER PEOPLE'S MONEY 62 (1914). *See* Bloomenthal, *Introductory Survey,* 13 SECURITIES L. REV. xi, xiv-xv (1981), where the author observed: "Even 'rapacious controlling management' with the power to carry out an action may not necessarily do so if, as the Second Circuit has put it in another case, it will have 'to hang its dirty linen out on the line.'" *Id.* at xv, *quoting,* Schlick v. Penn-Dixie Cement Corp., 507 F.2d 374, 384 (2d. Cir. 1974).

130. *See* note 106 *supra* and accompanying text.

131. *See, e.g.,* Rodman v. Grant Foundation, 608 F.2d 64, 70 (2d Cir. 1979); *Alabama Farm,* 606 F.2d at 611; Golub v. PPD Corp., 576 F.2d 759, 765 (8th Cir. 1978); Gluck v. Agemian, 495 F. Supp. 1209, 1214-16 (S.D.N.Y. 1980); Goldberger v. Baker, 442 F. Supp. 659, 667 (S.D.N.Y. 1977). As stated by the Fifth Circuit: "When the nature and scope of a transaction are clear, it is not necessary for the corporate instigators to characterize the various effects of the transaction as favorable or unfavorable or to evaluate its overall effect; such characterization is a matter of judgment, not fact." *Alabama Farm,* 606 F.2d at 611. *See also* note 139 *infra. But see* Vaughn v. Teledyne, Inc., in which the Ninth Circuit stated: "Corporate officials are under no duty to disclose their precise motive or purpose for engaging in a particular course of corporate action, *so long as* the motive is not manipulative or deceptive and the nature and scope of any stock transactions are adequately disclosed to those involved." 628 F.2d 1214, 1221 (9th Cir. 1980) (emphasis added). *But see* note 139 *infra.*

in which the board of directors is overreaching the minority stockholders.' You just have to give them the facts."[132]

For the lawyer consulted by a victim of corporate skullduggery, *Santa Fe* and its progeny demonstrate that the disclosures made by management must be examined with painful care; that, in certain situations, Rule 10b-5 is alive and well; that, although unfairness alone is an insufficient basis for a federal claim, there are circumstances, subject to certain limitations, in which unfairness coupled with either a failure to disclose or an affirmative deception remains a firm foundation for a federal claim; and that in such situations counsel may have a choice between a state forum and a federal one.

Counsel, however, should not leap to the conclusion that he has this choice of forum. He must remember the general rule that corporations are managed under the direction of their directors and not by their share-holders,[133] and that management's knowledge may be attributed to the corporation, thus precluding a finding of deception.[134] Even before *Santa Fe*, Rule 10b-5 claims alleging that a corporation had been deceived required proof that the corporation was "disabled from availing itself of an informed judgment on the part of its board regarding the merits of the transaction."[135] The need for a showing of disability is clearer today than ever before. For example, in *Biesenbach v. Guenther*,[136] a claim of deception based solely on the allegation that shareholders were not informed of management's breaches of state law fiduciary duties was dismissed for legal insufficiency. To hold otherwise, the Third Circuit reasoned, "would clearly circumvent the Supreme Court's holding in *Santa Fe*."[137] Similarly, in *Maldonado v.*

---

132. Ratner, *supra* note 6, at 322. *See also* Rodman v. Grant Foundation, 608 F.2d 64, 70-72 (2d Cir. 1979); Bertoglio v. Texas Int'l Co., 488 F. Supp. 630 (D. Del. 1980); Amalgamated Clothing and Textile Workers Union v. J. P. Stevens, 475 F. Supp. 328 (S.D.N.Y. 1979).

133. *See* Burks v. Lasker, 441 U.S. 471, 478 (1979); *Santa Fe*, 430 U.S. at 479; Cort v. Ash, 422 U.S. 66, 84 (1975).

134. *See* notes 104 and 105 *supra* and accompanying text.

135. Superintendent of Ins. v. Bankers Life & Cas. Co., 404 U.S. 6, 13 (1971) (quoting with approval Shell v. Hensley, 430 F.2d 819, 827 (5th Cir. 1970)).

136. 588 F.2d 400 (3d Cir. 1978).

137. *Id.* 402. Thus, the court stated:

Santa Fe made clear that absent deception, misrepresentation, or nondisclosure a breach of fiduciary duty does not violate the statute or Rule. . . . In effect, appellants are stating that the failure to disclose the breach of fiduciary duty is a misrepresentation sufficient to constitute a violation of the Act. We refuse to adopt this approach which would clearly circumvent the Supreme Court's holding in *Santa Fe*. As Judge Higginbotham has reiterated:

[I]t is bemusing, and ultimately pointless, to charge that directors perpetrated a "material omission" when they failed to (a) discover and adjudge faithless motives for their actions and (b) announce such a discovery in reporting the products of their managerial efforts and judgment. The securities laws, while their central insistence is upon disclosure, were never intended to attempt any such measures of

Flynn, the Second Circuit upheld the dismissal of a Rule 10b-5 claim based on the disinterested directors' decision to modify a stock option plan so as to benefit part of the corporation's management at the shareholders' expense.[138] In so holding, the Second Circuit reasoned that since the amendments modifying the stock option plan were "validly enacted by a vote of *disinterested* board members who had been *fully informed of all material facts,* their knowledge was attributable to the Corporation and no 'deception' occurred within the meaning of Rule 10b-5."[139]

Indeed, a careful reading of the *Goldberg* line of cases reveals that in actions alleging "deception" the courts have consistently required Rule 10b-5 claims to allege more than the bare availability of state court injunctive relief. In derivative actions, when shareholder approval of a transaction is

---

psychoanalysis or reported self-analysis. The unclean heart of a director is not actionable, whether or not it is "disclosed," unless the impurities are translated into actionable deeds or omissions both objective and external. . . .

Id. (quoting Stedman v. Storer, 308 F. Supp. 881, 887 (S.D.N.Y. 1969)), *quoted in* Lavin v. Data Systems Analysis, Inc., 443 F. Supp. 104, 107 (E.D. Pa. 1977), *aff'd,* 578 F.2d 1374 (3d Cir. 1978). *Accord,* Kirtz v. Wiggin, 483 F. Supp. 148, 151 (E.D. Mo. 1980) ("[t]he mere fact, if so, that plaintiffs, as minority stockholders, had not theretofore been told nor were aware of the alleged self-dealing may not be equated with 'deceptive practices' or 'omissions' in the Section 10(b) sense").

138. 597 F.2d 789 (2d Cir. 1979).

139. *Id.* 795 (emphasis added). *See* Selk v. St. Paul Ammonia Prods., Inc., 597 F.2d 635, 639 (8th Cir. 1979) (failure to disclose that purpose of merger was to freeze out minority shareholders not actionable under §§ 10(b) and 14(a)); O'Brien v. Continental Ill. Nat'l Bank & Trust Co., 593 F.2d 54, 60 (7th Cir. 1979) (failure to reveal that investment advice was self-serving not actionable under § 10(b)); *Goldberg,* 567 F.2d at 218 n.8 ("We do not mean to suggest that § 10(b) or Rule 10b-5 requires insiders to characterize conflict of interest transactions with pejorative nouns or adjectives"). Bucher v. Shumway, [1979-1980 Transfer Binder] FED. SEC. L. REP. (CCH) ¶ 97,142, at 96,299-300 (S.D.N.Y. 1979), *aff'd,* 622 F.2d 572 (2d Cir.), *cert. denied,* 101 S. Ct. 120 (1980) (failure to disclose that true purpose of tender offer was to consolidate management's control not actionable under §§ 10(b) and 14(e)); Hundahl v. United Benefit Life Ins. Co., 465 F. Supp. 1349, 1364 (N.D. Tex. 1979) (failure to disclose breach of fiduciary duty of scheme to undervalue company not actionable under § 10(b)). *See also* cases cited in note 131 *supra.*

Under certain limited circumstances, courts may require that management's "true purpose" be disclosed. Thus in Rodman v. Grant Foundation, 608 F.2d 64 (2d Cir. 1979), the Second Circuit stated that "[i]n the absence of some *ulterior wrongful design* hinging upon so-called 'entrenchment,' the directors were not required to put forth in proxy materials an analysis of their otherwise obvious interest in company control." *Id.* 71 (emphasis added). Similarly, in the *Alabama Farm* case, the Fifth Circuit concluded that an allegation that management had failed to disclose that it "had embarked on a program of maintaining control at the cost of inflating stock prices" involved material information under § 10(b). 606 F.2d at 614. Although difficult to pinpoint, these cases may stand for the proposition that when management has an ulterior wrongful design in embarking on a particular course of conduct, disclosure of that design is required. Language contained in the Ninth Circuit's Vaughn v. Teledyne, Inc., decision appears consistent with this assertion. *See* note 131 *supra.* Moreover, certain SEC disclosure requirements provide that purpose must be revealed. *See, e.g.,* Schedule 13D, Item 4, 17 C.F.R. § 240.13d-101 (1981); Schedule 13E-3, Item 7(a), 17 C.F.R. § 240.13e-100 (1981).

not required, the courts have reasoned that disclosure to a disinterested board of directors is equivalent to disclosure to the shareholders. Stated differently, the knowledge of the disinterested board is attributed to the corporation, thereby precluding a finding of deception.[140] Of course, in nonderivative actions, such as *Healey*, where an individual shareholder is the purchaser or seller of securities, a 10b-5 claim need only allege that the shareholder was deceived.[141] Under *Healey*, the deception requirement is satisfied by alleging that there was a material misrepresentation or nondisclosure in the flow of information between the majority and the individual shareholder that deprived the plaintiff of an opportunity under state law to enjoin the merger.[142]

A troublesome issue in determining whether a corporation has been deceived is the proper definition of a "disinterested" director. As the Second Circuit held in *Maldonado*, a director's "financial stake" in the subject transaction would clearly render him "interested."[143] What is not so clear is whether the presence of some other disability, such as a director's desire to maintain his position irrespective of the corporation's best interests, or the perpetration of improper influence or deception upon a director by a controlling person, including the failure to apprise a director of material facts, would likewise render the director "interested." Although some courts have held that only the existence of a financial conflict disqualifies the director,[144] the better view is that other disabilities have the same effect.[145] The crucial criterion should not be whether a director is financially interested, but whether he can exercise *independent judgment* on behalf of the corporation and its shareholders. Any conflict or disability that impairs a director's judgment poses the same threat to the best interests of the corporation and shareholders, regardless of whether it is financially based.[146] Thus, a

---

140. *See, e.g., Maldonado,* 597 F.2d at 793; Kaplan v. Bennett, 465 F. Supp. 555, 565-66 (S.D.N.Y. 1979).

141. *See* text accompanying notes 123-26 *supra.*

142. *Healey,* 616 F.2d at 646. The court further stated that "[b]ecause this result flows from misinformation that harms the plaintiff, it is precisely the type of situation to which rule 10b-5 is addressed." *Id.*

143. 597 F.2d at 793 (citing Falkenberg v. Baldwin, [1977-1978 Transfer Binder] FED. SEC. L. REP. (CCH) ¶ 96,086, at 91,911 (S.D.N.Y. 1977)).

144. *See, e.g.,* Tyco Labs., Inc. v. Kimball, 444 F. Supp. 292 (E.D. Pa. 1977) (directors held to be disinterested where their alleged interest in subject transaction was to perpetuate control).

145. Although in *Maldonado* the Second Circuit defined "disinterested" as the lack of any financial stake in the subject transaction, 597 F.2d at 793, the court also stated that "[d]omination or control of a corporation or of its board by those benefiting from the board's action may under some circumstances preclude its directors from being disinterested." *Id.* 795. *See* Kaplan v. Bennett, 465 F. Supp. 555, 565 (S.D.N.Y. 1979); Goldberger v. Baker, 442 F. Supp. 659, 665 (S.D.N.Y. 1977).

146. *See generally Maldonado,* 597 F.2d at 794 n.5 ("Nonattribution [of the directors' knowledge to the shareholders for purposes of Rule 10b-5] is justified when, because of the

showing that a director has a conflict of interest—whether financially related, status-oriented, or otherwise—or that he is acting under some other disability, should prevent him from representing the corporation for purposes of Rule 10b-5 disclosure.

Further, the term "disinterested" should be narrowly construed. For example, if a corporation's outside counsel sits on the board, there may be instances in which counsel will be subject to pressure from interested directors. This may occur if some directors have a strong interest in a contemplated transaction and if counsel derives substantial income from his representation. The same reasoning applies to major business suppliers of a corporation. Truly independent actions by either the lawyer or supplier might well signify a substantial reduction in revenue. This coercion, although arguably subtle, should foreclose labeling either the lawyer or the supplier "disinterested."[147]

The preceding discussion outlines a significant limitation of the *Goldberg* rationale. Only if corporate action requires shareholder approval, or if the

---

nature of the transaction, directors cannot be relied upon to represent the interests of shareholders fairly or when an external authority, the state, the incorporators, or the shareholders, have decreed that the directors cannot speak for the corporation"). *See also, e.g.,* Schoenbaum v. Firstbrook, 405 F.2d 215, 219-20 (2d Cir. 1968), *cert. denied,* 395 U.S. 906 (1969); Pappas v. Moss, 393 F.2d 865, 869 (3d Cir. 1968); Ruckle v. Roto Am. Corp., 339 F.2d 24, 29 (2d Cir. 1964).

147. In *Maldonado,* however, the Second Circuit concluded that a director who was a partner in a law firm that received substantial fees from the subject corporation was "disinterested." The court reasoned:

> [T]o label . . . [counsel] an "interested" director for purposes of Rule 10b-5 because of his relationship as the company's legal counsel would be to open the door to an unworkable standard for determining whether there has been deception practiced upon the corporation. . . . [W]e cannot assume that a counsel-director acts for reasons that are against the corporation's interest, as distinguished from the private interests of its officers.

597 F.2d at 794.

The role and number of outside directors is not a novel concern. Nearly a half-century ago, Justice Douglas described and offered a solution to the problem:

> [B]oards wholly or dominantly filled with "shirtsleeve" directors drawn from the executive management, without outside representation, are apt to suffer from myopia and lack of perspective. It is one thing to operate a business efficiently, but it is quite another to be sufficiently detached from the business to be able to see it in relation to its competitors, trade trends, and the like. . . . The minimal requirements in this regard are statutory provisions that a majority of the board shall be composed of stockholders who are not employees or officers of the corporation. . . .

Douglas, *Directors Who Do Not Direct,* 47 HARV. L. REV. 1305, 1313-15 (1934). *See* Speech by SEC Chairman Harold M. Williams, *The Role of Inside Counsel in Corporate Accountability,* [1981-1982 Transfer Binder] FED. SEC. L. REP. (CCH) ¶ 82,318, at 82,374-75 (Oct. 4, 1979).

directors are interested,[148] will nondisclosure provide the basis for a claim of deception of a corporation in a derivative action under Rule 10b-5.[149] Even in such cases, however, the bare allegation of nondisclosure will not suffice to state a federal claim.[150] A second limitation imposed by *Santa Fe* is that the aggrieved shareholder may also be required to allege that, had the corporate malfeasance been disclosed, state court remedies would have been available.[151] In this vein, a question left unanswered after *Santa Fe* is whether the complainant must show not only that a suit in state court could have been brought, but also that such a suit would have been won. The courts are split on this issue.[152] While the Ninth Circuit seems to require that the complainant show that he would have been awarded relief in the state court action,[153] the Second Circuit appears to require only the bare availability of such a state action.[154] Between these two extremes are the Third and Fifth Circuits. Whereas the Fifth Circuit requires the plaintiff to show "a reasonable *basis* for state relief,"[155] the Third Circuit's standard

---

148. *See* notes 139-47 *supra* and accompanying text.

149. *See* cases cited in note 100 *supra*.

150. *See Santa Fe,* 430 U.S. at 474 n.14; cases cited in note 100 *supra*.

151. 430 U.S. at 474 n.14.

152. *See* notes 153-66 *infra* and accompanying text.

153. *See Kidwell,* 597 F.2d at 1294.

154. *See* IIT v. Cornfeld, 619 F.2d 909 (2d Cir. 1980); *Goldberg,* 567 F.2d at 219.

155. *Alabama Farm,* 606 F.2d at 614 (emphasis added). The court stated:

> We hold that all that is required to establish 10b-5 liability is a showing that state law remedies were available and that the facts shown must make out a prima facie case for relief; it is not necessary to go further and prove that the state action would have been successful. . . . [T]he plaintiff must show that there is at least a reasonable basis for state relief, but need not prove that the state suit would in fact have been successful.

The Third Circuit's position taken in *Healey, see* note 156 *infra,* and the Fifth Circuit's position in *Alabama Farm,* appear more stringent than requiring the complainant to survive a Rule 12(b)(6) motion under the Federal Rules of Civil Procedure for failure to state a claim upon which relief can be granted, or to survive a motion under Rule 56 for summary judgment. Compare the *Healey* and *Alabama Farm* standards with the discussion below of Rules 12(b)(6) and 56:

> The Rule 12(b)(6) motion also must be distinguished from a motion for summary judgment under Rule 56, which goes to the merits of the claim and is designed to test whether there is a genuine issue of material fact. The Rule 12(b)(6) motion, as has been mentioned above, only tests whether the claim has been adequately stated in the complaint. Thus, on a motion under Rule 12(b)(6), the court's inquiry essentially is limited to the content of the complaint; summary judgment, on the other hand, involves the use of pleadings, depositions, answers to interrogatories, and affidavits. This distinction between the two provisions is not substantial, however, because Rule 12(b)(6) provides that if "matters outside the pleadings are presented to and not excluded by the court, the motion shall be treated as one for summary judgment. . . ."

5 C. WRIGHT & A. MILLER, FEDERAL PRACTICE AND PROCEDURE § 1356 (1969).

appears slightly more stringent, requiring the plaintiff to demonstrate "a reasonable *probability* of ultimate success."[156]

The formulation of a proper standard is a difficult task. The maintenance of actions along the lines of *Goldberg*[157] is dependent largely upon the applicable state law of fiduciary duty. Only if the relevant *state* law recognizes the viability of the plaintiff's claim will a *federal* claim be possible. Under such conditions, the success of the plaintiff's suit may well vary, even within a single federal circuit.[158] The incongruity of a federal claim—with federal law supposedly uniform and national in character—being dependent on state law is self-evident.

To ameliorate this incongruity, the Second Circuit requires that the complainant show only a bare availability of state court relief.[159] This approach recognizes the federal interest in full and fair disclosure.[160] Critics of this position contend that it may allow circumvention of state court processes, thereby inducing forum shopping. Under the Second Circuit's approach, a plaintiff who would have failed in state court may, by alleging the possibility of success, coupled with nondisclosure, state a valid claim of "deception" within the meaning of Rule 10b-5. This approach is quite expansive, and some courts have argued that it stretches *Santa Fe*'s footnote fourteen beyond its recognizable limits.[161] On the other hand, making a federal claim com-

---

156. *Healey,* 616 F.2d at 647 (emphasis added). Thus, the Third Circuit adopted a standard somewhat similar to that enunciated by the Fifth Circuit. The court stated:

> We . . . hold that in a case such as this the plaintiff must demonstrate that at the time of the misrepresentation or omission, there was a reasonable probability of ultimate success in securing an injunction had there been no misrepresentation or omission. . . . [W]e frame the test in terms of a reasonable probability for two reasons. First, we believe absolute certainty to be both an impossible goal as well as an impracticable standard for a jury to implement. Second, in most cases the state remedy will be a preliminary injunction, which looks to the likelihood of ultimate success.

Id. See also Wright v. Heizer Corp., 560 F.2d at 250, in which the Seventh Circuit apparently failed to specifically address this question.

157. *See generally* Campbell, *supra* note 106, at 192 ("*Meridor* and *Heizer* are really cases in which the very nub of the complaint was that the corporation has been treated unfairly by its fiduciaries").

158. For example, in the Ninth Circuit, which covers nine states, a number of different dispositions could result in cases having similar factual situations, due to the application of different state law.

159. *See* note 154 *supra* and accompanying text.

160. *See Santa Fe,* 430 U.S. at 477-78. *See generally* Note, *Suits for Breach of Fiduciary Duty Under Rule 10b-5 After* Santa Fe Industries, Inc. v. Green, 91 Harv. L. Rev. 1874, 1891-93 (1978).

161. *See* notes 153, 155 and 156 *supra* and accompanying text. *See generally* the commentators cited in note 106 *supra*.

pletely dependent on state law would emasculate the federal interest in uniformity,[162] and would place an extremely heavy burden on complainants under Rule 10b-5. Further, as noted by the Third Circuit, requiring the plaintiff to prove a state claim may well be an impossible standard to administer.[163]

Although the approaches of the Third and Fifth Circuits may ease the complainant's burden in proving his Rule 10b-5 claim, they, too, condition the recognition of such a claim on the status of the applicable state law.[164] Thus, these positions will encourage inconsistent results in similar situations, thereby negating the federal securities law's interest in maintaining uniformity.[165] Nevertheless, the Third and Fifth Circuits' views, although not a perfect solution, represent a workable compromise. That compromise seeks a balance between the Second Circuit's view, which may stretch *Santa Fe's* footnote fourteen beyond its intended meaning, and the Ninth Circuit's approach, which defines a federal right solely by reference to the application of state law.

An alternative approach would be to vary the degree of proof required according to the state of the record. For example, when no meaningful discovery has been conducted and the record is undeveloped, the Ninth Circuit's requirement of proof of success in a state action would be far too stringent. Conversely, where a complete trial has been held or a lengthy record has been compiled in federal court, a stricter standard arguably should apply.[166] Yet, looking to the state of the record evades the basic issues presented by the post-*Santa Fe* cases. This approach does nothing to address the tension between the federal interest in the uniform application of the federal securities laws and the rationale underlying *Santa Fe* and footnote fourteen.

---

162. *See* McClure v. Borne Chem. Co., 292 F.2d 824, 829-35 (3d Cir.), *cert. denied,* 368 U.S. 939 (1961); Note, *supra* note 160, at 1889.

163. *Healey,* 616 F.2d at 647 (3d Cir. 1980).

164. *See generally* Note, *Causation in Rule 10b-5 Actions for Corporate Mismanagement,* 48 U. Chi. L. Rev. 936 (1981); Note, Goldberg v. Meridor: *The Second Circuit's Resurrection of Rule 10b-5 Liability for Breaches of Corporate Fiduciary Duties to Minority Shareholders,* 64 Va. L. Rev. 765, 772-77 (1978).

165. *See* note 162 *supra* and accompanying text.

166. *See* Respondent's Brief in Opposition to the Petition for a Writ of Certiorari at 14-15, Alabama Fidelity Life Ins. Co. v. Alabama Farm Bureau Mut. Cas. Ins. Co., No. 79-1362 (October Term, 1979). Thus, the Ninth Circuit required proof of success on the state law claim where the facts were "gleaned from a lengthy record." *Kidwell,* 597 F.2d at 1278. The courts which have applied less stringent standards were presented with incomplete factual records.

VI. FURTHER REFLECTIONS ON FEDERALISM AND INVESTOR PROTECTION AFTER *SANTA FE*

What of federalism and investor protection after *Santa Fe?* With respect to Rule 10b-5 as well as other provisions of the federal securities laws, the degree of investor protection afforded will depend, in large part, on the applicable state law.[167] At first glance, it appears that the *Goldberg*-type[168] securities and corporation law cases that are brought in the federal courts alleging Section 10(b)/Rule 10b-5 violations present local law questions akin to those with which the federal judiciary grapples in diversity cases governed by the rule of *Erie Railroad Co. v. Tompkins*.[169] Significantly, however, unlike the *Erie* doctrine, under which federal courts apply state substantive law in order to recognize state created remedies and liabilities,[170] *Santa Fe's* footnote fourteen, as construed by the lower federal courts, conditions the existence of a *federal* right upon the applicable state law.[171]

---

167. *See* Burks v. Lasker, 441 U.S. 471 (1979); Cort v. Ash, 422 U.S. 66, 77–85 (1975). In *Burks,* its most recent pronouncement on this subject, the Court remarked that "Congress has never indicated that the entire corpus of state corporation law is to be replaced simply because a plaintiff's cause of action is based upon a federal statute." 441 U.S. at 478. The Court accordingly held that even in a case arising under the Investment Company Act "federal courts should apply state law governing the authority of independent directors to discontinue derivative suits to the extent such law is consistent with the policy of the [Investment Company and Investment Advisers Acts]." *Id.* 486.

168. Goldberg v. Meridor, 567 F.2d 209 (2d Cir. 1977), *cert. denied,* 434 U.S. 1069 (1978). *See* notes 101-06 *supra* and accompanying text.

169. 304 U.S. 64, 78 (1938) ("Except in matters governed by the Federal Constitution or by acts of Congress, the law to be applied in any case is the law of the state. And whether the law of the state shall be declared by its Legislature in a statute or by its highest court in a decision is not a matter of federal concern").

170. *See, e.g.,* Hanna v. Plumer, 380 U.S. 460 (1965); Byrd v. Blue Ridge Rural Elec. Coop., Inc., 356 U.S. 525 (1958); Guaranty Trust Co. v. York, 326 U.S. 99 (1945).

171. For example, in Goldberg v. Meridor, the majority's holding was bottomed on the proposition that the complainant could have gone to a New York state court for an injunction had the alleged facts been known to him in time. Judge Meskill, dissenting in part, doubted the validity of that premise. Noting that both the parent and its allegedly looted subsidiary were Panamanian corporations, Judge Meskill expressed the view that "it is not at all clear that New York law determines the availability of an injunction in this situation." 567 F.2d 209, 224 n.9 (2d Cir. 1977), *cert. denied,* 434 U.S. 1069 (1978) (Meskill, J., dissenting). The majority opinion responded that "[t]he doubts entertained by our brother as to the existence of injunctive remedies in New York are unfounded," and then observed that "defendants have not brought to our attention any Panamanian . . . prohibition against derivative actions." *Id.* 219-20 (citations omitted). Analogous language is contained in the Ninth Circuit's *Kidwell* decision instructing "the federal trial judge . . . [to] decide any legal issues that would have arisen in the hypothetical state suit." Kidwell *ex rel.* Penfold v. Meikle, 597 F.2d 1273, 1294 (9th Cir. 1979). Note in this context that, as under *Erie,* the federal court must not only apply state substantive law but must determine *which* state law to apply. *See generally* Day and Zimmerman, Inc. v. Challoner, 423 U.S. 3 (1975); Klaxon Co. v. Stentor Elec. Mfg. Co., Inc.,

This limitation, however, may be more apparent than real. In a large number of cases, the applicable state law may be unresolved: for example, the issue may be one of first impression, or the state's high court may not have considered the question.[172] In such a case, a federal court, although ostensibly predicting how the relevant state's high court would rule on the matter,[173] may take into account the federal interest in full and fair disclosure. Even if this result follows, the state's countervailing interest in maintaining areas of independence remains intact because the state high court is the final arbiter. The federal court's interpretation of state law is, in essence, merely a recommendation that the state high court can freely accept or reject when it ultimately determines the matter.

It can be argued that some federal courts applying *Santa Fe*'s footnote fourteen exception will deliberately ignore state law, even when such law has been construed by the relevant state's high court. Such a consequence is possible but unlikely. For example, the federal courts applying the *Erie* rule have, as a general proposition, satisfactorily determined relevant state law. In all likelihood, this tradition would be generally followed in a *Goldberg*-type action.[174]

Some commentators have asserted that this application of federalism ultimately will be detrimental to investor interests. Arguing that state fairness principles provide inadequate protection, they predict that concepts of federalism will lead to "[the denial of] effective relief to powerless shareholders."[175] It should be recognized, however, that the *Goldberg* line of

---

313 U.S. 487 (1941) (a federal court, in a case governed by the *Erie* rule, must apply whatever law the courts of the state in which the federal court sits would apply).

172. Other reasons may include confusion in the state court decisions, a developing line of authorities that casts doubt regarding the state of the law, *dicta* or ambiguities in state court opinions, and legislative developments that may undermine the judicial rule. Bernhardt v. Polygraphic Co. of Am., 350 U.S. 198, 205 (1956).

173. *See* Commissioner v. Estate of Bosch, 387 U.S. 456 (1967), in which the Court stated:

> [U]nder some conditions, federal authority may not be bound even by an intermediate state appellate court ruling. . . . [T]he State's highest court is the best authority on its own law. If there be no decision by that court then federal authorities must apply what they find to be the state law after giving "proper regard" to relevant rulings of other courts of the State.

Id. 465.

174. *See generally* C. WRIGHT, HANDBOOK OF THE LAW OF FEDERAL COURTS § 55, at 258 (3d ed. 1976). On the other hand, it can be argued that the Second Circuit's rationale in *Goldberg,* requiring the plaintiff to show only that state court remedies were available, obfuscates the application of state law and may induce forum shopping. *See* notes 159-61 *supra* and accompanying text.

175. Campbell, *supra* note 106, at 206. *See* Ratner, *supra* note 6, at 323 ("the approach the Supreme Court is following now will exclude from the federal courts cases for which there is no effective remedy under state law because of problems of service of process, venue, security

cases represents an accommodation between competing federal and state interests. On one hand, because business enterprises often have national investor constituencies and national economic significance, the law governing the relationship between these enterprises and constituencies should also be national and uniform.[176] On the other hand, the fiduciary duties of corporate management traditionally have been defined by state common law, which can be restated, reshaped, and adapted to contemporary local needs without legislative change.[177] Thus, the *Goldberg* and *Singer v. Magnavox*[178] lines of cases indicate that the degree of investor protection in this area may often depend on the interaction between federal and state law.

This conclusion is supported by the curious relationship that has existed in the past between state and federal regulation of corporate malfeasance. As suggested above, state inaction in the field may have been due in part to perceptions that the federal government was primarily responsible for the protection of shareholders.[179] *Santa Fe,* and other decisions cutting back on the scope of the "federal corporation law," have brought into question the continued validity of such views. Consequently, there may well be new pressures on the states to provide for the protection of investors, as state courts and legislatures may no longer perceive the federal government as the primary source of regulation. This observation of the state-federal relationship in the corporate area is consistent with the recent movement toward increased state court sensitivity to shareholder interests and suggests that state protections for investors may continue to develop.

VII. CONCLUSION

One approach in analyzing recent federal and state court decisions in the Rule 10b-5 and related corporate areas is from the perspective of federalism. These decisions may well underscore that the federal judiciary, particularly the Supreme Court, has become acutely aware that undue extension of the

---

for expenses, and other procedural obstacles"). Query whether the substance-procedure distinction applies in this situation, because the outcome is not the only consideration. Even though the application of state procedural mechanisms might preclude relief in the federal action, the federal judicial system, as an independent system, has a countervailing interest in applying its own procedural rules. As such, if the federal procedural mechanisms are constitutional, they may be controlling notwithstanding contrary state provisions. *See* Hanna v. Plumer, 380 U.S. 460 (1965); Byrd v. Blue Ridge Rural Elec. Coop., Inc., 356 U.S. 525 (1958).

176. *See* notes 162 and 165 *supra* and accompanying text.

177. *See generally* Burks v. Lasker, 441 U.S. at 477-78; *Santa Fe,* 430 U.S. at 477-78.

178. Singer v. Magnavox, 380 A.2d 969 (Del. 1977). *See* notes 80-84 *supra* and accompanying text.

179. *See* notes 44-47 *supra* and accompanying text.

Rule 10b-5 remedy into previously untouched areas may displace regulation that has traditionally been within the purview of the states. On the other hand, the *Goldberg* line of cases, particularly when viewed in conjunction with recent Delaware decisions, may well reflect a desirable accommodation between federal and state interests. The extent to which the federal and state courts may continue on this experimental path in federalism is not yet certain. Their journey, however, should receive the attention of the corporate community, corporate practitioners and academicians.

5

Duties of Boards of Directors and Management in Tender Offer Contests

I. INTRODUCTION

A good starting point for discussion of the duties of boards of directors and management in proxy and tender offer contests is Judge Friendly's admonition in *Electronic Speciality Co. v. International Controls Corp.*[1] There, Judge Friendly drew a parallel between proxy and tender offer battles. He stressed that these contests are not conducted " 'in the peace of a quiet chamber,'—but under the stresses of the marketplace."[2] Because management on both sides must "act quickly, sometimes impulsively, often in angry response to what they consider, whether rightly or wrongly, to be low blows by the other side," he concluded there will "[p]robably . . . no more be a perfect tender offer than a perfect trial."[3] Thus, according to Judge Friendly, Congress intended in enacting the Williams Act to assure basic fairness and fair dealing, not to impose "an unrealistic requirement of laboratory conditions."[4] As Judge Friendly remarked and as subsequent courts have held, the foregoing considerations bear on the kind of judgment to be applied in testing conduct on the part of both sides.[5]

---

1. 409 F.2d 937 (2d Cir. 1969).
2. *Id.* at 948 (quoting Hellenic Lines Ltd. v. Brown & Williamson Tobacco Corp., 277 F.2d 9, 13 (4th Cir.), *cert. denied,* 364 U.S. 879 (1960).
3. 409 F.2d at 948.
4. *Id.*
5. *Id. See* Seaboard World Airlines, Inc. v. Tiger Int'l, Inc., [1979 Transfer Binder] FED. SEC. L. REP (CCH) ¶ 96,877 at 95,590 (2d Cir.); Kennecott Copper Corp. v. Curtiss-Wright Corp., 584 F.2d 1195, 1200 (2d Cir. 1978); Ash v. LFE Corp., 525 F.2d 215, 221 (3d Cir. 1975); Gerstle v. Gamble-Skogmo, Inc., 478 F.2d 1281, 1300 (2d Cir. 1973); General Time Corp. v. Talley Indus., Inc., 403 F.2d 159, 162 (2d Cir. 1968), *cert. denied,* 393 U.S. 1026 (1969).

From this perspective, this chapter will address the duties of boards of directors and management in tender offer contests. In this regard, the discussion will examine such subjects as the general duty to disclose in the tender offer context, pertinent SEC tender offer rules, and the legitimacy of defensive tactics.

II. GENERAL DUTY TO DISCLOSE

Under federal law, the Williams Act provides the basic framework for assessing management's disclosure obligations in the tender offer context.[6] The legislative history of the Act indicates that it was designed to protect the legitimate interests of the target corporation, its management and its shareholders, and simultaneously to allow both the target and the bidder to present fairly their views to the shareholders.[7] Apparently, however, the Supreme Court took a more restrictive view of the Act's objective in *Piper v. Chris-Craft Industries, Inc.,*[8] where the Court stated that "[t]he sole purpose of the Williams Act was the protection of investors who are confronted with a tender offer."[9]

Section 14(e) of the Williams Act contains a broad antifraud provision prohibiting, among other things, all persons from making material misrepresentations or nondisclosures.[10] Regarding this duty, the Second Circuit, in *Chris-Craft Industries, Inc. v. Piper Aircraft Corp.,*[11] enunciated the following broad principle as it applies to the target corporation and its management:

> By reason of the special relationship between them, shareholders are likely to rely heavily upon the representations of corporate insiders when the shareholders find themselves in the midst of a battle for

---

6. 15 U.S.C. §§ 78m(d), (e), 78n(d), (e), (f) (1976) (added by Pub. L. No. 90-439, 82 Stat. 454 (1968)). The Williams Act amended the Securities Exchange Act of 1934 by adding §§ 13(d), (e) and 14(d), (e), (f). Unless otherwise stated, references herein are to the amended Securities Exchange Act of 1934.

7. As the Act's sponsor Senator Harrison Williams stated: "We have taken extreme care to avoid tipping the scales either in favor of management or in favor of the person making the takeover bid." 173 CONG. REC. 24,664 (1967) (remarks of Sen. Williams).

8. 430 U.S. 1 (1977).

9. *Id.* at 35.

10. 15 U.S.C. § 78n(e) (1976). Under certain circumstances, § 14(d) of the Williams Act and statutes in many states require both the bidder and target to disclose information relevant to the shareholders' decision to accept or reject a tender offer. *See generally* E. ARANOW, H. EINHORN & G. BERLSTEIN, DEVELOPMENTS IN TENDER OFFERS FOR CORPORATE CONTROL 207-25, 232-45 (1977).

11. 480 F.2d 341 (2d Cir.), *cert. denied,* 414 U.S. 910 (1973).

control. Corporate insiders therefore have a special responsibility to be meticulous and precise in their representations to shareholders.[12]

Moreover, under state law, full and fair disclosure may well be required in the tender offer context. For example, the Delaware Supreme Court has imposed a duty of "complete candor" in revealing the germane facts and circumstances surrounding a subject tender offer.[13]

A. Disclosure of Antitakeover Proposals

In October 1978, the Division of Corporation Finance issued a statement regarding disclosure in proxy and information statements of antitakeover or similar proposals.[14] Noting that the increased use to obtain corporate control has prompted many companies to consider defensive techniques to fend off hostile offers, the staff expressed concern over the adequacy of disclosure made to investors when the corporation seeks shareholder approval to amend its charter or by-laws to incorporate antitakeover or similar proposals.[15] Disclosure recommended by the staff included: (1) the reasons for the antitakeover proposals and basis for such reasons; (2) the overall effects of the proposal, including the impact upon management tenure; (3) the advantages and disadvantages of the proposal; (4) disclosure of how the proposal will operate; (5) whether the proposal was the subject of a

---

12. *Id.* at 364-65. Additional federal disclosure obligations may exist for boards of directors and management in the tender offer context. For further discussion, *see* Steinberg, *Fiduciary Duties and Disclosure Obligations in Proxy and Tender Contests for Corporate Control,* 30 EMORY L.J. 169, 217-19 (1981).

13. Lynch v. Vickers Energy Corp., 383 A.2d 278, 279-81 (Del. 1977). *See* Junker v. Crory, [1981 Transfer Binder] FED. SEC. L. REP. (CCH) ¶ 98,236, at 91,568 (5th Cir. 1981) (under Louisiana law, corporate officers and directors are obliged "to disclose facts within their knowledge to shareholders and to deal with them in an atmosphere of trust and confidence"); Nelson v. Gammon, 647 F.2d 710 (6th Cir. 1981) (Kentucky law).

14. Securities Exchange Act Release No. 15,230 [1978 Transfer Binder] FED. SEC. L. REP. (CCH) ¶ 81,748. The Division specifically identified fourteen kinds of defensive corporate charter amendments or provisions, including reincorporation in a state with an antitakeover statute, "supermajority" approval requirements for mergers, and favoring officers with long-term "sweetheart" contracts that cannot be abrogated or rescinded.

15. *Id.* As noted by one commentator, although in a number of cases antitakeover provisions have been challenged, few of these challenges have been successful. Moran, *Anti-Takeover Charter Changes Upheld by Courts,* Legal Times (Wash.), Mar. 24, 1980, at 32, col. 1. *See* discussion herein at page 32 *supra. See also* Pacific Realty Trust v. APC Investments, Inc., [1982 Transfer Binder] FED. SEC. L. REP. (CCH) ¶ 98,790 (9th Cir. 1982); Joseph E. Seagram & Sons, Inc. v. Conoco, Inc., 519 F. Supp. 506 (D. Del. 1981); Friedenberg, *Jaws III: The Impropriety of Shark-Repellent Amendments as a Takeovers Defense,* 7 DEL. J. CORP. L. 32 (1982); Comment, *Antitakeovers Maneuvers: Developments in Defense Tactics and Target Actions for Injunctive Relief,* 35 SW. L.J. 617 (1981).

vote of the issuer's board of directors and, if so, the result of such vote; and (6) a statement of the limitations or restrictions, if any, on the adoption of such proposals.[16]

B. Impact of *Santa Fe* and Its Progeny

In *Santa Fe Industries, Inc. v. Green*[17] the Supreme Court held that in order to state a cause of action under Section 10(b) and Rule 10b-5 of the Exchange Act, deception or manipulation must be alleged.[18] In other words, under Section 10(b) and Rule 10b-5, mere breaches of fiduciary duty that do not involve any misrepresentation or nondisclosure are not actionable. A number of district courts have read *Santa Fe* as signifying that the legitimacy of defensive tactics is not a matter within the purview of Section 14(e).[19] One such case is *Berman v. Gerber Products Co.*,[20] where the district court stated: "While actions of a board of directors or corporate officers might constitute internal mismanagement and breach of fiduciary duty even without deception, it is just such claims that are excluded from the purview of § 14(e) according to the standards set forth in [*Santa Fe Industries, Inc. v.] Green.*"[21]

Unquestionably, the *Santa Fe* decision presents obstacles to invoking a federal fiduciary duty upon target management under Section 14(e). The overwhelming philosophy of the Williams Act is that of disclosure—that shareholders should receive all information material to the operations of their companies so that they, in turn, can make informed investment de-

---

16. In particular, the staff expressed its opinion that "the issuer's proxy material or information statements should disclose in a prominent place that the overall effect of the proposal is to render more difficult the accomplishment of mergers or the assumption of control by a principal shareholder, and thus to make difficult the removal of management." [1978 Transfer Binder] FED. SEC. L. REP. (CCH) ¶ 81,748, at 80,985. For more discussion herein on this subject, *see* pages 32-33 *supra. See also* Steinberg, note 12 *supra,* at 223-25.

17. 430 U.S. 462 (1977).

18. *Id.* at 474.

19. *See, e.g.,* Altman v. Knight, 431 F. Supp. 309, 314 (S.D.N.Y. 1977). There the court noted:

> What plaintiff's claim boils down to, insofar as the acquisition itself is concerned, is that the [defendant directors] breached their fiduciary duties to [the subject company] when they voted to purchase Walworth for purely selfish motives at a grossly exaggerated price [solely to defeat a tender offer]. This is precisely the kind of claim the Supreme Court in *Santa Fe* felt should be decided under state corporate law.

See Vaughn v. Teledyne, Inc., 628 F.2d 1214, 1219-20 (9th Cir. 1980); Lewis v. McGraw, 495 F. Supp. 27, 30 (S.D.N.Y. 1979), *aff'd,* 619 F.2d 192, 195 (2d Cir. 1980).

20. 454 F. Supp. 1310 (W.D. Mich. 1978).

21. *Id.* at 1318. For further discussion on *Santa Fe* and its progeny herein, *see* pages 163-98 *supra.*

cisions.[22] On the other hand, an argument can be made that unlike Section 10(b), Section 14(e) proscribes "fraudulent acts or practices" and, hence, has a broader scope.[23] Moreover, under certain circumstances, as the Sixth Circuit has recently held, certain defensive tactics undertaken by target management may be "manipulative" practices proscribed by Section 14(e).[24] Further, it is arguable, based on the post-*Santa Fe* line of federal cases, that if a material nondisclosure or misrepresentation would have enabled a minority shareholder to bring suit in state court to enjoin the tender offer from being consummated, a remedy based partially on breach of fiduciary duty nevertheless would be actionable under Section 14(e).[25]

C. SEC Tender Offer Rules

In November 1979 the SEC adopted new tender offer rules.[26] In general, the rules are grouped into two regulations, Regulations 14D and 14E. If the tender offer is subject to Section 14(d)(1) of the Exchange Act, which

---

22. *See generally* Life Investors, Inc. v. AGO Holding, N.V., [1981-1982 Transfer Binder] FED. SEC. L. REP. (CCH) ¶ 98,356 (8th Cir. 1981); Panter v. Marshall Field & Co., 646 F.2d 271 (7th Cir.), *cert. denied,* 102 S. Ct. 658 (1981); Crouse-Hinds Co. v. InterNorth, Inc., [1980-1981 Transfer Binder] FED. SEC. L. REP. (CCH) ¶ 97,840 (N.D.N.Y. 1980).

23. *See generally* SEC v. Capital Gains Research Bureau, Inc., 375 U.S. 180, 195 (1963) (holding that "fraud" in the context of the Investment Advisers Act of 1940 includes equitable fraud). Moreover, § 14(e), by its terms, expressly applies to the making of false statements and half-truths. By comparison, § 10(b) applies only to manipulative and deceptive devices, or contrivances. Although Rule 10b-5 is phrased similar to § 14(e) in certain respects, as the Supreme Court held in Ernst & Ernst v. Hochfelder, 425 U.S. 185 (1976), the rule must be interpreted in conformity with its statutory source, § 10(b).

24. Mobil Corp. v. Marathon Oil Co., 669 F.2d 366 (6th Cir. 1981).

25. *See, e.g.,* Healey v. Catalyst Recovery, Inc., 616 F.2d 641 (3d Cir. 1980); Alabama Farm Bureau Mut. Cas. Co. v. Alabama Fidelity Life Ins. Co., 606 F.2d 602 (5th Cir. 1979), *cert. denied,* 101 S. Ct. 77 (1980); Kidwell *ex rel.* Penfold v. Meikle, 597 F.2d 1273 (9th Cir. 1979); Goldberg v. Meridor, 567 F.2d 209 (2d Cir. 1977), *cert. denied,* 434 U.S. 1069 (1978); Wright v. Heizer Corp., 560 F.2d 236 (7th Cir. 1977), *cert. denied,* 434 U.S. 1066 (1978). For further discussion herein on this subject, *see* pages 163-98 *supra. See also* Steinberg, note 12 *supra,* at 225-35.

26. SEC Securities Act Release No. 6,158, Securities Exchange Act Release No. 16,384, 44 FED. REG. 70,326 (1979). *See also* SEC Securities Act Release No. 6,108, Securities Exchange Act Release No. 16,112, [1979 Transfer Binder] FED. SEC. L. REP. (CCH) ¶ 82,182, in which the SEC adopted Rule 13e-4 which governs issuer tender offers for their own securities. In general, Rule 13e-4 requires that a disclosure Schedule 13E-4 be filed with the SEC, and establishes, *inter alia,* disclosure, dissemination, and compliance requirements. In addition, Rule 13e-4 proscribes manipulative, deceptive, and fraudulent conduct in connection with issuer tender offers. Note also that an issuer tender offer regulated by Rule 13e-4, that is also a going private transaction subject to Rule 13e-3, is required to be effected in compliance with both rules. Importantly, an issuer tender offer under state law "must be premised upon a valid business purpose consistent with the interests of the issuer's security holders and not with the primary objective of preserving management in office." Manges, *SEC Regulation of Issuer and Third-Party Tender Offers,* 8 SEC. REG. L.J. 275, 278 (1981).

concerns securities registered under Section 12 of that Act or securities of certain insurance and investment companies, both regulations are applicable. If the tender offer is not subject to Section 14(d)(1), only Regulation 14E is applicable. Some of the more pertinent provisions of the tender offer rules which concern the disclosure obligations of issuers and their boards of directors follow.

For example, Rule 14d-6(d) establishes an express obligation on a tender offeror to promptly disclose material changes in the information published, sent, or given to security holders.[27] In addition, Rule 14d-9 calls for the subject company to file with the SEC a Schedule 14D-9 which requires the disclosure of certain information.[28] This information includes, if material, a description of any contract, agreement, arrangement, or understanding, and any actual or potential conflict of interest between, among others, the bidder, the target, and their affiliates.[29] Also, Item 7 of Schedule 14D-9 requires disclosure with respect to certain negotiations and transactions by the subject company.[30] Further, the person filing the schedule, with the exception of the subject company's initial "stop-look-and-listen" letter,[31] is required to state the nature of the solicitation or recommendation and to specify whether the person is advising security holders to accept, reject, or

---

27. 17 C.F.R. § 240.14d-6(d) (1982). According to the SEC, this rule "comports with current practice and avoids any possible ambiguity, thus ensuring for disclosure of material information during the course of a tender offer." 44 FED. REG. at 70,333.

28. 17 C.F.R. § 240.14d-9 (1982); 44 FED. REG. at 70,327 ("the statement furnished under Rule 14e-2 [by the subject company] . . . would under Rule 14d-9 require the filing of Schedule 14D-9 with the Commission. . .").

29. SEC Schedule 14D-9, Item 3(b), 17 C.F.R. § 240.14d-101 (1982). In adopting Schedule 14D-9, the SEC "believe[d] that the disclosure elicited by the Schedule will assist security holders in making their investment decision and in evaluating the merits of a solicitation/recommendation." 44 FED. REG. at 70,336. See generally Chem-Nuclear Systems, Inc. v. Waste Management, Inc., [1982 Transfer Binder] FED. SEC. L. REP (CCH) ¶ 98,759 (W.D. Wash. 1982).

30. SEC Schedule 14D-9, Item 7, 17 C.F.R. § 240.14d-101 (1982). See Rowe, Tender Offer Regs: Changing the Game Rules, Legal Times (Wash.), Dec. 31, 1979, at 9, col. 1. See also 44 FED. REG. at 70,336.

31. "A subject company which is sending a 'stop-look-and-listen' letter is required to state that on or before a specified date (no later than 10 business days from the date of commencement) it will advise security holders of its position with respect to the tender offer." 44 FED. REG. at 70,335 (footnotes omitted). A "stop-look-and-listen" letter is the target company's initial limited communication regarding the tender offer. Id. In pertinent part, such a letter must only: (1) identify the bidder's tender offer; (2) state that the tender offer is being considered by the target's management; (3) represent that no later than ten days from the tender offer's commencement that the target will inform stockholders of its position and the reasons therefor, including its inability to assume a position; and (4) request that security holders delay making a decision whether to tender their shares until they have been informed of the target's position. Id. at 70,346.

take other action with respect to the tender offer.[32] Significantly, in order to comply with the disclosure obligation imposed by Rule 14e-2, a subject company will be required in the Schedule 14D-9 to state its position and the reasons therefor.[33] In this regard, Rule 14e-2 requires the subject company to publish or send to security holders a statement disclosing its position with respect to the tender offer within ten business days of the commencement of the tender offer by a person other than the issuer. The statement of position can take one of three forms: (1) recommendation or rejection of the tender offer; (2) no opinion, and will remain neutral toward the tender offer; or (3) the subject company is unable to take a position with respect to the tender offer. In addition, the company is required to include the reasons for its position with respect to the tender offer, including the inability to take a position.[34]

III. LEGITIMACY OF DEFENSIVE TACTICS

In a corporate world preoccupied with takeover attempts, attention naturally gravitates to the defensive tactics employed by target corporations attempting to fend off exchange or tender offers. In this regard, target

---

32. SEC Schedule 14D-9, Item 4, 17 C.F.R. § 240.14d-101 (1982). If the subject company is not making a recommendation it must state whether it is expressing no opinion and is remaining neutral toward the tender offer or is unable to take a position with respect to the offer. Note also that Item 4(b) of Schedule 14D-9 indicates that conclusory statements will not be considered sufficient disclosure.

33. *Id.*

34. SEC Rule 14e-2, 17 C.F.R § 240.14e-2 (1982). If the subject company changes its position or other material changes occur, the subject company is required to promptly publish, send, or give to security holders a statement disclosing such material change. *See* Sommer & Feller, *Takeover Rules: A Cohesive Comprehensive Code,* Legal Times (Wash.), Dec. 17, 1979, at 18, col. 1. In regard to Rule 14e-2, one source has stated:

> The Supreme Court's interpretation [in *Chris-Craft*] is consistent with the duty that rule 14e-2 imposes upon target directors to disclose affirmatively any information material to the tender offer. The failure to support the imposition of such a duty is inconsistent with the Act's goal of informing the investing public. Furthermore, a target management disclosure duty furthers the efficient market purposes of the Act. Information defines the fair market value of a security. When an investor chooses between the alternatives of tendering or holding, he needs to have all material information in order effectively and efficiently to assess his alternatives. With incomplete knowledge, the investor's decision will be inefficient.

Gelfond & Sebastian, *Reevaluating the Duties of Target Management in a Hostile Tender Offer,* 60 B.U.L. REV. 403, 410 (1980) (footnotes omitted). *But see* Berman v. Gerber Prods. Co., 454 F. Supp. 1310, 1325 (W.D. Mich. 1978) ("It is true that in general the Williams Act does not appear to impose upon the management of a target company an affirmative duty to respond to a tender offer at all"). For further discussion on the SEC tender offer rules, *see* pages 39-41 *supra*.

management has engaged in a wide variety of defensive tactics. For example, target management may advise the shareholders that the board of directors considers the tender offer "inadequate";[35] it may pursue active opposition such as an unprecedented dividend increase[36] or a defensive merger.[37] It may even take an action normally thought adverse to the shareholders' interest,[38] and assert that the tactic is now "in the best interests of the shareholders."[39] The variety of defensive tactics has been limited only by the fertile imagi-

---

In addition, § 13(d)(1) of the Exchange Act and Rule 13d-1 prescribed thereunder require any person or group of persons who acquire beneficial ownership of more than 5 percent of a class of equity securities registered under § 12 of the Act to disclose, within ten days, specific information by filing a Schedule 13D with the SEC and by sending copies to the issuer and to each exchange on which the security is traded. As stated by the Second Circuit, "the goal of § 13(d) is to alert the marketplace to every large, rapid aggregation or accumulation of securities . . . which might represent a potential shift in corporate control." Treadway Cos., Inc. v. Care Corp., 638 F.2d 357, 380 (2d Cir. 1980) (quoting GAF Corp. v. Milstein, 453 F.2d 709, 719 (2d Cir. 1971), cert. denied, 406 U.S. 910 (1972)). In this regard, it is clear that § 13(d) is a disclosure statute. In the view of Judge Gessell, however, such disclosure does not extend to indefinite or tentative possible plans. Hence, "[i]n judging the adequacy of a Schedule 13D statement, fair accuracy, not perfection, is the appropriate standard." Purolator, Inc. v. Tiger Int'l, Inc., [1981 Transfer Binder] FED. SEC. L. REP. (CCH) ¶ 97,867, at 90,369 (D.D.C.). But see SEC v. Savoy Indus., Inc., 587 F.2d 1149, 1165 (D.C. Cir. 1978) ("it is plain that section 13(d) requires the making of a completely truthful statement").

35. See, e.g, Panter v. Marshall Field & Co., 646 F.2d 271 (7th Cir.), cert. denied, 102 S. Ct. 658 (1981); Joseph E. Seagram & Sons, Inc. v. Abrams, 510 F. Supp. 860 (S.D.N.Y. 1981); Weeks Dredging & Cont., Inc. v. American Dredging Co., 451 F. Supp. 468, 471-72 (E.D. Pa. 1978); Emhart Corp. v. USM Corp., 403 F. Supp. 660, 661-62 (D. Mass.), vacated on other grounds, 527 F.2d 177 (1st Cir. 1975); Cauble v. White, 360 F. Supp. 1021, 1025-26 (E.D. La. 1973). For example, in Emhart, the target corporation communicated to its shareholders through press releases, advertisements, and letters that the tender offer was "quite inadequate" and was an attempt to seize control of the target "at bargain-basement prices." 403 F. Supp. at 662.

36. See, e.g, Humana, Inc. v. American Medicorp, Inc., [1977-1978 Transfer Binder] FED. SEC. L. REP. (CCH) ¶ 96,286 (S.D.N.Y Jan. 5, 1978). See also Klaus v. Hi-Shear Corp., 528 F.2d 225, 233 (9th Cir., 1975).

37. See, e.g., Applied Digital Data Sys., Inc. v. Milgo Elec. Corp., 425 F. Supp. 1145 (S.D.N.Y. 1977); Royal Indus., Inc. v. Monogram Indus., Inc., [1976-1977 Transfer Binder] FED. SEC. L. REP (CCH) ¶ 95,863 (C.D. Cal. Nov. 29, 1976); SEC v. Thermal Power Co., [1975-1976 Transfer Binder] FED. SEC. L. REP. (CCH) ¶ 95,265 (D.D.C. Aug. 1, 1975) (SEC complaint).

38. See, e.g., Donovan v. Bierwirth, 680 F.2d 263 (2d Cir. 1982) (trustees for target's pension plan purchased target's stock in attempt to thwart hostile tender offer); Mobil Corp. v. Marathon Oil Co., [1981-1982 Transfer Binder] FED. SEC. L. REP. (CCH) ¶ 98,399 (6th Cir. 1981) ("lock-up" options extended by target corporation to "white knight"); Crane Co. v. Harsco Corp., 511 F. Supp. 294 (D. Del. 1981) (target's purchase of block of its own stock from arbitrageurs); Applied Digital Data Sys., Inc. v. Milgo Elec. Corp., 425 F. Supp. 1145 (S.D.N.Y. 1977) (defensive sale of stock to friendly third party).

39. See notes 36-37 supra.

nations of the target's board, management, investment bankers, counsel, and other consultants.[40]

A. The Fiduciary Duty's Effect on Target Management's Response

Because they are fiduciaries, corporate directors and other insiders may resist a tender offer under state law only if they can objectively deem that the offer is inconsistent with the interests of the corporation and its shareholders.[41] Hence, resistance by members of management to preserve their jobs and status constitute breaches of their fiduciary duties.[42] Implicit in this assumption is that management, regardless of its good faith beliefs, must maintain objectivity when faced with a tender offer.[43]

---

40. *See* Butler, *Management's Responsibility in Responding to a Takeover,* in SEVENTH ANNUAL INSTITUTE ON SECURITIES REGULATION (PLI) 221 (R. Mundheim, A. Fleischer & B. Vandegrift eds., 1976):

> Counsel and public accountants should be retained immediately upon learning of an offer, both to evaluate the legal and financial aspects of the tender and to prepare and evaluate the defense possibilities. . . .
> . . . [R]etention of investment banking advisers is an open question. . . . If an exchange offer is made, it is almost mandatory to retain an investment banking firm to evaluate the fair value of the securities being offered. In a cash tender, the need is less clear.

Id. at 230-31.

41. *See* Northwest Indus., Inc. v. B. F. Goodrich Co., 301 F. Supp. 706 (N.D. Ill. 1969):

> [M]anagement has the responsibility [under state law] to oppose offers which, in its best judgment, are detrimental to the company or its stockholders. In arriving at such a judgment, management should be scrupulously fair in considering the merits of any proposal submitted to its stockholders. The officers' and directors' informed opinion should result in that strict impartiality which is required by their fiduciary duties.

Id. at 712-13. *See* E. ARANOW, H. EINHORN & G. BERLSTEIN, DEVELOPMENTS IN TENDER OFFERS FOR CORPORATE CONTROL 207-25, 232-45 (1977); Gruenbaum, *Defensive Tactics and the Business Judgment Rule,* 4 CORP. L. REV. 263 (1981).

42. *See* Commonwealth Oil Ref. Co. v. Tesoro Petro. Corp., 394 F. Supp. 267, 273-74 (S.D.N.Y. 1975). *See also* Singer v. Magnavox Co., 380 A.2d 969 (Del. 1977). Note the following statement of state fiduciary obligation issued by the Delaware Supreme Court in *Singer*:

> While technically not trustees, . . . [corporate directors] stand in a fiduciary relation to the corporation and its stockholders. . . . The rule that requires an undivided and unselfish loyalty to the corporation demands that there shall be no conflict between duty and self-interest. The occasions for the determination of honesty, good faith and loyal conduct are many and varied, and no hard and fast rule can be formulated. The standard of loyalty is measured by no fixed scale.

Id. at 977 (quoting Guth v Loft, Inc., 23 Del. 255, 5 A.2d 503, 510 (1939)).

43. *See* Northwest Indus., Inc. v. B. F. Goodrich Co., 301 F. Supp. 706, 712-13 (N.D. Ill. 1969).

While courts assessing the legality of defensive tactics under state law have adopted a variety of tests, most courts currently apply one of two tests: the "business purpose" test or the "primary purpose" test. Courts applying the business purpose test examine whether a valid business purpose exists for management's use of the maneuver.[44] In contrast, those courts that adhere to the primary purpose test determine whether the principal or primary purpose of the defensive maneuver was to benefit the subject corporation or to impede the bidder's tender offer.[45] In applying these tests, although a number of courts have declined to recognize the strong affinity of most corporate directors and other insiders toward their corporations, this factor merits consideration. Only a rare individual can affiliate closely with a corporation and still view an offeror's takeover attempt with detachment. Many insiders sincerely believe that the corporation is worth more than the offer. But even a sincere belief may have little basis in commercial reality.[46] Insiders must acknowledge that objectivity is difficult to maintain. Accordingly, management should take special care to make its assessment of the tender offer as neutral and thorough as possible. At the very least, management should employ independent investment bankers and legal counsel to scrutinize the offer.[47]

B. Management's Recommendation That the Tender Offer Should Be Rejected

Frequently, when management opposes a tender offer, it communicates to its shareholders that the offer is "inadequate" and "not in the best interests of the shareholders." By their nature, such communications fall within the scope of Section 14(e). In this context, perhaps the case that best focuses on the standards and responsibilities of target management under federal law is *Humana, Inc. v. American Medicorp, Inc.*[48] In *Humana* Medicorp issued a press release and a letter to its shareholders characterizing the

---

44. *See, e.g.*, Panter v. Marshall Field & Co., 646 F.2d 271, 293-95 (7th Cir.), *cert. denied*, 102 S. Ct. 658 (1981) (applying Delaware law); Berman v. Gerber Products Co., 454 F. Supp. 1310, 1319 (W.D. Mich. 1978) (applying Michigan law).

45. *See generally* Johnson v. Trueblood, 629 F.2d 287, 299-301 (Rosenn, J., concurring in part and dissenting in part) (construing Delaware law), *citing*, Petty v. Pentech Papers, Inc., 347 A.2d 140 (Del. Ch. 1975); Cheff v. Mathes, 41 Del. Ch. 494, 199 A.2d 548 (1964); Bennett v. Propp, 41 Del. Ch. 14, 187 A.2d 405 (1962).

46. Most shareholders do not share this strong attachment to the target corporation. Rather, they invest for the purpose of realizing as large a return as possible. In tender offer and exchange offer situations these shareholders consider seriously such factors as the premium offered by the bidder, the dividend policy of both the target and the offeror, and the future growth prospects of both corporations. Directors' unsubstantiated feelings that the tender offer is inadequate should be deemed irrelevant by the courts.

47. *Cf.* Zapata Corp. v. Maldonado, 430 A.2d 779 (Del. 1981).

48. [1977-1978 Transfer Binder] Fed. Sec. L. Rep. (CCH) ¶ 96,286 (S.D.N.Y. 1978).

Humana offer as "inadequate" and "not in the best interests of share-holders." In these statements, Medicorp did not communicate any of the positive aspects of the Humana offer, including the opinion of its own investment adviser, who valued the Humana preferred stock, which was one element of the exchange offer, at a clear premium over the market price of Medicorp stock.[49] Holding that Medicorp's description of the Humana offer violated Section 14(e), the district court stated:

> [O]nce Medicorp chose to communicate [to its shareholders] and, in particular, to characterize the offer as "inadequate," and "not in the best interests of" the stockholders, it was obligated to furnish its stockholders with all the information it had from Humana so that the stockholders would be sufficiently informed to react intelligently to the offer and would not be unfairly influenced by management's subjective presentation.[50]

C. Recent Decisions Regarding the Legitimacy of Defensive Tactics

Generally, a number of recent decisions dealing with duties of boards of directors and management assess the legitimacy of management's conduct and the scope of the business judgment rule. Although not a very recent case, *Berman v. Gerber Products Co.*[51] is an interesting starting point as it reflects the traditional perspective of the duties of target management under federal and state law in the tender offer setting. The case is first worthy of comment inasmuch as the plaintiffs alleged that Gerber violated Section 14(e) by failing to entertain inquiries from outside corporations regarding the potential acquisition of controlling interests in the company. The court rejected the plaintiffs' argument, concluding that the overtures were not firm offers, and hence were not "in connection with" a tender offer. Moreover, because such inquiries were not firm offers, they were not deemed material information required to be disclosed under Section 14(e).[52]

---

49. *Id.* at 92,833.

50. *Id. See also* Weeks Dredging & Contracting, Inc. v. American Dredging Co., 451 F. Supp. 468 (E.D. Pa. 1978); Cauble v. White, 360 F. Supp. 1021 (E.D. La. 1973).

51. 454 F. Supp. 1310 (W.D. Mich. 1978).

52. *Id.* at 1317-18. This holding appears to be consistent with the SEC's tender offer rules. *See* 44 FED. REG. 70,326, 70,336 (1979); note 161 *supra*. *See* Bucher v. Shumway, [1979-1980 Transfer Binder] FED. SEC. L. REP. (CCH) ¶ 97,142, at 96,302 (S.D.N.Y. 1979), *aff'd*, 622 F.2d 572 (2d Cir.), *cert. denied*, 101 S. Ct. 120 (1980) ("The law imposes no obligation upon the defendants to disclose mere inquiries or contacts made by those interested in acquiring the corporation or its stock"). *See also* Kennecott Corp. v. Smith, [1980 Transfer Binder] FED. SEC. L. REP. (CCH) ¶ 97,731 (3d Cir.), where the Third Circuit stated that once the offeror furnishes price and amount information to the target corporation's management, "[t]he target company in turn may be obliged to disseminate this information to its shareholders and to the securities markets in general under federal law, the rules of the New York Stock Exchange, and state law." *Id.* at 98,835.

The plaintiffs in *Gerber* also contended that the board's conduct in opposition to the takeover attempt was not motivated by legitimate business concerns and was contrary to the best interests of the shareholders. In short, as the court noted, the plaintiffs were alleging that the board had violated its fiduciary duty to the shareholders by attempting to block the tender offer.[53] Extending the strictures of *Santa Fe* to Section 14(e), the court rejected the shareholders' argument, reasoning that such claims are no longer cognizable under the antifraud provisions of the federal securities laws.[54] Furthermore, the court stated that assuming that plaintiffs' claims were cognizable under Section 14(e), the facts of the case indicated that the board had not, in fact, violated its fiduciary duty to the corporation's shareholders. The court concluded that the filing of a law suit alleging violations of the federal securities and antitrust laws by Gerber was in good faith, as the suit had a sufficient factual basis.[55] Also, the court noted that under the Michigan business judgment rule, management has relatively broad discretion to act in what it views to be the corporation's best interests.[56] Surprisingly, however, in light of two recent decisions which restrict the scope of Section 14(e),[57] *Gerber* ultimately may be used not by defendants but by plaintiffs in order to support the proposition that "[i]t is well settled that statements made by either the offeror or the target company prior to the actual effective date of a tender offer but after the announcement of the offer and preliminary

---

53. 454 F. Supp. at 1318.

54. *Id.*

55. *Id.* at 1318-19. The court also considered various allegations that the target corporation had failed to disclose a number of material facts to its stockholders. After considering each contention in turn, the court found them to be without merit. *Id.* at 1326-29. For example, in regard to one allegation, the court asserted that "under the facts of this case the information concerning Gerber's earnings during the previous two quarters would have had at best an infinitesimal effect upon a shareholder's decision to sell on the market or retain, and certainly would not meet the *TSC Industries* materiality standard." *Id.* at 1328. The court relied on TSC Industries, Inc. v. Northway, Inc., 426 U.S. 438 (1976), a case involving a proxy solicitation, in which the Supreme Court formulated a materiality standard that turned on whether there was a "substantial likelihood that a reasonable shareholder would consider [the omitted or misstated information] important in deciding how to vote." *Id.* at 449. For recent cases dealing with alleged Section 14(e) disclosure violations, *see, e.g.*, Life Investors, Inc. v. AGO Holding, N.V., [1980-1981 Transfer Binder] FED. SEC. L. REP. (CCH) ¶ 98,356 (8th Cir. 1981); Crane Co. v. Harsco Corp., 511 F. Supp. 294 (D. Del. 1981); Crouse-Hinds Co. v. InterNorth, Inc., [1980-1981 Transfer Binder] FED. SEC. L. REP. (CCH) ¶ 97,840 (N.D.N.Y. 1980).

56. *See* 419 F. Supp. at 1319 where the court stated that although

> corporate officers and directors have a high fiduciary duty of honesty and fair dealing with shareholders, it is also well established that corporate management may not be held liable for good faith errors in judgment. The so-called "business judgment rule" leaves relatively wide discretion in management to act in what it considers to be the best interests of the corporation.

57. Panter v. Marshall Field & Co., 646 F.2d 271 (7th Cir.), *cert. denied*, 102 S. Ct. 658 (1981); Lewis v. McGraw, 619 F.2d 192 (2d Cir. 1980).

filings fall within the purview of § 14(e)."[58] In this regard, the court stated that the plaintiffs could seek recovery under Section 14(e) on the theory that alleged inadequate disclosures misled them into retaining their shares when they could have sold them in the rising market.[59]

Lewis v. McGraw[60] and *Panter v. Marshall Field & Co.*[61] represent two very important tender offer cases that were recently decided. In *Lewis,* American Express made a proposed tender offer for the shares of McGraw-Hill. Through McGraw-Hill's opposition, the offer expired by its own terms without becoming effective.[62] Thereafter, a shareholder brought suit alleging that the conduct of McGraw-Hill's board violated Section 14(e) of the Williams Act.[63] The Second Circuit upheld the dismissal of the shareholder's claims against McGraw-Hill and its directors.[64] While there is arguably language in the opinion that a claim under Section 14(e) cannot be maintained unless a tender offer has, in fact, become effective,[65] the case should be read more narrowly as resting simply on the facts, or on the plaintiff's failure to show any realistic theory of causation or reliance.[66] Despite its possibly restrictive holding, which arguably has more limited practical application after the SEC's promulgation of Rule 14d-2,[67] and which, in any

---

58. 454 F. Supp. at 1318. *Gerber* also contained other significant issues, most notably the offeror's failure to adequately disclose to the target's shareholders its managerial practices relating to sensitive foreign payments. Also, the court recognized the disclosure responsibilities of the target's management. 454 F. Supp. at 1322-29. For further discussion, *see* Steinberg, note 12 *supra*, at 215-16.

59. 454 F. Supp. at 1325. According to the *Gerber* court:

> [I]f defendants misrepresented or omitted material facts in connection with their opposition to the Anderson Clayton proposal so that plaintiffs were induced to retain their shares in reliance upon the integrity and good judgment of the board of directors, but had they known the truth they would have sold their stock in the rising market, a direct causative link exists between defendants' acts and plaintiffs' investment decision.

Id. See O'Connor & Assoc. v. Dean Witter Reynolds, Inc., [1981-1982 Transfer Binder] FED. SEC. L. REP. (CCH) ¶ 98,433, at 92,631 (S.D.N.Y. 1982).

60. 619 F.2d 192 (2d Cir. 1980).

61. 646 F.2d 271 (7th Cir.), *cert. denied,* 102 S. Ct. 658 (1981).

62. 619 F.2d at 194.

63. *Id.* at 193-94.

64. *Id.* at 195-96.

65. *Id.* at 195 ("In the instant case, the target's shareholders simply could not have relied upon McGraw-Hill's statements, whether true or false, since they were never given an opportunity to tender their shares"). The majority of the *Panter* panel construed the decision as such. Significantly, Rule 14d-2 of the SEC's tender offer rules generally defines, with certain exceptions, the commencement of a tender offer as the date on which the offer is first published or sent or given to shareholders. 17 C.F.R. § 240.14d-2 (1982). *See* note 67 *infra*.

66. 619 F.2d at 195 ("Here . . . no reliance was possible under any imaginable set of facts. . .").

67. 44 FED. REG. 70,329 (1979). For further discussion herein on Rule 14d-2, *see* pages 39-41 *supra*.

event, appears to be confined to private claimants, the *Lewis* court remarked that its decision did not place statements made on the eve of a tender offer by a bidder or target outside the scope of the Williams Act. On the contrary, the court remarked that where "the offer ultimately becomes effective, and [the plaintiff's] reliance can be demonstrated or presumed, such statements [for private relief purposes] may well be made 'in connection with a tender offer. . . .' "[68] The court also stated that "[private] injunctive relief . . . may be available to restrain or correct misleading statements made during the period preceding a tender offer where it appears that such an offer is likely" to be forthcoming.[69]

Somewhat similar to the plaintiffs in *Lewis,* the plaintiffs in *Panter v. Marshall Field & Co.*[70] sought relief against directors of Marshall Field for allegedly embarking on a course of conduct which was designed to deceive the shareholders of the company and to defeat the tender offer that was to be made by Carter-Hawley, a national retail chain.[71] The case was before the Seventh Circuit on appeal from the district court's grant of the defendant's motion for a directed verdict.[72]

The plaintiffs' theory of recovery was premised on the contention that Marshall Field and its directors had illegally denied them an opportunity to tender their shares to Carter-Hawley or to sell them in the rising market by engaging in defensive tactics that prompted Carter-Hawley to withdraw its offer before becoming effective and by issuing misrepresentations that caused the shareholders not to dispose of their shares in the market. The allegations included, *inter alia,* that the defendants had violated federal and state law by maintaining a policy that Marshall Field would remain an independent business entity in order to perpetuate their control and failing to disclose such a policy to shareholders, engaging in a number of "defensive" acquisitions, filing an antitrust suit against Carter-Hawley, issuing misleading projections, and making material misstatements in press releases and letters in connection with the Carter-Hawley proposal.[73]

Turning first to the Section 14(e) claim, Judge Pell, relying on *Lewis,* held that because the tender offer was withdrawn before the plaintiffs had an opportunity to determine whether to tender their stock, they could not have

68. 619 F.2d at 195. *See* Berman v. Gerber Prods. Co., 454 F. Supp. at 1318 ("It is well settled that statements made by either the offeror or the target company prior to the actual effective date of a tender offer but after the announcement of the offer and preliminary filings fall within the purview of § 14(e)").

69. 619 F.2d at 195. The court also remarked that many of the violations alleged in the complaint could be recast as state law claims for breaches of fiduciary duty. *Id.*

70. 646 F.2d 271 (7th Cir.), *cert. denied,* 102 S. Ct. 658 (1981).

71. *Id.* at 277-82.

72. 486 F. Supp. 1168 (N.D. Ill. 1980).

73. 646 F.2d at 277-82, 287, 290-93.

relied on any of the defendants' alleged deceptions.[74] According to the court, the absence of the requisite element of reliance defeated the plaintiffs' claim.[75] The court also rejected the shareholders' contention that the defendants' misrepresentations or nondisclosures caused them not to sell their shares in the rising market, holding that "a *damages* remedy for investors who determine not to sell in the marketplace when no tender offer ever takes place was not intended to be covered by § 14(e). . . ."[76]

The court's holdings with respect to Section 14(e)'s limited scope can be read as applying only to private claimants.[77] At the outset of its discussion, the court stated that, under the plaintiffs' theory of recovery, total damages would exceed $200,000,000.[78] Hence, the court may have feared that application of Section 14(e) in this context would result in astronomical damages awards. Such a public policy rationale, however, would not extend to SEC suits for injunctive relief.[79] Accordingly, based on the court's reliance rationale which does not apply to SEC actions, the apparent public policy grounds, the statute's legislative history,[80] and the SEC's promulgation of

---

74. *Id.* at 283-87. Upon comparing § 14(e) with § 10(b), the court stated: "The two provisions are coextensive in their antifraud prohibitions, and differ only in their 'in connection with' language. They are therefore construed *in pari materia* by courts." *Id.* at 282. An argument can be made, however, that, unlike § 10(b), § 14(e) prohibits "fraudulent" acts or practices and, hence, should have a broader reach. Moreover, such conduct may be proscribed as "manipulative." *See* Mobil Corp. v. Marathon Oil Co., [1981-1982 Transfer Binder] FED. SEC. L. REP. (CCH) ¶ 98,399 (6th Cir. 1981).

75. 646 F.2d at 283-84, *distinguishing,* Affiliated Ute Citizens v. United States, 406 U.S. 128 (1972); Mills v. Electric Auto-Lite Co., 396 U.S. 375 (1970).

76. 646 F.2d at 285 (emphasis added). At another point, the court noted the judicial trend toward avoiding unduly broad interpretations of the securities acts, and stated that, consistent with this trend, it would refuse to provide a *damages* remedy for such misrepresentations when the proposed offer never became effective. *Id.* at 285-87.

77. *See id.* at 283-87. *But see id.* at 286 (court referred to its "finding that § 14(e) was not intended to remedy the conduct complained of here. . . ."); *id.* at 310 ("Management could speak without restraint knowing that once withdrawal is forced there is no Securities Act liability for deception practiced before withdrawal took place") (Cudahy, J., concurring in part and dissenting in part).

78. *Id.* at 283.

79. Unlike private monetary relief, SEC injunctions "are [equitable measures] designed to afford preventative relief only and not to redress past injuries." Steinberg, *SEC and Other Permanent Injunctions—Standards for Their Imposition, Modification, and Dissolution,* 66 CORNELL L. REV. 27, 28-29 (1980). *Cf.* Blue Chip Stamps v. Manor Drug Stores, 421 U.S. 723 (1975) (only purchasers and sellers have standing to bring implied private cause of action for damages under § 10(b) of the Exchange Act). The SEC is not precluded under *Blue Chip Stamps,* however, from bringing an enforcement action.

80. *See, e.g.,* Full Disclosure of Corporate Equity Ownership in Corporate Takeover Bids: Hearings on S. 510 Before the Senate Subcomm. on Securities of the Comm. on Banking and Currency, 90th Cong., 1st Sess. 15 (statement of SEC Chairman Cohen). Chairman Cohen testified that the purpose of the bill was "to provide the investor, the person who is required to make a decision, an opportunity to examine and to assess the relevant facts and to reach

Rule 14d-2,[81] it appears that, even under the *Panter* court's restrictive analysis, the type of illegal conduct alleged in that case would be within the purview of Section 14(e) insofar as SEC enforcement actions are concerned. Moreover, in practical effect, the court's holding may be somewhat curtailed by the application of Rule 14d-2, which, by its terms, defines the commencement of a tender offer.[82]

The gravamen of the plaintiffs' Section 10(b) and Rule 10b-5 claim was that the defendants' long-standing undisclosed policy of remaining independent and resisting all takeover efforts, designed to perpetuate the directors' control, was an omission of a material fact which rendered other statements and conduct of the defendants misleading. The court rejected this argument, reasoning that, even if such a policy existed, neither the policy nor the failure to disclose it constituted manipulation or deception as required by the statute and rule.[83] Moreover, the court held that the plaintiffs' allegation that, pursuant to such a policy, the defendants issued misleading statements and engaged in deceptive conduct, amounted to no more than an attempt to dress up a state claim for breach of fiduciary duty and to probe the "true purpose" of the defendants' actions.[84]

Turning to the plaintiffs' state law claims, the court held that the defendants' actions were protected by the business judgment rule. The court concluded that the directors gave appropriate consideration to each individual approach made to Marshall Field, that the defensive acquisitions were supported by business reasons, and that the filing of the antitrust suit against Carter-Hawley was made in good faith reliance on the advice of experienced antitrust counsel.[85]

---

a decision without being pressured and *without being subject to unwarranted techniques which are designed to prevent* that from happening" (emphasis added).

81. For a description of Rule 14d-2 herein, *see* pages 39-41 *supra*.

82. *See* notes 65, 67 *supra*.

83. 646 F.2d at 288. Interpreting the Supreme Court's decision in *Santa Fe,* the Seventh Circuit stated that "[t]he critical issue in determining whether conduct meets the requirement of deception . . . is whether the conduct complained of includes the omission or misrepresentation of a material fact, or whether it merely states a claim for a breach of a state law duty." *Id. See* Wright v. Heizer Corp., 560 F.2d 236 (7th Cir. 1977), *cert. denied,* 434 U.S. 1066 (1978). For other recent cases alleging disclosure violations in the tender offer context, *see* note 55 *supra*.

84. 646 F.2d at 289-93. For further discussion herein on the *Santa Fe* and true purpose lines of cases, *see* pages 94-98, 163-98 *supra*.

85. *Id.* at 293-98. *See* LTV Corp. v. Grumman Corp., [1981-1982 Transfer Binder] FED. SEC. L. REP. (CCH) ¶ 98,344 (E.D.N.Y. 1981) ("If the effect of a proposed takeover may be substantially to lessen competition, the target company is entitled to fend off its suitor"). The *Panter* court also rejected the plaintiffs' claim for interference with prospective advantage. 646 F.2d at 298-99. *See* Jewel Cos., Inc. v. Pay Less Drug Stores Northwest, Inc., 510 F. Supp. 1006 (N.D. Cal. 1981).

In a scathing dissent, Judge Cudahy asserted that "the majority here has moved one giant step closer to shredding whatever constraints still remain upon the ability of corporate directors to place self-interest before shareholder interest in resisting a hostile tender offer for control of the corporation."[86] Addressing first the plaintiffs' state law claims, Judge Cudahy contended that there was more than sufficient evidence for a jury to have decided in their favor.[87] In this regard, he particularly found troublesome the majority's broad construction of the business judgment rule.[88] Moreover, the dissent disagreed with the majority's interpretation of the scope of Section 14(e), reasoning that shareholders should have a damages remedy both in regard to the withdrawing of an offer prior to an opportunity to tender and to an election not to sell into the rising market in reliance on management's

---

86. *Id.* at 299 (Cudahy, J., concurring in part and dissenting in part). Although Judge Cudahy concurred in part of the majority's decision, the gist and tone of his opinion takes the form of a dissent.

87. In this regard, Judge Cudahy stated:

> There was abundant evidence from which a jury in this case could have concluded that Field's directors breached their fiduciary duties to the shareholders: 1) by pursuing a fixed, non-debatable and undisclosed policy of massive resistance to merger with, or acquisition by, a series of the nation's foremost retailers; 2) by making hasty and apparently imprudent defensive acquisitions to reduce Field's attractiveness as a takeover candidate and to force the withdrawal of the CHH offer; and 3) by hastily filing a major antitrust suit to further impair persistent acquisitive efforts of CHH.

Id. at 305 (Cudahy, J., concurring in part and dissenting in part).

88. *Id.* at 304-10 (Cudahy, J., concurring in part and dissenting in part) ("I emphatically disagree that the business judgment rule should clothe directors, battling blindly to fend off a threat to their control, with an almost irrebuttable presumption of sound business judgment, prevailing over everything but the elusive hobgoblins of fraud, bad faith or abuse of discretion"). *Id.* at 299.

In applying the business judgment rule, the majority remarked that the presumption of good faith that the "rule affords is heightened when the majority of the board consists of independent outside directors." *Id.* at 299. Responding to this assertion, Judge Cudahy stated:

> Directors of a New York Stock Exchange-listed company are, at the very least, "interested" in their own positions of power, prestige and prominence (and in their not inconsequential perquisites). They are "interested" in defending against outside attack the management which they have, in fact, installed or maintained in power—"their" management (to which, in many cases, they owe their directorships). And they are "interested" in maintaining the public reputation of their own leadership and stewardship against the claims of "raiders" who say that they can do better. Thus, regardless of their technical "independence," directors of a target corporation are in a very special position, where the slavish application of the majority's version of the good faith presumption is particularly disturbing.

Id. at 300-01 (Cudahy, J., concurring in part, dissenting in part).

misrepresentations and nondisclosures.[89] Otherwise, Judge Cudahy reasoned, incumbent management would have an open invitation "to make whatever claims and assertions may be expedient to force withdrawal of an offer."[90] Finally, in regard to the alleged violations of Section 10(b), the dissent concurred in the majority's holding that many of the claims were based on breaches of fiduciary duty.[91] However, in regard to a letter from Marshall Field's president to shareholders claiming a 13-percent increase in reported consolidated net earnings for a nine-month period when management in fact anticipated a decline in earnings for the full year, Judge Cudahy asserted that "this misleading use of the numbers created a serious question for the jury."[92] In conclusion, Judge Cudahy stated:

> To have taken this close case presenting a wide range of defensible inferences from the jury is a major disservice to stockholders everywhere. This case announces to stockholders (if they did not know it before) that they are on their own and may expect little consideration and less enlightenment from their board of directors when a tender offeror appears to challenge the directors for control. I believe that only the submission to jury verdict of cases like this one can restore confidence in our system of corporate governance.[93]

Although not involving a proxy or tender offer contest, *Johnson v. Trueblood*[94] is interesting from the perspective of the scope of the business judgment rule when control is a motive of a director in the operation of a corporation. In that case, the district court, construing Delaware law, stated in its jury instructions that the business judgment rule is rebutted only where

---

89. *Id.* at 310-12 (Cudahy J., concurring in part and dissenting in part). The SEC in its *amicus curiae* brief before the Seventh Circuit asserted that § 14(e) prohibits deception during the entire tender offer process, at least from the time of the public announcement of a tender offer proposal. Brief of the Securities Exchange Commission as *Amicus Curiae,* at 16-22, Panter v. Marshall Field & Co., [1981 Transfer Binder] FED. SEC. L. REP. (CCH) ¶ 97,929 (7th Cir.). The SEC said that "from the perspective of a public shareholder, once announcement of a tender offer proposal is made, it matters little whether fraud occurs before or after shareholders are given the opportunity to tender to the bidder, or whether they are ever given that opportunity." *Id.* at 21. *See* Berman v. Gerber Prods. Co., 454 F. Supp. 1310, 1324-25 (W.D. Mich. 1978).

90. 646 F.2d at 310 (Cudahy, J., concurring in part and dissenting in part).

91. *Id.* at 312.

92. *Id.* In regard to this claim, the majority stated: "We also find that because the projections of the five-year plan were tentative estimates prepared for the enlightenment of the management with no expectation that they would be made public, there was no duty to reveal them." *Id.* at 293. *See* Elkind v. Liggett & Myers, Inc., 635 F.2d 156, 164 (2d Cir. 1980); Vaughn v. Teledyne, Inc., 628 F.2d 1214, 1221 (9th Cir. 1980).

93. 646 F.2d at 312 (Cudahy, J., concurring in part and dissenting in part).

94. 629 F.2d 287 (3d Cir. 1980).

a director's sole or primary purpose for adopting a course of action or refusing to adopt another is to retain control.[95] In other words, according to the district judge's charge, the presumption of the business judgment rule is rebutted only if control is seen as a sole or primary purpose of the director's course of action. Thus, if a shareholder is only able to show that control was a motive, although not a primary motive, the rule is not rebutted.[96] On appeal, the majority of a Third Circuit Court of Appeals panel upheld the district court's charge.[97] Judge Rosenn, however, dissented, reasoning that placing the burden of justifying the fairness of the transaction on the defendants, once control is implicated as a motive, is consistent with the policies underlying the Delaware decisions.[98] Subsequently, a majority of the *Panter*

---

95. The district judge gave the following instruction to the jury in regard to the proper exercise of the business judgment rule:

> [T]he desire to retain control of a corporation in and of itself is an improper motive for a decision of a director. Therefore, if you find by a preponderance of the evidence that the defendants acted solely or primarily because of a desire to retain control of Penn Eastern, then the presumption of the sound business judgment rule has been rebutted. However, I further instruct you that a director may properly decline to adopt a course of action which would result in a shift of control, so long as his actions can be attributed to a rational business purpose. In other words, so long as other rational business reasons support a director's decision, the mere fact that a business decision involves a retention of control does not constitute a showing of bad faith to rebut the business judgment rule. *That rule is rebutted only where a director's sole or primary purpose for adopting a course of action or refusing to adopt another is to retain control.*

Id. at 292 (emphasis in original).

96. *Id.*

97. *Id.* at 292-93. The court noted that by the very nature of corporate life "a director has a certain amount of self-interest in everything he does." *Id.* at 292. Accordingly, to alleviate this conflict, "the rule achieves this purpose by postulating that if actions are arguably taken for the benefit of the corporation, then the directors are presumed to have been exercising their sound business judgment rather than responding to any personal motivations." *Id.* Furthermore, the majority found that the district judge's charge was consistent with Delaware case law. The court concluded:

> In short, we believe that under Delaware law, at a minimum the plaintiff must make a showing that the sole or primary motive of the defendant was to retain control. If he makes a showing sufficient to survive a directed verdict, the burden then shifts to the defendant to show that the transaction in question had a valid corporate business purpose.

Id. at 293. In support of its decision the court cited Petty v. Pentech Papers, Inc., 347 A.2d 140, 143 (Del. Ch. 1975); Cheff v. Mathes, 41 Del. Ch. 494, 199 A.2d 548 (1964); Bennett v. Propp, 41 Del. Ch. 14, 187 A.2d 405 (1962). *See generally* Comment, *Buying Out Insurgent Shareholders with Corporate Funds,* 70 YALE L.J. 308 (1960).

98. 629 F.2d at 299-301 (Rosenn, J., concurring in part and dissenting in part). Judge Rosenn summarized the issue before the court as follows:

> A major issue in this case is whether the defendants acted in good faith in managing Penn Eastern's affairs or whether they acted for an improper purpose—namely, the

panel, likewise interpreting Delaware law, adopted the Third Circuit's reasoning.[99]

The *Treadway Cos. v. Care Corp.*[100] and *Crouse-Hinds Co. v. InterNorth, Inc.*[101] cases involve the scope of the business judgment rule under state law in the proxy and tender offer contexts. In *Treadway* the Second Circuit, applying the New Jersey business judgment rule, reversed the district court's order which enjoined the voting at the annual meeting of a large block of shares sold by the subject corporation to a white knight.[102] The Second Circuit reasoned that the Treadway board, in approving the stock's sale, was moving towards a business combination with the white knight and with the exception of one director whose motives could not be attributed to the other directors, was not seeking to perpetuate its control over the corporation. Although acknowledging that a purpose of the stock sale to the white knight was to thwart the takeover attempt, the court nevertheless held that only if it were proved that the directors had acted improperly would the burden shift to them to show that the sale was fair and reasonable to the corporation.[103]

---

desire to retain control over Penn Eastern when it was not in its best interest. If the defendants acted in good faith, the business judgment rule would insulate them from any losses as a result of their decisions.

Id. at 299 (Rosenn, J., concurring in part and dissenting in part). According to Judge Rosenn, Delaware case law shows that once the record demonstrates that control is implicated in the transaction, a conflict of interest is created *ipso facto.* Once such a conflict of interest appears, the burden of proof then shifts to the defendants to justify the transaction as one primarily in the corporate interest. Concluding, Judge Rosenn stated:

Therefore, I believe that a standard requiring plaintiffs to show that control was the sole or primary purpose motivating the defendants' conduct imposes a burden on the plaintiff not consistent with Delaware law. Unlike the majority, I believe that under Delaware law, once plaintiff has shown that the desire to retain control was a motive in the particular business decision under challenge, the burden is then on the defendant to move forward with evidence justifying the transaction as primarily in the corporation's best interests.

Id. at 301 (Rosenn, J., concurring in part and dissenting in part).

99. 646 F.2d at 293-95. *But see* Treadway Cos. v. Care Corp., 638 F.2d 357, 382 (2d Cir. 1980) (under New Jersey law, "[o]nce a plaintiff demonstrates that a director had an interest in the transaction at issue, the burden shifts to the defendant to prove that the transaction was fair and reasonable to the corporation").

100. 638 F.2d 357 (2d Cir. 1980).

101. 518 F. Supp. 390 (N.D.N.Y. 1980), *rev'd,* 634 F.2d 690 (2d Cir. 1980), discussed in 581 Sec. Reg. & L. Rep. (BNA) A-1 (1980).

102. 490 F. Supp. 668 (S.D.N.Y.), *aff'd in part and rev'd in part and remanded,* 638 F.2d 357 (2d Cir. 1980).

103. 638 F.2d at 380-84. *See* Schwartz & Steinberger, *Proxy Contests for Corporate Control,* in Proxy Contests for Corporate Control: How to Mount the Attack or Defend the Citadel 51-52 (1980).

In applying the business purpose test, the Second Circuit concluded that the Treadway board had not acted for the purpose of maintaining its control over the corporation.[104] Particularly relevant to the court was that the result of the proposed business combination with the white knight was that all the directors of Treadway but one would lose their positions as directors and would not be offered new positions.[105] Thus, the perpetuation of control by Treadway's directors was not a motivation in seeking out the white knight. As such, the Second Circuit held that the plaintiff did not meet its burden of proving that the directors had an interest in the transaction, or acted in bad faith or for some improper purpose.[106] In its holding, however, the Second Circuit in *Treadway* ordered a new election, holding that the lower court had improperly ordered certain of its findings not to be disclosed in the respective parties' proxy statements.[107]

Crouse-Hinds Co. v. InterNorth, Inc.[108] involved an expedited appeal from a district court order which granted the motion of InterNorth for a preliminary injunction preventing Crouse-Hinds from performing an agreement with a third corporation, the Belden Corporation, pursuant to which Crouse-Hinds was to offer to purchase a portion of Belden's outstanding stock in exchange for stock of Crouse-Hinds.[109] The appeal was part of a rapid series of events relating to the announcement of a proposed merger between Crouse-Hinds and Belden. Shortly thereafter, InterNorth made an announcement of a tender offer for a majority of the stock of Crouse-Hinds.

---

104. 638 F.2d at 383.

105. *Id.*

106. *Id.* at 383-84. Dissenting in part, Chief Judge Feinberg stated:

> The majority states that the district court did not apply the "business judgment rule" to the Fair Lanes transaction. The majority then applies that rule, and concludes, contrary to the district court, that the transaction cannot be set aside. In reaching this conclusion, the majority argues that there is evidence in the record "that the directors did in fact exercise their independent judgment." But that is not the question before this court. Rather, the question for us is whether the district court, in the face of *some* evidence of independent judgment and reasonable diligence, could find the contrary evidence to be more weighty, and could reasonably conclude that the outside directors did not exercise sufficiently independent judgment and reasonable diligence. On the record before us, I am not prepared to hold as a matter of law that the issue can only be decided one way.

Id. at 385 (Feinberg, C. J., concurring in part and dissenting in part) (emphasis in original).

The *Treadway* case had other aspects. In regard to one such aspect, the Second Circuit held that the subject director, who was also the corporation's largest stockholder, did not breach his fiduciary duties by secretly selling his stock to the bidder without providing the subject corporation the opportunity to purchase it. *Id.* at 374-78. The Second Circuit also considered issues concerning the proxy provisions and § 13(d) of the Exchange Act.

107. 638 F.2d at 385. *See* Schwartz & Steinberger, note 102 *supra*, at 51-52.

108. 518 F. Supp. 390 (N.D.N.Y. 1980), *rev'd*, 634 F.2d 690 (2d Cir. 1980).

109. 634 F.2d at 692.

Subsequently, Crouse-Hinds and Belden agreed to a modification of the merger agreement pursuant to which Crouse-Hinds was to purchase a portion of Belden's outstanding stock in exchange for Crouse-Hinds' stock. InterNorth contended that the arrangement between Crouse-Hinds and Belden violated state law.[110]

Applying state law, the district court granted InterNorth's injunction motion, reasoning that the Crouse-Hinds board had acted to preserve its own control because the board was to remain in office after the consummation of the Belden merger.[111] In other words, the district court interpreted the Second Circuit's decision in *Treadway* to signify that a director was "interested" in a merger transaction for purposes of the business judgment rule if he would remain in office after consummation of the merger.[112] Accordingly, the district court concluded that the Crouse-Hinds board was interested in the exchange offer and held that the burden therefore shifted to the Crouse-Hinds directors to prove that the exchange agreement was fair and reasonable. In view of the evidence, the district court concluded that Crouse-Hinds did not sustain its burden of proof under the business judgment rule.[113]

On appeal, the Second Circuit reversed.[114] Significantly, the Second Circuit framed the issue to be whether the exchange offer between Crouse-Hinds and Belden had no valid business purpose and was designed merely to perpetuate Crouse-Hinds' management in office. Applying the business judgment rule and its decision in *Treadway,* the court concluded that InterNorth failed to carry its burden of demonstrating self-interest or bad faith on the

---

110. *Id.* at 692.

111. 518 F. Supp. at 410 ("the Crouse-Hinds board of directors, unlike the Treadway board in the Fair Lanes merger, will survive a Belden merger and retain its control of Crouse-Hinds").

112. *Id.* at 410-11.

113. *Id.* at 412. The district court stated:

> Although the independent investment advice sought and proffered by Crouse-Hinds is certainly some proof of its efforts to reach an objective determination about the merits of InterNorth's tender offer, in view of the strength of the evidence to the contrary, and of applicable case law, the court does not believe that Crouse-Hinds has sustained its burden of proof under the business judgment rule.

Id.

114. 634 F.2d at 704. The court stated:

> Thus, none of the proffered statements is sufficient to show director "interest" of the sort that is needed under the business judgment rule to shift the burden of proof to the directors. In short, when the tender offeror has presented the target company with an obvious reason to oppose the tender offer, the offeror cannot, on the theory that the target's management opposes the offer for some other, unstated, improper purpose, obtain an injunction against the opposition without presenting strong evidence to support its theory. We find no such evidence here.

Id.

part of the Crouse-Hinds directors.[115] Moreover, the Second Circuit took exception to the district judge's interpretation of *Treadway,* namely, that if the directors are to remain on the board after the merger, perpetuation of their control must be presumed to be their motivation. Responding to the district judge's interpretation of *Treadway,* the Second Circuit stated that the district court's "inference has no basis in either law or logic."[116] Therefore, the circuit court concluded that *Treadway* did not disturb the business judgment rule requirement that a complainant must present evidence of the directors' interest in order for the burden of proof to shift to those directors.[117]

Some of the more recent cases, however, have not been nearly as favorable to target management. For example, in *Conoco Inc. v. Seagram Company, Ltd.,*[118] Conoco sought a preliminary injunction to enjoin Seagram from purchasing Conoco's shares pursuant to a tender offer. The target corporation alleged that Seagram was estopped from going forward with the tender offer by reason of Seagram's promise not to make an "unfriendly offer," such promise allegedly being made during "friendly" negotiations between Seagram and Conoco.[119]

The district court denied Conoco's motion. In so doing, the court made clear that, in its view, the merit of the Seagram offer was a matter for Conoco's shareholders, not its management, to assess. The court stated:

> To be sure, the Board of Directors are under a duty to exercise their best business judgment with respect to any proposal pertaining to corporate affairs, including tender offers. They may be right; they may know what is best for the corporation, but their judgment is not conclusive upon the shareholders. What is sometimes lost sight of in these tender offer controversies is that the shareholders, not the directors, have the right of franchise with respect to the shares owned by them; "stockholders, once informed of the facts, have a right to make their own decisions in matters pertaining to their economic self-interest, whether consonant with or contrary to the advice of others, whether such advice is tendered by management or outsiders or those motivated by self-interest." In this instance, the shareholders now have the choice of acting upon the existing outstanding offers of Du Pont and Seagram. . . . The Directors are free to continue by proper legal means to express to the shareholders their objection and hostility to

---

115. *Id.* at 702.

116. *Id.*

117. *Id.* at 702-03. One author has stated that "[i]f properly structured and supported so as to clearly evidence a legitimate corporate purpose, the tactics authorized should withstand judicial scrutiny, even in the face of the argument that a motivating force was retention of control." Gruenbaum, *supra* note 41, at 267 (footnote omitted).

118. 517 F. Supp. 1299 (S.D.N.Y. 1981).

119. *Id.* at 1300-02.

the Seagram proposal, but they are not free to deny them their right to pass upon this offer or any other offer for the purchase of their shares.[120]

A similar rationale may be seen in *Joseph E. Seagram & Sons, Inc. v. Abrams*.[121] There, the directors of St. Joe, in opposition to the Seagram tender offer, announced that it was prepared to liquidate the company in order to thwart the takeover bid.[122] Seagram thereupon sought a temporary restraining order to prevent the St. Joe directors from implementing the plan. In granting Seagram's motion, the court found that an issue of triable fact had been raised, stating:

> It is inconceivable that an alleged flourishing enterprise has authorized its board to subject the assets and charter of the company to a scorched earth policy to be accomplished in the name of an exercise of business judgment but in fact, it is alleged, merely to thwart a change in the existing stock ownership which may end the tenure of the present directors and key officers of the company.[123]

Significantly, in its holding, although "fully mindful of the teachings of *Santa Fe*, the court implicitly concluded that the plaintiff had properly alleged "manipulation" within the meaning of Section 14()e).[124]

The conclusion that federal law places constraints on the use of defensive tactics in tender offers, beyond full and fair disclosure, became explicit in the Sixth Circuit's recent decision in *Mobil Corporation v. Marathon Oil Company*.[125] There, in response to Mobil's announced intention to take over Marathon, Marathon filed an antitrust action against Mobil and determined to seek a "white knight."[126] Subsequently, U.S. Steel came forward with an offer, which the Marathon directors recommended to its shareholders, and which was subject to two conditions. First, U.S. Steel required that it be given a present, irrevocable option to acquire ten million authorized but unissued shares which amounted to approximately 17 percent of Marathon's

---

120. *Id.* at 1303, *quoting*, American Crystal Sugar Co. v. Cuban-American Sugar Co., 276 F. Supp. 45, 50 (S.D.N.Y. 1967).

121. 510 F. Supp. 860 (S.D.N.Y. 1981).

122. *Id* at 861-62.

123. *Id.* at 861.

124. *Id.* (plaintiff's invocation of Section 14(e) is "presumably on the theory that an improper manipulation of the market is in progress by the moves of the St. Joe directors, designed to mislead and damage the true interests of stockholders and investors").

125. 669 F.2d 366 (6th Cir. 1981).

126. *Id.* at 367. Marathon was ultimately able to thwart the Mobil offer by means of its antitrust action. See 669 F.2d 378 (6th Cir. 1981), *cert. denied*, 102 S. Ct. 1490 (1982). See *also* 669 F.2d 384 (6th Cir. 1982).

outstanding shares. Second, it demanded an option to acquire Marathon's "crown jewel," namely, the company's 48-percent interest in oil and mineral rights in the Yates Field. The latter option could be exercised only if the U.S. Steel offer failed and if a third party obtained control of Marathon.[127]

Mobil thereupon brought suit, alleging, *inter alia,* that the options granted to U.S. Steel by Marathon violated Section 14(e) because they "served as a 'lock-up' arrangement to defeat any competitive offers of Mobil or third parties, thereby constituting a 'manipulative' practice 'in connection with a tender offer.' "[128] The Sixth Circuit agreed. Rejecting the contention that the conduct at issue involved "mere" breaches of fiduciary duty and, hence, were not actionable under the federal securities laws,[129] the court asserted that "it is difficult to conceive of a more effective and manipulative device than the 'lock-up' options employed here, options which not only artificially affect, but for all practical purposes completely block, normal healthy market activity."[130] Thus, because the option agreements, both individually and in combination, had the effect of deterring Mobil and other potential offerors from competing on a par with U.S. Steel, thereby creating an artificial ceiling on the value that Marathon stockholders could receive for their shares,[131] they were manipulative under Section 14(e).[132]

In concluding, the Sixth Circuit stressed that its holding did not signify that all forms of options which might deter competing offers constitute manipulative acts or practices under Section 14(e).[133] In this regard, however, it arguably appears from the decision's rationale that option agreements (particularly those entered into in response to a hostile takeover bid), which have the effect of precluding target shareholders from having an opportunity to consider competing offers, may well be proscribed. Phrased another way, the greater the deterrent effect that a particular option has on actual or potentially competing offerors, the more likely that such an option may be

---

127. 669 F.2d at 367-68.

128. *Id.* at 368.

129. *Id.* at 373-77. In this regard, the Sixth Circuit reversed the district court's holding that Mobil's claim "amounts to no more than a claim that the Marathon directors acted unfairly and breached their fiduciary [duty] to Marathon and its shareholders." *Id.* at 373. The Sixth Circuit also stated that "to find compliance with Section 14(e) solely by the full disclosure of a manipulative device as a *fait accompli* would be to read the 'manipulative acts and practices' language completely out of the Williams Act." *Id.* at 377.

130. *Id.* at 374.

131. *Id.* at 373-77 (Marathon shareholders "have had no real alternative to accepting the [U.S. Steel] offer, because Mobil's offer of $126 is conditional upon the invalidity of the options, and there is and could be no other comparable tender offer as long as the 'lock-up' options remain in effect." *Id.* at 377).

132. *Id.* at 373-77. *See also* SEC v. Grumman Corp., No. 81–3685 (E.D.N.Y.), SEC Litigation Release No. 9493 (Nov. 9, 1981).

133. 669 F.2d at 377.

viewed as a "manipulative" practice under Section 14(e).[134] In all practicality, therefore, although it may well be premature to venture a conclusion, the Sixth Circuit's decision may spell the death knell for certain types of lock-up agreements and will, at the very least, induce parties to such arrangements to be most circumspect.[135]

Further, although *Mobil* involved an action for injunctive relief under Section 14(e) and although the court expressly left undisturbed the district court's finding that the Marathon directors acted in good faith and with loyalty, the Sixth Circuit's decision can be read as permitting, or at least as

---

134. *See* Lynch and Steinberg, *The Legitimacy of Defensive Tactics in Tender Offers*, 64 Cornell L. Rev. 901 (1979).

135. *But see* Whittaker Corp. v. Edgar, 535 F. Supp. 933 (N.D. Ill. 1982). Faced with a hostile takeover bid by Whittaker, Brunswick entered into an agreement with American Home providing for the acquisition by American Home of Brunswick's Sherwood medical subsidiary and the stock of certain other Brunswick medical subsidiaries. Distinguishing the Sixth Circuit's decision in *Mobil*, the district court upheld the agreement. In pertinent part, the district court stated:

> The first distinction between *Mobil* and the present case is obvious—in *Mobil*, Marathon granted a lock-up option to U.S. Steel to be exercised if a third party gained control of Marathon while in the present case Brunswick sold a substantial asset to a third party in the face of a hostile tender offer. The fact that the Brunswick sale of Sherwood to American Home permits the acquisition to be made by way of tender offer, shares plus cash, or cash does not make the transaction fall within the definition of a lock-up under *Mobil*. Brunswick has not granted any lock-up option to American Home, nor did Whittaker revise its offer for Brunswick in an attempt to compete with the proposed sale of Sherwood as Mobil did in the *Mobil* case. Thus, the sale of Sherwood has not created an artificial price ceiling in the tender offer market for Brunswick common shares which would be a manipulative act in violation of the Williams Act. Indeed, the present American Home offer pays more to Brunswick shareholders at the front end of the deal than does the Whittaker offer. Moreover, the Sherwood sale, while in response to the Whittaker tender offer, cannot be construed as expressly designed solely for the purpose of completely blocking normal, healthy market activity as did the Yates Field lock-up in *Mobil*. A sale of a substantial asset by a corporation in the face of a hostile tender offer standing alone is not a violation of Section 14(e). Indeed the Sherwood sale might actually be characterized as part of healthy market activity, especially in light of the fact that Brunswick would receive more for Sherwood in the sale to American Home than what Sherwood was valued at by Whittaker—even assuming that the Sherwood sale is taxable to Brunswick. Moreover, there is no comparable threat to other bidders as in *Mobil* that, even if they gain control of Brunswick, they will lose Sherwood. Sherwood will be *sold* by Brunswick—not "locked-up"—and any potential bidders will be bidding for Brunswick without Sherwood. Accordingly, the court concludes that the proposed sale of Sherwood by Brunswick is not a manipulative act in violation of Section 14(e) of the Williams Act.

Id. at 949. *See also* Marshall Field & Co. v. Icahn, [1982 Transfer Binder] Fed. Sec. L. Rep. (CCH) ¶ 98,616 (S.D.N.Y. 1982). Such a basis for distinguishing *Mobil* appears questionable: Under the district court's rationale, a target company can arguably avoid the rigors of *Mobil* simply by entering into a contract to sell a substantial asset to a friendly party rather than providing an option to enter into such a transaction. Such a distinction may often be of little

not being antagonistic to, under appropriate circumstances, a damages remedy on behalf of target shareholders. Such a consequence, particularly if hostile offers have not become effective, although representing a departure from the Seventh Circuit's decision in *Panter,* would be consistent with the *Berman v. Gerber Products Co.* decision.[136]

D. A Recommended Analytical Framework

Once management decides to oppose a tender offer, it faces the delicate question of what defensive tactics to employ. In the selection process, management must consider several factors, including the likelihood of success by the bidder, the current market price and dividend rate of the target, and the number of target shares held by friendly and hostile stockholders. For example, if the insiders believe that shareholders are likely to approve the offer, management may enter into a defensive merger. Alternatively, if management controls only a small percentage of the outstanding stock, it may decide to issue or sell additional shares to a friendly third party, or even make its own tender offer to its shareholders, so that the bidder will be less likely to acquire the desired percentage of the target's stock.

Regardless of the defensive tactics employed, state law and the Williams Act mandate that target management owes its allegiance to the shareholders. Maneuvers used to perpetuate management's status or in some manner to prevent an informed decision by the target's shareholders violate these protective laws. Therefore, the legitimacy of a given defensive tactic should turn not only on the tactic used, but also on the effect of the tactic on the shareholders' right to decide, the reasons management relies upon for employing the tactic, and the extent of disclosure to the shareholders.

An equitable test to assess the legality of a defensive tactic should recognize the different practical effects that various defensive tactics have on the target's shareholders. Because the duty aspects of the Williams Act and state law frequently focus on the interest of shareholders to make an informed decision, target management's acts should be scrutinized in relation to their

---

consequence to a target who is fending off a hostile bid. Moreover, there can be little question that the sale of a profitable asset to a friendly party may well have the effect of inducing the competing offeror to withdraw its offer as well as to deter other potential bidders from entering the fray. As importantly, the consequence to target shareholders may well be the same: they will be precluded from accepting the competing bidder's offer and from considering offers from other parties which otherwise may have occurred. Accordingly, regardless of the soundness of the Sixth Circuit's approach in *Mobil,* to distinguish the decision on the above basis appears to be erroneous.

136. *See* 669 F.2d at 373-78. For discussion of *Panter* and *Berman, see* notes 51-59, 70-93 and accompanying text *supra. Cf.* O'Connor & Associates v. Dean Witter Reynolds, Inc., [1981-1982 Transfer Binder] Fed. Sec. L. Rep. (CCH) ¶ 98,443 (S.D.N.Y. 1982) (in insider trading action brought for alleged violation of Section 14(e) and Rule 14e-3, damages remedy proper even though no tender offer was made).

encroachment on this interest. A defensive tactic that effectively impedes or precludes the shareholders from considering a tender offer should not be judged by the same standards used to judge a defensive tactic that has little effect on such consideration. Although courts have applied different tests in evaluating defensive tactics, no distinctions have yet been drawn with respect to the effect of the particular tactic upon the shareholder.

The following two-tier analysis would effectuate the policies of the Williams Act[137] and possibly state law[138] and reflect the qualitative differences in the effect of defensive tactics: (1) Defensive tactics that have little effect on a shareholder's opportunity to consider the bidder's offer should not be construed to violate Section 14(e) or state law unless the target's management has made material misrepresentations or omissions with respect to the tactic;[139] (2) regarding defensive tactics that preclude or otherwise materially impede the target's shareholders' consideration of the offer, the challenging shareholder should initially be required to show that the tender offer was a factor in inducing the target management to take the particular action at that time, thereby giving rise to a presumption that the primary reason for the action was to block or impede the takeover bid. Target management may rebut this presumption by showing that the primary reason for the action was not to effectively impede shareholder consideration of the offer.[140]

---

137. The legislative history of the Williams Act evinces a clear congressional intent to protect shareholders who are faced with the difficult investment decision that must be made when presented with a tender offer. Congress chose to effectuate this end by making certain that a target's shareholders received all material information relating to their decision and rejected the notion that a target's management should make the decision for the corporation in line with its fiduciary duties to the shareholders. The assumption underlying Congress' approach to investor protection under the Williams Act was that an investor has the freedom to make his own decision after being fully informed. Disclosure, no matter how extensive, matters little if the target's management can employ defensive tactics that deprive or otherwise materially impede the investor's freedom of choice. The Williams Act, accordingly, provides shareholders with the right to hear a fair presentation of the material facts relating to their investment decision when confronted with a tender offer, and to make the investment decision upon receipt of the information. *See* authorities and legislative history cited in Lynch & Steinberg, note 134 *supra*, at 911-12.

138. It is arguable that the recommended framework herein is inappropriate under the fiduciary approach of state law which relies upon the business judgment of corporate directors in accord with the fiduciary duties owed to the corporation and shareholders. On the other hand, such a fiduciary approach does not necessarily signify that target management may preempt a decision that is designed to be made by the shareholders, such as a tender offer. *See* Conoco Inc. v. Seagram Company, Ltd., 517 F. Supp. 1299, 1303 (S.D.N.Y. 1981).

139. Of course, under state law, any such defensive tactic must be consistent with the directors' fiduciary obligations.

140. Rule 301 of the Federal Rules of Evidence provides:

In all civil actions and proceedings not otherwise provided for by Act of Congress or by these rules, a presumption imposes on the party against whom it is directed the burden of going forward with evidence to rebut or meet the presumption, but does not

In applying the proposed test, courts must decide, at the threshold, whether the defensive tactic has little effect on a shareholder's opportunity to consider the bidder's offer, or whether it precludes or otherwise materially impedes shareholder consideration of the offer. As a matter of definition, all defensive tactics arguably impede the bidder's offer. For practical application, however, this test should focus on whether the target's shareholders, rather than target management, will make the ultimate decision as to the disposition of their shares of stock and the future of the target corporation.

1. Defensive Tactics Not Precluding or Materially Impeding Shareholder Consideration

Examples of defensive tactics that generally will not affect a shareholder's right to consider a bidder's offer include dividend increases, and under certain circumstances, the identification and seduction of a "white knight."

a. Dividend Increases

Target management may raise dividend rates in order to discourage or help defeat tender offers. A dividend increase can cause an increase in the market price of the target's stock to rise in reflection of the increased return per share.[141] In the event of a tender offer, it can reduce the difference between the bidder's offer and the market price so that the offering price appears less attractive to the target's shareholders.

Shareholders usually benefit from this defensive maneuver; they obtain a greater return on their investment while retaining the option of accepting the offer. Thus, the target should not be required to absolutely freeze its dividend policy once an offer is announced. But to prevent misleading the shareholders, target management should point out that an increase in the stock's market price may be due to the dividend increase rather than to the market's perception of improved prospects for the corporation. Target management should also furnish the shareholders with full information regarding the dividend increase. This disclosure should include: (1) the reason for the increase, (2) prospects for continuing that dividend level, and (3) the effect of the dividend on the company's ability to sustain its current growth rate. Failure to provide this information, particularly when target management does not realistically expect to continue paying its higher dividend rate, should constitute a practice proscribed by Section 14(e) of the Williams Act.

---

shift to such party the burden of proof in the sense of the risk of nonpersuasion, which remains throughout the trial upon the party on whom it was originally cast.

141. *See* Schmults & Kelly, *Cash Take-Over Bids—Defensive Tactics*, 23 Bus. Law. 115, 117-18 (1967).

b. Defensive Mergers

Management may also resist a takeover bid by negotiating a merger with a third party, or "white knight." This tactic tends to be a last resort for management, and, frequently, can be successful. If the target's management believes that the bidder's tender offer will be successful when presented to its shareholders but also believes that a merger could be negotiated with a third party that would be more beneficial to the target's shareholders, management normally should not be precluded from seeking such a defensive merger.

Defensive mergers usually follow a rather predictable pattern. Because it knows the details of the original bid, the white knight typically offers more favorable terms to the target's shareholders. The bidder may parry this prospective defensive merger by (1) proceeding with its original tender or exchange offer, (2) raising the price of its offer, or (3) proposing its own merger with the target, to be considered in the same proxy vote as the white knight's proposal. Management must take care not to "stack the deck" with misleading disclosures regarding the tender offer, with misleading statements regarding the proposed merger, or through sales of stock to the white knight prior to the shareholders' vote.[142] The contest is ultimately decided by the shareholders, who select the offer that they prefer. In this context, it is important to note that while the proposal of a defensive merger may make it less likely that the bidder's offer will be accepted by the target's shareholders, the shareholders still retain the right to receive the bidder's offer and to make their own determination.

Although a defensive merger is generally a more effective tactic than a dividend increase, it does not usurp the decision-making power of the target's shareholders, nor does it harm them economically. It is therefore difficult to understand why a defensive merger should be prohibited even if its "primary purpose" is to block the likely success of the bidder's offer. So long as the shareholders are given full and accurate disclosure about both the bidder's offer and the proposed defensive merger with the white knight, they should be given the opportunity to choose the alternative which they deem most beneficial to their interests.

2. Defensive Tactics Which Preclude or Materially Impede Shareholder Determination

Defensive tactics that materially impede or preclude a target's shareholders from considering a bidder's offer should be judged under a more stringent standard than the disclosure test advanced for defensive tactics that allow shareholders to make their own investment decision. Currently, under the

---

142. *See* notes 146-47 and accompanying text *infra*.

primary purpose test, management all too often can prevail by obfuscating the actual reason for the tactic. This situation, however, can be easily remedied by altering the analytical framework of these situations. The party challenging the target's defensive tactics should have to demonstrate that the bidder's offer was a factor in inducing target management to take the defensive action at that time. Once the plaintiff proves the above, target management should be required to rebut the presumption by showing that the primary purpose of the particular defensive tactic was not to effectively impede or preclude shareholder consideration of the offer.[143]

Imposing a rebuttable presumption on the target corporation in this manner makes good sense. First, the target's management has the easiest access to information explaining the purpose of its tactics.[144] Second, this test does not interfere with a corporation's internal affairs; it merely requires the target corporation to explain its conduct, after the plaintiff establishes basic facts that tend to show a violation. If target management can rebut this presumption, then courts should hold that Section 14(e) and state law have not been violated.

Any management action that precludes or materially impedes the shareholders from considering a hostile takeover offer arguably arose from a desire to defeat the tender offer. Any other position ignores the realities of the corporate world. Management, however, may have seriously contemplated the challenged action before it knew of the takeover attempt.[145] Or a very attractive corporate opportunity may have arisen during the course of a tender offer, and management may have unquestionably pursued it even in the absence of the offer. In such situations, courts should focus on whether target management intended its actions to benefit the shareholders or to effectively impede or preclude their consideration of the bidder's offer.

Examples of defensive tactics that preclude or materially impede shareholder consideration of a bidder's offer include issuance of stock to a friendly party and defensive acquisitions.

---

143. The test proposed would apply only to civil actions, and not to criminal actions. The author expresses no opinion on the proper presumptions for criminal cases.

144. *See* McCormick's Handbook of the Law of Evidence § 343, at 806-07 (2d ed. E. Cleary, 1972); Morgan, *Some Observations Concerning Presumptions,* 44 Harv. L. Rev. 906, 911 (1931).

145. But the management's knowledge of the particular takeover attempt may be irrelevant. Where the bidder has made a prolonged effort to gain control, the relevant time frame should be the beginning of the bidder's struggles rather than the start of its last campaign. Thus, in Klaus v. Hi-Shear Corp., 528 F.2d 225, 233 (9th Cir. 1975), the Ninth Circuit affirmed the district court's finding that the principal purpose of the issuance of stock to a trust was to dilute the bidder's voting strength. This holding discounted evidence indicating that management had contemplated such a sale for over a year. *Id.* A possible reason for this outcome may be that the bidder sought control for approximately the same length of time.

a. Issuance of Stock

Issuing a substantial number of shares to a friendly party constitutes one defensive tactic open to management. This action might discourage a bidder from making an offer or reduce the probability that the bidder will acquire the desired percentage of the target's stock. While this hostile ownership of a large block of the target's stock may dull a bidder's enthusiasm, this tactic also directly dilutes the shareholders' ownership and voting rights. Consequently, this action lessens each shareholder's voice in determining whether the bidder will acquire the requisite ownership of shares. Accordingly, a target's sale of such stock to a third party should receive close scrutiny.[146]

A target choosing to sell stock will probably argue that it sought to infuse working capital into the corporation to take advantage of corporate opportunities. Certainly a sale of shares for cash will provide a corporation with additional funds to finance existing or proposed projects. In most instances, this fact will create difficulty in showing that the transaction has no business purpose. A management sensitive to the protection of shareholder interests, however, should recognize that sales of stock during the pendency of a takeover attempt can dramatically affect the balance of power within a corporation; such a management should give serious consideration to the suspension of sales of stock during this period. As one court noted, a target's management should not be permitted to sell stock if it would "deprive [the] shareholders of opportunities accruing to them by virtue of their stock ownership."[147] At the very least, the target's management should be required to demonstrate that the primary purpose of a stock sale during a takeover attempt was not to materially impede or preclude shareholder consideration of the bidder's offer.

b. Defensive Acquisition

A target corporation may decide to block the bidder's takeover attempt by acquiring another corporation. If the corporation is acquired through an exchange of stock, the number of outstanding shares in the target corporation will be increased. Just as in the direct issuance of stock for cash to friendly parties, this action may thwart a bidder because he may be unable to acquire a sufficient percentage of stock.

Alternatively, management may seek a defensive acquisition of a company in the bidder's business for the purpose of interposing an antitrust obstacle to the bidder. Either the target's management or the appropriate government

---

146. *See generally* Mobil Corp. v. Marathon Oil Co., 669 F.2d 366 (6th Cir. 1981); Applied Digital Data Systems, Inc. v. Milgo Electronic Corp., 425 F. Supp. 1145 (S.D.N.Y. 1977).

147. Applied Digital Data Systems, Inc. v. Milgo Electronic Corp., 425 F. Supp. 1145, 1158 (S.D.N.Y. 1977).

agency may institute suit to block the bidder's takeover attempt because of potential violations of the federal antitrust laws.[148]

Although sales of stock to friendly parties often materially impede the stockholders' ability to make their own determination about the future of the company by diluting their ownership interest, a defensive acquisition, by raising antitrust barriers, may totally preclude the shareholders from considering the offer. Thus, management should bear the burden of demonstrating that its primary purpose in making the defensive acquisition was not to materially impede or preclude shareholder consideration of the bidder's offer.[149]

IV. CONCLUSION

The objective of this chapter has been to examine the duties of management and boards of directors in tender offer contests for corporate control. As can be gathered from the foregoing discussion, these responsibilities, and the extent to which they are applicable in any particular situation, are subject to varied judicial interpretations. This chapter has accordingly attempted to delineate these obligations in an understandable, yet comprehensive, manner.

---

148. The Hart-Scott-Rodino Antitrust Improvements Act of 1976 imposes significant premerger notification requirements on certain tender offerors. 15 U.S.C. § 18a (1976). As summarized by one commentator:

> In general, the new program requires that "persons" meeting or exceeding a statutory "size of person" test who wish to acquire voting securities or assets in quantities meeting or exceeding a statutory "size of transaction" test must report their intentions prior to such acquisitions and provide information relevant to the transaction to the Antitrust Division of the Justice Department and to the FTC. Notification is defined as substantial completion of the Notification and Report Form promulgated by the FTC. After reporting, such "persons" must observe a stipulated waiting period before consummating the transaction. This waiting period may be extended by a request from either enforcement agency for additional information or documentary material. The Act exempts eleven classes of transactions from its requirements, and the FTC rules and regulations provide further exemption guidelines.

Comment, *Stop, Look and Listen: Premerger Notification Under the Hart-Scott-Rodino Antitrust Improvements Act*, 1979 DUKE L.J. 355, 359. For additional commentary on the Act, *see, e.g.*, S. AXINN, E. FOGG & N. STOLL, ACQUISITIONS UNDER THE HART-SCOTT-RODINO ANTITRUST IMPROVEMENTS ACT (1979); Kintner, Griffin & Goldston, *The Hart-Scott-Rodino Antitrust Improvements Act of 1976: An Analysis*, 46 GEO. WASH. L. REV. 1 (1976); Scher, *Emerging Issues Under the Antitrust Improvements Act of 1976*, 77 COLUM. L. REV. 679 (1977); Tomlinson, *Premerger Notification Under Hart-Scott-Rodino: Valuation of Assets and Voting Securities*, 26 UCLA L. REV. 1321 (1979); Comment, *The Goal of the New Premerger Notification Requirements: Preliminary Relief Against Anticompetitive Mergers*, 1979 DUKE L.J. 249.

149. *See, e.g.*, Royal Industries, Inc. v. Monogram Industries, Inc., [1976-1977 Transfer Binder] FED. SEC. L. REP. (CCH) ¶ 95,863 (C.D. Cal. 1976).

6

Application of the Business Judgment Rule and Related Judicial Principles—Reflections from a Corporate Accountability Perspective

I. INTRODUCTION

When one thinks of corporate accountability and internal affairs, attention naturally gravitates to the myriad of issues that have been discussed in this setting in recent years.[1] Yet, it is curious that, within this context, little attention has focused on the unduly broad application of certain judicial principles by a number of courts that permit boards of directors and management improperly to employ a relatively large number of procedures to insulate their actions from successful shareholder challenge.

This subject strikes at the very heart of corporate governance. Although shareholders may care, for example, about having independent directors on their boards or having the opportunity to present shareholder proposals,[2]

---

1. *See, e.g.,* Curzan & Pelesh, *Revitalizing Corporate Democracy: Control of Investment Managers' Voting on Social Responsibility Proxy Issues,* 93 HARV. L. REV. 670 (1980); Epstein, *Societal, Managerial, and Legal Perspectives on Corporate Social Responsibility—Product and Process,* 30 HASTINGS L.J. 1287 (1979); Ferrara & Steinberg, *The Role of Inside Counsel in the Corporate Accountability Process,* 4 CORP. L. REV. 3 (1981); Hetherington, *When the Sleeper Wakes: Reflections on Corporate Governance and Shareholder Rights,* 8 HOFSTRA L. REV. 183 (1979); Jones, *Corporate Governance: Who Controls the Large Corporation?* 30 HASTINGS L.J. 1261 (1979); Mace, *Directors: Myth and Reality—Ten Years Later,* 32 RUTGERS L. REV. 293 (1979); Schwartz, *Response: Some Thoughts on the Directors' Evolving Role,* 30 HASTINGS L.J. 1405 (1979); Small, *The Evolving Role of the Director in Corporate Governance,* 30 HASTINGS L.J. 1353 (1979); Stevenson, *The Corporation as a Political Institution,* 8 HOFSTRA L. REV. 39 (1979); Werner, *Management, Stock Market and Corporate Reform: Berle and Means Reconsidered,* 77 COLUM. L. REV. 388 (1977); Williams, *Corporate Accountability and the Lawyer's Role,* 34 BUS. LAW. 7 (1978).

2. *See, e.g.,* Securities Exchange Act Release No. 16356 (Nov. 23, 1979); Securities Exchange Act Release No. 15384 (Dec. 6, 1978); Securities Act Release No. 6003 (Dec. 4, 1978). *But see* Kripke, *The SEC, Corporate Governance and the Real Issues,* 36 BUS. LAW. 173 (1981).

these interests are relatively minute when compared to their ability to bring suit either individually or on behalf of the corporation when management has perpetrated an alleged wrong. Yet it is in the context of shareholder challenges to management actions that the courts have enunciated several principles which, if construed too broadly, serve as a subterfuge allowing recalcitrant management to rationalize and defend its otherwise illegal conduct. The principles permitting management to avoid shareholder scrutiny include the inveterate business judgment rule, the *Burks v. Lasker*[3] special litigation committee scenario, certain limitations on the *Goldberg v. Meridor*[4] rationale, the true purpose cases, and the somewhat related disclosure of antisocial, unethical or unlawful policies rationale. The above list, although by no means exhaustive,[5] will serve as the benchmark for this discussion.

Before delving into these areas, however, a caveat is in order. The author is not urging that the foregoing principles be abrogated. As the Supreme Court has noted, strike suits in this context are sometimes feared with good reason.[6] Mechanisms are undoubtedly required to combat vexatious and

---

3. 441 U.S. 471 (1979).

4. 567 F.2d 209 (2d Cir. 1977), *cert. denied,* 434 U.S. 1069 (1978).

5. For example, another such principle is the transactional causation requirement, described by one authority as follows:

> [W]hen a complaint alleges that the election of directors pursuant to allegedly deficient proxy materials results in a continuation of allegedly improper and undisclosed business practices, several courts have held that the subsequent acts are too remote from the election to provide the requisite causal nexus between the proxy solicitation and the alleged damage.

Block & Barton, *The Business Judgment Rule as Applied to Stockholder Proxy Derivative Suits Under the Securities Exchange Act,* 8 SEC. REG. L.J. 99, 115 (1980). *See, e.g.,* Nemo v. Allen, [1979 Transfer Binder] FED. SEC. L. REP. (CCH) ¶ 96,765 (S.D.N.Y. 1979); Herman v. Beretta, [1978 Transfer Binder] FED. SEC. L. REP. (CCH) ¶ 96,574 (S.D.N.Y. 1978); *In re* Tenneco Securities Litigation, [1978 Transfer Binder] FED. SEC. L. REP. (CCH) ¶ 96,492 (S.D. Tex. 1978); Lewis v. Elam, [1977-1978 Transfer Binder] FED. SEC. L. REP. (CCH) ¶ 96,013 (S.D.N.Y. 1977); Levy v. Johnson, [1976-1977 Transfer Binder] FED. SEC. L. REP. (CCH) ¶ 95,899 (S.D.N.Y. 1977). *But see* Weisberg v. Coastal States Gas Corp., 609 F.2d 650 (2d Cir. 1979), *cert. denied,* 100 S. Ct. 1600 (1980); Maldonado v. Flynn, 597 F.2d 789 (2d Cir. 1979).

6. *See* Blue Chip Stamps v. Manor Drug Stores, 421 U.S. 723 (1975):

> [I]n the field of federal securities laws governing disclosure of information even a complaint which by objective standards may have very little chance of success at trial has a settlement value to the plaintiff out of any proportion to its prospect of success at trial so long as he may prevent the suit from being resolved against him by dismissal or summary judgment. The very pendency of the lawsuit may frustrate or delay normal business activity of the defendant which is totally unrelated to the lawsuit.

Id. at 740 (citations omitted).

unfounded shareholder litigation.[7] Further, corporations are "managed under the direction of" their boards of directors.[8] As such, courts should normally respect, although not necessarily acquiesce in, directors' exercise of independent judgment.[9] Nevertheless, if these principles are construed too broadly, they provide recalcitrant management with potent weapons to insulate its otherwise illegal actions from successful shareholder attack.

II. JUDICIAL PRINCIPLES THAT INSULATE MANAGEMENT'S ACTIONS

A. The Business Judgment Rule

Few principles are as sacred or as deep-rooted in corporate law as the business judgment rule. The rule generally provides that corporate officers and directors, absent self-dealing or other personal interest,[10] shall be shielded from liability for harm to the corporation resulting from their decisions if such decisions "lie within the powers of the corporation and the authority of management and were reasonably made in good faith and with loyalty

---

7. Arguably, the courts may reduce the likelihood of vexatious litigation by such measures as requiring plaintiff to post security for expenses, requiring judicial review of derivative settlements, and granting summary judgment motions. A number of states require the posting of security for expenses. *See, e.g.,* CAL. CORP. CODE § 800(d) (West 1980); N.J. STAT. ANN. § 14A:3-6(3) (West Supp. 1980); N.Y. BUS. CORP. LAW § 627 (McKinney Supp. 1979); MODEL BUS. CORP. ACT § 49 (1979).

8. *See Corporate Director's Guidebook,* 33 BUS. LAW. 1591, 1606-07 (1978).

9. *See generally* United Copper Sec. Co., 244 U.S. 261 (1917); Joy v. North, [1982 Transfer Binder] FED. SEC. L. REP. (CCH) ¶ 98,860 (2d Cir.); Mobil Corp. v. Marathon Oil Co., 669 F.2d 366 (6th Cir. 1981); Cramer v. General Tel. & Elecs. Corp., 582 F.2d 259 (3d Cir. 1979); Genzer v. Cunningham, 498 F. Supp. 682 (E.D. Mich. 1980); Abella v. Universal Leaf Tobacco, Inc., 495 F.Supp. 713 (E.D. Va. 1980); Zapata Corp. v. Maldonado, 430 A.2d 779 (Del. 1981).

10. As one commentator stated:

> [W]here a director or controlling stockholder has a material personal interest in the outcome of a transaction or is engaged in self-dealing, it will fall to that individual to prove that the transaction he or she authorized is intrinsically fair to the corporation and its stockholders. Otherwise stated, where such a personal interest or self-dealing is shown to exist, a presumption of overreaching arises that can be overcome only by proof of intrinsic fairness. This has been denominated as the intrinsic fairness rule.

Arsht, *The Business Judgment Rule Revisited,* 8 HOFSTRA L. REV. 93, 115-16 (1979) (citations omitted). *See* Lewis v. S.L.&E., Inc., 629 F.2d 764, 769 (2d Cir. 1980); Blake v. National Research Assocs., Inc., 466 F.2d 570, 572 (4th Cir. 1972); Trans World Airlines, Inc. v. Summa Corp., 374 A.2d 5, 9 (Del. Ch. 1977).

and due care."[11] At least three strong policy considerations support this rule. First, if management were liable for mere good faith errors in judgment, few capable individuals would be willing to incur the financial and emotional risks of serving in such roles.[12] Second, courts are generally ill equipped to evaluate business judgments.[13] Finally, management has the expertise to discharge the responsibility of making such determinations.[14]

Because of these policy considerations, the business judgment rule is desirable if our society's economy is to function efficiently. Like any rule of general application, however, it can be construed so expansively that virtually any management action may be deemed reasonably made in good faith. For example, it is beyond peradventure that members of management should premise their decisions on what is in the corporation's best interests, rather than on preserving their jobs or status.[15] It thus arguably appears that, once the complainant demonstrates that retention of control was a motive in management's decision, the presumption of the rule should be rebutted and the burden should shift to management to justify the fairness of the transaction. Nonetheless, the Third and Seventh Circuits, in construing Delaware law, both recently held that the presumption is rebutted only where management's "sole or primary purpose" is to retain control.[16] Such

---

11. Dent, *The Power of Directors to Terminate Shareholder Litigation: The Death of the Derivative Suit?* 75 Nw. U.L. Rev. 96, 101 (1980). For other definitions of the rule, *see* 3A W. Fletcher, Cyclopedia of the Law of Private Corporations § 1039 (rev. perm. ed., 1975); Arsht, *supra* note 10, at 111-12. For recent applications of the rule, see Panter v. Marshall Field & Co., 646 F.2d 271 (7th Cir. 1981), *cert. denied,* 102 S. Ct. 658 (1981); Treadway Cos. v. Care Corp., 638 F.2d 357 (2d Cir. 1980).

12. *See Corporate Director's Guidebook, supra* note 8, at 1603-04, 1615.

13. *See* Abramowitz v. Posner, [1981-1982 Transfer Binder] Fed. Sec. L. Rep. (CCH) ¶ 98,458 (2d Cir. 1982); Auerbach v. Bennett, 47 N.Y.2d 619, 629, 393 N.E.2d 994, 1000, 419 N.Y.S.2d 920, 926 (1979).

14. Cases cited in note 13 *supra.*

15. *See, e.g.,* Commonwealth Oil Refining Co. v. Tesoro Petroleum Corp., 394 F. Supp. 267, 273-74 (S.D.N.Y. 1975). *See also* Singer v. Magnavox Co., 380 A.2d 969 (Del. 1977):

> "While technically not trustees [corporate directors] stand in a fiduciary relationship to the corporation and its stockholders. . . . This rule that requires an undivided and unselfish loyalty to the corporation demands that there shall be no conflict between duty and self-interest. The occasions for the determination of honesty, good faith and loyal conduct are many and varied, and no hard and fast rule can be formulated. The standard of loyalty is measured by no fixed scale."

Id. at 977, *quoting* Guth v. Loft, Inc., 5 A.2d 503, 510 (1939).

16. Panter v. Marshall Field & Co., 646 F.2d 271 (7th Cir.), *cert. denied,* 102 S. Ct. 658 (1981). In Johnson v. Trueblood, 629 F.2d 287 (3d Cir. 1980), the court asserted that by the very nature of corporate life "a director has a certain amount of self-interest in everything he does." *Id.* at 292. To alleviate this conflict, "the rule . . . postulate[s] that if actions are arguably taken for the benefit of the corporation, then the directors are presumed to have been exercising their sound business judgment rather than responding to any personal motivations." *Id.* The court concluded that

a holding unduly expands the business judgment rule and, as the dissents argued in the above cases, does not comport with other Delaware decisions.[17] Under such an expansive interpretation, management given the benefit of hindsight and the advice of expert counsel can practically always set forth some rational and proper purpose to explain its conduct. At the very least, once the complainant presents a *prima facie* case that control was a motive, management, in order to be entitled to the rule's presumption, should be required to come forward with evidence showing that a primary purpose underlying its conduct was to benefit the corporation.

The business judgment rule also receives excessively broad application in the tender offer setting. A number of courts have indicated that a target company's management may take certain actions to defeat a hostile tender offer if in its good faith judgment the offer is not in the corporation's best interests.[18] Target managements have consequently engaged in a wide variety

---

under Delaware law, at a minimum, the plaintiff must make a showing that the sole or primary motive of the defendant was to retain control. If he makes a showing sufficient to survive the directed verdict, the burden then shifts to the defendant to show that the transaction in question had a valid corporate business purpose.

Id. at 293, *relying on* Petty v. Pentech Papers, Inc., 347 A.2d 140, 143 (Del. Ch. 1975); Cheff v. Mathes, 41 Del. Ch. 494, 199 A.2d 548 (1964); Bennett v. Propp, 41 Del. Ch. 14, 187 A.2d 405 (1962). *But see* Treadway Cos. v. Care Corp., 638 F.2d 357, 382 (2d Cir. 1980) (under New Jersey law, "[o]nce a plaintiff demonstrates that a director had an interest in the transaction at issue, the burden shifts to the defendant to prove that the transaction was fair and reasonable to the corporation"). *See generally* Gruenbaum, *Defensive Tactics and the Business Judgment Rule,* 4 CORP. L. REV. 263 (1981); Comment, *Buying Out Insurgent Shareholders with Corporate Funds,* 70 YALE L.J. 308 (1960).

17. *See* Panter v. Marshall Field & Co., 646 F.2d 271, 301 (7th Cir. 1981) (Cudahy, J., dissenting); Johnson v. Trueblood, 629 F.2d 287, 301 (3d Cir. 1980) (Rosenn, J., dissenting). In his dissent in *Johnson,* Judge Rosenn stated:

Unlike the majority, I believe that under Delaware law, once plaintiff has shown that the desire to retain control was a motive in the particular business decision under challenge, the burden is then on the defendant to move forward with evidence justifying the transaction as primarily in the corporation's best interests.

Id. at 301, *relying on* Cheff v. Mathes, 41 Del. Ch. 494, 199 A.2d 548, 554 (1964); Bennett v. Propp, 41 Del. Ch. 14, 187 A.2d 405, 409 (1962). *See also* Treadway Cos. v. Care Corp., 638 F.2d 357 (2d Cir. 1980); Crouse-Hinds Co. v. InterNorth, Inc., 634 F.2d 690 (2d Cir. 1980).

18. *See, e.g.,* Panter v. Marshall Field & Co., 646 F.2d 271 (7th Cir.), *cert. denied,* 102 S. Ct. 658 (1981); Crouse-Hinds Company v. InterNorth, Inc., 634 F.2d 690 (2d Cir. 1980); Treadway Cos. v. Care Corp., 638 F.2d 357 (2d Cir. 1980); Berman v. Gerber Products Co., 454 F. Supp. 1310 (W.D. Mich. 1978). For commentary taking this position, *see* Fleischer, *Business Judgment Rule Protects Takeover Targets,* Legal Times (Wash.) Apr. 14, 1980, at 15; Herzel, Schmidt, & Davis, *Why Corporate Directors Have a Right to Resist Tender Offers,* 3 CORP. L. REV. 107 (1980); Lipton, *Takeover Bids in the Target's Boardroom,* 35 BUS. LAW. 101 (1979); Steinbrink, *Management's Response to the Takeover Attempt,* 28 CASE W. RES. L. REV. 882 (1978).

of defensive tactics to thwart takeover bids, such as announcing an unprecedented dividend increase, entering a defensive merger with a "white
knight," or acquiring another corporation.[19] To shareholders denied the
opportunity to tender their shares at a substantial premium, the courts'
unduly broad application of the business judgment rule appears inherently
unfair. Under such an interpretation, "[r]egardless of the tactic employed,
management can easily manufacture a 'legitimate' corporate purpose for its
action, even when it employed the tactic solely to perpetuate its own status."[20] Such a consequence seems practically assured when management
utilizes expert counsel and investment bankers to lay a foundation for and
to structure its antitakeover actions.

To avoid this perverse result, courts should at the very least inquire
whether the principal objective of management's actions was to benefit the
subject corporation or to impede the tender offer.[21] One significant (although
by no means determinative) consideration should be whether the decision
to oppose the takeover bid and to engage in defensive maneuvers was made
primarily by disinterested directors or by those directors whose very live-

---

19. *See* cases cited in note 18 *supra;* Humana, Inc. v. American Medicorp, Inc., [1977-
1978 Transfer Binder] FED. SEC. L. REP. (CCH) ¶ 96,286 (S.D.N.Y. Jan. 5, 1978); Applied
Digital Data Sys., Inc. v. Milgo Elec. Corp., 425 F. Supp. 1145 (S.D.N.Y. 1977); Royal Indus.,
Inc. v. Monogram Indus., Inc., [1976-1977 Transfer Binder] FED. SEC. L. REP. (CCH) ¶ 95,863
(C.D. Cal. Nov. 29, 1976).

20. Lynch & Steinberg, *The Legitimacy of Defensive Tactics in Tender Offers,* 64 CORNELL
L. REV. 901, 926 (1979). *See* Mobil Corp. v. Marathon Oil Co., 669 F.2d 366 (6th Cir. 1981);
Conoco, Inc. v. Seagram Co., Ltd., 517 F. Supp. 1299 (S.D.N.Y. 1981); Crane Co. v. Harsco
Corp., 511 F. Supp. 294 (D. Del. 1981). *See generally* Panter v. Marshall Field & Co., 646
F.2d 271 (7th Cir. 1981) (Cudahy, J., concurring in part and dissenting in part). Judge Cudahy
stated:

> Unfortunately, the majority here has moved one giant step closer to shredding whatever
> constraints still remain upon the ability of corporate directors to place self-interest
> before shareholder interest in resisting a hostile tender offer for control of the corpo-
> ration. There is abundant evidence in this case to go to the jury on the state claims for
> breach of fiduciary duty. I emphatically disagree that the business judgment rule should
> clothe directors, battling blindly to fend off a threat to their control, with an almost
> irrebuttable presumption of sound business judgment, prevailing over everything but
> the elusive hobgoblins of fraud, bad faith or abuse of discretion.

Id. at 299. Judge Cudahy asserted that "[t]his case announces to stockholders (if they did not
know it before) that they are on their own and may expect little consideration and less
enlightenment from their board of directors when a tender offeror appears to challenge the
directors for control." *Id.* at 312. Accordingly, "only the submission to jury verdict of cases
like this one can restore confidence in our system of corporate governance." *Id.*

21. *See, e.g.,* Klaus v. Hi-Shear Corp., 528 F.2d 225, 233 (9th Cir. 1975); Royal Indus.,
Inc. v. Monogram Indus., Inc., [1976-1977 Transfer Binder] FED. SEC. L. REP. (CCH) ¶ 95,863,
at 91,136 (C.D. Cal. Nov. 24, 1976).

lihood and economic interests depended on the continued separate existence of the subject corporation.[22]

B. The *Burks v. Lasker* Special Litigation Committee Scenario

A relatively new defensive strategy in response to a shareholders' derivative suit against members of a corporation's board of directors is for the corporation's board to appoint a special litigation committee composed of disinterested nondefendant directors. The extent to which such a committee can rely on the business judgment rule in terminating such suits is highly controversial and has been the subject of increasing scrutiny by both the courts[23] and commentators.[24] Further, it is important to keep in mind that

---

22. *See* Gelfond & Sebastian, *Reevaluating the Duties of Target Management in a Hostile Tender Offer,* 60 B.U.L. REV. 403, 472 (1980); Williams, *Role of Directors in Takeover Offers,* 13 REV. SEC. REG. 963 (1980). *See also* Panter v. Marshall Field & Co., 646 F.2d 271 (7th Cir. 1981), where Judge Cudahy stated:

> Directors of a New York Stock Exchange-listed company are, at the very least, "interested" in their own positions of power, prestige and prominence (and in their not inconsequential perquisites). They are "interested" in defending against outside attack the management which they have, in fact, installed or maintained in power—"their" management (to which, in many cases, they owe their directorships). And they are "interested" in maintaining the public reputation of their own leadership and stewardship against the claims of "raiders" who say that they can do better. Thus, regardless of their technical "independence," directors of a target corporation are in a very special position, where the slavish application of the majority's version of the good faith presumption is particularly disturbing.

Id. at 300-01 (Cudahy, J., concurring in part and dissenting in part). Moreover, it should be recognized that management will often be able to influence outside directors. *See* Mite Corp. v. Dixon, 633 F.2d 486, 495-96 (7th Cir. 1980), *aff'd,* 102 S. Ct. 2629 (1982). For further discussion on the legitimacy of defensive tactics herein, *see* pages 9-11, 205-31 *supra.*

23. *See, e.g.,* Joy v. North, [1982 Transfer Binder] FED. SEC. L. REP. (CCH) ¶ 98,860 (2d Cir.); Maldonado v. Flynn, [1981-1982 Transfer Binder] FED. SEC. L. REP. (CCH) ¶ 98,457 (2d Cir. 1982); Abramowitz v. Posner, [1981-1982 Transfer Binder] FED. SEC. L. REP. (CCH) ¶ 98,458 (2d Cir. 1982); Gaines v. Haughton, 645 F.2d 761 (9th Cir. 1981), *cert. denied,* 102 S. Ct. 1006 (1982); Galef v. Alexander, 615 F.2d 51 (2d Cir. 1980); Lewis v. Anderson, 615 F.2d 778 (9th Cir. 1979), *cert. denied,* 101 S. Ct. 206 (1980); Abbey v. Control Data Corp., 603 F.2d 724 (8th Cir. 1979), *cert. denied,* 444 U.S. 1017 (1980); Genzer v. Cunningham, 498 F. Supp. 682 (E.D. Mich. 1980); Maher v. Zapata Corp., 490 F. Supp. 348 (S.D. Tex. 1980); Siegal v. Merrick, 84 F.R.D. 106 (S.D.N.Y. 1979); Lewis v. Adams, No. 77-266C (N.D. Okla. Nov. 15, 1979); Zapata Corp. v. Maldonado, 430 A.2d 779 (Del. 1981); Auerbach v. Bennett, 47 N.Y.2d 619, 393 N.E.2d 994, 419 N.Y.S.2d 920 (1979).

24. *See, e.g.,* Coffee & Schwartz, *The Survival of the Derivative Suit: An Evaluation and a Proposal for Legislative Reform,* 81 COLUM. L. REV. 261 (1981). Dent, *The Power of Directors to Terminate Shareholder Litigation: The Death of the Derivative Suit?* 75 NW. U.L. REV. 96 (1980); Gammon, *Derivative Suits,* 12 REV. SEC. REG. 887 (1979); Steinberg, *The Use of Special Litigation Committees to Terminate Shareholder Derivative Suits,* 35 U. MIAMI L. REV. 1 (1980); Comment, *The Business Judgment Rule in Derivative Suits Against Directors,* 65 CORNELL L. REV. 600 (1980).

the application of the business judgment rule in this context "is an expansion of the traditional rule."[25]

In the seminal case of *Burks v. Lasker*,[26] the Supreme Court found two questions to be dispositive in determining whether federal court dismissal of shareholder derivative suits against board members is proper: (1) whether the applicable state law permits the disinterested directors to terminate shareholder derivative suits against fellow directors, and (2) whether such a state rule is consistent with the policies underlying the federal securities laws.[27] Of course, if dismissal is sought in state court, the only determination is whether relevant state law authorizes such dismissal.[28]

Subsequent to *Burks,* a number of federal and state courts have addressed this subject with varying results. As a generalization, at one end of the spectrum are decisions that construe state law so as to permit dismissal in any type of action, including those premised on self-dealing by defendant directors,[29] and that decline to recognize any federal policy as conflicting with such interpretation of state law.[30] A number of these decisions place the burden upon the shareholder to show that the special litigation committee was biased.[31] At the other end of the spectrum are decisions that construe state law so as to preclude dismissal in apparently all situations.[32] The middle position generally is occupied by those courts that assess the special litigation committee's independence and good faith, the reasonableness of the committee's decision, the type of conduct alleged to have been involved, and the presence of any strong federal policies.[33]

---

25. Genzer v. Cunningham, 498 F. Supp. 682, 689 (E.D. Mich. 1980).

26. 441 U.S. 471 (1979).

27. *Id.* at 480, 486.

28. *See, e.g.,* Zapata Corp. v. Maldonado, 430 A.2d 779 (Del. 1981); Auerbach v. Bennett, 47 N.Y.2d 619, 393 N.E.2d 994, 419 N.Y.S.2d 920 (1979).

29. *See, e.g.,* Maldonado v. Flynn, [1981-1982 Transfer Binder] FED. SEC. L. REP. (CCH) ¶ 98,457 (2d Cir. 1982); Gaines v. Haughton, 645 F.2d 761 (9th Cir. 1981), *cert. denied,* 102 S. Ct. 1006 (1982); Lewis v. Anderson, 615 F.2d 778 (9th Cir. 1979), *cert. denied,* 101 S. Ct. 206 (1980).

30. *See* cases cited in note 29 *supra.*

31. *See, e.g.,* Lewis v. Anderson, 615 F.2d at 783; Auerbach v. Bennett, 47 N.Y.2d at 633-35, 393 N.E.2d at 1002-03, 419 N.Y.S.2d at 928-29; Falkenberg v. Baldwin, SEC. REG. & L. REP. (BNA) No. 545, A-14 (N.Y. Sup. Ct. Mar. 3, 1980).

32. *See, e.g.,* Abella v. Universal Leaf Tobacco, Inc., 495 F. Supp. 713 (E.D. Va. 1980); Maher v. Zapata Corp., 490 F. Supp. 348 (S.D. Tex. 1980); Maldonado v. Flynn, 413 A.2d 1251 (Del. Ch. 1980), *reversed and remanded,* 430 A.2d 779 (Del. 1981).

33. *See, e.g.,* Joy v. North, [1982 Transfer Binder] FED. SEC. L. REP. (CCH) ¶ 98,860 (2d Cir.); Galef v. Alexander, 615 F.2d 51 (2d Cir. 1980); Abbey v. Control Data Corp., 603 F.2d 778 (8th Cir. 1979), *cert. denied,* 444 U.S. 1017 (1980); Cramer v. General Tel. & Elecs. Corp., 582 F.2d 259 (3d Cir. 1979); Genzer v. Cunningham, 498 F. Supp. 682 (E.D. Mich. 1980); Zapata Corp. v. Maldonado, 430 A.2d 779 (Del. 1981) (court should (1) inquire into independence and good faith of committee and bases supporting its conclusions and (2) apply its own independent business judgment).

It should be stressed that courts in the first group provide management with practically free reign to terminate shareholder derivative suits against directors.[34] Toward this end, management frequently appoints nondefendant disinterested directors to the special litigation committee and retains outside counsel of unimpeachable integrity. After hearing witnesses and examining documentary evidence, the committee, with the special counsel's concurrence, normally issues a comprehensive report concluding that the corporation's best interests would not be served by the suit due to its improbability of success, its exorbitant cost, and its tendency to disrupt company business and lower employee morale. Relying on the committee's report, the corporation seeks to dismiss the complaint.[35] With the burden of proof on the shareholders, these courts find an additional basis upon which to grant the motion.[36]

This is not to imply that special litigation committee investigations are necessarily shams. These committees and their special counsel may ferret out vexatious litigation as well as nonfrivolous actions that are not in the corporation's best interests. Nonetheless, the apparent pressure on committee members to discount the corporation's interests when fellow directors are sued should lead a court to scrutinize the type of conduct (*e.g.,* corporate mismanagement as opposed to self-dealing) alleged to have occurred and the reasonableness of the committee's determination.[37] Further, because the defendant directors selected the members of the committee, the appearance (and perhaps the presence) of impropriety and unfairness to the shareholders should place the burden of establishing the committee's independence upon the movant.[38] In this regard, to help ensure that the committee members

---

34. *See generally* Steinberg, *The Use of Special Litigation Committees to Terminate Shareholder Derivative Suits,* 35 U. MIAMI L. REV. 1 (1980).

35. *See* note 23 *supra;* Bishop, *Derivative Suits Against Bank Directors: New Problems, New Strategies,* 97 BANKING L.J. 158 (1980); Steinberg, *supra* note 34, at 1-2.

36. *See* note 31 *supra.*

37. *See* notes 32-33 *supra.* As the *Cramer* court stated:

> [W]e do not think that the business judgment of the directors should be totally insulated from judicial review. In order for the directors' judgment to merit judicial deference, that judgment must have been made in good faith and independently of any influence of those persons suspected of wrongdoing. In addition, where the shareholder contends that the directors' judgment is so unwise or unreasonable as to fall outside the permissible bounds of the directors' sound discretion, a court should, we think, be able to conduct its own analysis of the reasonableness of that business judgment.

582 F.2d at 275. *See* Steinberg, *supra* note 34, at 28 (when the directors' alleged actions involve conflicts of interests, fraud, or self-dealing, dismissal may not be proper). In such situations, a court "should, when appropriate, give special consideration to matters of law and public policy in addition to the corporation's best interests." Zapata Corp. v. Maldonado, 430 A.2d 779, 789 (Del. 1981).

38. *See, e.g.,* Genzer v. Cunningham, 493 F. Supp. 682, 693 (E.D. Mich. 1980); Gyrnberg

241

were not subject to the defendants' influence and had exercised independent judgment on the corporation's behalf, any prior contacts or relationships between committee members and defendants should be rigorously examined.[39]

C. Certain Limitations on the *Goldberg v. Meridor* Rationale

In *Santa Fe Industries, Inc. v. Green,*[40] the Supreme Court held that Section 10(b) and Rule 10b-5 did not reach breaches of fiduciary duty not involving deception or manipulation.[41] One argument advanced by the plaintiff-shareholders in that case was that the majority shareholder's failure to provide them with advance notice of an impending merger constituted a material nondisclosure. In what has become a most important footnote fourteen, the Court rejected this contention, reasoning that the plaintiffs had not indicated how they might have acted differently had they received such prior notice: "Indeed, they accept the conclusion of both courts below that under Delaware law they could not have enjoined the merger because an appraisal proceeding is their sole remedy in the Delaware courts for any alleged unfairness in the terms of the merger."[42] Accordingly, the Court concluded that the failure to provide advance notice was not a material nondisclosure within the meaning of Section 10(b) and Rule 10b–5.[43]

Significantly, however, after *Santa Fe,* the Delaware Supreme Court in *Singer v. Magnavox Co.*[44] held that appraisal is not a minority shareholder's sole remedy, stating that a long-form merger "made for the sole purpose of freezing out minority shareholders, is an abuse of the corporate process; and . . . states a cause of action for violation of a fiduciary duty."[45] Moreover, the court concluded that even if a valid business purpose were shown, the

---

v. Farmer, [1980 Transfer Binder] FED. SEC. L. REP. (CCH) ¶ 97,683, at 98,586 (D. Col. Oct. 8, 1980); Zapata Corp. v. Maldonado, 430 A.2d 779 (Del. 1981).

39. *See* Steinberg, *supra* note 34, at 25-26. For further discussion on this subject herein, *see* pages 133-62 *supra.*

40. 430 U.S. 462 (1977).

41. *Id.* at 473-74.

42. *Id.* at 474 n.14.

43. *Id.* The Court's decision was widely viewed by commentators as sharply curtailing the scope of Section 10(b). *See, e.g.,* Campbell, Santa Fe Industries, Inc. v. Green: *An Analysis Two Years Later,* 30 MAINE L. REV. 187 (1979); Jacobs, *Rule 10b-5 and Self-Dealing by Corporate Fiduciaries: An Analysis,* 48 U. CIN. L. REV. 643 (1979); Ratner, *"Federal Corporation Law" Before and After* Santa Fe Industries v. Green, in NINTH ANNUAL INSTITUTE ON SECURITIES REGULATION—CORPORATE TRANSCRIPT SERIES 305, 322 (Fleischer, Lipton & Vandegrift eds., 1978); Note, *Suits for Breach of Fiduciary Duty Under Rule 10b-5 After* Santa Fe Industries, Inc. v. Green, 91 HARV. L. REV. 1874 (1978).

44. 380 A.2d 969 (Del. 1977).

45. *Id.* at 980.

transaction must be scrutinized for its entire fairness.[46] Although subsequent Delaware case law has eliminated the business purpose requirement, *Singer*'s principles generally have been reaffirmed.[47] Decisions of other state courts, although not strictly in adherence with *Singer*,[48] also recognize that appraisal is not a minority shareholder's exclusive remedy when the merger has not been consummated.[49]

---

46. The court stated:

> On the contrary, the fiduciary obligation of the majority to the minority stockholders remains and proof of a purpose, other than such freeze-out, without more, will not necessarily discharge it. In such case the Court will scrutinize the circumstances for compliance with the *Sterling* rule of *"entire fairness"* and, if it finds a violation thereof, will grant such relief as equity may require.

Id.

47. *See* Weinberger v. UOP, Inc., 15 SEC. REG. & L. REP. (BNA) 327 (1983). As the author stated prior to *Weinberger:*

> *Singer* was the harbinger of a new era in Delaware. Subsequent Delaware cases have confirmed and extended the viability of *Singer*'s principles. From these decisions, a number of general principles can be proffered: a majority shareholder's fiduciary duty is not fulfilled simply by relegating the minority stockholders to their statutory appraisal remedy; majority shareholders cannot effect a merger solely for the purpose of eliminating the minority; such a merger must be for a proper purpose and must be entirely fair to the minority; a merger made primarily to advance the business purpose of a majority stockholder is proper so long as it has a bona fide purpose and is entirely fair to the minority; and where a complaint alleges that the purpose of the merger was to eliminate minority shareholders, such a complaint may often be immune from a motion to dismiss. The foregoing principles are applicable to short-form as well as long-form mergers.

Ferrara & Steinberg, *A Reappraisal of* Santa Fe: *Rule 10b-5 and the New Federalism,* 129 U. PA. L. REV. 263, 278-80 (1980), *citing,* Roland Int'l Corp. v. Najjar, 407 A.2d 1032 (Del. 1979); Tanzer v. International Gen. Indus., Inc., 379 A.2d 1121 (Del. 1977); Young v. Valhi, Inc., 382 A.2d 1372 (Del. Ch. 1978); Kemp v. Angel, 381 A.2d 241 (Del. Ch. 1977). For additional discussion of *Singer, see* Brudney & Chirelstein, *A Restatement of Corporate Freeze-outs,* 87 YALE L.J. 1354 (1978); Rothschild, *Going Private,* Singer, *and Rule 13e-3: What Are the Standards for Fiduciaries?* 7 SEC. REG. L.J. 195 (1979); Comment, *Delaware Reverses Its Trend in Going Private Transactions: The Forgotten Majority,* 11 LOY. L.A.L. REV. 567 (1978); Comment, Singer v. Magnavox *and Cash Take-Out Mergers,* 64 VA. L. REV. 1101 (1978).

48. *See, e.g., In re* Jones & Laughlin Steel Corp., 488 Pa. 524, 412 A.2d 1099 (1980) (state legislature intended that appraisal statute serve as sole postmerger remedy); Gabhart v. Gabhart, 267 Ind. 370, 370 N.E.2d 345 (1977) (adopting only the first prong of *Singer*). *But see* Perl v. IU Int'l Corp., 607 P.2d 1036 (Hawaii 1980) (following *Singer*). *See generally* Jones v. H. F. Ahmanson & Co., 1 Cal. 3d 93, 460 P.2d 464, 81 CAL. RPTR. 592 (1969) (as interpreted by the Hawaii Supreme Court, "[a]lthough *Ahmanson* did not involve a merger, it appears clear from the language of the opinion that the California Supreme Court would apply the fiduciary duty of good faith and inherent fairness to such a situation." 607 P.2d at 1047 n. 12).

49. *See* note 48 *supra;* Ferrara & Steinberg, *supra* note 47, at 281; Steinberg, *State Court Decisions After* Santa Fe, 9 SEC. REG. L.J. 85 (1981).

Based on these decisions and on *Santa Fe*'s footnote fourteen, the Second, Third, Fifth, Seventh and Ninth Circuits have generally held that, where there has been a material nondisclosure that would have enabled the shareholder to seek injunctive relief in a state court to prevent the consummation of a transaction, such nondisclosure constitutes "deception" within the meaning of Section 10(b).[50] The leading case adhering to this rationale is the Second Circuit's decision in *Goldberg v. Meridor.*[51]

There are, however, a number of limitations to the *Goldberg* rationale. For example, management is under no obligation to disclose to shareholders its own breaches of fiduciary duty. As the Third Circuit stated, to hold otherwise "would clearly circumvent the Supreme Court's holding in *Santa Fe.*"[52] Another limitation is that where a particular matter does not require shareholder approval, full disclosure to a disinterested board of directors is deemed equivalent to full disclosure to the shareholders. Stated differently, the disinterested directors' knowledge is attributed to the corporation, thereby precluding a finding of deception.[53] This limitation generally seems well-founded, since directors are elected to consider such matters.[54] However, if the term "disinterested" is defined too broadly, recalcitrant management will be able to undermine the *Goldberg* rationale in instances where shareholder approval is not required.

---

50. *See* Healey v. Catalyst Recovery, Inc., 616 F.2d 641 (3d Cir. 1980); Alabama Farm Bureau Mut. Cas. Co. v. American Fidelity Life Ins. Co., 606 F.2d 602 (5th Cir. 1979), *cert. denied,* 101 S. Ct. 77 (1980); Kidwell *ex rel.* Penfold v. Meikle, 597 F.2d 1273 (9th Cir. 1979); Goldberg v. Meridor, 567 F.2d 209 (2d Cir. 1977), *cert. denied,* 434 U.S. 1069 (1978); Wright v. Heizer Corp., 560 F.2d 237 (7th Cir. 1977), *cert. denied,* 434 U.S. 1066 (1978). A question that remains open is whether a shareholder must show not only that he could have brought suit in state court but also that he would have prevailed in the state court action. The courts are deeply split on this issue. *See* Ferrara & Steinberg, *supra* note 47, at 291-94.

51. 567 F.2d 209 (2d Cir. 1977), *cert. denied,* 434 U.S. 1069 (1978). The Second Circuit subsequently reaffirmed the *Goldberg* rationale in IIT v. Cornfeld, 619 F.2d 909, 917 (2d Cir. 1980).

52. Biesenbach v. Guenther, 588 F.2d 400, 402 (3d Cir. 1978). The court further reasoned:

> *Santa Fe* made clear that absent deception, misrepresentation, or nondisclosure a breach of fiduciary duty does not violate the statute or Rule. . . . In effect, appellants are stating that the failure to disclose the breach of fiduciary duty is a misrepresentation sufficient to constitute a violation of the Act. We refuse to adopt this approach which would clearly circumvent the Supreme Court's holding in *Santa Fe.*

Id.

53. Maldonado v. Flynn, 597 F.2d 789, 795 (2d Cir. 1979) (since the amendments modifying the stock option plan were "validly enacted by a vote of disinterested board members who had been fully informed of all material facts, their knowledge was attributable to the Corporation and no 'deception' occurred within the meaning of Rule 10b-5"). *See also* Kaplan v. Bennett, 465 F. Supp. 555, 565-66 (S.D.N.Y. 1979).

54. *See* notes 8-9 *supra* and accompanying text.

Accordingly, a director should not be deemed "disinterested" merely because he lacks a financial stake in the subject transaction.[55] Other disabilities, such as conflicts of interest, the design of "entrenchment," and the perpetration of improper influence by control persons, should also disqualify a director.[56] The presence of any such disability should be held to impair the director's ability to exercise independent judgment on the corporation's behalf, and should give rise to a requirement that management obtain shareholder approval of the transaction after full disclosure.[57]

Further, some courts have construed the term "disinterested" broadly to include directors who have other substantial contacts with the corporation, such as serving as outside counsel, as a major supplier, or having some other present or previous similar association.[58] This construction of "disinterested" leaves open the door for management to appoint such persons to the board and to delegate to them the decision-making functions whenever management is interested, such as in regard to particular remuneration benefits, and the determination is not relegated to the shareholders.[59] In such a situation, "[t]ruly independent actions by either the lawyer or the supplier might well signify a substantial reduction in income."[60] Yet, by labeling

---

55. See Tyco Labs., Inc. v. Kimball, 444 F. Supp. 292 (E.D. Pa. 1977); Falkenberg v. Baldwin, [1977-1978 Transfer Binder] FED. SEC. L. REP. (CCH) ¶ 96,086 (S.D.N.Y. 1977).

56. See Maldonado v. Flynn, 597 F.2d 789, 795 (2d Cir. 1979); Kaplan v. Bennett, 465 F. Supp. 555, 565 (S.D.N.Y. 1979); Goldberger v. Baker, 442 F. Supp. 659, 665 (S.D.N.Y. 1977).

57. See Ferrara & Steinberg, supra note 47, at 290.

58. See Panter v. Marshall Field & Co., 646 F.2d 271 (7th Cir.), cert. denied, 102 S. Ct. 658 (1981); Maldonado v. Flynn, 597 F.2d 789, 794 (2d Cir. 1979).

59. See 597 F.2d at 793-95 (amendments modifying stock option plan that inured to direct benefit of recipient-directors).

60. Ferrara & Steinberg, supra note 47, at 290.
In Maldonado, however, the Second Circuit concluded that a director who was a partner in a law firm that received substantial fees from the subject corporation was "disinterested." The court reasoned:

> [T]o label . . . [counsel] an 'interested' director for purposes of Rule 10b-5 because of his relationship as the company's legal counsel would be to open the door to an unworkable standard for determining whether there has been deception practiced upon the corporation. . . . [W]e cannot assume that a counsel-director acts for reasons that are against the corporation's interest, as distinguished from the private interests of its officers.

597 F.2d at 794.
For articles discussing Santa Fe and its progeny see, e.g., Block & Schwarzfeld, Corporate Mismanagement and Breach of Fiduciary Duty After Santa Fe v. Green, 2 CORP. L. REV. 91 (1979); Campbell, Santa Fe Industries, Inc. v. Green: An Analysis Two Years Later, 30 ME. L. REV. 187 (1979); Ferrara & Steinberg, A Reappraisal of Santa Fe: Rule 10b-5 and the New Federalism, 129 U. PA. L. REV. 263 (1980); Jacobs, Rule 10b-5 and Self Dealing by Corporate Fiduciaries: An Analysis, 48 CIN. L. REV. 643 (1979); Note, Suits for Breach of Fiduciary Duty Under Rule 10b-5 After Santa Fe Industries, Inc. v. Green, 91 HARV. L. REV. 1874 (1978);

such persons "disinterested," the courts forever foreclose shareholders from challenging the propriety of these transactions. Such a broad construction is contrary both to the federal disclosure policy underlying the *Goldberg* rationale and to the maintenance of corporate accountability.

D. True Purpose Cases

The true purpose cases stand for the proposition that the securities laws require objective disclosure rather than subjective revelation.[61] Nearly twenty-five years ago, Judge Rifkind posed the following question, then answered it in the negative: "Assuming that data are supplied, is the proxy statement nevertheless false if it omits a confession of selfish motive?"[62] As one authority has remarked: "It is not necessary to say, 'this is a grossly unfair transaction in which the board of directors is overreaching the minority shareholders.' You just have to give them the facts."[63] Or, as the Third Circuit put it: "[T]he unclean heart of a director is not actionable, whether or not it is disclosed, unless the impurities are translated into actionable deeds or omissions both objective and external."[64] Thus, management is under no obligation to describe a particular matter in pejorative terms[65] or to disclose its true purpose or motivation.[66]

The problem in this context principally occurs when management undertakes a course of conduct designed to maintain its own control. Although corporate control is acknowledged to be of universal interest to incumbent management,[67] when management embarks on a program or adopts a policy for the purpose of perpetuating its control, the nondisclosure of such purpose

---

Note, Goldberg v. Meridor: *The Second Circuit's Resurrection of Rule 10b-5 Liability for Breaches of Corporate Fiduciary Duties to Minority Shareholders,* 64 VA. L. REV. 765 (1978). For further discussion herein on this subject, *see* pages 163-98 *supra.*

61. *See, e.g.,* Selk v. St. Paul Ammonia Products, Inc., 597 F.2d 635, 639 (8th Cir. 1979) (failure to disclose that purpose of merger was to freeze out minority shareholders not actionable under Sections 10(b) and 14(a)); O'Brien v. Continental Illinois Nat'l Bank & Trust Co., 593 F.2d 54, 60 (7th Cir. 1979) (failure to reveal that investment advice was self-serving not actionable under Section 10(b)); Gluck v. Agemian, [1980 Transfer Binder] FED. SEC. L. REP. (CCH) ¶ 97,582, at 98,090 (S.D.N.Y. 1980) ("disclosure of subjective motive is not required under the federal securities laws"); Hundahl v. United Benefit Life Ins. Co., 465 F.Supp. 1349, 1364 (N.D. Tex. 1979) (failure to disclose breach of fiduciary duty or scheme to undervalue company not actionable under Section 10(b)).

62. Doyle v. Milton, 73 F. Supp. 281, 286 (S.D.N.Y. 1947).

63. Ratner, *supra* note 43, at 322.

64. Biesenbach v. Guenther, 588 F.2d 400, 402 (3d Cir. 1978).

65. *See* Goldberg v. Meridor, 567 F.2d 209, 218 n.8 (2d Cir. 1977), *cert. denied,* 434 U.S. 1069 (1978).

66. *See* notes 62-65 *supra* and accompanying text.

67. *See* Rodman v. The Grant Foundation, 608 F.2d 64, 71 (2d Cir. 1979).

can ultimately harm the corporation and its shareholders. Recognizing this fact, the Fifth Circuit found actionable under Section 10(b) an allegation that management had failed to disclose that it "had embarked on a program of maintaining control at the cost of inflating stock prices."[68] Further, the Second Circuit has implied that when management's design hinges upon so-called "entrenchment," rather than its obvious interest in company control, then disclosure of such design will be required.[69]

As a general proposition, if these true purpose cases are construed too broadly, management can undertake practically any course of action to perpetuate its control and never be required to disclose its ultimate design. For example, in order to maintain control, management may decide that the corporation should remain an independent entity. To this end, management may embark on a stock repurchase program for the purpose of raising stock prices to deter potential acquirors, may enter other lines of business to pose antitrust obstacles for potential bidders, and may seek shareholder approval for adoption of a number of antitakeover amendments to further solidify its position.[70] Yet, under a broad true purpose construction, management is under no obligation to disclose that it has engaged in these actions in order to perpetuate its control.

On the other hand, it is contrary to management's self-interest to reveal its intent in such a context, and, with the advice of counsel, legitimate business reasons can be formulated to justify the action taken. As asserted in an earlier chapter, however, the same beneficial disclosure result can usually be achieved by requiring that the *effect* of the action be disclosed. Thus, in each of the examples above, management should be required to disclose that the effect of its action is to solidify management's control and to render hostile takeover bids less probable and, if made, less likely to

---

68. Alabama Farm Bureau Mut. Cas. Co., Inc. v. American Fidelity Life Ins. Co., 606 F.2d 602, 614 (5th Cir. 1979), *cert. denied*, 101 S. Ct. 77 (1980).

69. Rodman v. The Grant Foundation, 608 F.2d at 71. *See also* Vaughn v. Teledyne, Inc., 628 F.2d 1214, 1221 (9th Cir. 1980) ("Corporate officials are under no duty to disclose their precise motive or purpose for engaging in a particular course of corporate action, so long as the motive is not manipulative or deceptive and the nature and scope of any stock transactions are adequately disclosed to those involved"); Steinberg, *Fiduciary Duties and Disclosure Obligations in Proxy and Tender Contests for Corporate Control*, 30 EMORY L.J. 169 (1981). *See also* SEC v. C & R Clothiers, Inc., [1980 Transfer Binder] FED. SEC. L. REP. (CCH) ¶ 97,650 (D.D.C. 1980) (consent).

70. *See generally* Panter v. Marshall Field & Co., 646 F.2d 271 (7th Cir.), *cert. denied*, 102 S. Ct. 658 (1981); Treadway Cos. v. Care Corp., 638 F.2d 357 (2d Cir. 1980); Berman v. Gerber Prod. Co., 454 F. Supp. 1310 (W.D. Mich. 1978); Johnson, *Disclosure in Tender Offer Transactions: The Dice Are Still Loaded*, 42 U. PITT. L. REV. 1, 33-34 (1980); Lynch & Steinberg, *supra* note 20, at 928-38. For further discussion on this subject herein, *see* pages 94-98 *supra*.

succeed.[71] If such disclosure is made, the shareholder generally will receive all the information he needs to make an informed decision regarding whether, for example, to sell or retain his stock, to seek the removal of incumbent management, or even to bring suit in state court alleging that management has breached its fiduciary duty.

E. Disclosure of Antisocial, Unethical, or Unlawful Policies

A troublesome issue is whether management must disclose, particularly in proxy solicitations for the election of directors, antisocial, unethical or unlawful corporate policies. The rationale supporting nondisclosure is that claims for requiring such disclosures are in fact simply a means by which shareholders can question management's business judgment. To mandate disclosure would open the floodgates for litigious shareholders to bring suit whenever they disagreed with the efficacy or wisdom of management's policies.[72] Moreover, a rule requiring disclosure of such policies is unworkable, since management is unlikely to accuse itself of pursuing antisocial or illegal policies.[73]

Nonetheless, a number of reasonable shareholders would often consider antisocial policies material to their investment and voting decisions, particularly if they have caused significant economic harm. Such information might be important to shareholders in deciding, for example, which directors to vote for or whether to tender stock in a takeover bid setting.[74] Moreover,

---

71. *See* Securities Exchange Act Release No. 15230 (Oct. 1978): "[T]he issuer's proxy material or information statements should disclose in a prominent place that the overall effect of the proposal is to render more difficult the accomplishment of mergers or the assumption of control by a principal stockholder, and thus to make difficult the removal of management."

72. *See* Amalgamated Clothing and Textile Workers Union, AFL-CIO v. J. P. Stevens & Co., 475 F. Supp. 328 (S.D.N.Y. 1979), *dismissed as moot,* [1981 Transfer Binder] FED. SEC. L. REP. (CCH) ¶ 97,814 (2d Cir. Jan. 9, 1981): "As to plaintiffs' allegation that [defendant's] labor policy has resulted in significant expenses, management is clearly not required to submit in proxy statements seeking reelection of directors all business judgments whenever it would be possible for shareholders to disagree with their efficacy or wisdom." *Id.* at 331. *See also* Gaines v. Haughton, 645 F.2d 761 (9th Cir. 1981), *cert. denied,* 102 S. Ct. 1006 (1982).

73. 475 F. Supp. at 332-33. *See* SEC v. Chicago Helicopter Industries, Inc., Civ. No. 79CO469 (N.D. Ill. 1980) ("It is unlikely that the materiality requirement of § 10(b) was ever intended to require management to accuse itself of antisocial behavior"), *discussed in* SEC. REG. & L. REP. (BNA) No. 595, A-4 (Mar. 18, 1981).

74. *See* Brief of the SEC in Amalgamated Clothing and Textile Workers Union, AFL-CIO v. J. P. Stevens & Co., [1981 Transfer Binder] FED. SEC. L. REP. (CCH) ¶ 97,814 (2d Cir. Jan. 9, 1981):

> The Commission submits that the district court erred in concluding that the alleged omissions were non-material as a matter of law because the trier of fact could reasonably conclude, first, that the illegal policy which caused significant economic harm reflected adversely on the way in which Stevens was being managed and, second, that this information would be important to shareholders' decisions about whether to retain Stevens' directors.

while many shareholders undeniably wish only to maximize their investments, others seek to invest in companies adhering to ethical, social, and legal norms. Failure to require disclosure on the ground that these shareholders are "unreasonable" or that the information they seek is "immaterial" is inconsistent with fundamental principles of corporate accountability.[75] Further, as noted in an earlier chapter, although courts should be circumspect regarding adoption of principles that would require management to accuse itself of antisocial behavior, to permit nondisclosure on the broad ground that management is not disposed to reveal such policies ignores the fact that, under well-established disclosure standards, management must disclose much that is contrary to its interests.[76]

III. CONCLUSION

This chapter has focused on a number of judicial principles that, if construed too broadly, serve to insulate recalcitrant management's otherwise illegal actions from successful shareholder challenge. If interpreted properly, these principles advance both the corporation's and shareholders' best interests. If courts are unduly solicitous toward management, however, corporate accountability will needlessly suffer. In this regard, before holding that a particular action taken by management is insulated from challenge by one of these principles, courts should scrutinize the purposes underlying the relevant principle and determine whether applying the principle in that

---

75. *See* Natural Resources Defense Council, Inc. v. SEC, 389 F. Supp. 689, 700 (D.D.C. 1974):

> There are many so-called "ethical investors" in this country who want to invest their assets in firms which are concerned about and acting on environmental problems of the nation. This attitude may be based purely on a concern for the environment, but it may also proceed from the recognition that awareness of and sensitivity to environmental problems is the mark of intelligent management. Whatever their motive, this Court is not prepared to say that they are not rational investors and that the information they seek is not material information within the meaning of the securities laws.

76. *See, e.g.,* Item 401(f) of Regulation S-K, 17 C.F.R. § 229.401 (1982). *See generally* Brief of the SEC, Amalgamated Clothing and Textile Workers Union v. J. P. Stevens & Co., [1981 Transfer Binder] FED. SEC. L. REP. (CCH) ¶ 97,814 (2d Cir. Jan. 9, 1981):

> [I]t is clear that future plans of a corporation must be disclosed where they are material and *legal,* and there is no basis for concluding that disclosure obligations may be avoided by making future *illegal* plans. The very concept of disclosure may be contrary to human nature, in that management might prefer to conceal all unfavorable information about a company, including such matters as financial losses. Nevertheless, the essence of the federal securities laws, as stated in the preamble to the Securities Act of 1933, is "to provide full and fair disclosure."

Id. (emphasis in original). For further discussion on this subject herein, *see* pages 99-104 *supra.*

setting would effectuate its purposes. Moreover, the importance of affording shareholders, suing either derivatively or individually, the opportunity for redress should be a relevant consideration in determining whether a particular principle should be applied in a given case. Thus, although courts should apply the business judgment rule and related judicial principles in appropriate situations to shield management's conduct, they should be careful to ensure that their processes are not used as a sword by recalcitrant management to pierce legitimate shareholder interests.

7

The Role of Inside Counsel

I. INTRODUCTION

In today's complex and ever-changing corporate world, the role of inside counsel is by no means an easy one. Today, inside counsel plays an active role in shaping corporate events as they occur, in assessing and determining corporate policies, and in establishing the tone and standard for what may be called "the conduct of corporations." As former SEC Chairman Harold M. Williams has remarked, the responsibility and prestige of inside counsel have increased dramatically in recent years.[1]

The consequences of this increased responsibility are twofold. First, societal expectations have risen regarding the role of counsel in the corporate accountability process.[2] Second, there has been a tendency at times to look

---

1. *See* Williams, *The Role of Inside Counsel in Corporate Accountability,* [1979-1980 Transfer Binder] FED. SEC. L. REP. (CCH) ¶ 82,318, at 82,369 (Oct. 4, 1979) (hereinafter cited as Williams).

2. As stated by Dean Redlich:

> We may sometimes resent the fact that the public is pointing to the lawyers and holding us responsible for many of the moral shortcomings of the country, but there is no way that the legal profession can avoid bearing this burden. We play too crucial a role in government and corporate life to avoid this responsibility. . . .
>
> It is both our burden and our glory that we are expected to live by a high professional standard and earn a living at the same time. We do not have the luxury of the clergy who can live in the temple and condemn the market place. Nor do we have the more flexible standard of those who live solely in the market place. We have to carry the standards of the temple into the market place and practice our trade there. That is why a country which questions its moral behavior inevitably questions its lawyers.

Redlich, *Lawyers, the Temple and the Market Place,* 30 BUS. LAW. 65 (1975).

to the federal government to set appropriate standards of professional conduct. Examples of such federal involvement include the Ethics in Government
Act of 1978,[3] the debate on Rule 2(e) of the SEC's Rules of Practice,[4] the
rulemaking petition submitted by the Institute for Public Representation,[5]

---

3. Pub. L. 95-521, 18 U.S.C. §§ 207 et seq.

4. See, e.g., Touche Ross & Co. v. SEC, 609 F.2d 570 (2d Cir. 1979); In the Matter of
Carter and Johnson, Securities Exchange Act Release No. 17597, [1981 Transfer Binder] FED.
SEC. L. REP. (CCH) ¶ 82,847 (March 17, 1981); In re Keating, Muething & Klekamp, Securities
Exchange Act Release No. 15982, [1979–1980 Transfer Binder] FED. SEC. L. REP. (CCH)
¶ 82,124 (July 2, 1979). For law review articles that enter this Rule 2(e) debate, see, e.g.,
Downing & Miller, The Distortion and Misuse of Rule 2(e), 54 NOTRE DAME LAW. 774 (1979);
Gruenbaum, Client's Frauds and Their Lawyers' Obligations, 68 GEO. L.J. 191 (1979); Johnson,
The Expanding Responsibilities of Attorneys in Practice Before the SEC: Disciplinary Proceedings Under Rule 2(e) of the Commission's Rules of Practice, 25 MERCER L. REV. 637
(1974); Kramer, Clients' Frauds and Their Lawyers' Obligations: A Study in Professional
Irresponsibility, 67 GEO. L.J. 991 (1979); Comment, Reassessing the Validity of SEC Rule
2(e) Discipline of Accountants, 39 B.U.L. REV. 968 (1979); Comment, SEC Disciplinary Rules
and the Federal Securities Laws: The Regulation, Role and Responsibilities of the Attorney,
1972 DUKE L.J. 969; Comment, Attorney Liability Under SEC Rule 2(e): A New Standard?
11 TEX. TECH L. REV. 83 (1979); Note, SEC Disciplinary Proceedings, 5 J. CORP. LAW 433
(1980).

5. On July 25, 1978, the Commission requested public comments on the petition, without
taking any position on the merits of the proposal. Securities Exchange Act Release No. 16045,
15 SEC DOCKET 1376 (July 25, 1979). In general terms, the petition would have required
disclosure of certain information regarding the relationships between registrants and their
attorneys as well as disclosure regarding resignations and dismissals of any securities attorney
or general counsel of a registrant. In addition, the proposal would have required disclosure
by each registrant of certification by the board of directors that it has instructed all attorneys
employed or retained by the corporation to report to the board certain corporate activities
discovered by counsel, which, in counsel's opinion, violate or probably violate the law.

On April 30, 1980, the Commission denied the petition. In so acting, the Commission stated:

> The Commission believes that companies and the legal profession currently are de-
> voting considerable attention to many of the issues raised in the Institute's petition. The
> business community is focusing on the role and responsibilities of the board of directors,
> including problems relating to information flow to the board. Moreover, the American
> Bar Association and its Commission on Evaluation of Professional Standards is ad-
> dressing issues of professional responsibility related to the petition. For example, that
> Commission is holding public hearings on its Discussion Draft of Model Rules of
> Professional Conduct which deals with the issue of when a lawyer, in, or for, an
> organization should refer a matter to a higher authority.
>
> In light of the concerns expressed by the commentators, particularly with respect to
> the impracticability of the proposal and its effect on attorney-client relationships, and
> the initiatives in this area being taken by the legal profession and the business community,
> the Commission does not believe it would be appropriate, at this time, to consider
> further the rules proposed by the Institute. Moreover, to modify the proposals sufficiently
> to meet the practical problems identified above, assuming it is possible, would require
> a significant amount of staff time and effort. As you know, the Commission's staff
> resources are greatly limited and are being devoted at present to other projects. The

and the introduction in Congress of the Corporation Democracy Act of 1980.[6]

As a result of both the increased role of inside counsel and the consequences deriving therefrom, inside counsel is confronted with a number of complex questions. These questions may be divided into five general subject areas: (1) who is inside counsel's client, (2) counsel's role as an adviser as opposed to an advocate, (3) counsel's general duty to inquire and to offer advice, (4) counsel's obligation to take appropriate action when a corporate fraud or crime is discovered, and (5) the propriety of inside counsel serving as a director to the corporation.

Before reaching these specific questions, it should be acknowledged that inside counsel, because he is employed and receives his entire compensation from the corporate entity, is in a different posture from outside counsel. In reality, there can be little doubt that when inside counsel discloses his client's fraud or takes other action that questions the client's integrity, he is taking a greater risk in losing the means to his livelihood than outside counsel. At worst, outside counsel may be deprived of a single client, but inside counsel may, in the end, have to find another job.[7]

Nevertheless, it should be recognized that the inside counsel to a corporation is a member of the bar and must therefore adhere to the profession's responsibilities and obligations. In this regard, inside counsel's adherence to his professional obligations are not lessened by the fact of his employee status. Although this may seem somewhat harsh, it should be remembered that inside counsel is bound by the duties and obligations that go along with the privilege of being an attorney.[8]

Commission will continue to monitor developments in this area and will, of course, bring enforcement actions or disciplinary proceedings in appropriate cases.

Securities Exchange Act Release No. 16769, 19 SEC DOCKET 1300 (April 30, 1980). For further discussion herein on this subject, *see* pages 62-63 *supra*.

6. H.R. 7010, 96th Cong., 2d Sess. (1980). Another such bill, the Protection of Shareholders' Rights Act of 1980, S. 2567, 96th Cong., 2d Sess. (1980), introduced by Senator Metzenbaum, had comparable provisions. *See* SEC. REG. & L. REP. (BNA) No. 550, F-1 (April 23, 1980). Pertinent provisions of these bills, if enacted, would have required that a majority of a corporation's board be composed of independent directors, that the audit and nominating committees be composed solely of independent directors, that each director has a "duty of loyalty" and a "duty of care" to the corporation and its shareholders, that cumulative voting be required, that shareholders be entitled to vote on major corporate transactions, and that extensive disclosure be required in regard to such matters as employment discrimination, compliance with environmental controls, tax rates, cost of legal and accounting fees, and planned plant closings. For further discussion herein on this subject, *see* pages 21-22 *supra*.

7. *See* Hershman, *Special Problems of Inside Counsel for Financial Institutions*, 33 BUS. LAW. 1435, 1436 (1978).

8. *See* Forrow, *The Corporate Law Department Lawyer—Counsel to the Entity*, 34 BUS. LAW. 1797, 1804 (1979); Williams, *Corporate Accountability and the Lawyer's Role*, 34 BUS. LAW. 7, 13 (1978).

II. WHO IS INSIDE COUNSEL'S CLIENT?

The American Bar Association's rules of professional conduct provide that "[a] lawyer employed or retained by a corporation or similar entity, owes his allegiance to the entity and not to a stockholder, director, officer, employee, representative or other person connected with the entity." In any particular situation, however, this guideline may be less than helpful. Some commentators have advocated that inside counsel owes his primary allegiance to management or to the corporation's board of directors.[9] Such a conclusion, however, should not be reached in a number of situations. This point is well illustrated by the Fifth Circuit's decision in *Garner v. Wolfinbarger*.[10] That case involved a shareholder derivative suit where the corporation sought to invoke the attorney-client privilege in order to preclude the shareholders from obtaining the requested documents. In holding that the corporation could not invoke the attorney-client privilege, the Fifth Circuit stated:

> It must be borne in mind that management does not manage for itself, and that the beneficiaries of its actions are the stockholders. Conceptualistic phrases describing the corporation as an entity separate from its stockholders are not useful tools of analysis. They serve only to obscure the fact that management has duties which run to the benefit ultimately of stockholders. There may be situations in which the corporate entity or its management, or both, have interests adverse to those of some or all its stockholders. And when all is said and done, management is not managing for itself.[11]

The end result is that there are no easy answers to this question. It appears that inside counsel should take into account a number of factors, such as,

---

9. *See, e.g.,* Taylor, *The Role of Corporate Counsel,* 32 RUTGERS L. REV. 237, 241-245 (1979).

10. 430 F.2d 1093 (5th Cir. 1970).

11. *Id.* at 1101. *See* Valente v. Pepsico, Inc., 68 F.R.D. 361, 367-368 (D. Del. 1975); Bailey v. Meister Brau, Inc., 55 F.R.D. 211, 213-214 (N.D. Ill. 1972). As stated by the district court in *Valente, Garner* and *Bailey* "stand generally for the proposition that where a corporation seeks advice from legal counsel, and the information relates to the subject of a later suit by a minority shareholder in the corporation, the corporation is not entitled to claim the privilege as against its own shareholder, absent some special cause." Valente v. Pepsico, Inc., *supra,* at 367. The basis of those decisions, according to the *Valente* court, "rest[ed] in each case on the understanding that a corporation is, at least in part, the association of its shareholders, and it owes to them a fiduciary obligation which is stronger than the societal policy favoring privileged communications." *Id.* at 367-368. *See also* Garrett, SEC. REG. & L. REP. (BNA) No. 223, A-16 (Oct. 17, 1973) (general counsel's responsibilities are owed to the corporation's shareholders as well as to management).

what is best for the corporate entity as a whole, what are the interests of management and the directors in this situation, are management and the directors noninterested or do they have a conflict of interest, what are the interests of the present shareholders of the corporation, are the interests of the future shareholders of the corporation to be considered as well, and, finally, in certain situations, are the interests of the employees of the corporation, and even the community as a whole, to be considered as relevant in inside counsel's determination of the interests of the corporate entity. In other words, it can be argued that the interests of the corporate entity cannot be considered apart from these various, and sometimes far-reaching, considerations which have just been enumerated.

III. ADVOCATE VS. ADVISER—INSIDE COUNSEL AS ADVISER

A. Distinguishing the Roles

The role of an attorney in an advisory role as opposed to an adversary role is fundamentally different. The Code of Professional Responsibility[12] correctly distinguishes between these roles. The Code vests an attorney in an advisory role with much greater discretion to withdraw from representation than one in an advocate's role. Indeed, when a matter is before a tribunal, the disciplinary rules generally permit counsel to withdraw only if permission of the tribunal is obtained.[13] Further, the rules make clear that all permissible doubts in a litigation setting are to be resolved in favor of the client.[14] In the context of the advisory setting, however, the Code provides that counsel may withdraw if his client does not follow the advice rendered. Indeed, withdrawal is permitted even though the client intends to commit no fraud, no crime, and the attorney's continued representation will not breach any of the disciplinary rules.[15] The proposed final draft of the ABA's

---

12. ABA Code of Professional Responsibility (as amended Aug. 1977).

13. *See* DR 2-110(B), DR 2-110(C); EC 7-8.

14. *See* EC 7-4 which permits counsel to "urge any permissible construction of the law favorable to his client, without regard to his professional opinion as to the likelihood that the construction will ultimately prevail." As an advocate, counsel's "conduct is within the bounds of the law, and therefore permissible, if the position taken is supported by the law or is supportable by a good faith argument for an extension, modification, or reversal of the law." *Id.*

15. *See* EC 7-8 which provides:

> A lawyer should exert his best efforts to insure that decisions of his client are made only after the client has been informed of relevant considerations. A lawyer ought to initiate this decision-making process if the client does not do so. Advice of a lawyer to his client need not be confined to purely legal considerations. A lawyer should advise his client of the possible effect of each legal alternative. A lawyer should bring to bear

Model Rules of Professional Conduct similarly distinguishes between the role of an attorney acting as adviser rather than advocate.[16]

The reason for this distinction is fairly clear. In an advocate setting an attorney is dealing with past conduct, while in an advisory setting counsel is concerned with present or contemplated conduct. As such, counsel in the advisory setting has a much greater role in shaping the future course of his client's conduct. Former Chairman Williams had occasion to comment on the different roles of counsel as advocate versus adviser:

> As an advocate—*e.g.*, in the courtroom—except in unusual situations, [the lawyer's] job is to vindicate the client's position, to justify what the client did in the past or wishes to do in the future. In the adviser capacity, however, the lawyer's role is different. It is there that he has the opportunity to bring considerations of both ethics and law to bear on the corporation's future conduct.[17]

---

upon this decision-making process the fullness of his experience as well as his objective viewpoint. In assisting his client to reach a proper decision, it is often desirable for a lawyer to point out those factors which may lead to a decision that is morally just as well as legally permissible. He may emphasize the possibility of harsh consequences that might result from assertion of legally permissible positions. In the final analysis, however, the lawyer should always remember that the decision whether to forego legally available objectives or methods because of non-legal factors is ultimately for the client and not for himself. In the event that the client in a non-adjudicatory matter insists upon a course of conduct that is contrary to the judgment and advice of the lawyer but not prohibited by Disciplinary Rules, the lawyer may withdraw from the employment.

Id. See DR 2-110(C)(1)(e).

16. *See, e.g.,* Rule 1.16 of the proposed final draft of the ABA's Commission on Evaluation of Professional Standards on the Model Rules of Professional Conduct (May 30, 1981).

17. Williams, note 8 *supra,* at 13. *See generally* Stone, *The Public Influence of the Bar,* 48 HARV. L. REV. 1 (1934), where the former Chief Justice stated:

> We must remember, nevertheless, that the very conditions which have caused specialization, which have drawn so heavily upon the technical proficiency of the Bar, have likewise placed it in a position where the possibilities of its influence are almost beyond calculation. . . . Without the constant advice and guidance of lawyers business would come to an abrupt halt. And whatever standards of conduct in the performance of its function the Bar consciously adopts must at once be reflected in the character of the world of business and finance. Given a measure of self conscious and cohesive professional unity, the Bar may exert a power more beneficent and farreaching than it or any other non-governmental group has wielded in the past.

Id. at 9-10. *See also* Gruenbaum, *Corporate/Securities Lawyers: Disclosure, Responsibility, and Liability to Investors, and National Student Marketing Corp.,* 54 NOTRE DAME LAW. 795, 800-04 (1979).

B. Advisers Should Consider Relevant Implications

The concept that counsel's role as an adviser should require thorough consideration of the implications of his client's contemplated conduct, including the effect on the investing public, has been recognized by both the courts and the Commission. As succinctly framed by the Second Circuit in *SEC v. Spectrum, Ltd:*[18] "The securities laws provide a myriad of safeguards designed to protect the interests of the investing public. Effective implementation of these safeguards, however, depends in large measure on the members of the bar who serve in an advisory capacity to those engaged in securities transactions."[19] This theme has been reiterated by the Commission on a number of occasions. In *In re Emanuel Fields,*[20] the Commission stated:

> Very little of a securities lawyer's work is adversary in character. He doesn't work in courtrooms where the pressure of vigilant adversaries and alert judges checks him. He works in his office where he prepares prospectuses, proxy statements, opinions of counsel, and other documents that we, our staff, the financial community, and the investing public must take on faith.[21]

The above commentary aptly illustrates that the attorney's role as adviser is particularly relevant when applied to inside counsel. Normally, inside counsel is rendering advice in the context of present or future contemplated conduct. In this context, the word of approval by inside counsel may frequently constitute the "passkey" by which corporate transactions are con-

---

18. 489 F.2d 535 (2d Cir. 1973).

19. *Id.* at 536. *See* SEC v. Coven, 581 F.2d 1020 (2d Cir. 1978), *cert. denied,* 99 S. Ct. 1432 (1979); SEC v. National Student Marketing, 457 F. Supp. 682 (D.D.C. 1978); Felts v. National Accounting Sys. Assocs., Inc., [1979 Transfer Binder] Fed. Sec. L. Rep. (CCH) ¶ 96,890 (N.D. Miss. 1978).

20. [1972-1973 Transfer Binder] Fed. Sec. L. Rep. (CCH) ¶ 79,407 (1973), *aff'd without opinion,* 495 F.2d 1075 (D.C. Cir. 1974).

21. *Id.* at 83,174-83, 175 n.20. *See In re* Arthur Andersen & Co., [1973-1974 Transfer Binder] Fed. Sec. L. Rep. (CCH) ¶ 79,900 (1974), where the Commission remarked:

> Professionals involved in the disclosure process are in a very real sense representatives of the investing public served by the Commission, and as a result, their dealings with the Commission and its staff must be permeated with candor and full disclosure. It cannot resemble an adversary relationship more appropriate to litigants in court, because the Commission is not an adverse party in this context.

Id. at 84,263. *See also* In the Matter of Carter and Johnson, Securities Exchange Act Release No. 17597, [1981 Transfer Binder] Fed. Sec. L. Rep. (CCH) ¶ 82,847 (March 17, 1981); Gruenbaum, note 17 *supra,* at 802.

summated.[22] Because of this fact, the responsibilities of inside counsel are substantial. Inside counsel should not only counsel by the strict letter of the law but also by the spirit of the law. Moreover, inside counsel should take into regard the effect that the contemplated action will have not only on the corporate entity per se but also on other affected parties. Otherwise, the result may well be that although the corporate entity may benefit in the short run by the contemplated transaction, it will be injured in the long run.[23]

IV. INSIDE COUNSEL'S DUTY TO INQUIRE AND TO OFFER ADVICE

In rendering legal advice, should inside counsel accept the facts as they are presented or, alternatively, does he have a duty to inquire? Implicit in the position of inside counsel to a major corporation is an assumption of responsibility for the substantial legal issues faced by the corporation. Inherent in this responsibility, it appears, is the right and obligation to ascertain the facts essential to the pertinent issues involved in a particular decision-making process. Thus, it seems fairly clear that inside counsel cannot always

---

22. *See generally* Sommer, *The Emerging Responsibilities of the Securities Lawyer,* [1974 Transfer Binder] FED. SEC. L. REP. (CCH) ¶ 79,631, at 83,689:

> In a word, and the word is Professor Morgan Shipman's, the professional judgment of the attorney is often the "pass key" to securities transactions. If he gives an opinion that an exemption is available, securities get sold; if he doesn't give the opinion, they don't get sold. If he judges that certain information must be included in a registration statement, it gets included (unless the client seeks other counsel or the attorney crumbles under the weight of client pressure); if he concludes it need not be included, it doesn't get included.

23. *See* Loeb, *The Corporate Chiefs' New Class,* TIME, April 14, 1980, at 87, where one former general counsel, Irving Shapiro, stated:

> In the past businessmen wore blinders. After hours they would run to their club, play golf with other businessmen, have a martini—and that was about it. They did not see their role as being concerned with public policy issues. In a world where government simply took taxes from you and did not interfere with your operations, maybe that idea was sensible. In today's world it is not.

See also Redlich, *Lawyers, the Temple and the Market Place,* 30 BUS. LAW. note 2 *supra,* at 65-72. *See generally* REPORT OF THE HOUSE OF REPRESENTATIVES SUBCOMM. ON OVERSIGHT AND INVESTIGATION OF THE COMM. ON INTERSTATE AND FOREIGN COMMERCE, No. 95-134, 95th Cong., 1st Sess. (Oct. 1976); REPORT OF THE SENATE SUBCOMM. ON REPORTS, ACCOUNTING AND MANAGEMENT OF THE COMM. ON GOVERNMENT RELATIONS, 94TH CONG., 2D SESS. (Comm. Print, Dec. 1976). For discussion on these Reports, see page 67 n.269 *supra.*

advise on the basis of facts furnished by the corporate manager with whom he deals. In other words, there may be a duty to inquire under some circumstances.[24]

A. Scope of Inquiry

Of course, the next question is what are the proper boundaries of an inside lawyer's duty to inquire in this context. Surely, for instance, inside counsel cannot be expected to conduct a full-fledged investigation whenever he renders a legal opinion. On the other hand, he should not wait for information to trickle his way. At the least, inside counsel should take reasonable steps to be informed of the company's affairs and should not wait for "red flags" to serve as notice for action.[25] As a means of keeping reasonably informed, counsel should texture internal control mechanisms so that at least some issues that may need more detailed attention will surface.[26]

B. Counsel's Role Under the FCPA

The Foreign Corrupt Practices Act (FCPA) serves as an example of the foregoing principles. Under the FCPA, it appears that inside counsel should recommend written policies and procedures and also monitor their implementation for internal control. Such a role is particularly appropriate since the special position occupied by inside counsel enables him to be aware of what constitutes an adequate internal control environment. In like manner, he should also be aware of the specific aspects of the business and personalities that are likely to cause problems in regard to compliance with the FCPA.[27]

---

24. *See* Williams, note 1 *supra,* at 82,371.

25. *Id.* at 82,375. *See* Evans, "Investor Protection and the Securities Bar," before the Securities Law Committee of the Chicago Bar Association, at 11 (May 15, 1980) ("We and the investing public have a right to expect that the securities lawyer acting as adviser, unlike the advocate, will not always accept the facts presented to him but must inquire sufficiently to determine a state of facts which can support his legal opinion").

26. *See* Williams, "Freedom, Free Enterprise and the Accountability Process," before the Banking, Corporation and Business Law Section of the New York State Bar Association, at 20 (Jan. 24, 1980) ("Although not the only officer who deals with corporate problems which are not exclusively related to the profit and revenue producing activities of the corporation, he is one of the few corporate officers who is likely to hear from all of the corporation's internal and external constituencies").

27. *See* Forrow, *The Corporate Law Department Lawyer—Counsel to the Entity,* 34 Bus. Law. 1806 (1979); Williams, note 1 *supra,* at 82,372.

C. Counsel's Duty to Offer Advice

Counsel's duty to stay reasonably informed is closely related to another concept—that is, the duty to offer advice irrespective of whether he is asked to do so. It may well be true that the client's ire will be aroused by gratuitous legal advice. Nonetheless, when a client contemplates conduct that the lawyer knows has a substantial likelihood of causing serious legal consequences, counsel may well have a duty to warn the client regarding the legal implications of the proposed conduct.[28] Moreover, this concept has the beneficial aspect of enabling the client to confront legal problems through preventive counseling.[29]

V. INSIDE COUNSEL'S RESPONSIBILITIES UPON DISCOVERING A CLIENT'S FRAUD OR CRIME

Perhaps the most controversial area of attorney responsibility is the extent of the attorney's obligation to take appropriate action upon learning of his client's fraud or crime. Predictably, a plethora of legal literature has been written on this subject.[30] In addition, the district court's opinion in *National Student Marketing*,[31] as well as the Commission's decision in the *Carter-Johnson* case,[32] lend guidance.

---

28. *See generally* discussion draft of the ABA's Commission on Evaluation of Professional Standards on the Model Rules of Professional Conduct, Rule 2.4 (Jan. 30, 1980), which provides: "A lawyer who knows that a client contemplates a course of action which has a substantial likelihood of serious legal consequences shall warn the client of the legal implications of the conduct, unless a client has expressly or by implication asked not to receive such advice."

29. *See* Taylor, *The Role of Corporate Counsel,* 32 RUTGERS L. REV. 245-50 (1979); Williams, note 1 *supra,* at 82,375-76.

30. *See, e.g.,* authorities cited in note 4 *supra.*

31. 457 F. Supp. 682 (D.D.C. 1978).

32. Securities Exchange Act Release No. 17597, [1981 Transfer Binder] FED. SEC. L. REP. (CCH) ¶ 82,847 (March 17, 1981). In that Rule 2(e) proceeding, two attorneys were charged with having violated, and having aided and abetted violations of, the antifraud provisions of the Securities Exchange Act in connection with their representation of National Telephone Co. After a full hearing on the merits, Administrative Law Judge Tracy found that the attorney respondents "(a) assisted management in its efforts to conceal material facts concerning its financial condition; and (b) failed to inform the board of directors concerning management's unwillingness to make such disclosures." [1979 Transfer Binder] FED. SEC. L. REP. (CCH) ¶ 82,175, at 82,169 (1979). The Commission granted the petition filed by the respondents pursuant to Section 17 of the Commission's Rules of Practice, 17 C.F.R. § 201.17, and in a separate order advised the public and the bar that the Commission would permit the filing of *amicus curiae* briefs on the legal and policy issues involved in the proceeding (six such briefs were filed). Subsequently, the Commission reversed the findings of the Administrative Law Judge.

A. ABA Proposed Final Draft

The proposed final draft (of the ABA's Commission on Evaluation of Professional Standards) on the Model Rules of Professional Conduct[33] deals with counsel's obligation to seek higher authority. Perhaps the most pertinent rule is 1.13 which provides, in relevant part, that if the lawyer for an organization knows that an officer, employee, or other person associated with that organization is engaged in, intends to engage in, or fails to act "in a matter related to the representation that is a violation of a legal obligation to the organization, or a violation of law which reasonably might be imputed to the organization, and is likely to result in material injury to the organization, the lawyer shall proceed as is reasonably necessary in the best interest of the organization." The rule provides that the measures taken by counsel shall be designed to minimize disruption and the risk of disclosing confidences. Such measures may include:

1. Asking reconsideration of the matter;

2. Advising that a separate legal opinion on the matter be sought for presentation to appropriate authority in the organization; and

3. Referring the matter to higher authority in the organization, including, if warranted by the seriousness of the matter, referral to the highest authority that can act in behalf of the organization as determined by applicable law.

The rule thereafter states that if despite counsel's efforts to remedy the situation, the highest authority that can act on behalf of the organization insists upon action or refuses to act, and such action or refusal thereto is clearly a violation of a legal obligation to the organization and is likely to result in substantial injury to the organization, then counsel may take further remedial action. The rule expressly provides, however, that disclosure of information relating to the representation is permitted only if counsel reasonably believes that:

1. The highest authority in the organization has acted to further the personal or financial interests of members of that authority which are in conflict with the interests of the organization; and

2. Revealing the information is necessary in the best interest of the organization.[34]

---

33. *See* note 16 *supra.*

34. Rule 1.13 of the discussion draft did not contain these conditions. The provision stated that, under such circumstances, counsel may disclose client confidences to the extent necessary, if counsel reasonably believes that such action is in the best interests of the organization. ABA discussion draft, note 28 *supra.* This provision was in marked contrast to an even earlier draft which required "the lawyer [to] take further measures necessary to prevent the violation, including giving notice to the injured persons, making the lawyer's resignation known publicly, or reporting the matter to appropriate regulatory authority." *Text of Initial Draft of Ethics Code Rewrite Committee,* Legal Times (Wash.), Aug. 27, 1979, at 33, Rule 1.13(b).

Thus, Rule 1.13 of the ABA proposed final draft places a number of conditions on corporate counsel's authority to report the client's fraud to the SEC or other appropriate official. Moreover, the rule does not extend to third persons. In this regard, however, Rule 1.6(b) implicitly recognizes the severe consequences that can be visited upon such persons. The rule vests counsel with discretion to disclose information to the extent believed necessary "[t]o prevent the client from committing a criminal or fraudulent act that the lawyer believes is likely to result in . . . substantial injury to the

---

As this book was in the proofing process, the ABA's House of Delegates approved substantial revisions to Rule 1.13. As revised, Rule 1.13 provides:

(a) A lawyer employed or retained by an organization represents the organization, including its directors, officers, employees, members, shareholders or other constituents, as a group, except where the interests of any one or more of the group may be adverse to the organization's interest.

(b) If a lawyer for an organization knows that an officer, employee or other person associated with the organization is engaged in action, intends to act or refuses to act in a matter related to the representation that is a violation of a legal obligation to the organization, or a violation of law which reasonably might be imputed to the organization, and is likely to result in substantial injury to the organization, the lawyer shall proceed as is reasonably necessary in the best interest of the organization. In determining how to proceed, the lawyer shall give due consideration to the seriousness of the violation and its consequences, the scope and nature of the lawyer's representation, the responsibility in the organization and the apparent motivation of the person involved, the policies of the organization concerning such matters and any other relevant considerations. Any measures taken shall be designed to minimize disruption of the organization and the risk of revealing information relating to the representation to persons outside the organization. Such measures may include among others: (1) asking reconsideration of the matter; (2) advising that a separate legal opinion on the matter be sought for presentation to appropriate authority in the organization; and (3) referring the matter to higher authority in the organization, including, if warranted by the seriousness of the matter, referral to the highest authority that can act in behalf of the organization as determined by applicable law.

(c) If, despite the lawyer's efforts in accordance with paragraph (b), the highest authority that can act on behalf of the organization insists upon action, or a refusal to act, that is clearly a violation of law and is likely to result in substantial injury to the organization, the lawyer may resign in accordance with Rule 1.16.

(d) In dealing with an organization's directors, officers, employees, members, shareholders or other constituents, a lawyer shall explain the identity of the client when it is apparent that the organization's interests are adverse to those of the constituents with whom the lawyer is dealing.

(e) A lawyer representing an organization may also represent any of its directors, officers, employees, members, shareholders or other constituents, subject to the provisions of Rule 1.7. If the organization's consent to the dual representation is required by Rule 1.7, the consent shall be given by an appropriate official of the organization other than the individual who is to be represented or by the shareholders.

See "ABA House of Delegates Approves Revisions to Proposed Conduct Rules," 15 Sec. Reg. & L. Rep. (BNA) 346 (1983).

financial interest or property of another [or] [t]o rectify the consequences of a client's criminal or fraudulent act in the commission of which the lawyer's services had been used." Significantly, Rule 1.6(b) appears to signify that corporate counsel has greater discretion to disclose information relating to the representation where third persons, rather than the organization itself, is likely to incur substantial injury.[35]

B. In the Matter of Carter and Johnson

For the purpose of this discussion, the two pertinent issues that the Commission addressed in *Carter-Johnson* were (1) whether the respondents had violated Rule 2(e) of the Commission's Rule of Practice[36] by aiding and abetting violations of the federal securities laws and (2) whether they had violated Rule 2(e) by engaging in unethical and improper professional conduct. Turning to the attorneys' liability under an aiding and abetting rationale, the Commission stressed that mere errors in judgment or even carelessness is not a sufficient predicate on which to impose Rule 2(e) liability:

It is axiomatic that a lawyer will not be liable as an aider and abettor merely because his advice, followed by the client, is ultimately determined to be wrong. What is missing in that instance is a wrongful

---

35. *See also* ABA proposed draft Rules 1.2(d) and 4.1(b). Rule 1.2(d) states that "[a] lawyer shall not counsel or assist a client in conduct that the lawyer knows or reasonably should know is criminal or fraudulent." Rule 4.1(b)(2) provides that "[i]n the course of representing a client a lawyer shall not knowingly fail to disclose a fact to a third person when disclosure is necessary to prevent assisting a criminal or fraudulent act, as required by Rule 1.2(d)." For further discussion on this subject herein, *see* pages 62-67 *supra*.

As this book was in the proofing process, the ABA's House of Delegates approved substantial revisions to Rule 1.6(b). As revised, Rule 1.6(b) provides:

(b) A lawyer may reveal such information to the extent the lawyer reasonably believes necessary: (1) to prevent the client from committing a criminal act that the lawyer believes is likely to result in imminent death or substantial bodily harm; or (2) to establish a claim or defense on behalf of the lawyer in a controversy between the lawyer and the client, to establish a defense to a criminal charge or civil claim against the lawyer based upon conduct in which the client was involved, or to respond to the client's allegations in any legal proceeding concerning the lawyer's professional conduct for the client.

See "ABA House of Delegates Approves Revisions to Proposed Conduct Rules," 15 Sec. Reg. & Rep. (BNA) 346 (1983).

36. Rule 2(e), 17 C.F.R. § 201.2(e)(1), authorizes the Commission to deny, temporarily or permanently, the privilege of appearing or practicing before it in any way to any person, including an attorney, who is found by the Commission "(i) not to possess the requisite qualifications to represent others, or (ii) to be lacking in character or integrity or to have engaged in unethical or improper professional conduct, or (iii) to have willfully violated, or willfully aided and abetted the violations of any provisions of the Federal securities laws . . . or the rules and regulations thereunder."

intent on the part of the lawyer. It is that element of intent which provides the basis for distinguishing between those professionals who may be appropriately considered as subjects of professional discipline and those who, acting in good faith, have merely made errors of judgment or have been careless.

Significant public benefits flow from the effective performance of the securities lawyer's role. The exercise of independent, careful and informed legal judgment on difficult issues is critical to the flow of material information to the securities markets. Moreover, we are aware of the difficulties and limitations attendant upon that role. In the course of rendering securities law advice, the lawyer is called upon to make difficult judgments, often under great pressure and in areas where the legal signposts are far apart and only faintly discernible.[37]

Turning next to the Administrative Law Judge's finding that the respondents had violated Rule 2(e) by engaging in unethical and improper professional conduct, the Commission reversed.[38] The Commission then focused on the lawyer's professional obligations when he gives essentially correct disclosure advice to a client but the client does not follow such advice, and as a consequence, violates the federal securities laws. After discussing from a general perspective the lawyer's responsibility in this context, the Commission formulated the following standard:

The Commission is of the view that a lawyer engages in "unethical or improper professional conduct" under the following circumstances: When a lawyer with significant responsibilities in the effectuation of a company's compliance with the disclosure requirements of the federal securities law becomes aware that his client is engaged in a substantial and continuing failure to satisfy those disclosure requirements, his continued participation violates professional standards unless he takes prompt steps to end the client's noncompliance. . . . [39]

---

37. FED. SEC. L. REP. (CCH) ¶ 82,847, at 84,167. The Commission concluded that, although "it is a close question," there was not a sufficient basis for upholding the respondents' liability as aiders and abettors. *Id.* at 84,167-69.

38. *Id.* at 84,169-73.

39. *Id.* at 84,172. Elaborating, the Commission stated:

We do not imply that a lawyer is obliged, at the risk of being held to have violated Rule 2(e), to seek to correct every isolated disclosure action or inaction which he believes to be at variance with applicable disclosure standards, although there may be isolated disclosure failures that are so serious that their correction becomes a matter of primary professional concern. It is also clear, however, that a lawyer is not privileged to unthinkingly permit himself to be co-opted into an ongoing fraud and cast as a dupe or a shield for a wrongdoing client.

Thus, while declining to discipline the respondent attorneys, the Commission set forth a standard for ethical conduct that had prospective application.[40] In that decision, the Commission also stated that it intended to solicit public comment in regard to the standard adopted[41] which it subsequently did.[42]

Initially, counselling accurate disclosure is sufficient, even if his advice is not accepted. But there comes a point at which a reasonable lawyer must conclude that his advice is not being followed, or even sought in good faith, and that his client is involved in a continuing course of violating the securities laws. At this critical juncture, the lawyer must take further, more affirmative steps in order to avoid the inference that he has been co-opted, willfully or unwillfully, into the scheme of non-disclosure.

The lawyer is in the best position to choose his next step. Resignation is one option, although we recognize that other considerations, including the protection of the client against foreseeable prejudice, must be taken into account in the case of withdrawal. A direct approach to the board of directors or one or more individual directors or officers may be appropriate; or he may choose to try to enlist the aid of other members of the firm's management. What is required, in short, is some prompt action that leads to the conclusion that the lawyer is engaged in efforts to correct the underlying problem, rather than having capitulated to the desires of a strong-willed, but misguided client.

Some have argued that resignation is the only permissible course when a client chooses not to comply with disclosure advice. We do not agree. Premature resignation serves neither the end of an effective lawyer-client relationship nor, in most cases, the effective administration of the securities laws. The lawyer's continued interaction with his client will ordinarily hold the greatest promise of corrective action. So long as a lawyer is acting in good faith and exerting reasonable efforts to prevent violations of the law by his client, his professional obligations have been met. In general, the best result is that which promotes the continued, strong-minded and independent participation by the lawyer. We recognize, however, that the "best result" is not always obtainable, and that there may occur situations where the lawyer must conclude that the misconduct is so extreme or irretrievable, or the involvement of his client's management and board of directors in the misconduct is so thoroughgoing and pervasive that any action short of resignation would be rare and of an egregious nature.

Id. at 84,172-73. In a separate opinion, Commissioner Evans concurred with the dismissal of charges against Johnson but contended that Carter was an aider and abettor of National's violations relating to the Form 8-K for December 1974 that was filed in January 1975 and the December 20, 1974 press release. In addition, Commissioner Evans took issue with the majority's method of articulating professional standards to be applied by the Commission in the future. *Id.* at 84,173-78.

    40. *Id.* at 84,172 ("The Commission has determined that this interpretation will be applicable only to conduct occurring after the date of this opinion").

    41. *Id.* at 84,170 ("The Commission intends to issue a release soliciting comment from the public as to whether this interpretation should be expanded or modified").

    42. Securities Act Release No. 6344, [1981-1982 Transfer Binder] FED. SEC. L. REP. (CCH) ¶ 83,026 (Sept. 21, 1981). After issuing the release soliciting public comment, the Commission at this time has taken no further action. For further discussion herein on *Carter-Johnson* and subsequent Commission action, *see* pages 62-67 *supra.*

C. Rule 1.13 as Client Discovery Mechanism

As a general proposition, Rule 1.13 may be useful as a client discovery mechanism. The rule recognizes that although management runs the affairs of the corporation on a day-to-day basis, the highest authority within the corporate structure is generally viewed as the board of directors.[43] When a particular matter assumes sufficient significance, it may well be counsel's duty to refer the matter to the board. The rule implicitly acknowledges, moreover, that situations may arise when the board fails to act in the best interests of the shareholders and the corporation.[44] Examples include where the directors have conflicts of interest or other disabilities[45] or where a receiver has been appointed.[46] In such situations, counsel should recognize that his responsibilities may well extend to the shareholders of the corporation.[47]

VI. THE PROPRIETY OF INSIDE COUNSEL AS DIRECTOR

The last issue that will be addressed is the propriety of inside counsel to sit on the corporation's board of directors. The ABA proposed final draft

---

43. *See generally* Burks v. Lasker, 441 U.S. 471, 477-78 (1979); Santa Fe Indus., Inc. v. Green, 430 U.S. 462, 479 (1979); Cort v. Ash, 422 U.S. 66, 84 (1975).

44. *See* Commentary to Rule 1.13, note 16 *supra*, at 93 ("where the board's conduct is motivated by the personal interests of its members, an assumption that the organization has made an informed decision in the matter may be untenable"). *See also* notes 33-34 and accompanying text *supra*.

45. *See generally* Healey v. Catalyst Recovery of Pa., Inc., 616 F.2d 641 (3d Cir. 1980); Alabama Farm Bureau Mut. Cas. Co., Inc. v. American Fidelity Life Ins. Co., 606 F.2d 602 (5th Cir. 1979); Kidwell *ex rel.* Penfold v. Meikle, 597 F.2d 1273 (9th Cir. 1979); Goldberg v. Meridor, 567 F.2d 209 (2d Cir. 1977); Wright v. Heizer Corp., 560 F.2d 236 (7th Cir. 1977); Shoenbaum v. Firstbrook, 405 F.2d. 215 (2d Cir. 1968); Pappas v. Moss, 393 F.2d 865 (2d Cir. 1968); Ruckle v. Roto Am. Corp., 339 F.2d 24 (2d Cir. 1964).

46. *See generally* SEC v. Investors Sec. Corp., 510 F.2d 561 (3d Cir. 1977); SEC v. Charles Plohn & Co., 448 F.2d 1167 (2d Cir. 1970); SEC v. Bowler, 427 F.2d 190 (4th Cir. 1970).

47. *See generally* Felts v. National Accounting Sys. Ass'ns., Inc., [1979 Transfer Binder] Fed. Sec. L. Rep. (CCH) ¶ 96,890 (N.D. Miss. 1978), where the court stated:

> The legal services performed or which should have been performed by [the lawyer] were undertaken not only for the benefit of the issuer but also, under the securities laws, for the benefit of the purchasers of securities. The plaintiffs here were foreseeable and intended third-party beneficiaries of [the lawyer's] legal services and skill. It was foreseeable (and, indeed, known) to [the lawyer] and [the issuer] that the plaintiffs and all purchasers of these securities would rely on him. [The lawyer] voluntarily assumed a relationship not only with [the issuer] but also with the purchasers of these securities. The law and public policy require that the attorney exercise his position of trust and superior knowledge responsibly so as not to adversely affect persons whose rights and interests are certain and foreseeable. [The lawyer's] duty to these plaintiffs was breached by his reckless and grossly negligent conduct.

Id. at 95,520.

generally provides that inside counsel may sit on the corporate board if there is no serious risk of conflict between the lawyer's responsibilities as counsel and those as director.[48] A number of authorities apparently disagree with this provision.[49] They argue that inside counsel's status as director constitutes an *inherent* conflict between his independent status as counsel to the corporation, which calls for the need of professional legal judgment, and that of an inside director, which involves a very different set of duties and responsibilities. Indeed, it is plausible that the lawyer-director may more than infrequently have to pass on questions regarding the legality of the board of directors' conduct.[50]

Apart from this concern is the possibility that counsel's position on the board of directors may raise attorney-client problems. Indeed, from a practical standpoint, this issue has raised great concern among a number of corporations. A finding that inside counsel acted as director, rather than counsel, will render inapplicable the viability of the attorney-client privilege.[51] Because of this possibility, corporate counsel should be careful not to place his employer-client in a position from which it cannot defend its communications with counsel. Perhaps the best solution is for counsel to attend all the board meetings and participate as appropriate only in the role of counsel. This way, counsel keeps informed and the board has the benefit of his advice, but without the burdens carried by a directorship.[52]

---

48. *See* commentary to Rule 1.7, note 16 *supra*, at 50.

49. *See, e.g.,* Hershman, note 49 *supra*, at 1439-40; Riger, *The Lawyer-Director—"A Vexing Problem,"* 33 Bus. Law. 2381 (1978); Williams, note 1 *supra*, at 82,374-75. *But see* Nelson & Moses, *Lawyers Still Taking Directorships with Clients*, Legal Times (Wash.), July 21, 1980, at 1.

50. *See Shareholder Communications, Shareholder Participation in the Corporate Electoral Process and Corporate Governance Generally*, Securities Exchange Act Release No. 15384 (Dec. 6, 1978), SEC Docket 348, 354 (Dec. 19, 1978), wherein the Commission noted "the inherent conflicts faced by lawyers who serve both as directors and as counsel to corporations." *See* authorities cited in note 49 *supra*.

51. *See* Hershman, note 49 *supra*, at 1440. Also, serving in dual roles may increase counsel's exposure to liability. As Hershman points out, "as a director, the General Counsel is likely to be held to a higher standard of care than other directors because of his unique access to information and expertise; as the court pointed out in *Escott v. BarChris* [283 F. Supp. 643, 687 (S.D.N.Y. 1968)] with respect to the culpability of BarChris inside counsel on account of action taken by him after his election to the Board." *Id. See* Riger, note 49 *supra*, at 2383. Such a conclusion appears to be supported by the SEC's recent promulgation of Rule 176, 17 C.F.R. § 230.176 (1982), which provides that "the presence or absence of another relationship to the issuer when the person is a director or proposed director" is a factor to be taken into account in determining whether the subject party has fulfilled its due diligence responsibilities pursuant to Section 11.

52. *See* Williams, note 1 *supra*, at 82,375.

VII. INSIDE COUNSEL AS A SHAPER
OF CORPORATE CONDUCT

In conclusion, a number of additional points will be proffered. First, because inside counsel plays a vital part in the shaping of corporate policy, he has a distinct advantage over outside counsel in the advisory role. On the other hand, ethical problems surely will arise if corporate management expects inside counsel to be a team supporter of corporate policies at all times. As was discussed previously, inside counsel's professional responsibilities are not diminished, nor should his judgment be obscured, by the fact that he is a corporate employee. In this respect, he should continue to exercise independent professional judgment, even when such judgment is contrary to the prevailing thinking of either corporate management or the board. Hence, the advantage inside counsel possesses, unlike that of outside counsel, is that he is in a better position to shape the events as they occur in determining corporate policies and standards for conduct. Counsel has this advantage because he is on the scene and in daily contact with corporate management. As a final general caveat, as long as inside counsel does not assist the corporate client in fraudulent or illegal conduct, he should not feel obligated to resign. Rather, his energies should be channeled into advising and prompting corporate management and the board of directors to engage in conduct that is both legal and ethical.

8

Conclusion

This book has examined many of the difficult corporate and securities law issues that impact on corporate internal affairs. Although the subjects addressed are quite diverse, there are important themes that they share.

One such theme is the relationship between state corporation and federal securities law. As discussed earlier, prior to recent Supreme Court decisions which have narrowed the scope of the federal securities laws, the federal courts actively sought to vindicate shareholder rights[1] while the state courts were engaged in a "race for the bottom."[2] After such decisions as *Santa Fe*[3] and *Burks*,[4] however, some state courts, particularly in Delaware, have responded by providing significant safeguards for shareholders.[5] Perhaps this intriguing interplay between fiduciary duties under state law and federal disclosure obligations is best exemplified by *Santa Fe* and its progeny. Under the post-*Santa Fe* framework, as seen by recent federal and state court decisions, it is by showing that a potential state court action would have

---

1. *See, e.g.,* Affiliated Ute Citizens v. United States, 406 U.S. 128 (1972); Superintendent of Ins. v. Bankers Life & Cas. Co., 404 U.S. 6 (1971); SEC v. Geon Indus., Inc., 531 F.2d 39 (2d Cir. 1976); SEC v. Texas Gulf Sulphur Co., 401 F.2d 833 (2d Cir. 1968) (*en banc*), *cert. denied,* 394 U.S. 976 (1969); McClure v. Borne Chem. Co., 292 F.2d 824 (3d Cir.), *cert. denied,* 368 U.S. 939 (1961).

2. *See, e.g.,* Cary, *Federalism and Corporate Law: Reflections Upon Delaware,* 83 YALE L.J. 663 (1974).

3. 430 U.S. 462 (1977).

4. 441 U.S. 471 (1979).

5. *See, e.g.,* Zapata Corp. v. Maldonado, 430 A.2d 779 (Del. 1981); Perl v. IU Int'l Corp., 607 P.2d 1036 (Hawaii 1980); Gabhart v. Gabhart, 267 Ind. 377, 370 N.E.2d 345 (1977); Singer v. Magnavox Co., 380 A.2d 969 (Del. 1979).

existed for breach of fiduciary duty that a federal cause of action for disclosure violations will arise.[6]

Another common theme is the extent to which the business judgment rule is being construed by courts to uphold the validity of actions taken by management. While some courts interpret the rule broadly,[7] others appear to be reexamining the doctrine.[8] For example, certain courts, particularly in the special litigation committee, *Santa Fe-Goldberg*, and tender offer contexts, have declined to apply rigorously the business judgment rule.[9] Whether these decisions reflect merely minor exceptions to the general broad application of the doctrine or a more fundamental rethinking of its propriety in given contexts is an issue that must await further judicial clarification.

Moreover, while some of the subjects addressed herein apply to only a particular context, others conceivably extend to any corporate-related transaction. In a book concerning corporate internal affairs, such a broad scope is necessarily required. A significant unifying theme, however, is the application of important principles of corporation-securities law in a number of different settings. Such an application focuses on the extent to which courts are construing these principles to protect corporate, shareholder, and other interests.

In sum, the book has attempted to focus, from a corporate and securities law perspective, on many of the recurrent and perplexing issues that confront corporations and their counsel. In this regard, the subjects addressed extend beyond the theme of corporate accountability and governance to encompass the much broader concept of corporate internal affairs. Hopefully, the analysis provided herein will serve as a useful framework for assessing these significant issues.

---

6. *See, e.g.,* Healey v. Catalyst Recovery, Inc., 616 F.2d 641 (3d Cir. 1980); Alabama Farm Bureau Mut. Cas. Co. v. American Fidelity Life Ins. Co., 606 F.2d 602 (5th Cir. 1979), *cert. denied,* 446 U.S. 933 (1980); Kidwell v. Meikle, 597 F.2d 1273 (9th Cir. 1979); Goldberg v. Meridor, 567 F.2d 209 (2d Cir. 1977), *cert. denied,* 434 U.S. 1069 (1978); Wright v. Heizer Corp., 560 F.2d 236 (7th Cir. 1977), *cert. denied,* 434 U.S. 1066 (1978). *See also* United States v. Margala, [1981-1982 Transfer Binder] FED. SEC. L. REP. (CCH) ¶ 98,363 (9th Cir. 1981).

7. *See, e.g.,* Panter v. Marshall Field & Co., 646 F.2d 271 (7th Cir.), *cert. denied,* 102 S. Ct. 658 (1981); Gaines v. Haughton, 645 F.2d 761 (9th Cir. 1981), *cert. denied,* 102 S. Ct. 1006 (1982); Treadway Cos. v. Care Corp., 638 F.2d 357 (2d Cir. 1980); Lewis v. Anderson, 615 F.2d 778 (9th Cir. 1979), *cert. denied,* 101 S. Ct. 206 (1980); Berman v. Gerber Products, Co., 454 F. Supp. 1310 (W.D. Mich. 1978); Auerbach v. Bennett, 47 N.Y.2d 619, 393 N.E. 2d 994, 419 N.Y.S.2d 920 (1979).

8. *See, e.g.,* Mobil Corp. v. Marathon Oil Co., 669 F.2d 366 (6th Cir. 1981); Conoco Inc. v. Seagram Company Ltd., 517 F. Supp. 1299 (S.D.N.Y. 1981); Joseph E. Seagram & Sons, Inc. v. Abrams, 510 F. Supp. 860 (S.D.N.Y. 1981); Abella v. Universal Leaf Tobacco, Inc., 495 F. Supp. 713 (E.D. Va. 1980); Maher v. Zapata Corp., 490 F. Supp. 348 (S.D. Tex. 1980); Zapata Corp. v. Maldonado, 430 A.2d 779 (Del. 1981); Singer v. Magnavox Co., 380 A.2d 969 (Del. 1977).

9. *See* cases cited in note 8 *supra.*

Bibliography

ACQUISITIONS

Books

BUSINESS ACQUISITIONS: PLANNING AND PRACTICE (J. Herz & C. Baller eds., 1981).
FOX, BYRON E., & FOX, ELEANOR M. CORPORATE ACQUISITIONS AND MERGERS (1968).

Articles

Chazen, Leonard. *Fairness from a Financial Point of View in Acquisitions of Public Companies: Is "Third Party Sale Value" the Appropriate Standard?* 36 BUSINESS LAWYER 1439 (1981).
Fleischer, Arthur, Jr., & Sternberg, Daniel. *Corporate Acquisitions.* 12 REVIEW OF SECURITIES REGULATION 937 (1979).
Freund, James C., & Easton, Richard L. *The Three-Piece Suitor: An Alternative Approach to Negotiated Corporate Acquisitions.* 34 BUSINESS LAWYER 1679 (1979).
Freund, James C., & Greene, Edward F. *Substance Over Form S-14: A Proposal to Reform SEC Regulation of Negotiated Acquisitions.* 36 BUSINESS LAWYER 1483 (1981).
Herzel, Leo, Sherck, Timothy C., & Colling, Dale E. *Sales and Acquisitions of Divisions.* 5 CORPORATION LAW REVIEW 3 (1982).
Note, *The Conflict Between Managers and Shareholders in Diversifying Acquisitions: A Portfolio Theory Approach.* 88 YALE LAW JOURNAL 1238 (1979).
Note, *Partial and Selective Reacquisitions of Corporate Securities.* 15 CALIFORNIA WESTERN LAW REVIEW 264 (1979).

BUSINESS JUDGMENT RULE

Articles

Arsht, S. Samuel. *The Business Judgment Rule Revisited.* 8 HOFSTRA LAW REVIEW 93 (1980).
Carney, William J. *Fundamental Corporate Changes, Minority Shareholders, and Business Purposes.* AMERICAN BAR FOUNDATION RESEARCH JOURNAL 69 (1980).

Comment, *Director Liability Under the Business Judgment Rule: Fact or Fiction?* 35 SOUTH-
WESTERN LAW JOURNAL 775 (1981).

Gruenbaum, Samuel H. *Defensive Tactics and the Business Judgment Rule.* 4 CORPORATION
LAW REVIEW 263 (1981).

Pitt, Harvey L., & Israel, Carol Herndon. *Recent Cases Chart Use of Business Judgment Rule.*
Legal Times (Washington) Jan. 29, 1981, at 33, col. 1.

Steinberg, Marc I. *Application of the Business Judgment Rule and Related Judicial Principles—
Reflections from a Corporate Accountability Perspective.* 56 NOTRE DAME LAWYER 903
(1981).

CORPORATE ACCOUNTABILITY AND GOVERNANCE

Books

AMERICAN LAW INSTITUTE. PRINCIPLES ON CORPORATE GOVERNANCE AND STRUCTURE: RESTATE-
MENT AND RECOMMENDATIONS (Tentative Draft No. 1 1982).

COMMENTARIES ON CORPORATE STRUCTURE AND GOVERNANCE (D. Schwartz ed., 1976).

CORPORATIONS AT THE CROSSROADS: GOVERNANCE AND REFORM (D. DeMott ed., 1980).

EISENBERG, MELVIN A. THE STRUCTURE OF THE CORPORATION (1976).

MILSTEIN, IRA M., & KATSH, SALEM M. THE LIMITS OF CORPORATE POWER: EXISTING CON-
STRAINTS ON THE EXERCISE OF CORPORATE DISCRETION (1981).

THE MODERN CORPORATE MANAGER: RESPONSIBILITY AND REGULATION (W. Groening ed., 1981).

NADER, RALPH, GREEN, MARK, & SELIGMAN, JOEL. TAMING THE GIANT CORPORATION (1976).

SECURITIES AND EXCHANGE COMMISSION STAFF REPORT ON CORPORATE ACCOUNTABILITY (1980).

STANDARDS FOR REGULATING CORPORATE INTERNAL AFFAIRS, THE RAY GARRETT, JR., CORPORATE
AND SECURITIES LAW INSTITUTE (sponsored by Northwestern University School of Law)
(D. Fischel ed., 1981).

Articles

Anderson, Alison Grey. *Conflicts of Interest: Efficiency, Fairness and Corporate Structure.* 25
UCLA LAW REVIEW 738 (1978).

Cary, William L. *Federalism and Corporate Law, Reflections Upon Delaware.* 83 YALE LAW
JOURNAL 663 (1974).

Coffee, John C., Jr. *Beyond the Shut-Eyed Sentry: Toward a Theoretical View of Corporate
Misconduct and an Effective Legal Response.* 63 VIRGINIA LAW REVIEW 1099 (1977).

Comment, *Law for Sale: A Study of the Delaware Corporation Law of 1967.* 117 UNIVERSITY
OF PENNSYLVANIA LAW REVIEW 861 (1969).

Epstein, Edwin M. *Societal, Managerial, and Legal Perspectives on Corporate Social Responsibility—Product and Process.* 30 HASTINGS LAW JOURNAL 1287 (1979).

Ferrara, Ralph C. *Federal Intervention into Corporate Governance.* 36 BUSINESS LAWYER 759
(1981).

Filer, John H. *Responsible Corporate Philanthropy.* THE CORPORATE DIRECTOR 8 (March/April
1980).

Fischel, Daniel R. *The "Race to the Bottom" Revisited: Reflections on Recent Developments
in Delaware's Corporation Law.* 76 NORTHWESTERN UNIVERSITY LAW REVIEW 913 (1982).

Hetherington, J. A. C. *Where the Sleeper Wakes: Reflections on Corporate Governance and
Shareholder Rights.* 8 HOFSTRA LAW REVIEW 183 (1979).

Jones, Thomas M. *Corporate Governance: Who Controls the Large Corporation.* 30 HASTINGS
LAW JOURNAL 1261 (1979).

Knauss, Robert L. *Corporate Governance—A Moving Target.* 70 MICHIGAN LAW REVIEW 478
(1981).

Kripke, Homer. *The SEC, Corporate Governance, and the Real Issues.* 36 BUSINESS LAWYER 173 (1981).

Loomis, Philip A., Jr., & Rubman, Beverly K. *Corporate Governance in Historical Perspective.* 8 HOFSTRA LAW REVIEW 141 (1979).

Manning, Bayless. *Building the Modern Board.* THE CORPORATE DIRECTOR 20 (March/April 1980).

Metzenbaum, Howard M. *Legislative Approaches to Corporate Governance.* 56 NOTRE DAME LAWYER 926 (1981).

Miller, Arthur S. *A Modest Proposal for Helping to Tame the Corporate Beast.* 8 HOFSTRA LAW REVIEW 79 (1979).

Millspaugh, Peter E. *The Corporate Democracy Act—A Renaissance or Death Knell for the Corporate World?* 4 CORPORATION LAW REVIEW 291 (1981).

Note, *Stock Exchange Listing Agreements as a Vehicle for Corporate Governance.* 129 UNIVERSITY OF PENNSYLVANIA LAW REVIEW 1427 (1981).

Reich, Robert B. *Corporate Accountability and Regulatory Reform.* 8 HOFSTRA LAW REVIEW 5 (1979).

Rockefeller, David. *Ethics and the Corporation.* 8 HOFSTRA LAW REVIEW 135 (1979).

Ruder, David S. *Private Sector Responses to Proposals for Federal Intervention into Corporate Governance.* 36 BUSINESS LAWYER 771 (1981).

Schwartz, Donald E. *Federal Chartering of Corporations: An Introduction.* 61 GEORGETOWN LAW JOURNAL 71 (1972).

Soderquist, Larry D. *Reconciling Shareholders' Rights and Corporate Responsibility: Close and Small Public Corporations.* 33 VANDERBILT LAW REVIEW 1387 (1980).

Soderquist, Larry D., & Vecchio, Robert P. *Reconciling Shareholders' Rights and Corporate Responsibility: Guidelines for Management.* DUKE LAW JOURNAL 819 (1978).

Steinberg, Marc I. *Application of the Business Judgment Rule and Related Judicial Principles—Reflections from a Corporate Accountability Perspective.* 56 NOTRE DAME LAWYER 903 (1981).

———. *The ALI Draft Restatement on Corporate Governance—The Business Judgment Rule, Related Principles and Some General Observations.* 37 U. MIAMI L. REV. (Special Issue 1983).

Stevenson, Russell B., Jr. *The Corporation as a Political Institution.* 8 HOFSTRA LAW REVIEW 39 (1979).

Stone, Christopher D. *The Place of Enterprise Liability in the Control of Corporate Conduct.* 90 YALE LAW JOURNAL 1 (1980).

Vaghts, Detler F. *The Governance of the Corporation: The Options Available and the Power to Prescribe.* 31 BUSINESS LAWYER 929 (1976).

Weiss, Elliott J. *Social Regulation of Business Activity: Reforming the Corporate Governance System to Resolve an Institutional Impasse.* 28 UCLA LAW REVIEW 343 (1981).

Werner, Walter. *Corporation Law in Search of Its Future.* 81 COLUMBIA LAW REVIEW 1611 (1981).

Williamson, Oliver E. *On the Governance of the Modern Corporation.* 8 HOFSTRA LAW REVIEW 63 (1979).

DERIVATIVE SUITS

Articles

Buxbaum, Richard M. *Conflict-of-Interest Statutes and the Merit for a Demand on Directors in Derivative Suits.* 68 CALIFORNIA LAW REVIEW 1122 (1980).

Comment, *The Demand and Standing Requirements in Stockholder Derivative Actions.* 44 UNIVERSITY OF CHICAGO LAW REVIEW 168 (1976).

Note, *Demand on Directors and Shareholders as a Prerequisite to a Derivative Suit.* 73 HARVARD LAW REVIEW 729 (1960).

Prunty, B. S., Jr. *The Shareholder's Derivative Suit: Notes on Its Derivation.* 32 NEW YORK UNIVERSITY LAW REVIEW 980 (1957).

DISCLOSURE

Books

KRIPKE, HOMER. THE SEC AND CORPORATE DISCLOSURE: REGULATION IN SEARCH OF A PURPOSE (1979).

REPORT OF THE ADVISORY COMMITTEE ON CORPORATE DISCLOSURE TO THE SECURITIES AND EXCHANGE COMMISSION (1977).

STEVENSON, RUSSELL B., JR. CORPORATIONS AND INFORMATION—SECRECY, ACCESS & DISCLOSURE (1980).

Articles

Bauman, Jeffrey D. *Rule 10b-5 and the Corporation's Affirmative Duty to Disclose.* 65 GEORGETOWN LAW JOURNAL 935 (1979).

Brudney, Victor. *Dividends, Discretion, and Disclosure.* 66 VIRGINIA LAW REVIEW 85 (1980).

Comment, *Disclosure of Regulatory Violations Under the Federal Securities Laws: Establishing the Limits of Materiality.* 30 AMERICAN UNIVERSITY LAW REVIEW 225 (1980).

Ferrara, Ralph C., Starr, Richard M., & Steinberg, Marc I. *Disclosure of Information Bearing on Management Integrity and Competency.* 76 NORTHWESTERN UNIVERSITY LAW REVIEW 555 (1981).

Kripke, Homer. *Where Are We on Corporate Disclosure After the Advisory Committee Report.* 6 SECURITIES REGULATION LAW JOURNAL 99 (1978).

Note, *Disclosure of Material Inside Information: An Affirmative Corporate Duty?* ARIZONA STATE LAW JOURNAL 795 (1980).

Note, *Mandatory Disclosure of Corporate Projections and the Goals of Securities Regulation.* 81 COLUMBIA LAW REVIEW 1525 (1981).

Pozen, Robert C. *Disclosure and Trading in an International Securities Market.* 15 INTERNATIONAL LAWYER 84 (1981).

Roiter, Eric D. *Illegal Corporate Practices and the Disclosure Requirements of the Federal Securities Laws.* 50 FORDHAM LAW REVIEW 781 (1982).

Stevenson, Russell B., Jr. *The SEC and the New Disclosure.* 62 CORNELL LAW REVIEW 50 (1976).

Weiss, Elliott J. *Disclosure and Corporate Accountability.* 34 BUSINESS LAWYER 575 (1979).

ENFORCEMENT

Articles

Comment, *Equitable Remedies in SEC Enforcement Actions.* 123 UNIVERSITY OF PENNSYLVANIA LAW REVIEW 1188 (1975).

Comment, *Scope of Review or Standards of Proof—Judicial Control of SEC Sanctions & Steadman v. SEC.* 93 HARVARD LAW REVIEW 1845 (1980).

Eisenberg, Jonathan. *SEC Injunctive Actions.* 14 REVIEW OF SECURITIES REGULATION 901 (1981).

Farrand, James R. *Ancillary Remedies in SEC Civil Enforcement Suits.* 89 HARVARD LAW REVIEW 1779 (1976).

Hazen, Thomas L. *Administrative Enforcement: An Evaluation of the Securities and Exchange Commission's Use of Injunctions and Other Enforcement Methods.* 31 HASTINGS LAW JOURNAL 427 (1979).

Long, Joseph C. *A Guide to the Investigative and Enforcement Provisions of the Uniform Securities Act.* 37 WASHINGTON AND LEE LAW REVIEW 739 (1980).

Mathews, Arthur F. *Effective Defense of SEC Investigations: Laying the Foundation for Successful Disposition of Civil Administrative and Civil Proceedings.* 24 EMORY LAW JOURNAL 567 (1975).

———. *Litigation and Settlement of SEC Administrative Proceedings.* 29 CATHOLIC UNIVERSITY LAW REVIEW 215 (1980).

Pitt, Harvey L., & Markham, Jerry W. *SEC Injunctive Actions.* 6 REVIEW OF SECURITIES REGULATION 955 (1973).

Steinberg, Marc I. *SEC and Other Permanent Injunctions—Standards for Their Imposition, Modification, and Dissolution.* 66 CORNELL LAW REVIEW 27 (1980).

———. *Steadman v. SEC—Its Implications and Significance.* 6 DELAWARE JOURNAL OF CORPORATE LAW 1 (1981).

Treadway, William E. *SEC Enforcement Techniques: Expanding and Exotic Forms of Ancillary Relief.* 32 WASHINGTON AND LEE LAW REVIEW 637 (1975).

FOREIGN CORRUPT PRACTICES ACT

Articles

Atkeson, Timothy. *The Foreign Corrupt Practices Act of 1977: An International Application of SEC's Corporate Governance Reforms.* 12 INTERNATIONAL LAWYER 703 (1978).

Baker, Thomas E. *Accounting and Accountability: Overview of the Accounting Provisions of the Foreign Corrupt Practices Act of 1977.* 36 WASHINGTON AND LEE LAW REVIEW 809 (1979).

Baruch, Hurd. *Foreign Corrupt Practices Act.* 57 HARVARD BUSINESS REVIEW 32 (1979).

Best, Judah. *The Foreign Corrupt Practices Act.* 11 REVIEW OF SECURITIES REGULATION 975 (1978).

Comment, *The Accounting Provisions of the Foreign Corrupt Practices Act: An Alternative Perspective on SEC Intervention in Corporate Governance.* 89 YALE LAW JOURNAL 1573 (1980).

Comment, *Materiality and Internal Accounting Controls Under the Foreign Corrupt Practices Act.* ARIZONA STATE LAW JOURNAL 931 (1980).

Elden, Gary M., & Sableman, Mark S. *Negligence Is Not Corruption: The Scienter Requirement of the Foreign Corrupt Practices Act.* 49 GEORGE WASHINGTON LAW REVIEW 819 (1981).

Goelzer, Daniel L. *The Accounting Provisions of the Foreign Corrupt Practices Act—The Federalization of Corporate Record Keeping and Internal Control.* 5 JOURNAL OF CORPORATION LAW 1 (1979).

Herlihy, Edward D., & Levine, Theodore A. *Corporate Crisis: The Overseas Payment Problem.* 8 LAW AND POLICY IN INTERNATIONAL BUSINESS 547 (1976).

Note, *Effective Enforcement of the Foreign Corrupt Practices Act.* 32 STANFORD LAW REVIEW 561 (1980).

Olson, John. *Surprising Degree of Accord Found on FCPA Change.* Legal Times (Washington), June 29, 1981, at 33.

Roth, Allan. *International Business—The Foreign Corrupt Practices Act of 1977: Background and Summary*. 1 CORPORATION LAW REVIEW 347 (1978).

Siegel, Mary. *The Implication Doctrine and the Foreign Corrupt Practices Act*. 79 COLUMBIA LAW REVIEW 1085 (1979).

Stevenson, Russell B., Jr. *The SEC and Foreign Bribery*. 32 BUSINESS LAWYER 53 (1976).

Timmeny, Wallace. *SEC Enforcement of the Foreign Corrupt Practices Act*. 2 LOYOLA OF LOS ANGELES INTERNATIONAL AND COMPARATIVE LAW ANNUAL 25 (1979).

GOING PRIVATE/MERGERS

Books

BORDEN, ARTHUR M. GOING PRIVATE (1981).

FREUND, JAMES C. ANATOMY OF A MERGER: STRATEGIES AND TECHNIQUES FOR NEGOTIATING CORPORATE ACQUISITIONS (1980).

KINTNER, EARL W. PRIMER ON THE LAW OF MERGERS (1973).

LIPTON, MARTIN, & STEINBERGER, ERICA H. TAKEOVERS AND FREEZEOUTS (1981).

Articles

Brudney, Victor, & Chirelstein, Marvin A. *Fair Shares in Corporate Mergers and Takeovers*. 88 HARVARD LAW REVIEW 297 (1974).

———. *A Restatement of Corporate Freezeouts*. 87 YALE LAW JOURNAL 1354 (1978).

Comment, Singer v. Magnavox *and Cash Takeout Mergers*. 64 VIRGINIA LAW REVIEW 1101 (1978).

Comment, *Rule 13e-3 and the Going-Private Dilemma: The SEC's Quest for a Substantive Fairness Doctrine*. 58 WASHINGTON UNIVERSITY LAW QUARTERLY 883 (1980).

Connolly, Leonard L. *New Going-Private Rule*. 13 REVIEW OF SECURITIES REGULATION 975 (1980).

Elfin, Rodman M. *Changing Standards and the Future Course of Freezeout Mergers*. 5 JOURNAL OF CORPORATION LAW 261 (1980).

Gannon, Christopher R. *An Evaluation of the SEC's New Going Private Rule*. 7 JOURNAL OF CORPORATION LAW 55 (1981).

Greene, Edward F. *Corporate Freeze-Out Mergers: A Proposed Analysis*. 28 STANFORD LAW REVIEW 487 (1976).

Lorne, Simon M. *A Reappraisal of Fair Shares in Controlled Mergers*. 126 UNIVERSITY OF PENNSYLVANIA LAW REVIEW 955 (1978).

Manning, Bayless. *The Shareholder's Appraisal Remedy: An Essay for Frank Coker*. 72 YALE LAW JOURNAL 223 (1962).

Moore, Charles L. *Corporate Freezeouts—1980*. 13 REVIEW OF SECURITIES REGULATION 939 (1980).

Note, *Regulating Going Private Transactions: SEC Rule 13e-3*. 80 COLUMBIA LAW REVIEW 782 (1980).

Note, *Shareholders' Rights in Short-Form Mergers: The New Delaware Formula*. 64 MARQUETTE LAW REVIEW 687 (1981).

Rothschild, Steven J. *Going Private*, Singer, *and Rule 13e-3: What Are the Standards for Fiduciaries*. 7 SECURITIES REGULATION LAW JOURNAL 195 (1979).

Steinberg, Marc I. *State Court Decisions After* Santa Fe. 8 SECURITIES REGULATION LAW JOURNAL 79 (1981).

INSIDER TRADING

Articles

Barry, John F. III. *The Economics of Outside Information and Rule 10b-5.* 129 University of Pennsylvania Law Review 1307 (1981).

Branson, Douglas M. *Discourse on the Supreme Court Approach to SEC Rule 10b-5 and Insider Trading.* 30 Emory Law Journal 263 (1981).

Brudney, Victor. *Insiders, Outsiders, and Informational Advantages Under the Federal Securities Laws.* 93 Harvard Law Review 322 (1979).

Dooley, Michael P. *Enforcement of Insider Trading Restrictions.* 66 Virginia Law Review 1 (1980).

Gruenbaum, Samuel H. *The New Disclose or Abstain from Trading Rule: Has the SEC Gone Too Far?* 4 Corporation Law Review 350 (1981).

Heller, Harry. Chiarella, *SEC Rule 14e-3 and Dirks: "Fairness" versus Economic Theory.* 37 Business Lawyer 517 (1982).

Langevoort, Donald C. *Insider Trading and the Fiduciary Principle: A post-Chiarella Restatement.* 70 California Law Review 1 (1982).

Levmore, Saul. *Securities and Secrets: Insider Trading and the Law of Contracts.* 68 Virginia Law Review 117 (1982).

Morrison, Peter H. *Silence Is Golden: Trading on Nonpublic Market Information.* 8 Securities Regulation Law Journal 211 (1980).

Note, *Damages for Insider Trading Violations in an Impersonal Market Context.* 7 Journal of Corporation Law 97 (1981).

Note, *Trading on Material, Nonpublic Information Under Rule 14e-3.* 49 George Washington Law Review 539 (1981).

Wang, William K. S. *Trading on Material Nonpublic Information on Impersonal Stock Markets: Who Is Harmed and Who Can Sue Whom Under SEC Rule 10b-5?* 54 Southern California Law Review 1217 (1981).

OFFICERS AND DIRECTORS

Books

Berle, Adolf A., Jr., & Means, Gardiner C. The Modern Corporation and Private Property (1932).

Bishop, Joseph W. Law of Corporate Officers and Directors (1981).

Corporate Director's Guidebook. Reprinted in 33 Business Lawyer 1591 (rev. ed., 1979).

Knepper, William E. Liability of Officers and Directors (1978).

Mace, Myles L. Directors: Myth and Reality (1971).

Articles

ABA Committee on Corporate Laws. *The Overview Committees of the Board of Directors.* 35 Business Lawyer 1335 (1980).

Anderson, Allison Grey. *Conflicts of Interest: Efficiency, Fairness and Corporate Structure.* 25 UCLA Law Review 738 (1978).

Berle, Adolf A., Jr. *For Whom Corporate Managers Are Trustees: A Note.* 45 Harvard Law Review 1365 (1933).

Brudney, Victor. *The Independent Director—Heavenly City or Potemkin Village.* 95 HARVARD LAW REVIEW 597 (1981).

Brudney, Victor, & Clark, Robert C. *A New Look at Corporate Opportunities.* 94 HARVARD LAW REVIEW 997 (1981).

Dent, George W., Jr. *The Revolution in Corporate Governance, the Monitoring Board, and the Director's Duty of Care.* 61 BOSTON UNIVERSITY LAW REVIEW 623 (1981).

Dodd, E. Merrick, Jr. *For Whom Are Corporate Managers Trustees?* 45 HARVARD LAW REVIEW 1145 (1932).

Gillerman, Gerald. *The Corporate Fiduciary Under State Law.* 3 CORPORATION LAW REVIEW 299 (1980).

Golden, Bruce P. *Corporate Law for Financial Institutions and Directors' Duties When Forming a Bank Holding Company.* 99 BANKING LAW JOURNAL 146 (1982).

Goldstein, Elliott, & Shepherd, Michael L. *Directors' Duties and Liabilities Under the Securities Act and Corporation Law.* 36 WASHINGTON AND LEE LAW REVIEW 739 (1979).

Haft, Robert J. *Business Decisions by the New Board: Behavioral Science and Corporate Law.* 80 MICHIGAN LAW REVIEW 1 (1981).

Hershman, Mendes. *Liabilities and Responsibilities of Corporate Officers and Directors.* 33 BUSINESS LAWYER 263 (1977).

Joffe, Edward M. *The Outside Director: Standards of Care Under the Securities Laws.* 24 EMORY LAW JOURNAL 669 (1975).

Leech, Noyes E., & Mundheim, Robert H. *The Outside Director of the Publicly Held Corporation.* 31 BUSINESS LAWYER 1799 (1976).

Mace, Myles L. *Directors: Myth and Reality—Ten Years Later.* 32 RUTGERS LAW REVIEW 293 (1979).

Manning, Bayless. *Building the Modern Board.* THE CORPORATE DIRECTOR 20 (March/April 1980).

Marsh, Harold, Jr. *Are Directors Trustees?* 22 BUSINESS LAWYER 35 (1976).

Phillips, David Morris. *Managerial Misuse of Property: The Synthesizing Thread in Corporate Doctrine.* 32 RUTGERS LAW REVIEW 184 (1979).

The Role and Composition of the Board of Directors of the Large Publicly Owned Corporation—Statement of the Business Roundtable. 33 BUSINESS LAWYER 2083 (1978).

Schwartz, Donald E. *Some Thoughts on the Directors' Evolving Role.* 30 HASTINGS LAW JOURNAL 1405 (1979).

Shaneyfelt, Donald L *The Personal Liability Maze of Corporate Directors and Officers.* 58 NEBRASKA LAW REVIEW 692 (1979).

Small, Marshall L. *The Evolving Role of the Director in Corporate Governance.* 30 HASTINGS LAW JOURNAL 1353 (1979).

Soderquist, Larry D. *Toward a More Effective Corporate Board: Reexamining Roles of Outside Directors.* 52 NEW YORK UNIVERSITY LAW REVIEW 1341 (1977).

Solomon, Lewis D. *Restructuring the Corporate Board of Directors: Fond Hope—Faint Promise?* 76 MICHIGAN LAW REVIEW 581 (1978).

PROFESSIONALS

Accountants

Books

CAUSEY, DENZIL Y. DUTIES AND LIABILITIES OF PUBLIC ACCOUNTANTS (1979).

GORMLEY, JAMES R. THE LAW OF ACCOUNTANTS AND AUDITORS: RIGHTS, DUTIES, AND LIABILITIES (1981).

Articles

Adams, Albert T. *Lessening the Legal Liability of Auditors.* 32 BUSINESS LAWYER 1037 (1977).

Burton, John C. *The Developing Role of the Independent Auditor in Corporate Governance.* 56 NOTRE DAME LAWYER 813 (1981).

Fiflis, Ted J. *Current Problems of Accountants' Responsibilities to Third Persons.* 28 VAN-DERBILT LAW REVIEW 31 (1975).

Gruenbaum, Samuel H., & Steinberg, Marc I. *Accountants' Liability and Responsibility: Securities, Criminal and Common Law.* 13 LOYOLA OF LOS ANGELES LAW REVIEW 247 (1980).

Hawes, Douglas W. *Stockholder Appointment of Independent Auditors: A Proposal.* 74 COLUMBIA LAW REVIEW 1 (1974).

Margolis, Stuart A. *Sanctions Against Accountants for Violations of the Securities Laws: A Reappraisal.* 4 DELAWARE JOURNAL OF CORPORATE LAW 399 (1979).

Mess, Michael A. *Accountants and the Common Law: Liability to Third Parties.* 52 NOTRE DAME LAWYER 838 (1977).

Metzger, Michael B., & Heintz, James A. *Hochfelder's Progeny: Implications for the Auditor.* 63 MINNESOTA LAW REVIEW 79 (1978).

Note, *Accountants' Liability For Negligence—A Contemporary Approach for a Modern Profession.* 48 FORDHAM LAW REVIEW 401 (1979).

Roberts, Roy. *Work Papers, Evidence, Fraud and Third Party Liability.* THE NATIONAL PUBLIC ACCOUNTANT 30 (June 1980).

Sommer, A. A., Jr. *Corporate Governance: Its Impact on the Profession.* 150 JOURNAL OF ACCOUNTANCY 52 (1980).

Vernava, Anthony M., & Hepp, Gerald W. *Responsibility of the Accountant Under the Federal Securities Exchange Act of 1934.* 6 JOURNAL OF CORPORATION LAW 317 (1981).

Walker, Craig M. *Accountants' Liability—The Scienter Standard Under Section 10(b) and Rule 10b-5 of the Securities Exchange Act of 1934.* 63 MARQUETTE LAW REVIEW 243 (1979).

Attorneys

Duties and Responsibilities

Articles

Block, Dennis J., & Barton, Nancy E. *Attorneys' Responsibilities—Professional Ethics and the Federal Securities Laws.* 8 SECURITIES REGULATION LAW JOURNAL 333 (1981).

Burke, Maureen H. *The Duty of Confidentiality and Disclosing Corporate Misconduct.* 36 BUSINESS LAWYER 239 (1981).

Curzan, Myron P., & Pelesh, Mark L. *The Changing Role of Outside Counsel: A Proposal for a Legal "Audit."* 56 NOTRE DAME LAWYER 838 (1981).

Frank, Harvey. *A Higher Duty: A New Look at the Ethics of the Corporate Lawyer.* 26 CLEVELAND STATE LAW REVIEW 337 (1977).

Gruenbaum, Samuel H. *Clients' Frauds and Their Lawyers' Obligations: A Response to Professor Kramer.* 68 GEORGETOWN LAW JOURNAL 197 (1974).

———. *Corporate/Securities Lawyers: Disclosure, Responsibility, Liability to Investors, and National Student Marketing Corp.* 54 NOTRE DAME LAWYER 795 (1979).

Hoffman, Junius. *On Learning of a Corporate Client's Crime of Fraud—The Lawyer's Dilemma.* 33 BUSINESS LAWYER 1389 (1978).

Kaplan, Stanley F. *Some Ruminations on the Role of Counsel for a Corporation.* 56 NOTRE DAME LAWYER 873 (1981).

Karmel, Roberta S. *Attorneys' Securities Law Liabilities.* 27 BUSINESS LAWYER 1153 (1975).

Kramer, Victor H. *Clients' Frauds and Their Lawyers' Obligations: A Study in Professional Irresponsibility.* 67 GEORGETOWN LAW JOURNAL 991 (1979).

Lorne, Simon M. *The Corporate and Securities Adviser, the Public Interest, and Professional Ethics.* 76 MICHIGAN LAW REVIEW 425 (1978).

Lowenfels, Lewis D. *Expanding Public Responsibilities of Securities Lawyers: An Analysis of the New Trend in Standard of Care and Priorities of Duties.* 74 COLUMBIA LAW REVIEW 412 (1974).

Mathews, Arthur F. *Liabilities of Lawyers Under the Federal Securities Laws.* 30 BUSINESS LAWYER 105 (1975).

Note, *The Duties and Obligations of the Securities Lawyer: The Beginning of a New Standard for the Legal Profession?* DUKE LAW JOURNAL 121 (1975).

Patterson, L. Ray. *The Limits of the Lawyer's Discretion and the Law of Legal Ethics:* National Student Marketing *Revisited.* DUKE LAW JOURNAL 1251 (1979).

Pollack, Irving M. *The SEC Lawyer: Who Is His Client and What Are His Responsibilities.* 49 GEORGE WASHINGTON LAW REVIEW 453 (1981).

Shipman, Morgan E. *The Need for SEC Rules to Govern the Duties and Civil Liabilities of Attorneys Under the Federal Securities Statutes.* 34 OHIO STATE LAW JOURNAL 231 (1973).

Small, Marshall L. *An Attorney's Responsibilities Under Federal and State Securities Laws: Private Counselor or Public Servant?* 61 CALIFORNIA LAW REVIEW 1189 (1973).

Sonde, Theodore. *The Responsibility of Professionals Under the Federal Securities Laws— Some Observations.* 68 NORTHWESTERN UNIVERSITY LAW REVIEW 1 (1973).

Williams, Harold M. *Corporate Accountability and the Lawyer's Role.* 34 BUSINESS LAWYER 7 (1978).

Attorney-Client Privilege

Articles

Block, Dennis J., & Barton, Nancy E. *Internal Corporate Investigations: Maintaining the Confidentiality of a Corporate Client's Communications with Investigative Counsel.* 35 BUSINESS LAWYER 5 (1979).

Burke, Maureen H. *The Duty of Confidentiality and Disclosing Corporate Misconduct.* 36 BUSINESS LAWYER 239 (1981).

Gruenbaum, Samuel H., & Oppenheimer, Martin A. *Special Investigative Counsel: Conflicts and Roles.* 33 RUTGERS LAW REVIEW 865 (1981).

Note, *Application of the Attorney-Client Privilege to Corporations: New Directions and a Proposed Solution.* 20 BOSTON COLLEGE LAW REVIEW 953 (1979).

Note, *The Attorney-Client Privilege and the Corporation in Shareholder Litigation.* 50 SOUTHERN CALIFORNIA LAW REVIEW 303 (1977).

Note, *The Implications of* Upjohn. 56 NOTRE DAME LAWYER 887 (1981).

Note, Upjohn v. United States: *Death Knell for the Control Group Test and a Plea for a Policy-Oriented Standard of Corporate Discovery.* 31 SYRACUSE LAW REVIEW 1043 (1980).

Patton, S. Kendall. *Disqualification of Corporate Counsel in Derivative Actions—*Jacuzzi *and the Inadequacy of Dual Representation.* 31 HASTINGS LAW JOURNAL 347 (1979).

Pitt, Harvey L. *The "Upjohn" Decision: "To Thine Own Self Be True."* Legal Times (Washington), Jan. 26, 1981, at 20.

Counsel as Director

Articles

Comment, *Corporate Counsel on the Board of Directors: An Overview.* 10 CUMBERLAND LAW REVIEW 791 (1980).

Hawes, Douglas W. *Should Counsel to a Corporation Be Barred from Serving as a Director?— A Personal View.* 1 CORPORATION LAW REVIEW 14 (1978).

Knepper, William E. *Liability of Lawyer-Directors.* 40 OHIO STATE LAW JOURNAL 341 (1978).

Lorne, Simon M. *Why Outside Counsel Should Stay Outside.* DIRECTORS & BOARDS 26 (Fall 1981).

Note, *Should Lawyers Serve as Directors of Corporations for Which They Serve as Counsel?* UTAH LAW REVIEW 711 (1978).

Riger, Martin. *The Lawyer-Director—"A Vexing Problem."* 33 BUSINESS LAWYER 2381 (1978).

Inside Counsel

Articles

Driver, Albert W., Jr. *The Inside General Counsel's Response to Auditors' Inquiries.* 30 BUSINESS LAWYER 217 (1975).

Ferrara, Ralph C., & Steinberg, Marc I. *The Role of Inside Counsel in the Corporate Accountability Process.* 4 CORPORATION LAW REVIEW 3 (1981).

Forrow, Brian D. *Special Problems of Inside Counsel for Industrial Companies.* 33 BUSINESS LAWYER 1453 (1978).

————. *The Corporate Law Department Lawyer: Counsel to the Entity.* 34 BUSINESS LAWYER 1979 (1979).

Hershman, Mendes. *Special Problems of Inside Counsel for Financial Institutions.* 33 BUSINESS LAWYER 1435 (1978).

McKinney, Luther. *Relationship with Outside Counsel.* 34 BUSINESS LAWYER 921 (1979).

Rast, L. Edmund. *What the Chief Executive Looks for in His Corporate Law Department.* 33 BUSINESS LAWYER 811 (1978).

Schaefer, C. Barry. *Proposed Model Rule 5.4: Is It Necessary for Corporate Staff Counsel?* 15 CREIGHTON LAW REVIEW 639 (1982).

Subak, John T. *Special Problems of Inside Counsel.* 33 BUSINESS LAWYER 1433 (1978).

Taylor, John C. III. *The Role of Corporate Counsel.* 32 RUTGERS LAW REVIEW 237 (1979).

Rule 2(e)

Articles

Comment, *Attorney Liability Under SEC Rule 2(e): A New Standard?* 11 TEXAS TECH LAW REVIEW 83 (1979).

Comment, *Reassessing the Validity of SEC Rule 2(e) Discipline of Accountants.* 59 BOSTON UNIVERSITY LAW REVIEW 968 (1979).

Comment, *SEC Disciplinary Rules and the Federal Securities Laws: The Regulation, Role and Responsibilities of the Attorney.* DUKE LAW JOURNAL 969 (1972).

Dolin, Mitchell F. *SEC Rule 2(e) After* Carter-Johnson *and Toward a Reconciliation of Purpose and Scope.* 9 SECURITIES REGULATION LAW JOURNAL 331 (1982).

Downing, Robert A., & Miller, Richard L., Jr. *The Distortion and Misuse of Rule 2(e).* 54 NOTRE DAME LAWYER 774 (1979).

Gross, Kent. *Attorneys and Their Corporate Clients, SEC Rule 2(e) and the Georgetown "Whistle Blowing" Proposal.* 3 CORPORATION LAW REVIEW 197 (1980).

Gruenbaum, Samuel H. *The SEC's Use of Rule 2(e) to Discipline Accountants and Other Professionals.* 56 NOTRE DAME LAWYER 120 (1981).

Johnson, Norman S. *The Expanding Responsibilities of Attorneys in Practice Before the SEC: Disciplinary Proceedings Under Rule 2(e) of the Commission's Rules of Practice.* 25 MERCER LAW REVIEW 637 (1974).

Kelleher, John J. *Scourging the Moneylenders from the Temple: The SEC, Rule 2(e), and the Lawyers.* 17 SAN DIEGO LAW REVIEW 501 (1980).

Krane, Steven C. *The Attorney Unshackled: SEC Rule 2(e) Violates the Client's Sixth Amendment Right to Counsel.* 57 Notre Dame Lawyer 50 (1981).
Marsh, Harold, Jr. *Rule 2(e) Proceedings.* 35 Business Lawyer 987 (1980).
Note, *SEC Disciplinary Proceedings Against Attorneys Under Rule 2(e).* 79 Michigan Law Review 1270 (1981).

PROXY CONTESTS

Books

Aranow, Edward Ross, & Einhorn, Herbert A. Proxy Contests for Corporate Control (1968).
Proxy Contests and Battles for Corporate Control (PLI, 1981).
Proxy Litigation and Contests (Law Journal Seminars Press, 1981).

Articles

Hazen, Thomas L. *Corporate Mismanagement and the Federal Securities Act's Antifraud Provisions: A Familiar Path with Some New Detours.* 20 Boston College Law Review 819 (1979).
Steinberg, Marc I. *Fiduciary Duties and Disclosure Obligations in Proxy and Tender Contests for Corporate Control.* 30 Emory Law Journal 169 (1981).

SANTA FE AND ITS PROGENY

Articles

Block, Dennis J., & Schwarzfeld, Neal. *Corporate Mismanagement and Breach of Fiduciary Duty After* Santa Fe v. Green. 2 Corporation Law Review 91 (1979).
Campbell, Rutherford B., Jr. Santa Fe Industries, Inc. v. Green: *An Analysis Two Years Later.* 30 Maine Law Review 187 (1979).
Comment, Santa Fe Industries v. Green *Revisited: A Critique of Circuit Court Application of Rule 10b-5 to Breaches of Fiduciary Duty to Minority Shareholders.* 28 UCLA Law Review 564 (1981).
Ferrara, Ralph C., & Steinberg, Marc I. *A Reappraisal of* Santa Fe: *Rule 10b-5 and the New Federalism.* 129 University of Pennsylvania Law Review 263 (1980).
———. *The Interplay Between State Corporation and Federal Securities Law—*Santa Fe, Singer, Burks, Maldonado, *Their Progeny, and Beyond.* 7 Delaware Journal of Corporate Law 1 (1982).
Gorman, Thomas O. *At the Intersection of Supreme Avenue and Circuit Street: The Focus of Section 10(b) and* Santa Fe's *Footnote Fourteen.* 7 Journal of Corporation Law 199 (1981).
Hazen, Thomas L. *Corporate Mismanagement and the Federal Securities Act's Anti-Fraud Provisions: A Familiar Path with Some New Detours.* 20 Boston College Law Review 819 (1979).
Jacobs, William R. *Rule 10b-5 and Self Dealing by Corporate Fiduciaries: An Analysis.* 48 University of Cincinnati Law Review 643 (1979).

Krendl, Cathy S. *Progeny of* Santa Fe v. Green: *An Analysis of the Elements of a Fiduciary Duty Claim Under Rule 10b-5 and a Case for a Federal Corporation Law.* 59 NORTH CAROLINA LAW REVIEW 231 (1981).

Note, Goldberg v. Meridor: *The Second Circuit's Resurrection of Rule 10b-5 Liability for Breaches of Corporate Fiduciary Duties to Minority Shareholders.* 64 VIRGINIA LAW REVIEW 765 (1978).

Note, *Liability for Corporate Mismanagement Under Rule 10b-5 After* Santa Fe v. Green. 27 WAYNE LAW REVIEW 269 (1980).

Note, *Suits for Breach of Fiduciary Duty Under Rule 10b-5 After* Santa Fe Industries, Inc. v. Green. 91 HARVARD LAW REVIEW 1874 (1978).

Roberts, William M. *The Status of Minority Shareholders' Remedies for Oppression After* Santa Fe *and* Singer *and the Question of "Reasonable Investment Expectation" Valuation.* 6 DELAWARE JOURNAL OF CORPORATE LAW 16 (1981).

Sherrard, Thomas J. *Federal Judicial and Regulatory Responses to* Santa Fe Industries, Inc. v. Green. 35 WASHINGTON AND LEE LAW REVIEW 695 (1978).

Steinberg, Marc I. *State Court Decisions After* Santa Fe. 8 SECURITIES REGULATION LAW JOURNAL 79 (1981).

SECURITIES AND EXCHANGE COMMISSION

Books

KARMEL, ROBERTA S. REGULATION BY PROSECUTION—THE SECURITIES AND EXCHANGE COMMISSION VERSUS CORPORATE AMERICA (1982).

PHILLIPS, SUSAN M., & ZECHER, J. RICHARD. THE SEC AND THE PUBLIC INTEREST (1981).

Articles

Steinberg, Marc I. *The Securities and Exchange Commission's Administrative, Enforcement, and Legislative Programs and Policies—Their Influence on Corporate Internal Affairs* 58 NOTRE DAME LAW REVIEW 173 (1982).

Wolfson, Nicholas. *A Critique of the Securities and Exchange Commission.* 39 EMORY LAW JOURNAL 119 (1981).

SPECIAL LITIGATION COMMITTEES

Articles

Bishop, Joseph W., Jr. *Derivative Suits Against Bank Directors: New Problems, New Strategies.* 97 BANKING LAW JOURNAL 158 (1980).

Block, Dennis J., & Barton, Nancy E. *The Business Judgment Rule as Applied to Shareholder Proxy Derivative Suits Under the Securities Exchange Act.* 8 SECURITIES REGULATION LAW JOURNAL 99 (1980).

Block, Dennis J., & Prussin, H. Adam. *The Business Judgment Rule and Shareholder Derivative Actions: Viva* Zapata? 37 JOURNAL OF CORPORATION LAWYER 27 (1981).

Brown, Meredith M., & Phillips, William J. *The Business Judgment Rule:* Burks v. Lasker *and Other Recent Developments.* 6 JOURNAL OF CORPORATION LAW 453 (1981).

Brown, Richard C. *Shareholder Derivative Litigation and the Special Litigation Committee.* 43 UNIVERSITY OF PITTSBURGH LAW REVIEW 601 (1982).

Coffee, John C., Jr., & Schwartz, Donald E. *The Survival of the Derivative Suit: An Evaluation and a Proposal for Legislative Reform.* 81 COLUMBIA LAW REVIEW 261 (1981).

Comment, *Director Dismissal of Shareholder Derivative Suits Under the Investment Company Act:* Burks v. Lasker. 11 LOYOLA OF LOS ANGELES LAW REVIEW 519 (1980).

Comment, *A Procedural Treatment of Derivative Suit Dismissals by Minority Directors.* 69 CALIFORNIA LAW REVIEW 885 (1980).

DeMott, Deborah A. *Defending the Quiet Life: The Role of Special Counsel in Director Terminations of Derivative Suits.* 56 NOTRE DAME LAWYER 850 (1981).

Dent, George W., Jr. *The Power of Directors to Terminate Shareholders Litigation: The Death of the Derivative Suit?* 75 NORTHWESTERN UNIVERSITY LAW REVIEW 96 (1980).

Ferrara, Ralph C., & Steinberg, Marc I. *The Interplay Between State Corporation and Federal Securities Law*—Santa Fe, Singer, Burks, Maldonado, *Their Progeny and Beyond.* 7 DELAWARE JOURNAL OF CORPORATE LAW 1 (1982).

Gammon, Elinor W. *Derivative Suits.* 12 REVIEW OF SECURITIES REGULATION 887 (1979).

Gorman, Thomas O. *Federalism and the* Burks *Factors: When Can Directors Dismiss Derivative Suits?* 5 CORPORATION LAW REVIEW 120 (1982).

Johnson, Janet. *The Business Judgment Rule: A Review of Its Application to the Problem of Illegal Foreign Payments.* 6 JOURNAL OF CORPORATION LAW 481 (1981).

Kim, Kon Sik. *The Demand on Directors. Requirement and the Business Judgment Rule in the Shareholder Derivative Suit: An Alternative Framework.* 6 JOURNAL OF CORPORATION LAW 511 (1981).

Note, *The Business Judgment Rule in Derivative Suits Against Directors.* 65 CORNELL LAW REVIEW 600 (1980).

Note, *Zapata Corporation v. Maldonado: A Limitation on the Use of Delaware's Business Judgment Rule in Stockholder Derivative Suits.* 6 DELAWARE JOURNAL OF CORPORATE LAW 80 (1981).

Steinberg, Marc I. *Dismissing Derivative Suits.* THE CORPORATE DIRECTOR 1 (July/Aug. 1980).

———. *The Use of Special Litigation Committees to Terminate Shareholder Derivative Suits.* 35 UNIVERSITY OF MIAMI LAW REVIEW 1 (1980).

———. Maldonado *in Delaware: Special Litigation Committees—An Unsafe Haven.* 9 SECURITIES REGULATION LAW JOURNAL 381 (1982).

Zolezzi, Richard V. *Director Good Faith Marches On: A California Analysis of Director Termination of Shareholder Derivative Suits Under* Burks v. Lasker. 32 HASTINGS LAW JOURNAL 519 (1980).

STOCKHOLDER PROPOSALS

Articles

Black, Lewis S., Jr., & Sparks, A. Gilchrist III. *SEC Rule 14a-8: Some Changes in the Way the SEC Staff Interprets the Rule.* 11 TOLEDO LAW REVIEW 957 (1980).

Curzan, Myron P., & Pelesh, Mark L. *Revitalizing Corporate Democracy: Control of Investment Manager's Voting on Social Responsibility Proxy Issues.* 94 HARVARD LAW REVIEW 670 (1980).

Eisenberg, Jonathan. *Current Applications of the Shareholder Proposal Rule.* 15 REVIEW OF SECURITIES REGULATION 903 (1982).

Warwick, Kathleen A. *Shareholder Proposals.* TWELFTH ANNUAL INSTITUTE ON SECURITIES REGULATION 89 (Transcript Series) (A. Fleischer, M. Lipton, R. Mundheim & R. Santoni eds., 1980).

Williams, Crystal. *Improper Shareholder Proposals.* 13 REVIEW OF SECURITIES REGULATION 841 (1980).

TENDER OFFERS

Generally

Books

Aranow, Edward Ross, Einhorn, Herbert A., & Berlstein, George. Developments in Tender Offers for Corporate Control (1977).

Fleischer, Arthur, Jr. Tender Offers: Defenses, Responses and Planning (1981).

Lipton, Martin, & Steinberger, Erica H. Takeovers and Freezeouts (1981).

Articles

Bloomenthal, Harold S. *The New Tender Offer Regimen, State Regulation, and Preemption.* 30 Emory Law Journal 35 (1981).

Johnson, Henry F. *Disclosure in Tender Offer Transactions: The Dice Are Still Loaded.* 42 University of Pittsburgh Law Review 1 (1980).

Leiser, Harvey. *The SEC: A Black Knight for Target Management—An Analysis of Some Recent SEC Rules and Proposed Rules.* 7 Journal of Corporation Law 21 (1981).

Steinberg, Marc I. *Fiduciary Duties and Disclosure Obligations in Proxy and Tender Contests for Corporate Control.* 30 Emory Law Journal 169 (1981).

Management's Conduct

Articles

Easterbrook, Frank H., & Fischel, Daniel R. *The Proper Role of a Target's Management in Responding to a Tender Offer.* 94 Harvard Law Review 1161 (1981).

———. *Takeover Bids, Defensive Tactics, and Shareholders' Welfare.* 36 Business Lawyer 1733 (1981).

Gelfond, Richard L., & Sebastian, Steven B. *Reevaluating the Duties of Target Management in a Hostile Tender Offer.* 60 Boston University Law Review 403 (1980).

Gilson, Ronald. *A Structural Approach to Corporations: The Case Against Defensive Tactics in Tender Offers.* 33 Stanford Law Review 819 (1981).

Herzel, Leo, Schmidt, John R., & Davis, Scott J. *Why Corporate Directors Have a Right to Resist Tender Offers.* 3 Corporation Law Review 107 (1980).

Lipton, Martin. *Takeover Bids in the Target's Boardroom.* 35 Business Lawyer 101 (1979).

———. *Takeover Bids in the Target's Boardroom: An Update After One Year.* 36 Business Lawyer 1017 (1981).

Lynch, Gary G., & Steinberg, Marc I. *The Legitimacy of Defensive Tactics in Tender Offers.* 64 Cornell Law Review 901 (1979).

Note, *Tender Offer Decisions: Effect of the Business Judgment Rule.* 45 Albany Law Review 1122 (1981).

Steinbrink, William H. *Management's Response to a Takeover Attempt.* 28 Case Western Reserve Law Review 882 (1978).

Williams, Harold M. *Role of Directors in Takeover Offers.* 13 Review of Securities Regulation 963 (1980).

General Subject Index

Index to Cases

This index contains references to cases discussed in the text sections of the book.

293

About the Author

MARC I. STEINBERG is Associate Professor of Law at The University of Maryland School of Law. His prior teaching experience includes serving as Visiting Associate Professor of Law at The National Law Center, George Washington University, and as Adjunct Professor of Law at The Georgetown University Law Center. Professor Steinberg previously served as Special Projects Counsel and confidential legal advisor to the General Counsel at the U.S. Securities and Exchange Commission. He is the author of numerous law review articles, and serves on the advisory board of *The Corporation Law Review, The Delaware Journal of Corporate Law, The Journal of Corporation Law,* and *The Securities Regulation Law Journal.*